Professional Financial Computing Using Excel and VBA

Professional Financial Computing Using Excel and VBA

HUMPHREY K. K. TUNG,
DONNY C. F. LAI, and
MICHAEL C. S. WONG

with STEPHEN NG

WILEY

John Wiley & Sons (Asia) Pte. Ltd.

Other Wiley Editorial Offices

John Wiley & Sons, 111 River Street, Hoboken, NJ 07030, USA
John Wiley & Sons, The Atrium, Southern Gate, Chichester, West Sussex, P019 8SQ,
    United Kingdom
John Wiley & Sons (Canada) Ltd., 5353 Dundas Street West, Suite 400, Toronto, Ontario,
    M9B 6HB, Canada
John Wiley & Sons Australia Ltd., 42 McDougall Street, Milton, Queensland 4064, Australia
Wiley-VCH, Boschstrasse 12, D-69469 Weinheim, Germany

Library of Congress Cataloging-in-Publication Data
ISBN 978–0–470–82439–9

Typeset in 10.5/13pt Sabon-Roman by Thomson Digital, India
Printed in Singapore by Toppan Security Printing Pte. Ltd.
10 9 8 7 6 5 4 3 2 1

Contents

Preface

This book is a good company to Master degree programs in Financial Engineering, Financial Risk Management, Quantitative Investment, Computational Finance, or Mathematical Finance. Also, risk managers, traders, IT analysts, quantitative analysts working in investment banks and hedge fund will find it to be a good reference.

The book provides VBA examples on some widely-used finance and risk models. We expect that readers have prior training on these models because some of them require strong mathematical foundation. Through the examples, readers can easily build their implementable analytics and apply similar skills to other complex models.

Feedback from professors, students, analysts, and risk professionals are warmly welcome.

Humphrey Tung
Donny Lai
Michael Wong
Stephen Ng
Email: efmcw103@gmail.com

## CHAPTER 1

Financial Engineering and Computing

1.1 FINANCIAL ENGINEERING AND SPREADSHEET MODELING

"Spreadsheet Modeling for Finance" has long been a popular course in the MSc Financial Engineering program at the university we served in Hong Kong. The course is different from introductory Excel courses in financial management. It is an advanced course offered mainly to students with solid training in mathematical finance, option pricing, and risk modeling. Most of the students in the course have been designated a chartered financial analyst (CFA) or certified as a financial risk manager (FRM). The financial engineering program mainly recruits part-time students working in various financial institutions. There are around 40 to 60 new recruits each year. Many of them are derivatives traders, bank risk managers, bank IT specialists, fund managers, product structurers, bank regulators, and product auditors. In 1997–2008, the program trained more than 500 graduates. Most of them successfully applied the knowledge gained to their daily work.

Some may ask why no "quantitative analysts" are mentioned. Loosely speaking, these financial engineering graduates are quantitative analysts in nature. Strictly speaking, none of them carries the job title "quantitative analyst." A global investment bank may have one or two quantitative analysts and/or financial engineers in Hong Kong. Given the presence of 15 global institutions, there are a maximum of 10 quantitative analyst job vacancies a year. This number cannot satisfy the continuous supply of financial engineering graduates every year. Although our graduates are not called quantitative analysts, their training in financial engineering did help their fast career development. Also, their quantitative skills have enabled Hong Kong to excel in financial services.

When we planned this book in 2007, the financial market in Hong Kong was very bullish. Many China initial public offering (IPO) deals were completed in Hong Kong. The Hang Seng Index reached over 30,000 points. Structured products and hedge funds were prevalent in corporate banking and private banking. Equity-linked notes, minibonds, and currency-linked products were common in retail banking.

In addition to sizable financial institutions, Hong Kong is a hub of boutique hedge funds. It is believed that there are 600 or more. These hedge funds employ few people, but their asset under management (AUM) can be over US$100 million each. In these hedge funds, financial and risk analysis is mostly based on Excel and Visual Basic for Applications (VBA) programming. This is a reason why the course "Spreadsheet Modeling" is very popular.

Our progress in writing this book was hindered by the financial tsunami in 2008. High market volatility, depreciation of wealth, and massive layoffs in the banking sector brought a lot of frustration to financial practitioners and financial educators. When we completed this book in June 2009, the market remained very weak. Many wealthy individuals suffered huge losses in the past 12 months; financial institutions cut their manpower seriously; selling complex products became difficult; and new regulations were enacted relating to structured products. In 2009, students in the course "Spreadsheet Modeling" still enjoyed the class but were slightly worried outside of the class. This is because the next round, which would be the fourth or fifth round, of massive layoffs would affect them. Investment banking follows obvious business cycles. This applies to study programs in financial engineering as well.

Mature students are always pragmatic in acquiring knowledge. Complex mathematics is very fancy, but our mature students tend to take it for granted and focus mostly on the applications of the mathematics. The course "Spreadsheet Modeling" makes those fancy mathematical concepts more easily applicable. From the perspective of educators, this mindset of the students is not harmful. After using Excel and VBA to build their models, some students become more interested in complex mathematics. What we would like them to know is not simply building models for financial analysis. We wish that they could understand model risks and estimate when these risks are likely to occur. The increased curiosity of our students after the course made us feel satisfied about our educational efforts.

Many new financial products have no mathematical models. Due to the advancement of technology, an analyst can easily apply Monte Carlo simulation on related variables and find out an average value. Our students especially like this analytical approach because there is less of a mathematical foundation required. In fact, Excel and VBA can easily handle Monte Carlo simulation.

1.2 LEHMAN BROTHERS' PRODUCTS FOR RETAIL INVESTORS

Since 2005, Lehman Brothers began actively distributing a wide range of structured products via retail banks in Hong Kong, as well as in Singapore. One of our former financial engineering students came from France. After graduation, he worked in Lehman Brothers (Tokyo). A major part of his job was to structure products, which were finally sold to Hong Kong retail investors via local retail banks.

These products included equity-linked notes, minibonds (collateralized debt obligation [CDO] with total return swaps), and index-linked guaranteed notes. The equity-linked notes could provide an annual yield of 30 percent. Obviously the distribution of stock returns at that time was asymmetric with high upside potential and limited downside risk. The minibonds offered yields much better than bank deposits and the principle was guaranteed by an AA/A-rated institution—Lehman Brothers. This rating is better than that of many local banks.

Unfortunately, Lehman Brothers collapsed in September 2008. More than 40,000 retail investors in Hong Kong became victims. Some lost almost all their wealth. These victims continuously demonstrated in the street, at the front doors of various banks, and at the entrance of the Hong Kong Monetary Authority. Regulators encouraged banks to buy back the Lehman products. Banks were unwilling to do so. The Hong Kong banking industry experienced unprecedented exposure to reputational risk. In fact, this risk has never been discussed seriously and measured properly.

The Lehman incident made financial regulators extremely busy. Many of our financial engineering students are working for the regulatory bodies in Hong Kong. They were under serious pressure in the six-month period after September 2008. To mitigate regulatory risk, the regulators in Hong Kong announced a series of measures to prevent ordinary citizens from mistakenly buying high-risk products. These measures included mystery shopper programs (that is somebody pretending to be a bank client in order to test the selling process of frontline people) and audio-recording all relevant transactions. At the same time, the legal risk of banks intensified. Misrepresentation and insufficient duty of care became the words surrounding all financial institutions in Hong Kong. As a result, one of our authors was appointed to be an expert witness in some legal disputes relating to complex products. Risk management in banks suddenly became crisis management. Quantitative risk measures seemed less appealing.

1.3 RISK MANAGEMENT AND BASEL II

This book does not cover much about Basel II, which is the standard of risk management for the banking sector. There is a chapter about value-at-risk (VaR) and a chapter about probability of default (PD). Both VaR and PD are fundamental to bank capital charge. This book intends to share how complex financial products can be priced properly with simple programming tools. Asset pricing is a cornerstone of risk management. If an asset does not have any pricing model, we find it hard to measure its risk and evaluate its fair value. A pricing model facilitates scenario analysis: how much the asset will gain or lose in different scenarios, including some stress scenarios.

After the financial tsunami, Basel II has lost its credibility. Regulators obviously underestimated the impact of pro-cyclicality on credit risk. In 2002–2006, our university worked closely with the Hong Kong Monetary Authority to promote Basel II discussion in the Hong Kong banking sector. One of our authors was also an architect of the first internal-ratings-based system in Hong Kong. Basel II did help banks save capital charge. This could be an incentive for banks to invest heavily in risk management systems. This is also a reason why banks were undercapitalized in the crisis.

Basel II imposes capital requirements on market risk, credit risk, and operational risk. However, the interrelationship of these three risks has not been considered seriously. The VaR methodology assumes normal distribution of asset returns. Many credit-linked products, such as CDOs, collateralized mortgage obligations (CMOs), and others, are marketable securities subject to both interest rate risk plus credit migration risk. Actual or expected increase in credit risk can substantially lower asset prices. It seems that the Basel II capital requirement does not adequately address this issue. How should the correlation of credit risk and market risk be modeled? That is beyond the scope of this book.

Liquidity risk and stress testing risk are key issues in the collapse of banks. These risks are covered in Pillar II of Basel II. How can liquidity risk be modeled? Excel and VBA may help, but there is no consensus on what assumptions should be adopted. Stress testing usually involves many assumptions and a subjective selection of scenarios. Stress tests can be easily done and regulators usually find it hard to challenge those test results.

1.4 ABOUT THE BOOK

The main topic of this book is the practical implementation of financial models using Excel and VBA programming. Too often, books on spreadsheet modeling provide only quick-and-dirty implementations of financial models that have very little use in real-world applications. This book focuses on the programming practices and skills to perform real-world implementation of financial models that are robust, reusable, and flexible. It takes an in-depth look at how to implement financial models using both Excel and VBA, and discusses the essential programming practices and skills in structuring complex financial models through advanced VBA features. It provides comprehensive coverage of financial models in the areas of derivatives pricing, market and credit risk modeling, and advanced interest rate modeling. Each of the later chapters on model implementation starts with a review of all the necessary financial theory and concepts from a practitioner's perspective. Step-by-step instructions on the implementation are then provided to explain the programming techniques involved for models with different complexities. Alternative approaches are also discussed to enable readers a comprehensive understanding of different techniques.

This book is suitable for those who have solid backgrounds in financial engineering, financial modeling, and financial risk management; a master's degree in financial mathematics, financial engineering, or computational finance is preferable. CFA, FRM, or professional risk manager (PRM) qualifications will be helpful to readers, but these readers must have prior training in calculus and matrix algebra. When we wrote this book, we surveyed books with relevant titles. None of them were advanced enough for our MSc (Financial Engineering) students. Most books with titles such as *Financial Modeling*, *Excel Modeling in Finance*, or *Spreadsheet Modeling in Finance* are targeted at undergraduate students in Finance or MBA students. Our book is targeted at financial engineering or mathematical finance students at business schools or engineering schools.

The book title "Financial Computing" is modified from "Computational Finance." When our MSc (Financial Engineering) program was first launched in the 1990s, a number of professors from Carnegie Mellon University (CMU) served as our program advisors and teaching fellows. CMU offers a well-known program—MSc (Computational Finance). Computational Finance focuses on financial models that are based on mathematical theories and computational intelligence. Our book places less emphasis on financial models although we provide brief summaries on the theories mentioned in the book. We place more emphasis on how to implement these advanced models with Excel and VBA programming. This helps quantitative analysts quickly develop some models for their analytical work. This is the reason we named the book "Financial Computing" instead of "Computational Finance." Our book covers a small number of well-known models and illustrates how Excel and VBA programming can be applied to implement these models. Through these models, readers can pick up Excel and VBA skills easily and apply these skills to other complex models. We believe that the book will be a good companion to any degree program in financial engineering or financial mathematics.

1.5 CHAPTER HIGHLIGHTS

Chapter 2 deals with the GARCH(1,1) model, which is used to predict the volatility of asset prices. Volatility estimates are critical for derivatives pricing and the volatility index can be traded. We introduce an effective way to use Solver in conjunction with VBA routines to enhance the functionality of Solver. Chapter 3 looks at the finite difference model, which is frequently used in derivatives pricing based on the Black–Scholes partial differential equation. We discuss the use of matrix manipulation under Excel as well as the VBA programming environment. A general framework that may be used to price a variety of options is formulated. Chapter 4 turns to portfolio mean-variance optimization. This is the base of modern investment theory and investment portfolio formation. We pay particular attention to the implementation of the Markowitz algorithm under short-selling restrictions. In all these chapters, we discuss the deficiency in taking a simple Excel implementation and demonstrate the necessity of using VBA programming in efficiently coping with complex conditions.

Chapter 5 introduces the Newton–Raphson method. This numerical procedure is powerful in solving a system of equations, and the routine developed here will be useful throughout the book. Chapter 6 discusses yield curve construction with cubic spline interpolation. We describe a generalized bootstrapping method, a computer-intensive statistical method, in the construction of a smooth yield curve given any available data set of bond prices. This enables the construction of an interest rate tree discussed in later chapters.

Chapters 7 and 8 deal with two different tree models in option pricings: the binomial model and the Black–Derman–Toy model. The binomial model can be applied to a wide range of equity derivatives. It can be implemented very easily using VBA programming. The Black–Derman–Toy model is particularly useful for pricing interest rate derivatives. We introduce an effective way to implement this model in VBA taking bond options as our working example.

Chapter 9 discusses option pricing using the Monte Carlo simulation method, which is a powerful tool in the valuation of exotic options with complex payoff conditions. We discuss various important issues regarding this method and look at the implementation for a number of exotic options.

In particular, we take a closer look at the Monte Carlo pricing of American-style options with early exercising features.

Chapter 10 applies simulation techniques to determine portfolio value-at-risk. This chapter aims at providing the necessary programming skills to build a flexible and expandable risk engine for portfolio risk simulation.

Chapter 11 looks at the state-of-the-art Hull–White model of interest rates, which is commonly adopted by the industry for pricing interest rate derivatives. We discuss an effective way to implement the complex structure of this model taking bond options again as an example.

Chapters 12 and 13 discuss two well-known credit risk models: the CreditMetrics model and the KMV–Merton model. We start the discussion of the CreditMetrics model with a single issuer and then move to credit migration risk of credit portfolios. Chapter 12 focuses on the implementation of the credit RiskMetrics framework with the use of Monte Carlo simulation. In Chapter 13 we introduce the structural model developed by Robert C. Merton and extend our discussion to the KMV–Merton model. The KMV–Merton model is best applied to publicly traded firms and its underlying methodology predicts the probability of default of a firm within a given time horizon.

Appendices A to G provide a review of Excel and VBA programming. Many engineering school graduates may be familiar with Fortran, C, or Java and seldom touch Excel or VBA. The appendices will help these readers.

In all chapters, mathematical models are briefly mentioned. Our focus is to share with readers how to write relevant VBA programs. There is no standard programming route for a single problem. Readers may find faster programming methods to achieve the same outcome. These readers are welcome to contact us and share your better approaches with us. Practical exercises are provided at the end of each chapter that allow the readers to apply their technical skills acquired from the chapter. The solutions to these questions can be downloaded through the FTP link given by http://www.cs.cityu.edu.hk/~donny/humphrey/financial_computing.

1.6 OTHER REMARKS

We would like to thank our students in Hong Kong for asking us challenging questions in class. This helps improve our thinking and sharpen our teaching performance. Among all the authors, Dr. Humphrey Tung contributed the most. He carefully reviewed every equation in the book. The other three authors would like to thank him for his passion in this project.

## CHAPTER 2

The GARCH(1,1) Model

2.1 THE MODEL

In this chapter, we discuss what is known as the GARCH(1,1) model, introduced by Bollerslev.[1] The distinctive feature of this model is that volatilities of asset price returns are not constant. Under the stochastic regime, price return r_t between, for example, the end of previous day $t - 1$ and the end of day t can be generated through random normal drawings as:

$$r_t = \varepsilon(\mu, \sigma_t) \qquad (2.1)$$

with dynamical volatility σ_t and constant mean μ. The model attempts to keep track and forecast the variations in the volatility through time. Applications of this so-called GARCH (generalized autoregressive conditional heteroscedasticity) volatility are widespread especially in the assessment of portfolio risk exposure over a short period of time.

In GARCH(1,1), future variance σ_{t+1}^2 is a weighted average of its immediate past estimation σ_t^2, the most recent observation of squared residual $(r_t - \mu)^2$, and a long-run average variance V_L. It follows an iteration equation given by:

$$\sigma_{t+1}^2 = \gamma V_L + \alpha(r_t - \mu)^2 + \beta\sigma_t^2 \qquad (2.2)$$

with weight factors $\alpha > 0$, $\beta > 0$, and $\gamma > 0$. Since the total weight must sum up to one, we have:

$$\gamma = 1 - \alpha - \beta.$$

Note that the constant mean μ in equation (2.2) can be estimated based on its historical average. There are all together three parameters in the model, namely (V_L, α, β) that satisfy the constraints,

$$V_L > 0, \ \alpha > 0, \ \beta > 0, \ \text{and}\ \alpha + \beta < 1. \qquad (2.3)$$

They can be estimated under the notion of maximum likelihood of seeing the historical data. Given the historical time series of price returns $\{r_1, r_2, \ldots, r_n\}$, we can first estimate the constant mean historically as:

$$\mu \cong (1/n)(r_1 + \ldots + r_n).$$

For a particular choice of model parameters, GARCH volatilities $\{\sigma_1, \sigma_2, \ldots, \sigma_n\}$ can be generated through equation (2.2) where the iteration starts off from observation r_1 and estimate $\sigma_1^2 \cong (r_1 - \mu)^2$. According to the random normal assumption in equation (2.1), the likelihood or chance of the entire historical data set being observed is proportional to:

$$L \propto \frac{\exp\{-\frac{1}{2}(r_1 - \mu)^2/\sigma_1^2\}}{\sqrt{2\pi\sigma_1^2}} \times \ldots \times \frac{\exp\{-\frac{1}{2}(r_n - \mu)^2/\sigma_n^2\}}{\sqrt{2\pi\sigma_n^2}}. \qquad (2.4)$$

The best model parameters should therefore generate the volatilities $\{\sigma_1, \sigma_2, \ldots, \sigma_n\}$ that maximize the likelihood L in (2.4) or equivalently the logarithm of likelihood $\ln(L)$ given by:

$$\ln(L) = -\frac{1}{2}\sum_{t=1}^{n}\left[\ln(\sigma_t^2) + \frac{(r_t - \mu)^2}{\sigma_t^2}\right] \qquad (2.5)$$

where all constant terms irrelevant to the maximization are ignored in the equation.

2.2 EXCEL IMPLEMENTATION

Figure 2.1 illustrates how the above calculation could be organized in an Excel spreadsheet.[2] The table analyzes daily returns of the Dow Jones Industrial Average (DJI) between March 22, 1990 and December 6, 2006. The leading segment from 19900322 to 19940302 will be taken as in-sample data for the determination of model parameters. The rest will be used as out-of-sample data to back test the accuracy of the model. From row 13 onward, column A in the table records the date, column B shows the closing of the DJI on each of these dates, while column C calculates the corresponding daily returns. For example, the formula adopted in C14 = (B14 − B13)/B13. The cell C2 defines the range "C14:C1011" of the entire in-sample historical returns $\{r_1, r_2, \ldots, r_n\}$. The cell C3 = **AVERAGE(INDIRECT**(C2)) calculates the corresponding constant mean μ in the model. Trial values of the model parameters (V_L, α, β) are input through cells F5, F6, and F7,

	A	B	C	D	E	F	G
1	GARCH(1,1) Parameters:						
2		In-sample Range	C14:C1011	Precision	0.010	Estimate Parameters	
3		Historical Mean (μ)	0.00038395			and call Solver	
4					Estimated		
5	Backtesting Confidence:			V_L	0.00007515	0.00006666	
6		Out of Sample Range	C1012:C4227	α	0.04000000	0.03713742	
7		Confidence Level (z)	1	β	0.95000000	0.94934303	
8		Nominal	0.6827	α + β		0.98648045	
9		Model	0.6937				
10					Total in-sample Ln(L)	4374.4682	
11							
12	Date	Closings	Returns	Residuals	GARCH Variances	Ln(L)	Backtesting
13	19900322	2695.72					
14	19900323	2704.28	0.003175404	2.79145E-03	7.79220E-06	5.38119	1
15	19900326	2707.66	0.001249871	8.65918E-04	8.58812E-06	5.78891	1
16	19900327	2736.94	0.010813765	1.04298E-02	9.08219E-06	-0.18410	0
17	19900328	2743.69	0.002466258	2.08231E-03	1.35632E-05	5.44423	1
18	19900329	2727.70	-0.005827918	-6.21187E-03	1.39385E-05	4.20623	0
19	19900330	2707.21	-0.007511823	-7.89578E-03	1.55667E-05	3.53273	0
20	19900402	2700.45	-0.002497036	-2.88099E-03	1.79947E-05	5.23209	1

FIGURE 2.1 Excel Implementation of GARCH(1,1).

respectively. We may define several named cells to enhance the readability of the formulae: C3(mu), F5(longvar), F6(alpha), F7(beta), and C7(zvalue).

The fourth column from D14 onward calculates the residuals $(r_t - \mu)$ for each of these returns using the formula D14 = (C14 − mu), for example. GARCH variances σ_t^2 are recorded in the fifth column from E14. They are generated iteratively using the formula (see equation [2.2]):

$$E15 = (1 - \text{alpha} - \text{beta}) * \text{longvar} + \text{alpha} * D14\char94 2 + \text{beta} * E14$$

starting off with the value in E14 = D14^2. To determine the best model parameters, we need to first evaluate the likelihood value associated with each trial parameter set. Column F under the data caption implements term-by-term the expression for ln(L) in equation (2.5) using the formula:

$$F14 = (-0.5) * (\text{LN}(E14) + D14\char94 2/E14)$$

such that the total in-sample ln(L) is given by cell F10 = SUM(OFFSET (INDIRECT(C2),0,3)). For example, consider the trial model parameters of $(V_L = 0.00005, \alpha = 0.02, \beta = 0.95)$ that satisfy the constraints in (2.3), we have the likelihood value being ln(L) = 4365.5993.

Here, we are interested in choosing (V_L, α, β) that maximize ln(L) under the constraints in (2.3). Such a task can be achieved by using the Solver algorithm in Excel. We can simply go to Tools, then Solver, and the **Solver Parameters** screen will pop up as shown in Figure 2.2. **Set Target Cell** is the cell F10 that is the likelihood value ln(L), check **Equal To** as **Max** for maximizing, and input the cells F5:F7 in **By Changing Cells** for the trial values of V_L, α, and β.

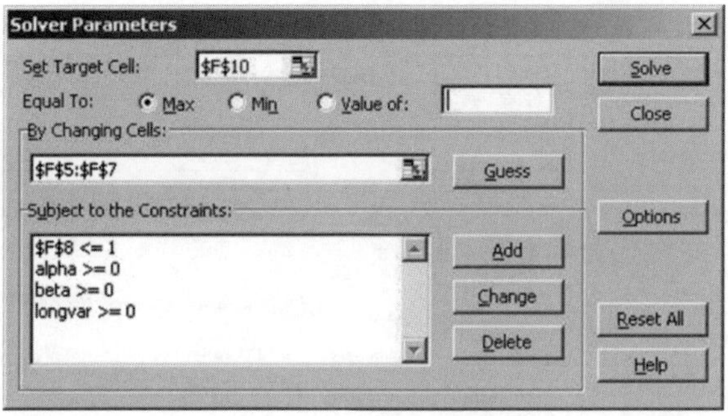

FIGURE 2.2   Solver Parameters screen.

The constraints in (2.3) can easily be included in the Solver algorithm under the **Subject to the Constraints** field. Click **Add** and, as shown in Figure 2.3, enter the following through the **Add Constraint** screen:

$$\text{longvar} >= 0, \text{ alpha} >= 0, \text{ beta} >= 0, \text{ and } F8 <= 1$$

for the constraints $V_L > 0$, $\alpha > 0$, $\beta > 0$, and $\alpha + \beta < 1$, respectively. In the spreadsheet, we have defined the cell F8 = alpha + beta to be the sum of α and β. Note that Solver provides only the choices ">=" and "<=" for our purpose. Under a floating point environment, they work effectively in the same way as the strictly greater and strictly smaller operators ">" and "<." The non-negative constraints can also be included through an alternative setup. We can click **Options** to open the **Solver Options** screen and check **Assume Non-Negative** that applies the constraints to the cells F5:F7 specified in **By Changing Cells.**

Solver adapts a gradient search algorithm specified by the **Estimates, Derivatives,** and **Search** fields in the **Solver Options** screen as shown in Figure 2.4. For the current problem, we need to insert a maximum running time in **Max Time,** the number of iterations in the search in **Iterations,** and in **Precision** the required precision in the cells F5:F7 in **By Changing Cells.**

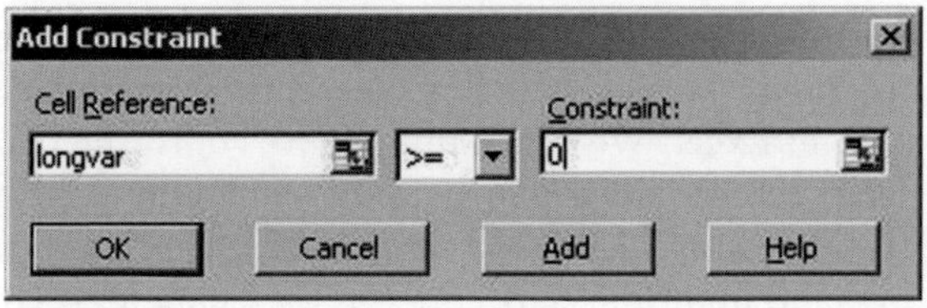

FIGURE 2.3   Add Constraint screen.

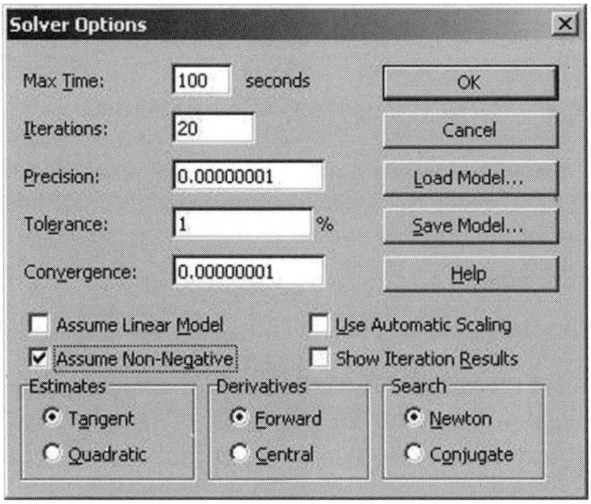

FIGURE 2.4 Solver Options screen.

Depending on the problem, this represents only the maximum achievable precision if there is enough iterations. Here, Solver will normally require 10 to 20 iterations to achieve the precision of 10^{-8}. To start off the search algorithm, we need to provide initial values for the cells F5:F7. Suppose we initiate the search with F5 = 0.00007, F6 = 0.04, and F7 = 0.90. By clicking **Solve**, Solver returns the optimal solutions to be F5 = 0.00006663, F6 = 0.03714556, and F7 = 0.94929286 after the search with a maximum likelihood of F10 = 4374.46820612.

How good is the GARCH(1,1) model with these optimal parameters? To answer this question, we will backtest the model with out-of-sample historical data. In columns A and B we have included historical closings of the DJI up to the trading day 20061206 with about 3,000 backtesting points right after the in-sample data. The out-of-sample historical returns are located in C1012 to C4227 as defined in cell C6, and the GARCH variances are located in E1012 to E4227. Recall in the model, known values of r_t and σ_t^2 will allow us to forecast the new variance σ_{t+1}^2 the next day when the actual r_{t+1} will be observed subsequently. According to the random normal assumption in equation (2.1), the confidence interval of r_{t+1} is given by $[\mu - z\sigma_{t+1}, \mu + z\sigma_{t+1}]$ with z being the confidence level. In this respect, we can backtest the accuracy of the model by checking the percentage that the forecasted interval has included the observation for the entire out-of-sample data. In Figure 2.1, the cell C7 defines the chosen value of z, while the cell C8 calculates the nominal confidence of the interval based on standard cumulative probability as:

$$C8 = \textbf{NORMSDIST}(C7) - \textbf{NORMSDIST}(-C7).$$

Column G under the data caption records on each day the success (1) or failure (0) of whether the forecast confidence interval has included the observation using the formula:

$$G14 = \textbf{IF(AND}(C14 <= mu + zvalue * \textbf{SQRT}(E14), C14 >= mu$$
$$- zvalue * \textbf{SQRT}(E14)), 1, 0).$$

The cell C9 = **AVERAGE(OFFSET(INDIRECT**(C6),0,4)) then accumulates the backtesting confidence for the entire out-of-sample data. To check the accuracy of GARCH(1,1), we can compare this value with the nominal value as given by C8.

There are critical issues on the choice of initial values that are relevant to the current problem. Without going into a detailed discussion of its search algorithm, we consider the following example to simply demonstrate an important shortfall of Solver. For arbitrary choice of initial values, there is indeed no guarantee of finding the correct optimal solution by Solver. The initial values should be as close to the solution as possible.

EXAMPLE 2.1

Consider the single-variable function given by $f(x) = \frac{1}{3} x^3 - \frac{1}{2} x^2 + 1$. The local maximum and minimum are located at $x = 0$ and $x = 1$, respectively, where $f(0) = 1$ and $f(1) = 0.8333$. The function is strictly increasing to the right of the local minimum, and it is strictly decreasing to the left of the local maximum.

Suppose we want to use Solver to determine the overall maximum and minimum points of the function under the constraints $x \geq -0.4$ and $x \leq 1.4$.

The values of the function at both edges are given by $f(-0.4) = 0.8987$ and $f(1.4) = 0.9347$. They are neither the maximum point nor the minimum point of our concern. The solution should clearly be the points $x = 0$ and $x = 1$, respectively (see Figure 2.5).

Depending on the initial value of x, Solver determines only the nearest maximum or minimum point that is not necessarily the overall solution. In particular, if the initial value is chosen to be $x = 1.2$, the

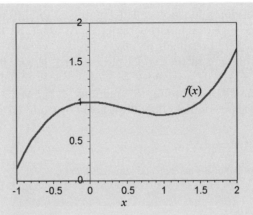

FIGURE 2.5 The plot of $f(x)$ between $x = 1$ and $x = 2$.

nearest maximum is located at $x = 1.4$ (the right edge). Upon maximizing, Solver returns this point to be the solution rather than $x = 0$ as expected. Similarly, if the initial value is chosen to be $x = -0.2$ for minimizing, Solver returns the nearest minimum at $x = -0.4$ (the left edge) not $x = 1$ (see Table 2.1).

TABLE 2.1 Set Iterations $= 20$ and Precision $= 10^{-8}$.

Initial value	Maximum by Solver	Minimum by Solver
$x = 0.5$	$x = -0.00000001$	$x = 0.99999996$
$x = 1.2$	$x = 1.40000000$	$x = 1.00000000$
$x = -0.2$	$x = -0.00000000$	$x = -0.40000000$

2.3 EXCEL PLUS VBA IMPLEMENTATION

In general, there is no *a priori* information on the model parameters in GARCH(1,1). A preliminary procedure for the purpose of determining the proper initial values for Solver would definitely be required in view of the shortfall as demonstrated in the above example. An effective way to perform such an integrated task is to write additional VBA routines underneath the spreadsheet in Figure 2.1 such that Solver can be initiated immediately after the preliminary procedure.

We first develop a function called TotalLikelihood() that calculates the likelihood value with trial model parameters. As input, the function reads in the historical squared residuals $\{h_1, h_2, \ldots, h_n\}$ where $h_t = (r_t - \mu)^2$, the number of terms n, and the model parameters (V_L, α, β). Iteratively, it generates the GARCH variances $\{\sigma_1^2, \sigma_2^2, \ldots, \sigma_n^2\}$ and accumulates the likelihood value $\ln(L)$ according to equations (2.2) and (2.5), respectively. The pseudo code of TotalLikelihood() is given by Code 2.1 as follows:

TotalLikelihood(h(1:n), n , α , β , V_L)

\# define $v_1 = \sigma_1^2$ to start off the iteration and accumulate $ln(L)$
   v(1) = h(1)

   sum = $ln($ v(1) $)$ + h(1) / v(1)

\# generate { $v_2 = \sigma_2^2$, $\ldots$, $v_n = \sigma_n^2$ } by iteration and accumulate $ln(L)$
   For (i = 1 to n − 1){ v(i + 1) = (1 − α − β) V_L + α h(i) + β v(i)

        sum = sum + $ln($ v(i + 1) $)$ + h(i + 1) / v(i + 1)   }

   TotalLikelihood = −½ sum

Code 2.1: Pseudo code of the TotalLikelihood() function.

We want to develop a search routine called EstimateBestParameters() that scans through the valid region of the model parameters and identifies the spot with the largest $\ln(L)$, which utilizes the above likelihood function. Define in cell E2 the required precision *prec* of the parameters in this preliminary procedure. According to the constraints in (2.3), the search for a proper α and β should run through all points given by the double-loop as:

$$\alpha = i \times prec, \ i = 1, 2, \ldots, N - 1 \qquad (2.6)$$

$$\beta = j \times prec, \ j = 1, 2, \ldots, N - i - 1$$

where $N = (1/prec)$ is defined to be the number of grids between zero and one with precision *prec*. We should always choose *prec* such that $(1/prec)$ is an integer. It can be shown[3] that V_L is simply the unconditional variance $E[(r_t - \mu)^2]$ of price returns. Numerically, it should be close to the historical variance given by:

$$V_{historical} = (1/n)[(r_1 - \mu)^2 + \ldots + (r_n - \mu)^2].$$

In practice, the search for a proper V_L can be confined within the region

$$0.8 V_{historical} \leq V_L \leq 1.2 V_{historical}$$

and run through the loop as:

$$V_L = (k \times prec) \, V_{historical}, \ k = k_{low}, \ldots, k_{high} \qquad (2.7)$$

where k_{low} and k_{high} are the nearest integers to 0.8N and 1.2N, respectively. The pseudo code of EstimateBestParameters() is given by Code 2.2. As input, the routine reads in historical price returns $\{r_1, r_2, \ldots, r_n\}$, the number of terms n, and the search precision *prec*. As output, it returns the best model parameters (V_L, α, β) taken to be the initial values for Solver. We can set the precision to 0.01 in EstimateBestParameters() and then use Solver to fine-tune the model parameters. Alternatively, we can set the precision to be very small and estimate the model parameters directly from EstimateBestParameters(), but this will be numerically intensive.

EstimateBestParameters( )

```
# input historical price returns and precision parameter
    Read n, r(1:n), and prec

# estimate the historical mean and variance
    μ = AVERAGE( r(1:n) )
    V_historical = VAR( r(1:n) )

# construct the squared residuals
    For ( i = 1 to n ) {   h(i) = ( r(i) − μ )²   }

# determine the number of grids given precision
    N = Int(1/prec)

# scan through the valid region of the parameters for the largest ln(L)
    maxlnL = −10⁸

For ( i = 1 to N − 1 ) {
    For ( j = 1 to N − i − 1 ) {
        For ( k = Int(0.8N) to Int(1.2N) ) {

            α = i prec ,   β = j prec   , V_L = k prec V_historical

            lnL = Totallikelihood( h(1:n) , n , α , β , V_L )

            If( lnL ≥ maxlnL ){ maxlnL = lnL
                              bestα = α , bestβ = β , bestV_L = V_L   }

            } } }

# output best model parameters
    Output bestV_L, bestα, and bestβ
```

Code 2.2: Pseudo code of the EstimateBestParamters() routine.

The main routine EstimateBestParameters() can be invoked through the button in the spreadsheet. In the VBA coding as shown in Code 2.3, it contains three subroutines and one function designed to tackle specific tasks so that it can be maintained easily. The first statement will display a message box asking for confirmation to start the calculation. It is always a good practice to include a message box to avoid mis-invoking a long-running procedure. The GetInputs() routine will read in historical price returns and the precision parameter from the Excel spreadsheet and generate both the squared residuals and historical variance for the evaluation of likelihood values below. In the GetInputs() routine, the ByRef declaration denotes that the particular variable will be evaluated internally and taken as output of the routine. The first statement in GetInputs() inputs historical price returns from the range of in-sample data defined in C2. The triple-loop will scan through the valid region of the model parameters (V_L, α, β) and identify the best spot with maximum likelihood utilizing the TotalLikelihood() function. The PutBestValues() routine will then return the estimated values of the parameters to the cells E5:E7 for display, as well as to the cells F5:F7 for Solver input. The final statement triggers Solver to perform further optimization based on these initial values. Certainly, it must be configured properly ahead of time as described in Section 2.2. As it will be used in this implementation, we need to add Solver in the VBA reference section by clicking on **References** in the **Tools** menu and checking **Solver** in the Reference dialogue. The TRUE parameter of the SolverSolve function suspends the display of the resulting dialogue at the end of Solver execution.

```
Sub EstimateBestParameters()
    If MsgBox("Start calculation?", vbYesNo + vbInformation) = vbNo Then Exit Sub
    'Read inputs
    Dim residualSq() As Double, hVar As Double, prec As Double
    Call GetInputs(residualSq, hVar, prec)
    'initialize values
    Dim bestAlpha As Double, bestBeta As Double, bestLongVar As Double
    Dim i As Integer, j As Integer, k As Integer
    Dim nFrac As Integer: nFrac = Int(Round(1/prec,15))
    Dim maxlnL As Double: maxlnL = -100000000#
    'Iterate by the increment of alpha, beta, and longVar
    Dim alpha As Double, beta As Double, longVar As Double, lnL As Double
    For i = 1 To (nFrac -1)
        alpha = i * prec
        For j = 1 To (nFrac - i - 1)
            beta = j * prec
            For k = Int(0.8 * nFrac) To Int(1.2 * nFrac)
                longVar = k * prec * hVar
                lnL = TotalLikelihood(residualSq, alpha, beta, longVar)
                If lnL < maxlnL Then
                    maxlnL = lnL
                    bestAlpha = alpha
                    bestBeta = beta
```

```
            bestLongVar = longVar
        End If
      Next k
    Next j
  Next i
  'Write outputs
  Call PutBestValues(bestAlpha, bestBeta, bestLongVar)
  'Call solver and turn off the final Solver Results dialog
  'Solver must be configured ahead of time
  SolverSolve (True)
End Sub


'Read inputs from excel
Sub GetInputs(ByRef residualSq() As Double, ByRef hVar As Double, ByRef prec As Double)
  Dim priceReturn As Range: Set priceReturn =Range(Range("C2").Text)
  Dim mu As Double
  With WorksheetFunction
    mu = .Average(priceReturn)
    hVar = .Var(priceReturn)
  End With
  ReDim residualSq(1 To priceReturn.Count)
  Dim i As Integer
  For i = 1 To priceReturn.Count
    residualSq(i) = (priceReturn(i) - mu) ^ 2
  Next
  prec = Range("E2").Value
End Sub


'Write outputs to excel
Sub PutBestValues(alpha As Double, beta As Double, longVar As Double)
  Range("E5:F5").Value = longVar
  Range("E6:F6").Value = alpha
  Range("E7:F7").Value = beta
End Sub


'Calculate the total log of likelihood
Function TotalLikelihood(residualSq() As Double, alpha As Double, beta As Double, longVar
                         As Double) As Double
  Dim garchVar() As Double: ReDim garchVar(1 To UBound(residualSq))
  garchVar(1) = residualSq(1)
  Dim sum As Double: sum = Log(garchVar(1)) + residualSq(1)/garchVar(1)
  Dim i As Integer
  For i = 1 To (UBound(residualSq) - 1)
    garchVar(i + 1) = (1 - alpha - beta) * longVar + alpha * residualSq(i) + beta * garchVar(i)
    sum = sum + Log(garchVar(i + 1)) + residualSq(i + 1)/garchVar(i + 1)
  Next
  TotalLikelihood = -0.5 * sum
End Function
```

Code 2.3: VBA codes of the EstimateBestParameters() routine, GetInputs() routine, PutBestValues() routine, and TotalLikelihood () function.

REVIEW QUESTION

1. In the Exponentially Weighted Moving Average model (EWMA), future variance is a weighted average of its immediate past estimation and the most recent observation of squared residual. It follows an iteration equation given by

$$\sigma_{t+1}^2 = (1 - \lambda)(r_t - \mu)^2 + \lambda\sigma_t^2$$

with weight factor $1 > \lambda > 0$. Modify the implementation in garch11.xls to include the EWMA model. The factor λ should be determined based on maximum likelihood analysis starting from a preliminary search using VBA and following by a fine tuning procedure using Solver.

ENDNOTES

1. T. Bollerslev, "Generalized Autoregressive Conditional Heteroscedasticity," *Journal of Econometrics*, 31 (1986): 307–27. See also Robert Engle, "GARCH 101: The Use of ARCH/GARCH Models in Applied Econometrics," *Journal of Economic Perspectives*, Vol. 15, No. 4 (2001): 157–68.
2. Refer to garch11.xls
3. Stephen J. Taylor, "ARCH Models: Definitions and Examples," in *Asset Price Dynamics, Volatility, and Prediction*, (Princeton: Princeton University Press, 2005), 197–234.

## CHAPTER 3

Finite Difference Methods

3.1 DIFFERENCE EQUATIONS

In this chapter, we consider a numerical technique known as finite difference method capable of solving differential equations by difference equations.[1] It relies on discretizing continuous variables into a grid of points that spans the domain of interest and approximating differential operators by finite differences. In this way, we can approximate a differential equation by a difference equation that relates the function values at different points on the grid. Hence, it can be solved numerically through iteration starting from the initial condition. Suppose for example that variable x takes on discrete values of $\{0, \Delta x, 2\Delta x, \ldots\}$ with grid size Δx. Derivative with respect to x can be approximated by the finite difference as:

$$y'(x) \cong \frac{y(x + \Delta x) - y(x)}{\Delta x}.$$

Thus, we can numerically solve a general first-order differential equation $y'(x) = g(x, y)$ by the difference equation $y(x + \Delta x) = y(x) + \Delta x \, g(x, y(x))$ given an initial value of $y(0) = c$ for example.

The Black–Scholes partial differential equation in (3.1) describes the option price $F(S, t)$ with respect to its underlying asset price S and time t:

$$\frac{\partial}{\partial t} F(S, t) + rS \frac{\partial}{\partial S} F(S, t) + \tfrac{1}{2}\sigma^2 S^2 \frac{\partial^2}{\partial S^2} F(S, t) = rF(S, t), \; F(S, t) = \psi(S) \quad (3.1)$$

Together with the differential equation, there are payoff condition $\psi(S)$ at maturity T and intermediate boundary conditions at any time t prior to maturity. The parameters r and σ are, respectively, the risk-free interest rate and volatility of the logarithmic price return of the asset. In particular, we are interested in solving the Black–Scholes equation for the current values $F(S, 0)$ based on the difference equation in this method. Note that the asset

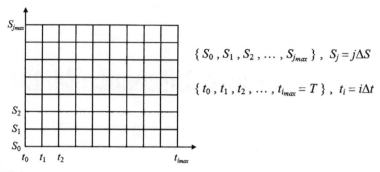

FIGURE 3.1 Two-dimensional grid for the finite difference method.

price S is always positive and the option ceases to exist after it has matured. In the finite difference method, we partition the domain of interest in asset price and time using a two-dimensional grid with sizes ΔS and Δt as shown in Figure 3.1.

For interior point (S_j, t_i) on the grid, partial derivatives with respect to asset price in equation (3.1) can be approximated to the second order of price grid ΔS by the finite differences as:

$$\frac{\partial}{\partial S} F(S_j, t_i) \cong \frac{F(S_{j+1}, t_i) - F(S_{j-1}, t_i)}{2\Delta S}. \tag{3.2}$$

$$\frac{\partial^2}{\partial S^2} F(S_j, t_i) \cong \frac{F(S_{j+1}, t_i) - 2F(S_j, t_i) + F(S_{j-1}, t_i)}{(\Delta S)^2}. \tag{3.3}$$

For the derivative with time, we adopt a forward difference approximation to the first order of time grid Δt given by:

$$\frac{\partial}{\partial t} F(S_j, t_i) \cong \frac{F(S_j, t_{i+1}) - F(S_j, t_i)}{\Delta t}. \tag{3.4}$$

Replacing also the asset price terms in (3.1) by $S_j = j\Delta S$, we can approximate the Black–Scholes partial differential equation by the difference equation:

$$F(S_j, t_{i+1}) = a_j F(S_{j-1}, t_i) + b_j F(S_j, t_i) + c_j F(S_{j+1}, t_i), \quad \begin{aligned} &\text{for } j = 1, \ldots, j_{max} - 1 \\ &i = 0, \ldots, i_{max} - 1 \end{aligned}$$

$$\tag{3.5}$$

where

$$a_j = \tfrac{1}{2}rj\Delta t - \tfrac{1}{2}\sigma^2 j^2 \Delta t$$
$$b_j = 1 + r\Delta t + \sigma^2 j^2 \Delta t$$
$$c_j = -\tfrac{1}{2}rj\Delta t - \tfrac{1}{2}\sigma^2 j^2 \Delta t.$$

Note that the boundary values $F(S_0, t_{i+1})$ and $F(S_{jmax}, t_{i+1})$ are both missing in the iteration. For completeness, we include in equation (3.5) the corresponding transformations:

$$F(S_0, t_{i+1}) = b_0 \, F(S_0, t_i) \tag{3.6}$$

$$F(S_{jmax}, t_{i+1}) = b_{jmax} \, F(S_{jmax}, t_i) \tag{3.7}$$

where $b_{jmax} = 1$ and $b_0 = e^{r\Delta t}$ or 1 for European or American-style options,[2] respectively. The difference equation can now be written in matrix representation as:

$$\begin{pmatrix} F(S_0, t_{i+1}) \\ F(S_1, t_{i+1}) \\ \vdots \\ F(S_{jmax-1}, t_{i+1}) \\ F(S_{jmax}, t_{i+1}) \end{pmatrix} = G \begin{pmatrix} F(S_0, t_i) \\ F(S_1, t_i) \\ \vdots \\ F(S_{jmax-1}, t_i) \\ F(S_{jmax}, t_i) \end{pmatrix} \tag{3.8}$$

where G is a $(j_{max} + 1) \times (j_{max} + 1)$ tridiagonal matrix given by:

$$\begin{pmatrix} b_0 & 0 & 0 & \ldots & & & & \\ a_1 & b_1 & c_1 & 0 & \ldots & & & \\ 0 & a_2 & b_2 & c_2 & 0 & & \ldots & \\ \vdots & \vdots & \vdots & \vdots & \vdots & \vdots & \vdots & \vdots \\ & & & & \ldots & a_{jmax-1} & b_{jmax-1} & c_{jmax-1} \\ & & & & \ldots & 0 & 0 & b_{jmax} \end{pmatrix} \tag{3.9}$$

It is clear that equation (3.8) is iterating forward in time. To solve the Black–Scholes equation, we need to iterate backward in time instead, starting from the option's payoff values at maturity to its current values at t_0. This can be done *implicitly* by reverting equation (3.8) through the inverse matrix G^{-1} such that numerically it is given by the difference equation:[3]

$$\begin{pmatrix} F(S_0, t_i) \\ F(S_1, t_i) \\ \vdots \end{pmatrix} = G^{-1} \begin{pmatrix} F(S_0, t_{i+1}) \\ F(S_1, t_{i+1}) \\ \vdots \end{pmatrix} \tag{3.10}$$

for $i = 0, \ldots, i_{max} - 1$ and with payoff condition $F(S_j, t_{imax}) = \psi(S_j)$ at maturity. For exotic options with intermediate boundary conditions, we need to adjust each $F(S_j, t_i)$ on the left side of equation (3.10) according to the boundary conditions before the next iteration with G^{-1} to an earlier time. For example, an American put option has the payoff condition at maturity given by:

$$\psi(S_j) = max\{K - S_j, 0\}$$

with a strike price K. The option can be exercised at any time prior to its maturity based on the same payoff function. We should therefore compare each $F(S_j, t_i)$ with its intrinsic value $\psi(S_j)$ and perform the update according to the early exercising condition as:

$$F(S_j, t_i) = max\{F(S_j, t_i), \psi(S_j)\}.$$

The errors involved in the use of equation (3.10) are proportional to the time grid Δt and to the square of the price grid ΔS. Numerically, the iteration is unconditionally stable in the sense that the solution remains well behaved for arbitrarily large values of Δt and ΔS despite being less precise. A more accurate procedure is given by the Crank–Nicholson scheme for which the errors are proportional to $(\Delta t)^2$ and $(\Delta S)^2$. The difference equation in this scheme can be found in Section 3.4 and the iteration is unconditionally stable but it is numerically more intensive.

3.2 EXCEL IMPLEMENTATION

Figures 3.2 to 3.4 illustrate how the difference equation in (3.10) could be implemented in an Excel spreadsheet.[4] As shown in Figure 3.2, option parameters (T, K, r, σ) are input through cells B4, B5, B6, and B7, respectively. In the finite difference method, the price grid is configured by the grid number j_{max} and the grid size ΔS. There is also the requirement that boundary value S_{jmax} should presumably be far away from the strike price K. Thus, the grid size cannot be chosen arbitrarily in order to improve accuracy. Numerically, it is sufficient to consider $S_{jmax} > 2K$ such that we have a soft lower bound on the grid size as:

$$\Delta S > 2K/j_{max}.$$

It is then clear that the grid number j_{max} should be defined to the full extent of Excel in order to maximize precision. As j_{max} also governs the size of the matrix G, we can at most take $j_{max} = 50$ under the maximum capacity of matrix operations in Excel. Thus, $j_{max} = 50$ in B2 is a rigid parameter and

▲	A	B	C	D	E
1					
2	*jmax* =	50			
3	*imax* =	100			
4	*Maturity* (*T*) =	5	(*year*)		
5	*Strike* (*K*) =	5			
6	*Risk-free Rate* (*r*) =	0.05	(*per year*)		
7	*Volatility* (*σ*) =	0.25	(*per year*)		
8	*Price Inc.* (*ΔS*) =	0.25		*Min :*	0.2
9	*Time Inc.* (*Δt*) =	0.05	(*year*)		
10					

FIGURE 3.2 Option parameters and grid configuration.

the grid size ΔS is input through B8 with reference to its lower bound in E8 = 2*B5/B2. For the time grid configurated by i_{max} and Δt, the boundary value t_{imax} is defined to be the option maturity. Similarly, a large grid number $i_{max} \leq 250$ should be inserted in B3 utilizing the full column space in Excel. The corresponding grid size Δt is presumably small and determined in B9 = B4/B3.

We now construct the tridiagonal matrix **G** as given by (3.9). We may define several named cells to enhance the readability of the formulae: F5 (strike), F6(riskfree), F7(sigma), F8(dprice), and F9(dtime). Note that $j_{max} = 50$ is a rigid setup in the implementation, the size of the matrix is 51×51, and it is defined in cells B66:AZ116 from top-left to bottom-right. It is convenient to first create the row and column labels of **G** such that all entries can be defined with reference to the labeling. As is partially shown in Figure 3.3, cells B65:AZ65 label the column number L_c: (0 − 50) of the matrix, while A66:A116 label the row number L_r: (0 − 50) of the matrix. For the top row and bottom row of the matrix, the nonzero entries are defined according to (3.9) as:

$$G(L_r = 0, L_c = 0) = b_0 = e^{r\Delta t} \text{ or } 1$$

$$G(L_r = 50, L_c = 50) = b_{jmax} = 1.$$

▲	A	B	C	D	E	F	G	H	I	J
64	**Matrix G :**									
65	$L_r \backslash L_c$	0	1	2	3	4	5	6	7	8
66	0	1.0025	0.0000	0.0000	0.0000	0.0000	0.0000	0.0000	0.0000	0.0000
67	1	-0.0003	1.0056	-0.0028	0.0000	0.0000	0.0000	0.0000	0.0000	0.0000
68	2	0.0000	-0.0038	1.0150	-0.0088	0.0000	0.0000	0.0000	0.0000	0.0000
69	3	0.0000	0.0000	-0.0103	1.0306	-0.0178	0.0000	0.0000	0.0000	0.0000
70	4	0.0000	0.0000	0.0000	-0.0200	1.0525	-0.0300	0.0000	0.0000	0.0000
71	5	0.0000	0.0000	0.0000	0.0000	-0.0328	1.0806	-0.0453	0.0000	0.0000
72	6	0.0000	0.0000	0.0000	0.0000	0.0000	-0.0488	1.1150	-0.0638	0.0000
73	7	0.0000	0.0000	0.0000	0.0000	0.0000	0.0000	-0.0678	1.1556	-0.0853
74	8	0.0000	0.0000	0.0000	0.0000	0.0000	0.0000	0.0000	-0.0900	1.2025

FIGURE 3.3 The matrix G (partially) together with row and column labels.

	A	B	C	D	E	F	G	H	I	J
11	L_r	*Asset*	*Option*	5.00	4.95	4.90	4.85	4.80	4.75	4.70
12	0	0.00	3.89	5.00	4.99	4.98	4.96	4.95	4.94	4.93
13	1	0.25	3.65	4.75	4.74	4.73	4.71	4.70	4.69	4.68
14	2	0.50	3.40	4.50	4.49	4.48	4.46	4.45	4.44	4.43
15	3	0.75	3.15	4.25	4.24	4.23	4.21	4.20	4.19	4.18
16	4	1.00	2.90	4.00	3.99	3.98	3.96	3.95	3.94	3.93
17	5	1.25	2.66	3.75	3.74	3.73	3.71	3.70	3.69	3.68
18	6	1.50	2.42	3.50	3.49	3.48	3.46	3.45	3.44	3.43
19	7	1.75	2.19	3.25	3.24	3.23	3.21	3.20	3.19	3.18
20	8	2.00	1.98	3.00	2.99	2.98	2.96	2.95	2.94	2.93
21	9	2.25	1.79	2.75	2.74	2.73	2.71	2.70	2.69	2.68
22	10	2.50	1.60	2.50	2.49	2.48	2.46	2.45	2.44	2.43
23	11	2.75	1.44	2.25	2.24	2.23	2.21	2.20	2.19	2.18

FIGURE 3.4 The two-dimensional structure for price iteration together with time and column labels.

In the case of a European-style option, we set B66 = **EXP**(riskfree∗ dtime), AZ116 = 1, and elsewhere zero in the two rows. For all the interior rows of the matrix, the entries can be defined according to the rules:

If $(L_c = L_r - 1)$, then $G(L_r, L_c) = a_{j=L_r}$ $\qquad(3.11)$

If $(L_c = L_r)$, then $G(L_r, L_c) = b_{j=L_r}$

If $(L_c = L_r + 1)$, then $G(L_r, L_c) = c_{j=L_r}$

Elsewhere $G(L_r, L_c) = 0$

where a_j, b_j, and c_j are given by equation (3.5). We can use the row and column labels as references and apply the following expression for B67 to each of the cells B67:AZ115 in the interior rows.

$$\text{IF(B\$65} = \text{\$A67} - 1, \; 0.5 * \text{riskfree} * \text{\$A67} * \text{dtime} - 0.5 * \text{sigma} \wedge 2 *$$
$$(\text{\$A67}) \wedge 2 * \text{dtime},$$
$$\text{IF(B\$65} = \text{\$A67}, \; 1 + \text{riskfree} * \text{dtime} + \text{sigma} \wedge 2 * (\text{\$A67}) \wedge 2 * \text{dtime},$$
$$\text{IF(B\$65} = \text{\$A67} + 1, \; -0.5 * \text{riskfree} * \text{\$A67} * \text{dtime} - 0.5 * \text{sigma} \wedge 2 *$$
$$(\text{\$A67}) \wedge 2 * \text{dtime}, 0)))$$

The difference equation in (3.10) requires instead the inverse matrix G^{-1}. It is efficient to explicitly calculate all the entries in G^{-1} for successive usage as it is static in the iteration. The size of G^{-1} is also 51×51 and it is defined in cells B119:AZ169. The entries can be determined based on the matrix inverse operation adopted in these cells as **MINVERSE**(B66:AZ116) where B66:AZ116 denotes the input matrix **G**. It is also convenient to name G^{-1} in cells B119:AZ169 as inverseG.

To iterate equation (3.10) backward in time, we first construct a two-dimensional structure catering for arrays of option prices evaluated at different times. As is partially shown in Figure 3.4, the row labels L_r: $(0 - 50)$ of the array are defined in cells A12:A62, while the underlying asset prices are determined in B12:B62 according to the common expression B12 = \$A12*dprice. We also create the time labels starting from D11 and run toward the right end of the spreadsheet. We assign D11 = B4 to be the option maturity t_{imax} and subtract one Δt per step to the right by applying recursively the common expression E11 = **ROUND**(D11 − dtime, 8). Here, the **ROUND** function rounds off each time label to 8 decimal places to avoid a possible floating point problem in the procedure below. The time label will hit the current time t_0 at column offset from D11 with the grid number i_{max}, and will become negative thereafter. To initiate the iteration, we define in D12:D62 the option's payoff values at maturity with respect to the asset prices in B12:B62. Suppose it is a put option with the strike price defined in B5, then the payoff values can be defined using the common expression:

$$D12 = \textbf{MAX}(\text{strike} - B12, 0).$$

For one Δt prior to maturity, the option values in E12:E62 can be determined according to equation (3.10) through the matrix multiplication of G^{-1} with the values D12:D62 at maturity. Iterating backward in time in the same way, option values at different time labels can be determined through their previous values in the immediate left-hand array using the same G^{-1}. For the arrays of option values under the time labels starting from E11, we apply the common matrix operation as:

$$\{E12 : E62 = \textbf{IF}(E\$11 >= 0, \textbf{MMULT}(\text{inverseG}, D\$12 : D\$62), "")\}$$

$$(3.12)$$

where { . . . } denotes the condition that it is applied to the array in a collective sense through **Ctrl-Shift-Enter**. The iteration will terminate at the point when the time label reaches the current time of exactly zero as ensured by the **ROUND** function.[5] As discussed above, this will appear at column offset of i_{max} from D11. The current option values are then displayed in C12:C62 adjacent to the asset prices based on the common expression C12 = **OFFSET**(D12, 0, \$B\$3).

Figure 3.4 depicts only the pricing of a plain vanilla European-style option. For exotic options with intermediate boundary conditions, we need to adjust the generated option values in (3.12) according to some extra conditions depending on the underlying asset prices in B12:B62. Since (3.12) is collectively applied to the array of option prices, it is quite difficult to include in the expression any dynamic update condition with reference to the row labels. However, we can replace the collective structure in (3.12) by a flexible expression given by:

E12 = **IF**(E$11 >= 0, **INDEX** (**MMULT**(inverseG, D$12 : D$62), $A12 + 1, 1), " ")

where the **INDEX** function returns exclusively the entry defined by the row labels within a single column in the generated array. In this way, an intermediate condition such as an early exercising condition in an American-style option can be included easily as:

E12 = **IF**(E$11 >= 0, **MAX**(**INDEX**(**MMULT**(inverseG, D$12 : D$62),

$A12 + 1, 1), **MAX**(strike − $B12, 0)), " ")

The common expression is applied to the entire array in cells E12:E62 and to every array of option values under the time labels. The same matrix multiplication will be repeated in each cell along an array creating a numerical burden in the implementation.[6] Thus, it is efficient to implement the difference equation in (3.10) with intermediate conditions through VBA.

3.3 VBA IMPLEMENTATION

In general, the same matrix operations can also be performed under the VBA environment. It will be shown below that the difference equation in (3.10) can be implemented in an effective way for which intermediate boundary conditions can also be included efficiently in the iteration. We can adopt the same input screen as depicted in Figure 3.2 for both the option parameters (T, K, r, σ) and grid configuration $(i_{max}, j_{max}, \Delta S)$. We then develop a routine called CalOptionPrices() that takes the above inputs and returns an array of the current option values $F(L_r = 0: j_{max})$ with respect to asset prices $\{S_0, S_1, S_2, \ldots, S_{jmax}\}$. The pseudo code of CalOptionPrices() is given by Code 3.1 as follows:

CalOptionPrices($T, K, r, \sigma, i_{max}, j_{max}, \Delta S, F(0 : j_{max})$)

determine the grid size of time
  $\Delta t = T / i_{max}$

construct the matrix **G** according to the rules in (3.11)
  $G(0, 0) = Exp(r\Delta t)$ or 1
  For ($L_c = 1$ to j_{max}) { $G(0, L_c) = 0$ }

  $G(j_{max}, j_{max}) = 1$

For ($L_c = 0$ to $j_{max} - 1$) { $G(j_{max} , L_c) = 0$ }

For ($L_r = 1$ to $j_{max} - 1$) {
      For ($L_c = 0$ to j_{max}) {   If($L_c = L_r - 1$) then
                              $G(L_r , L_c) = ½ r L_r \Delta t - ½ \sigma^2 L_r^2 \Delta t$
                    Elseif($L_c = L_r$) then
                              $G(L_r , L_c) = 1 + r \Delta t + \sigma^2 L_r^2 \Delta t$
                    Elseif($L_c = L_r + 1$) then
                              $G(L_r , L_c) = -½ r L_r \Delta t - ½ \sigma^2 L_r^2 \Delta t$
                    Else
                              $G(L_r , L_c) = 0$
                    Endif   }
      }

# initiate the option values at maturity based on the payoff condition
    For ($L_r = 0$ to j_{max}) { $F(L_r) = $ payoff(K , $L_r \Delta S$) }

perform the backward iterations in (3.10) i_{max} number of times up to current option values in
   conjunction with update according to intermediate boundary conditions
    For ($i = 1$ to i_{max}) { $\mathbf{F}(0 : j_{max}) = \mathbf{G}^{-1} (0 : j_{max} , 0 : j_{max}) \mathbf{F}(0 : j_{max})$

        call Boundary($F(0 : j_{max})$, j_{max} , $\Delta S, K$) }

Code 3.1: Pseudo code of the CalOptionPrices() routine.

In Code 3.1, the matrix multiplication is only performed once per iteration in time followed by an update of the entire array of option values. Intermediate conditions are thus executed efficiently in the implementation. To be flexible, we define both the payoff and intermediate boundary conditions external to this routine. The payoff condition is defined through the user function payoff(K, S) that evaluates according to the strike and asset prices. The intermediate conditions are defined using the routine Boundary() that updates an input array of option values. In the case of an American-style option with an early exercising condition, for example, the pseudo code of the Boundary() routine is given by Code 3.2 as follows:

Boundary($F(0 : j_{max})$, j_{max} , ΔS , K)

  For ($L_r = 0$ to j_{max}) { $F(L_r) = $ MAX($F(L_r)$, *payoff(K , $L_r \Delta S$)*) }

Code 3.2: Pseudo code of the Boundary() routine for an early exercising condition.

Figure 3.5 depicts the spreadsheet design for this VBA implementation.[7] The input section from row 1 to row 10 is taken to be the same as in Figure 3.2 with a new button labeled "Calculate" that triggers the underlying VBA procedures. The option pricings are displayed from row 12 onward in

	A	B	C	D
1				
2	$jmax$ =	50		
3	$imax$ =	100		
4	Maturity (T) =	5	(year)	
5	Strike (K) =	5		
6	Risk-free Rate (r) =	0.05	(per year)	
7	Volatility (σ) =	0.25	(per year)	
8	Price Inc. (ΔS) =	0.25	Min :	0.2
9	Time Inc. (Δt) =	0.05	(year)	
10			Calculate	
11	L_r	Asset	American Put Option	
12	0	0.00	5.000000	
13	1	0.25	4.750000	
14	2	0.50	4.500000	
15	3	0.75	4.250000	
16	4	1.00	4.000000	
17	5	1.25	3.750000	
18	6	1.50	3.500000	

FIGURE 3.5   Spreadsheet design for the implementation of the finite difference method.

the same way as the first three columns in Figure 3.4. The main VBA routine IFD() can be invoked through the "Calculate" button in the spreadsheet. As shown in Code 3.3, we have divided the whole algorithm into three parts handling the input, matrix calculation, and output tasks. The input statements will read in both the option parameters and grid configuration from cells B2:B8. The matrix calculations are performed through a single call to the CalOptionPrices() routine. The output statements will then return the resulting option prices to column C starting from row 12 with respect to the underlying asset prices in column B.

The CalOptionPrices() routine first generates the matrix G according to the rules in (3.11). By default, all elements in a declared VBA array are initialized to zero. Thus, we need to assign only the tridiagonal entries of G in the actual coding. The routine then initiates and iterates the array of option prices together with the intermediate update conditions. The matrix operation $G^{-1}F$ for the iteration is performed by calling a user-defined routine SolveAxb() that calculates the column vector $x(n \times 1) = A^{-1}b$ given square matrix $A(n \times n)$ and column vector $b(n \times 1)$. The two external functions Payoff() and Boundary() will serve to define the type of option to be considered. Here, we consider an example of an American put option with an early exercising boundary condition. For convenience, we have also defined the function Max() to handle the maximum operation in the payoff function.

The routine SolveAxb() will be useful for the implementations throughout this book. The VBA coding of SolveAxb() is given in Code 3.4. The parameters $\{n, iptr, jptr, kptr\}$ define the entries of $A(iptr: iptr + n - 1, jptr: jptr + n - 1)$, $b(kptr: kptr + n - 1)$, and $x(kptr: kptr + n - 1)$ to be involved in the matrix calculation. The vector $x = A^{-1}b$ can be calculated very easily by making a call to the Excel matrix functions **MINVERSE** and **MMULT**. For Excel matrix functions, input and output are considered to be two-dimensional spreadsheet objects with row and column labels starting off from one. To avoid confusion in making cell references with the use of Excel matrix functions, it is convenient to distinguish between VBA arrays and spreadsheet objects by first making the conversion. We adopt the naming convention with prefix "ws," which will denote a spreadsheet object. In Code 3.4, we have converted the VBA matrix A and vector b into spreadsheet objects before calling the Excel functions. The output is a spreadsheet object that should convert back into VBA vector x.

```
Sub IFD()
    'Input parameters from worksheet
    Dim iMax As Integer: iMax = Range("B3").Value
    Dim jMax As Integer: jMax = Range("B2").Value
    Dim maturity As Double: maturity = Range("B4").Value
    Dim strike As Double: strike = Range("B5").Value
    Dim riskFree As Double: riskFree = Range("B6").Value
    Dim sigma As Double: sigma = Range("B7").Value
    Dim dprice As Double: dprice = Range("B8").Value

    'Perform the matrix calculation
    Dim Fvec() As Double: ReDim Fvec(0 To jMax)
    Call CalOptionPrices(maturity, strike, riskFree, sigma, iMax, jMax, dprice, Fvec())

    'Put results back to worksheet
    Dim i As Integer
    For I = 0 To jMax: Range(``C12").Offset(i, 0) = Fvec(i): Next i
End Sub
```

```
Sub CalOptionPrices(maturity As Double, strike As Double, riskFree As Double, sigma As Double, _
        iMax As Integer, jMax As Integer, dprice As Double, ByRef Fvec() As Double)

    Dim dtime As Double: dtime = maturity / iMax
    Dim Lr As Integer, i As Integer

    'Construct the matrix G
    Dim Gmatrix() As Double: ReDim Gmatrix(0 To jMax, 0 To jMax)
    Gmatrix(0, 0) = 1
    Gmatrix(jMax, jMax) = 1
    For Lr = 1 To jMax - 1
```

```
    Gmatrix(Lr, Lr - 1) = 0.5 * ((Lr * riskFree * dtime) - (Lr ^ 2 * sigma ^ 2 * dtime))
    Gmatrix(Lr, Lr) = 1 + (riskFree * dtime) + (Lr ^ 2 * sigma ^ 2 * dtime)
    Gmatrix(Lr, Lr + 1) = -0.5 * ((Lr * riskFree * dtime) + (Lr ^ 2 * sigma ^ 2 * dtime))
    Next Lr


    'Initialize the option vector according to the payoff condition
    For Lr = 0 To jMax: Fvec(Lr) = Payoff(strike, Lr * dprice): Next Lr


    'Perform the iteration
    For i = 1 To iMax
        Call SolveAxb(Gmatrix, Fvec, Fvec, jMax + 1, 0, 0, 0)
        Call Boundary(Fvec, jMax, dprice, strike)
    Next i

End Sub
```

```
'Put option payoff condition
Function Payoff(strike As Double, price As Double) As Double
    Payoff = Max(strike - price, 0)
End Function
```

```
'Early exercising condition for American-style option
Sub Boundary(ByRef Fvec() As Double, jMax As Integer, dprice As Double, strike As Double)
    Dim intrinsicValue As Double, Lr As Integer
    For Lr = 0 To jMax
      intrinsicValue = Payoff(strike, Lr * dprice)
      Fvec(Lr) = Max(Fvec(Lr), intrinsicValue)
    Next Lr
End Sub
```

```
Function Max(x As Double, y As Double) As Double
    If x > y Then Max = x Else Max = y
End Function
```

Code 3.3: VBA codes of the IFD() routine, CalOptionPrices() routine, Payoff() function, Boundary() routine, and Max() function.

```
Sub SolveAxb(Amatrix() As Double, bvec() As Double, ByRef xvec() As Double, _
             n As Integer, iptr As Integer, jptr As Integer, kptr As Integer)

    Dim wsAmatrix As Variant: ReDim wsAmatrix(1 To n, 1 To n)
    Dim row As Integer, column As Integer
    For row = 1 To n
        For column = 1 To n: wsAmatrix(row, column) = Amatrix(iptr + row - 1, jptr + column - 1):
        Next column
    Next row
```

```
Dim wsbvec As Variant: ReDim wsbvec(1 To n, 1 To 1)
For row = 1 To n: wsbvec(row, 1) = bvec(kptr + row - 1): Next row

Dim wsxvec As Variant:
With Application.WorksheetFunction
    wsxvec = .MMult(.MInverse(wsAmatrix), wsbvec)
End With

Dim i As Integer
If n = 1 Then
    For i = kptr To kptr + n - 1: xvec(i) = wsxvec(i - kptr + 1): Next i
Else
    For i = kptr To kptr + n - 1: xvec(i) = wsxvec(i - kptr + 1, 1): Next i
End If

End Sub
```

Code 3.4: VBA codes of the SolveAxb() routine. Note that when n equals one, the (1 × 1) spreadsheet output "wsxvec" has been degenerated into a variant with only one index.

3.4: CRANK–NICHOLSON SCHEME

In the Crank–Nicholson scheme, we adopt forward difference approximation for the time derivative and adjust accordingly all the other terms in the differential equation by forward averaging. Using the two-dimensional grid as depicted in Figure 3.1, we can approximate the time derivative in the Black–Scholes equation (3.1) by forward difference as:

$$\frac{\partial}{\partial t} F(S_j, t_i) \cong \frac{F(S_j, t_{i+1}) - F(S_j, t_i)}{\Delta t}$$

and adjust the F, $(\partial F/\partial S)$, and $(\partial^2 F/\partial S^2)$ terms by averaging over the same forward time as:

$$F(S_j, t_i) \quad \rightarrow \frac{[F(S_j, t_{t+1}) + F(S_j, t_i)]}{2}$$

$$\frac{\partial}{\partial S} F(S_j, t_i) \quad \rightarrow \frac{\partial}{\partial S} \left(\frac{[F(S_j, t_{i+1}) + F(S_j, t_i)]}{2} \right)$$

$$\cong \frac{F(S_{j+1}, t_{i+1}) - F(S_{j-1}, t_{i+1}) + F(S_{j+1}, t_i) - F(S_{j-1}, t_i)}{4\Delta S}$$

$$\frac{\partial^2}{\partial S^2} F(S_j, t_i) \quad \rightarrow \quad \frac{\partial^2}{\partial S^2}\left(\frac{[F(S_j, t_{i+1}) + F(S_j, t_i)]}{2}\right)$$

$$\cong \frac{\begin{array}{l}F(S_{j+1}, t_{i+1}) - 2F(S_j, t_{i+1}) + F(S_{j-1}, t_{i+1})\\ + F(S_{j+1}, t_i) - 2F(S_j, t_i) + F(S_{j-1}, t_i)\end{array}}{(2\Delta S)^2}$$

The difference equation now reads:

$$(-\tfrac{1}{2}a_j)F(S_{j-1}, t_{i+1}) + (1 - \tfrac{1}{2}d_j)F(S_j, t_{i+1}) + (-\tfrac{1}{2}c_j)F(S_{j+1}, t_{i+1})$$
$$= (\tfrac{1}{2}a_j)F(S_{j-1}, t_i) + (1 + \tfrac{1}{2}d_j)F(S_j, t_i) + (\tfrac{1}{2}c_j)F(S_{j+1}, t_i)$$

$$\text{for } j = 1, \ldots, j_{max} - 1$$
$$i = 0, \ldots, i_{max} - 1$$

where:

$$a_j = \tfrac{1}{2}rj\Delta t - \tfrac{1}{2}\sigma^2 j^2 \Delta t$$
$$d_j = r\Delta t + \sigma^2 j^2 \Delta t$$
$$c_j = -\tfrac{1}{2}rj\Delta t - \tfrac{1}{2}\sigma^2 j^2 \Delta t.$$

For completeness, we also include the transformations in (3.6) and (3.7) such that the difference equation can be written in matrix representation as:

$$Q\begin{pmatrix} F(S_0, t_i + 1) \\ F(S_1, t_{i+1}) \\ \vdots \\ F(S_{jmax-1}, t_{i+1}) \\ F(S_{jmax}, t_{i+1}) \end{pmatrix} = P\begin{pmatrix} F(S_0, t_i) \\ F(S_1, t_i) \\ \vdots \\ F(S_{jmax-1}, t_i) \\ F(S_{jmax}, t_i) \end{pmatrix}$$

where P and Q are $(j_{max} + 1) \times (j_{max} + 1)$ tridiagonal matrices given by:

$$P = \begin{pmatrix} b_0 & 0 & 0 & \cdots & & & & \\ \tfrac{1}{2}a_1 & 1 + \tfrac{1}{2}d_1 & \tfrac{1}{2}c_1 & 0 & \cdots & & & \\ 0 & \tfrac{1}{2}a_2 & 1 + \tfrac{1}{2}d_2 & \tfrac{1}{2}c_2 & 0 & \cdots & & \\ \vdots & \vdots & \vdots & \vdots & \vdots & \vdots & \vdots & \vdots \\ & & & & \cdots & \tfrac{1}{2}a_{jmax-1} & 1 + \tfrac{1}{2}d_{jmax-1} & \tfrac{1}{2}c_{jmax-1} \\ & & & & \cdots & 0 & 0 & b_{jmax} \end{pmatrix}$$

$$Q = \begin{pmatrix} 1 & 0 & 0 & \cdots & & & & \\ -\frac{1}{2}a_1 & 1-\frac{1}{2}d_1 & -\frac{1}{2}c_1 & 0 & \cdots & & & \\ 0 & -\frac{1}{2}a_2 & 1-\frac{1}{2}d_2 & -\frac{1}{2}c_2 & 0 & \cdots & & \\ \vdots & \vdots & \vdots & \vdots & \vdots & \vdots & \vdots & \vdots \\ & & & & \cdots & -\frac{1}{2}a_{jmax-1} & 1-\frac{1}{2}b_{jmax-1} & -\frac{1}{2}c_{jmax-1} \\ & & & & \cdots & 0 & 0 & 1 \end{pmatrix}$$

The difference equation can be iterated forward or backward in time by inverting Q or P, respectively. It is unconditionally stable and the errors are proportional to $(\Delta t)^2$ and $(\Delta S)^2$.

REVIEW QUESTIONS

1. Implement the implicit finite difference method under the Crank–Nicholson scheme to price an American put option written on equity with the following input parameters:

On option:	r – Risk free interest rate
	σ – Volatility of the underlying equity
	T – Time to maturity of the option
	K – Strike price of the option
On precision:	i_{max} – Number of steps to maturity
	j_{max} – Size parameter of the tridiagonal matrix
	ΔS – Price increment in the lattice

2. Modify the implementation in Question 1 to include the pricing of a double barrier put option written on same underlying and with upper and lower barriers, H and L, respectively.

ENDNOTES

1. W.H. Press, S.A. Teukolsky, W.T. Vetterling, and B.P. Flannery, "Partial Differential Equations," in *Numerical Recipes in C : The Art of Scientific Computing*, 2nd Edition, (Cambridge: Cambridge University Press, 1997), 827–888. For application on Black–Scholes pricings, see John C. Hull, "Mechanics of Options Markets," in *Options, Futures, and Other Derivatives*, (New Jersey: Prentice Hall, 2006), 181–203.
2. Assume S_{jmax} to be sufficiently large such that the change in time premium between t_i and t_{i+1} is insignificant. This gives:

$$b_{jmax} = F(S_{jmax}, t_{i+1})/F(S_{jmax}, t_i) \cong 1.$$

For European and American call options, we have $F(S_0, t_i) = 0$ and b_0 is thus arbitrary. For European put options, $F(S_0, t_i) = Ke^{-r(T-t_i)}$ from put-call parity. This gives $b_0 = e^{r\Delta t}$. For American put options, $F(S_0, t_i) = K$ due to early exercise and $b_0 = 1$.

3. For backward difference approximation of the time derivative in equation (3.1),

$$\partial F(S_j, t_i)/\partial t \cong [F(S_j, t_i) - F(S_j, t_{i-1})]/\Delta t.$$

The resulting difference equation is *explicitly* iterating backward in time starting from the option's maturity with a known payoff condition. However, it is numerically stable only with very small time grid $\Delta t < (\sigma^2 j_{max}^2)^{-1}$. The scaling is also practically inconvenient as doubling the price grids would require quadrupling the time grids to maintain stability.

4. Refer to implicitfd_ep.xls.

5. Under double precision, there is a possible floating point problem that zero will only be quoted up to 15 decimal places with an undesirable negative sign such as -0.0000000000000011.

6. Refer to implicitfd_ap.xls.

7. Refer to implicitfd_ap_vba.xls.

## CHAPTER 4

Portfolio Mean-Variance Optimization

4.1 PORTFOLIO SELECTION

The fundamental goal of portfolio selection is to optimally allocate investments between different assets by considering the trade-off between risk and return. In this chapter, we discuss the implementation of a quantitative tool known as Mean-Variance Optimization (MVO) using the matrix operation in Excel and VBA. Consider a portfolio consisting of n assets with prices $\{S_1, \ldots, S_n\}$ and quantities $\{q_1, \ldots, q_n\}$. If it is to be kept for a period of time, the portfolio value at the end of the period will be subjected to uncertain asset price changes $\{\Delta S_1, \ldots, \Delta S_n\}$. The potential gain or loss of the portfolio in this period can be summed up as:

$$\Delta S_P = \sum_{i=1}^{n} q_i \, \Delta S_i. \qquad (4.1)$$

The objective of MVO is to determine the optimal portfolio content within a budget so as to minimize the risk exposure in this period under an expected growth in value. The idea relies on the correlation among asset price changes under a stochastic regime for which the statistics can be inferred from historical data.

It is convenient to rewrite equation (4.1) in terms of asset price returns $r_i = \Delta S_i / S_i$ over the investment horizon for which portfolio return r_P in this period can be written as a weighted sum of asset returns in the basket. This gives:

$$r_P = \sum_{i=1}^{n} w_i \, r_i, \quad \sum_{i=1}^{n} w_i = 1 \qquad (4.2)$$

where the weight factor w_i represents the fraction of the total portfolio budget that will be invested in the i-th asset. In the stochastic model, uncertain asset returns in (4.2) can all be considered random variables parameterized by historical means and variances. Written as the linear combination of the asset returns in (4.2), portfolio return can also be considered a random variable with mean and variance defined through (4.2) as:

$$\mu_P = \sum_{i=1}^{n} w_i \mu_i \qquad (4.3)$$

$$\sigma_P^2 = \sum_{i=1}^{n} \sum_{j=1}^{n} w_i w_j \sigma_{ij} \qquad (4.4)$$

where μ_i and $\sigma_i^2 = \sigma_{ii}$ respectively denote the mean and variance of individual asset return r_i, and σ_{ij} for $i \neq j$ denotes the covariance between two different returns r_i and r_j. Under this framework, the task of MVO is to determine the optimal portfolio content that minimizes the random variation of the portfolio return in (4.4) given an expected return in (4.3) and that should also be feasible under the portfolio budget. The variance terms $w_i^2 \sigma_i^2$ in (4.4) are strictly positive and they are adding up. The idea of MVO relies on the fact that the covariance terms $w_i w_j \sigma_{ij}$ in (4.4) could possibly be negative and thus diversify the total portfolio variance.

It is efficient to express equations (4.3) and (4.4) in matrix multiplication and formulate MVO as the determination of the column vector **w** that:

$$\begin{aligned} & \text{minimize } \sigma_P^2 = \mathbf{w}^T \mathbf{\Sigma}\, \mathbf{w} \\ & \text{subject to } \mathbf{w}^T \boldsymbol{\mu} = \mu_P \text{ and } \mathbf{u}^T \mathbf{w} = 1 \end{aligned} \qquad (4.5)$$

where

$$\mathbf{w} = \begin{bmatrix} w_1 \\ \vdots \\ w_n \end{bmatrix}, \quad \boldsymbol{\mu} = \begin{bmatrix} \mu_1 \\ \vdots \\ \mu_n \end{bmatrix}, \quad \mathbf{u} = \begin{bmatrix} 1 \\ \vdots \\ 1 \end{bmatrix}, \quad \mathbf{\Sigma} = \begin{pmatrix} \sigma_1^2 & \sigma_{12} & \cdots & \sigma_{1n} \\ \sigma_{21} & \sigma_2^2 & \cdots & \sigma_{2n} \\ \vdots & & & \vdots \\ \vdots & & & \vdots \\ \sigma_{n1} & \sigma_{n2} & \cdots & \sigma_n^2 \end{pmatrix}.$$

The entries in the mean vector $\boldsymbol{\mu}$ and the variance-covariance matrix $\mathbf{\Sigma}$ can presumably be estimated using historical asset returns over the same horizon as the portfolio. The optimization in (4.5) allows both long and short positions for which w_i can be positive or negative. It can be solved very easily using the method of Lagrange multipliers and the optimal solution was first worked out by Merton[1] as:

$$\mathbf{w} = \frac{(C\mu_P - A)(\mathbf{\Sigma}^{-1}\boldsymbol{\mu}) + (B - A\mu_P)(\mathbf{\Sigma}^{-1}\mathbf{u})}{BC - A^2} \qquad (4.6)$$

$$\sigma_P^2 = \frac{C\mu_P^2 - 2A\mu_P + B}{BC - A^2} \qquad (4.7)$$

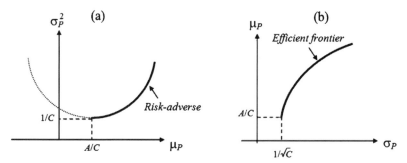

FIGURE 4.1 (a) Optimal portfolio mean-variance relation with risky assets only, and (b) Portfolio efficient frontier.

where $A = \mathbf{u}^T\boldsymbol{\Sigma}^{-1}\boldsymbol{\mu}$, $B = \boldsymbol{\mu}^T\boldsymbol{\Sigma}^{-1}\boldsymbol{\mu}$, and $C = \mathbf{u}^T\boldsymbol{\Sigma}^{-1}\mathbf{u}$. Since the variance-covariance matrix $\boldsymbol{\Sigma}$ is symmetric, it can be shown that the two quadratic forms, B and C, and the denominator $BC - A^2$ are all positive. The optimal portfolio mean-variance relation in (4.7) is strictly convex as shown in Figure 4.1(a). It is usual to invert (4.7) and present the risk-adverse domain ($\mu_P \geq A/C$) of the mean-variance relation in terms of the so-called portfolio efficient frontier as shown in Figure 4.1(b) with the following optimal relation.

$$\mu_P = \frac{A}{C} + \frac{1}{C}\sqrt{(BC - A^2)(C\sigma_P^2 - 1)}. \tag{4.8}$$

The above discussion analyzes the case in which all the available assets are risky. We can extend the analysis to include risk-free cash that provides a guaranteed return μ_0 over the investment period. Consider w_0 to be the fraction of the total portfolio budget that will be held as cash. Reformulate the MVO in (4.5) as the determination of the column vector $\mathbf{w}$ and w_0 that:

$$\begin{aligned} &\text{minimize } \sigma_P^2 = \mathbf{w}^T\boldsymbol{\Sigma}\,\mathbf{w} \\ &\text{subject to } \mathbf{w}^T\boldsymbol{\mu} + w_0\,\mu_0 = \mu_P \text{ and } \mathbf{u}^T\mathbf{w} + w_0 = 1. \end{aligned} \tag{4.9}$$

Again, it can be solved very easily using the method of Lagrange multipliers[2] and the optimal portfolio content is given by:

$$w_0 = 1 - \frac{(\mu_P - \mu_0)(A - \mu_0 C)}{C\mu_0^2 - 2A\mu_0 + B}, \quad \mathbf{w} = \frac{(\mu_P - \mu_0)(\boldsymbol{\Sigma}^{-1}\boldsymbol{\mu} - \mu_0\boldsymbol{\Sigma}^{-1}\mathbf{u})}{C\mu_0^2 - 2A\mu_0 + B} \tag{4.10}$$

that generates the efficient frontier as shown in Figure (4.2) with the following linear optimal relation.[3]

$$\mu_P = \mu_0 + \sigma_P\sqrt{C\mu_0^2 - 2A\mu_0 + B} \tag{4.11}$$

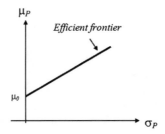

FIGURE 4.2 Efficient frontier of a portfolio with cash and risky assets.

We have considered so far MVO that allows both long and short positions on the risky assets for which w_i can be positive or negative. Suppose there are short-selling restrictions on the risky assets due to market constraint or internal policy. In such a long-only portfolio, the asset positions w_i are all limited to be non-negative in the optimization. Accordingly, the MVO in (4.9) should be appended with additional constraints as:

$$minimize\ \sigma_P^2 = \mathbf{w}^T \mathbf{\Sigma}\,\mathbf{w}$$
$$subject\ to\ \mathbf{w}^T \mathbf{\mu} + w_0\,\mu_0 = \mu_P,\ \mathbf{u}^T \mathbf{w} + w_0 = 1,\ and\ w_1, \ldots, w_n \geq 0. \tag{4.12}$$

It should be noted that the cash position w_0 remains unconstrained in (4.12) where it can be positive, zero, or negative. In principle, (4.12) can again be solved using the method of Lagrange multipliers.[4] However, the evaluation of the optimal portfolio content would be non-trivial because of the inequality constraints in the Kuhn-Tucker conditions.

Markowitz has developed an efficient algorithm[5] that allows us to solve the MVO in (4.12) simply using the optimal result in (4.10). Consider another MVO related to (4.12) for which we delete the non-negative constraints $w_{1, 2, \ldots, n} \geq 0$ and instead constrain a certain subset of $\{w_1, \ldots, w_n\}$, called the OUT subset, to be zero. The basic idea in the Markowitz algorithm is that the optimal solution of this related problem could possibly be a particular solution of the original problem for a specific segment of the efficient frontier. The optimal solution can simply be obtained from (4.10) by modifying the array entries in $\{\mathbf{\Sigma}, \mathbf{\mu}, \mathbf{u}\}$ associated with the OUT subset. If w_i is in the OUT subset, we set the i-th row of both the vectors $\mathbf{\mu}$ and $\mathbf{u}$ to zero, and also the i-th row and i-th column of the matrix $\mathbf{\Sigma}$ to zero except the diagonal entry which we set to be one.

$$\mu_i \to 0,\ u_i \to 0$$
$$\Sigma_{i1}, \ldots, \Sigma_{in} \to 0,\ \Sigma_{1i}, \ldots, \Sigma_{ni} \to 0,\ except\ \Sigma_{ii} \to 1 \tag{4.13}$$

Suppose $\{\Sigma_m, \mu_m, u_m\}$ are the modified arrays according to the OUT subset. The optimal solution of the related problem is then given by:

$$w_0 = 1 - \frac{(\mu_P - \mu_0)(A_m - \mu_0 C_m)}{C_m \mu_0^2 - 2A_m \mu_0 + B_m}, \quad \mathbf{w} = \frac{(\mu_P - \mu_0)(\Sigma_m^{-1} \mu_m - \mu_0 \Sigma_m^{-1} \mathbf{u}_m)}{C_m \mu_0^2 - 2A_m \mu_0 + B_m}$$

$$(4.14)$$

with multipliers:

$$\lambda_1 = \frac{(\mu_P - \mu_0)}{C_m \mu_0^2 - 2A_m \mu_0 + B_m}, \quad \lambda_2 = \frac{-\mu_0(\mu_P - \mu_0)}{C_m \mu_0^2 - 2A_m \mu_0 + B_m}$$

where $A_m = \mathbf{u}_m^T \Sigma_m^{-1} \mu_m$, $B_m = \mu_m^T \Sigma_m^{-1} \mu_m$, and $C_m = \mathbf{u}_m^T \Sigma_m^{-1} \mathbf{u}_m$. It is clear in (4.14) that $w_i = 0$ inside the OUT subset. If all w_i outside the OUT subset are non-negative for a particular value of μ_P, (4.14) could possibly be a solution of the MVO in (4.12) that also satisfies the Kuhn–Tucker conditions as:

$$\partial L / \partial w_0 = -\lambda_1 \mu_0 - \lambda_2 = 0 \tag{4.15}$$

$$\partial L / \partial w_i = (\Sigma \mathbf{w} - \lambda_1 \mu - \lambda_2 \mathbf{u})_i = 0 \text{ when } w_i \geq 0$$
$$> 0 \text{ when } w_i = 0, \text{ for } i = 1, \ldots, n. \tag{4.16}$$

It should be noted that $\partial L / \partial w_0 = 0$ in (4.15) would automatically be satisfied with the multipliers defined in (4.14). Given portfolio return $\mu_P > \mu_0$, we can determine the optimal portfolio content by solving the MVO in (4.12) through the Markowitz algorithm as:

1. Define an OUT subset and construct the modified arrays $\{\Sigma_m, \mu_m, \mathbf{u}_m\}$ according to (4.13).
2. Check that all the entries of $\mathbf{w}$ in (4.14) are non-negative. If so, proceed to step (3). If this is not the case, return to step (1) and try another OUT subset.
3. Check that condition (4.16) has been satisfied. If so, w_0 and $\mathbf{w}$ defined in (4.14) will be an optimal solution given portfolio return μ_P. Otherwise, return to step (1) and try another OUT subset.

In step (1), the size of the OUT subset can be chosen from $N_{out} = 0$ to $N_{out} = n - 1$. When $N_{out} = n$, there is only one OUT subset namely the entire risky content $\{w_1, \ldots, w_n\}$. The algorithm will not work as well in this case as the denominator in (4.14) vanishes with μ_m and $\mathbf{u}_m$ being zero vectors. However, this corresponds to the trivial portfolio content with $\mathbf{w} = 0$ and $w_0 = 1$. The algorithm is guaranteed to find a solution before we exhaust the list of all *OUT* subsets. Also, the optimal portfolio content is unique given the return. We should quit the routine once we obtain a solution.

4.2 EXCEL IMPLEMENTATION

It is always convenient to separate the raw data from the actual calculations using different worksheets defined as:[6]

dayclose—Historical daily closing prices of all risky assets to be considered.

return—Historical price returns generated through "dayclose" for specific time horizon.

MVO—Actual calculations of the mean-variance optimization based on "return."

Figure 4.3 depicts the layout of the worksheet "dayclose" with historical daily closing prices of 35 commonly traded commodities from the year 1998 to 2005. Sequences of closing prices are recorded in one column per asset starting from column B onward with the corresponding time stamp given by column A. In each column, the top cell records the asset name with its ticker symbol in the following cell. For example, column B records the daily closing prices of Crude Oil with the ticker symbol CL.

Figure 4.4 displays the worksheet "return," which contains the historical price returns of the assets. They are generated dynamically using the raw data in "dayclose" and according to the investment horizon defined in cell K16 (named horizon) of worksheet "MVO." Again, return sequences are arranged one column per asset starting from column A onward with the corresponding ticker symbol defined in the top cell. Such row labels can be

	A	B	C	D	E	F	G	H	I	J	K
1		CRUDE OIL	HEATING OIL	UNL.GASOLINE	NATURAL GAS	ALUMINIUM	COPPER	GOLD	ZINC	SILVER	LEAD
2	Date	CL	HO	HU	NG	LMAH	HG	GC	LMZS	SI	LMPB
3	19980101	17.64	49.08	52.81	2.264	1552	76.9	289.9	1107	5.933	564
4	19980102	17.43	49.41	53.26	2.153	1552	76.2	289.4	1107	5.9	564
5	19980105	16.89	47.92	51.86	2.207	1502	75.35	282.7	1082	5.873	559
6	19980106	16.91	47.76	52.35	2.182	1504	75.4	282.3	1084	6.015	560
7	19980107	16.82	47.33	51.94	2.145	1504	75	284.7	1089	5.973	562
8	19980108	16.97	47.75	52.62	2.046	1492	74.6	281.8	1120	5.728	580
9	19980109	16.63	46.7	52.81	2.046	1490	74.15	279.1	1087	5.593	570
10	19980112	16.47	46.21	52.03	2.002	1472	74	278.9	1077	5.46	546
11	19980113	16.43	46.09	51.39	2.014	1504	78.1	283.8	1124	5.653	547
12	19980114	16.45	46.28	51.05	2.016	1512	76.5	282.4	1142	5.658	542
13	19980115	16.34	46.23	50.39	2.094	1507	77.2	286.4	1132	5.783	527
14	19980116	16.51	46.75	50.99	2.176	1498	76.3	291.1	1152	5.758	528
15	19980119	16.51	46.75	50.99	2.176	1503	78.3	281.1	1116	5.758	513

FIGURE 4.3   The layout of the worksheet "dayclose" with daily closing prices.

	A	B	C	D	E	F	G	H	I	J
1	CL	HO	HU	NG	LMAH	HG	GC	LMZS	SI	LMPB
2	-0.073696	-0.058068	-0.045825	-0.075088	-0.028995	0.003901	-0.012073	0.022584	-0.025282	-0.065603
3	0.090575	0.065974	0.090693	0.003343	0.021234	0.036269	0.057263	0.007067	0.042711	0.001898
4	-0.104377	-0.095576	-0.099709	0.089005	-0.019168	-0.043125	-0.011559	-0.051754	0.160862	-0.007576
5	-0.038221	-0.031860	-0.038197	-0.001748	-0.036767	-0.007185	-0.013030	-0.034228	-0.122143	0.041985
6	-0.074919	-0.066976	-0.012398	-0.065674	0.013067	0.086842	-0.001016	0.012452	0.000488	0.023810
7	0.185211	0.135867	0.145106	0.095595	-0.008826	-0.046610	0.022704	0.042573	0.032531	0.035778
8	-0.075460	-0.052482	-0.065775	0.136441	-0.014726	0.026032	0.020543	0.039927	0.008192	0.010363
9	-0.023779	-0.011309	0.000199	-0.123824	0.025374	0.046411	0.021104	-0.013962	-0.017969	-0.008547
10	0.003292	0.017274	0.037781	-0.072595	-0.056271	-0.068007	-0.047377	-0.016814	-0.055211	-0.034483
11	-0.040026	-0.086966	-0.063422	-0.042612	0.010776	-0.037437	0.005007	-0.034203	-0.115022	0.005357
12	0.033493	-0.007288	0.020663	-0.022738	-0.034115	-0.008570	-0.026237	-0.020503	-0.006660	-0.035524
13	-0.221561	-0.065570	-0.081179	0.061386	-0.010670	-0.016622	-0.001364	-0.012369	0.007663	-0.009208
14	0.231946	0.066920	0.061300	0.137593	-0.034213	-0.019608	0.007514	-0.017341	0.008365	0.016729
15	0.001379	-0.022092	-0.064543	-0.125871	0.025029	0.046897	-0.003390	0.051961	0.000000	-0.007313

FIGURE 4.4   The layout of the worksheet "return" with price returns over a specific investment horizon.

constructed through a direct mapping from "dayclose" using the common expression A1 = dayclose!B2 along the row. The investment horizon should be defined in number of days. Suppose, for example, it is taken to be five days (horizon = 5). The cell A2 should correspond to the price return of CL with opening price dayclose!B3 and closing price dayclose!B8 five days later. In the same way, the following cell A3 should correspond to the price return from dayclose!B8 to dayclose!B13 in the subsequent five days. In general, this can be done very easily using the **OFFSET** function with the leftmost corner cell dayclose!$A$3 being the reference location in worksheet "dayclose." In each column of worksheet "return," price returns in each cell can be calculated by identifying the opening and closing prices through row offset from the reference location according to its row number **ROW**() as:

opening price = **OFFSET**(dayclose!$A$3, (**ROW**() − 2) ∗ horizon, **COLUMN**())
closing price = **OFFSET**(dayclose!$A$3, (**ROW**() − 1) ∗ horizon, **COLUMN**())
price return = (closing price − opening price)/opening price

The column number **COLUMN**() will provide a column offset from the reference location to match the ticker symbol in the two worksheets. Running down the row of "return," price returns should be calculated until the location of the closing price has exceeded the data range of "dayclose." this happens when the closing price is pointing to a blank cell thereafter, and where we simply insert a blank cell in "return." The following expression can be applied to every column of "return" with a ticker symbol:

IF(**OFFSET**(dayclose!$A$3, (**ROW**() − 1) ∗ horizon, **COLUMN**()) = "", "",
(**OFFSET**(dayclose!$A$3, (**ROW**() − 1) ∗ horizon, **COLUMN**())
− **OFFSET**(dayclose!$A$3, (**ROW**() − 2) ∗ horizon, **COLUMN**()))
/**OFFSET**(dayclose!$A$3, (**ROW**() − 2) ∗ horizon, **COLUMN**())).

H	I	J	K	L	M	N	O	P	Q	R	S	T
		Var-Covar										
	Tickers:	HG	LMAH	CL	GC	W						
		6	5	1	7	15						
HG	6	0.00188739	0.00089565	0.00038696	0.00030496	0.00017046	0.00000000	0.00000000	0.00000000	0.00000000	0.00000000	
LMAH	5	0.00089565	0.00086633	0.00037601	0.00019351	0.00006943	0.00000000	0.00000000	0.00000000	0.00000000	0.00000000	
CL	1	0.00038696	0.00037601	0.00567581	0.00012155	0.00059209	0.00000000	0.00000000	0.00000000	0.00000000	0.00000000	
GC	7	0.00030496	0.00019351	0.00012155	0.00100378	0.00019257	0.00000000	0.00000000	0.00000000	0.00000000	0.00000000	
W	15	0.00017046	0.00006943	0.00059209	0.00019257	0.00273249	0.00000000	0.00000000	0.00000000	0.00000000	0.00000000	
		0.00000000	0.00000000	0.00000000	0.00000000	0.00000000	1.00000000	0.00000000	0.00000000	0.00000000	0.00000000	
		0.00000000	0.00000000	0.00000000	0.00000000	0.00000000	0.00000000	1.00000000	0.00000000	0.00000000	0.00000000	
		0.00000000	0.00000000	0.00000000	0.00000000	0.00000000	0.00000000	0.00000000	1.00000000	0.00000000	0.00000000	
		0.00000000	0.00000000	0.00000000	0.00000000	0.00000000	0.00000000	0.00000000	0.00000000	1.00000000	0.00000000	
		0.00000000	0.00000000	0.00000000	0.00000000	0.00000000	0.00000000	0.00000000	0.00000000	0.00000000	1.00000000	
	Nasset :	5										
	Horizon :	10	(days)		Nsample :	197						
	A :	3.494774989										
	B :	0.030080053										
	C :	2052.936879										

FIGURE 4.5 The layout of the variance-covariance matrix in worksheet "MVO."

In worksheet "MVO," we first construct the variance-covariance matrix Σ using the asset price returns in "return." Figure 4.5 depicts the layout of the matrix with user-defined portfolio contents. As shown in the figure, the number of assets to be included in the portfolio is arbitrary, with the maximum size limited to ten. The choice of assets can be specified through the cells J3:S3 by entering their ticker symbols. The total number of assets in the portfolio is given by K15 = **COUNTA**(J3:S3) that counts the number of non-empty cells in this array. The adjacent cells J4:S4 will identify the corresponding column location of data in worksheet "return" to facilitate calculation of the matrix. For an unused blank cell in J3:S3, the adjacent cell will also be blank in J4:S4. The following expression can be used to define J4 and apply to all other cells in J4:S4:

$$J4 = \textbf{IF}(J3 = \text{""}, \text{""}, \textbf{MATCH}(J3, \text{return!}1 : 1, 0)).$$

In Figure 4.5, the ticker symbol in J3 is defined as HG. The above function will search for this item in array return!1:1 (row 1 of "return") and report in J4 its relative position (the sixth column) in this array. We can use the column locations acquired in cells J4:S4 to construct the variance-covariance matrix defined in cells J5:S14 (named as vcmatrix). We first repeat the same sequence vertically in cells I5:I14 based on the common expression I5 = **IF**(J4 = "" , "" , J4). Thus, each matrix entry Σ_{ij} will be associated with the target column locations of two assets from I5:I14 (for $i = 1, 2, \ldots$) and J4:S4 (for $j = 1, 2, \ldots$). For example, the entry in J5 has target locations given by I5 and J4. The corresponding return data to be included in the covariance calculation can be identified using the **OFFSET** function with the cell return!$A$2 in the leftmost column of "return" being the reference location.

$$\textbf{COVAR}(\textbf{OFFSET}(\text{return!}\$A\$2, 0, \$I5 - 1, \text{nsample}), \\ \textbf{OFFSET}(\text{return!}\$A\$2, 0, J\$4 - 1, \text{nsample})) \qquad (4.17)$$

For both target locations, the row and column offsets from the reference location aim at the leading entry of the data set, the height parameter (named nsample) then defines the downward range to be included in the calculation. The height parameter is simply the size of the return data given an investment horizon. It is defined in N16 = COUNT(return!A:A) by counting the number of numeric cells in column A of "return." If there are blank cells in J4:S4 (and so I5:I14), the variance-covariance matrix will have redundant columns (and rows) relative to the unused cells. With respect to such redundancy, the matrix should be augmented with zero columns (and zero rows) except one at diagonal entries. We can use the following formula to define J5 and all other matrix entries:

J5 = IF(OR($I5 = "" , J$4 = ""),
        IF(ROW() − ROW($J$5) = COLUMN() − COLUMN($J$5), 1, 0),
        COVAR(OFFSET(return!$A$2, 0, $I5 − 1, nsample),
        OFFSET(return!$A$2, 0, J$4 − 1, nsample))).

As shown in Figure 4.6, the mean vector μ is defined in C5:C14 (named mvec) of worksheet "MVO." Similar to (4.17), it can be constructed with reference to the target locations given by I5:I14. For example, the mean return in C5 can be calculated according to the target location in I5 as:

AVERAGE(OFFSET(return!$A$2, 0, $I5 − 1, nsample)).

Again, the mean vector will have zero redundant entries if there are blank cells in I5:I14. This is also true for the **u** vector defined in B5:B14 (named uvec). The following expressions can be used to define the mean vector and

	A	B	C	D	E	F	G	H	I
1									
2									
3				(Long/Short)	(Long/Short with cash)	(Long with cash)	(Solver)	Tickers :	
4		u	Mean	w	w & w0	w & w0	w & w0		
5		1	0.00475002	0.54865170	0.58967960	0.42523893	0.42523891	HG	6
6		1	0.00122930	-0.32003669	-0.83602452	0.00000000	0.00000000	LMAH	5
7		1	0.00885418	0.26791066	0.21825540	0.38147271	0.38147270	CL	1
8		1	0.00243828	0.46379599	0.05626889	0.00000000	0.00000000	GC	7
9		1	0.00134965	0.03967834	-0.10011259	0.00000000	0.00000000	W	15
10		0	0.00000000	0.00000000	0.00000000	0.00000000	0.00000000		
11		0	0.00000000	0.00000000	0.00000000	0.00000000	0.00000000		
12		0	0.00000000	0.00000000	0.00000000	0.00000000	0.00000000		
13		0	0.00000000	0.00000000	0.00000000	0.00000000	0.00000000		
14		0	0.00000000	0.00000000	0.00000000	0.00000000	0.00000000		
15					1.07193323	0.19328836	0.19328839		
16			(daily)			Markowitz			
17		Risk-free rate :	0.00019231	0.00192308					
18		Portfolio mean :	0.00057692	0.00576923			0.00576923		
19		Portfolio variance :		0.00117253	0.00061050	0.00129279	0.00129279		
20									

FIGURE 4.6 The layout of the optimal output in worksheet "MVO."

the **u** vector, respectively, as:

C5 = **IF**($I5 = "" , 0, **AVERAGE**(**OFFSET**(return!$A$2, 0, $I5 − 1, nsample)))
B5 = **IF**($I5 = "" , 0, 1).

Consider first the MVO problem in (4.5) that allows both long and short positions in risky assets. As shown in Figure 4.5, we have evaluated the factors A, B, and C in cells K17 (named Avalue), K18 (named Bvalue), and K19 (named Cvalue), respectively, through Excel matrix operations as:

K17 = **MMULT**(**TRANSPOSE**(uvec), **MMULT**(**MINVERSE**(vcmatrix), mvec))
K18 = **MMULT**(**TRANSPOSE**(mvec), **MMULT**(**MINVERSE**(vcmatrix), mvec))
K19 = **MMULT**(**TRANSPOSE**(uvec), **MMULT**(**MINVERSE**(vcmatrix), uvec)).

In Figure 4.6, the expected portfolio return μ_P is defined in D18 (named mport) by scaling the choice of daily rate in C18 with the investment horizon as D18 = C18*horizon. The optimal portfolio content **w** in (4.6) can be determined in cells D5:D14 using the formula:

{D5 : D14 = ((Cvalue * mport − Avalue) * **MMULT**(**MINVERSE**(vcmatrix), mvec)
 + (Bvalue − Avalue * mport) * **MMULT**(**MINVERSE**(vcmatrix), uvec))
 /(Bvalue * Cvalue − Avalue^2)}.

The minimized portfolio variance σ_P^2 can be calculated in D19 based on the optimal content as:

D19 = **MMULT**(**TRANSPOSE**(D5 : D14), **MMULT**(vcmatrix, D5 : D14)).

Consider the MVO problem in (4.9) with the inclusion of cash. In Figure 4.6, the risk-free return μ_0 is defined in D17 = C17*horizon (named riskfree) by scaling the daily rate in C17. The optimal portfolio content **w** and cash w_0 in (4.10) can be determined in cells E5:E14 and E15, respectively, using the formula:

{E5 : E14 = (mport − riskfree) * (**MMULT**(**MINVERSE**(vcmatrix), mvec)
 − riskfree * **MMULT**(**MINVERSE**(vcmatrix), uvec))
 /(Cvalue * riskfree^2 − 2 * Avalue * riskfree + Bvalue)}
E15 = 1 − (mport − riskfree) * (Avalue − riskfree * Cvalue)
 /(Cvalue * riskfree^2 − 2 * Avalue * riskfree + Bvalue).

As before, the minimized portfolio variance can also be calculated in E19 based on the optimal content.

Consider now the MVO problem in (4.12) with short-selling restrictions on risky assets. We defer our discussion on the implementation of the Markowitz algorithm to section 4.3 with the use of VBA. Here, we consider solving this problem using Excel Solver despite the fact that there are critical issues when initializing the algorithm. In Figure 4.6, the portfolio content $\mathbf{w}$ to be optimized is defined in cells G5:G14. The corresponding cash position w_0 in G15 can be related to this content through the budget constraint $w_0 = 1 - \mathbf{u}^T\mathbf{w}$ in (4.12) as:

$$G15 = 1 - \mathbf{MMULT}(\mathbf{TRANSPOSE}(\text{uvec}), \text{G5} : \text{G14}).$$

In G18 and G19, we explicitly evaluate the expected return $\mathbf{w}^T\boldsymbol{\mu} + w_0\,\mu_0$ and variance $\mathbf{w}^T\boldsymbol{\Sigma}\,\mathbf{w}$ of the portfolio, respectively, relative to this content as:

$$G18 = \mathbf{MMULT}(\mathbf{TRANSPOSE}(\text{G5} : \text{G14}), \text{mvec}) + \text{G15} * \text{riskfree}$$
$$G19 = \mathbf{MMULT}(\mathbf{TRANSPOSE}(\text{G5} : \text{G14}), \mathbf{MMULT}(\text{vcmatrix}, \text{G5} : \text{G14})).$$

In the **Solver Parameters** screen as shown in Figure 4.7, we set the **Target Cells** to be the portfolio variance in G19 and check **Equal To** as **Min** for minimizing. We take in the **By Changing Cells** the portfolio content in cells G5:G14 and include in the **Subject to the Constraints** field the condition that the so-evaluated portfolio return in G18 must equal the prescribed value mport in D18. In the **Solver Options** screen as shown in Figure 4.8, we check **Assume Non-Negative** that imposes the non-negative constraints in (4.12) on the portfolio content specified in the **By Changing Cells**. It is sufficient to consider in **Precision** the required precision of 10^{-8} for the algorithm and limit the number of iterations within 20. To start off the search algorithm, we need to provide initial values for G5:G14 as close to

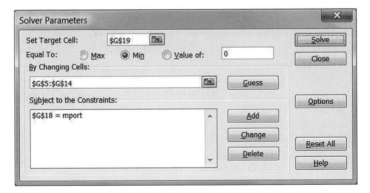

FIGURE 4.7 Solver Parameters screen.

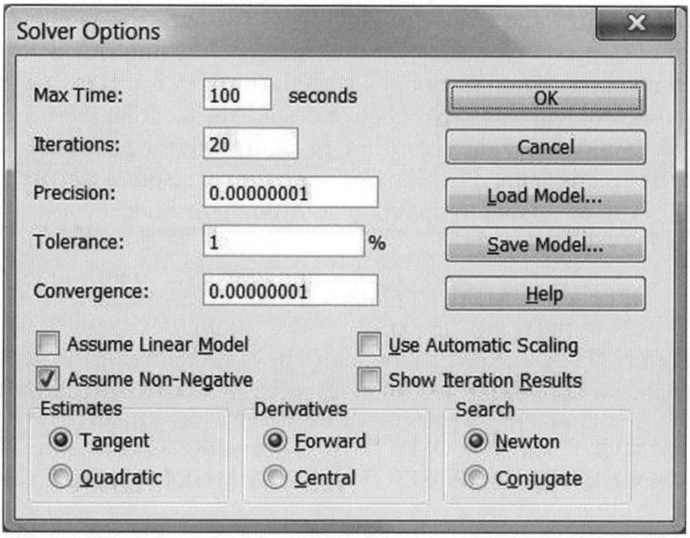

FIGURE 4.8 Solver Options screen.

the solution as possible. A proper choice would be a cash portfolio with no risky assets $\{w_1 = 0, \ldots, w_n = 0\}$. However, there is no guarantee of finding the correct optimal solution.

4.3 EXCEL PLUS VBA IMPLEMENTATION

An effective and reliable way to solve the MVO problem in (4.12) is to implement the Markowitz algorithm as discussed in section 4.1 using VBA. It is guaranteed to find the correct optimal solution that is unique given the portfolio return. The idea is to examine all possible OUT subsets and identify the particular case that generates the optimal solution of the original problem. The size of the OUT subset can run from $N_{out} = 0$ to $N_{out} = n - 1$. For each N_{out}, there are N_c (equals n choose N_{out}) OUT subsets with different combinations:

N_{out}	OUT subsets	N_c
0	$\{\phi\}$	1
1	$\{w_1\}, \{w_2\}, \ldots, \{w_n\}$	n
2	$\{w_1, w_2\}, \{w_1, w_3\}, \ldots \{w_1, w_n\}, \{w_2, w_3\}, \ldots,$ $\{w_2, w_n\}, \ldots, \{w_{n-1}, w_n\}$	$\frac{1}{2}n(n-1)$
$\vdots$		
$n - 1$	$\{w_2, w_3, \ldots, w_n\}, \{w_1, w_3, \ldots, w_n\}, \ldots, \{w_1, w_2, \ldots, w_{n-1}\}$	n

Among all possible OUT subsets above, there is a unique combination for which the corresponding optimal content w given by (4.14) will be non-negative and will satisfy the Kuhn-Tucker conditions in (4.16).

We first develop a routine called GetOutSubset() capable of generating all OUT subsets given its size $N_{out} = k$. Consider the array $I_k(L, 1:k)$ that provides in ascending order the pointers to all elements in different OUT subsets labeled as $L = 1, \ldots, N_c(k)$. When $k = 2$, for example, we have $I_2(1, 1) = 1$ and $I_2(1, 2) = 2$ that define the first OUT subset $\{w_1, w_2\}$. Pointer arrays of size k can be generated by appending every pointer array of size $k - 1$ with an additional entry of higher value. Given pointer array $I_{k-1}(l', 1:k-1)$ of size $k - 1$, we can generate several pointer arrays of size k (labeled consecutively as $L = l, l + 1, \ldots$); each with an additional entry of a separate value greater than the last entry in the given array:

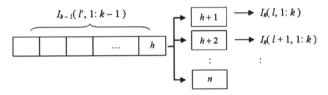

In this way, the entire set of pointer arrays $I_k(L, 1:k)$ for $L = 1, \ldots, N_c(k)$ can be generated iteratively by considering every $I_{k-1}(L', 1:k-1)$ for $L' = 1, \ldots, N_c(k-1)$. The pseudo code of GetOutSubset() is given by Code 4.1 which performs such tasks. As input, the routine reads in all pointer arrays for size $k - 1$ and the number of combinations. As output, it generates the arrays for size k and updates the number of combinations. The iteration should start off from $k = 1$ with $N_c(1) = n$ pointer arrays, namely, $I_1(1, 1) = 1$, $I_1(2, 1) = 2$, $\ldots$, and $I_1(n, 1) = n$. The VBA code of GetOutSubset() is given by Code 4.2. Note that "nmax" and "Ncmax" are parameters that configure the maximum possible size of n and N_c, respectively, in the module. In worksheet "MVO," the number of assets to be included in the portfolio is limited to below ten. We should set nmax = 10, and the maximum number of OUT subsets should correspondingly be Ncmax = 252 (10 choose 5).

GetOutSubset (n, k, N_c, I(1: N_c, 1: k))

```
l = 0

# input Nc and I for size k − 1, and consider every input array
  For( L' = 1 to Nc ) {

# for particular array I, generate several Inew for size k with consecutive labeling
    For( j = I( L', k − 1 ) + 1 to n ) { l = l + 1
```

$$\text{For}(\, i = 1 \text{ to } k - 1\,)\{\ I_{new}(\, l, i\,) = l(\, L', i\,)\ \}$$
$$I_{new}(\, l, k\,) = j\ \}$$
$$\}$$

\# return I_{new} as I and update N_c
For($\, L = 1 \text{ to } l\,$) { For($\, i = 1 \text{ to } k\,$){ $l(\, L, i\,) = I_{new}(\, L, i\,)$ } } }
$$N_c = l$$

Code 4.1: Pseudo code of the GetOutSubset() routine.

```
Sub GetOutSubset(n As Integer, k As Integer, ByRef Nc As Integer, ByRef Iout() As Integer)
    Dim Icount As Integer, L As Integer, Lprime As Integer
    Dim i As Integer, j As Integer
    Dim Inew(1 To Ncmax, 1 To nmax) As Integer

    Icount = 0
    For Lprime = 1 To Nc
        For j = Iout(Lprime, k - 1) + 1 To n
            Icount = Icount + 1
            For i = 1 To k - 1
                Inew(Icount, i) = Iout(Lprime, i)
            Next i
            Inew(Icount, k) = j
        Next j
    Next Lprime

    For L = 1 To Icount
        For i = 1 To k
            Iout(L, i) = Inew(L, i)
        Next i
    Next L

    Nc = Icount
End Sub
```

Code 4.2: VBA code of the GetOutSubset() routine.

We now want to develop a routine called Markowitz() that considers every OUT subset generated from GetOutSubset() and performs the checking in steps 1–3 as stated at the end of section 4.1. The pseudo code of Markowitz() is given by Code 4.3. As input, it reads in the total number of risky assets n, the data arrays $\{\boldsymbol{\Sigma}, \boldsymbol{\mu}, \mathbf{u}\}$, the expected portfolio return μ_P, and the risk-free return μ_0. As output, it returns the optimal portfolio content $\mathbf{w}$ and cash position w_0. To examine all possible OUT subsets, we have considered in the outer loop the values of N_{out} from 0 to $n - 1$. For each N_{out}, we generate all the OUT subsets and perform the checking on every combination in the inner loop of L. The checking will proceed to higher values of N_{out} until an optimal solution has been identified whereupon the procedure will be stopped immediately.

For $N_{out} = 0$, there is $N_c(0) = 1$ OUT subset $\{\phi\}$ with no modification on the entries in $\{\Sigma, \mu, u\}$. For $N_{out} \geq 1$, the OUT subsets are generated iteratively through GetOutSubset() starting off from $N_{out} = 1$ with $N_c(1) = n$ subsets as defined above. For each OUT subset, the modified arrays $\{\Sigma_m, \mu_m, u_m\}$ will be constructed according to the generated pointer array, and the portfolio content defined in (4.14) will also be calculated. The checking of non-negative and Kuhn–Tucker conditions for such portfolio content will subsequently be conducted.

It should be noted that the denominator $D_m = C_m \mu_0^2 - 2A_m \mu_0 + B_m$ in (4.14) is strictly positive. However, it could possibly be negative due to floating point precision that renders the sign of (4.14) to be misidentified. Under double precision, a real number will only be quoted up to 15 decimal places; it is therefore essential to adjust the denominator by a floating precision of $\varepsilon = 10^{-14}$. The same factor should also be used in checking whether a real number x is negative ($x < -\varepsilon$), nonnegative ($x \geq -\varepsilon$), positive ($x > \varepsilon$), or zero ($|x| \leq \varepsilon$). Using the first "Next L," we skip those OUT subsets with negative portfolio content in (4.14) if $w_i < -\varepsilon$ for either component of w. Then, for the Kuhn-Tucker conditions in (4.16), we skip again using the second "Next L" if neither ($\eta_i > \varepsilon$) $\cap$ ($|w_i| \leq \varepsilon$) or ($|\eta_i| \leq \varepsilon$) $\cap$ ($w_i \geq -\varepsilon$) is true (that is if *testflag* = .False.) for either component of w and $\eta = (\Sigma w - \lambda_1 \mu - \lambda_2 u)$. It runs through all L and proceeds to higher values of N_{out}. If an OUT subset has not been filtered out by these two exit conditions, the corresponding portfolio content in (4.14) will be the optimal solution of the MVO in (4.12). The entire procedure will be stopped immediately by "Exit N_{out}" that bypasses two nested loops.

Markowitz(n, μ(1: n), u(1: n), Σ(1: n, 1: n), μ_P, μ_0, w(1: n), w$_0$)

$\varepsilon = 1 \times 10^{-14}$

For (N_{out} = 0 to n – 1) {

# generate the *OUT* subsets
    If(N_{out} = 0) then
        N_c = 1
    elseif(N_{out} = 1) then
        N_c = n
        For (L = 1 to N_c) { I(L, 1) = L }
    else
        Call *GetOutSubset*(n, N_{out}, N_c, I(1: N_c, 1: N_{out}))
    endif

    For (L = 1 to N_c) {

construct the modified arrays according to (4.13)
    For $(i=1$ to n){ $\mu_m(i)=\mu(i),\ u_m(i)=u(i)$
                     For $(j=1$ to n) do{ $\Sigma_m(i,j)=\Sigma(i,j)$ } }

    For $(k=1$ to N_{out}){ $i=I(L,k)$
                     $\mu_m(i)=0,\ u_m(i)=0$
                     For $(j=1$ to n){ $\Sigma_m(i,j)=0, \Sigma_m(j,i)=0$ }
                     $\Sigma_m(i,i)=1$ }

calculate A_m, B_m, and C_m

$$A_m = u_m^T(1:n)\,\Sigma_m^{-1}(1:n,1:n)\,\mu_m(1:n)$$
$$B_m = \mu_m^T(1:n)\,\Sigma_m^{-1}(1:n,1:n)\,\mu_m(1:n)$$
$$C_m = u_m^T(1:n)\,\Sigma_m^{-1}(1:n,1:n)\,u_m(1:n)$$

calculate the portfolio content defined in (4.14)
$$D_m = C_m\,\mu_0^2 - 2A_m\,\mu_0 + B_m + \varepsilon$$
$$\lambda_1 = (\mu_P-\mu_0)/D_m\ ,\quad \lambda_2 = -\mu_0\,(\mu_P-\mu_0)/D_m$$
$$w(1:n) = \lambda_1\,\Sigma_m^{-1}(1:n,1:n)\,\mu_m(1:n) + \lambda_2\,\Sigma_m^{-1}(1:n,1:n)\,u_m(1:n)$$
$$w_0 = 1 - \lambda_1\,(A_m - \mu_0\,C_m)$$

check that all the entries of **w** in (4.14) are non-negative
    For $(i=1$ to n){ If$(w(i)<-\varepsilon)$ { Next L } }

check that the KKT condition (4.16) has been satisfied
    $\eta(1:n) = \Sigma(1:n,1:n)\,w(1:n) - \lambda_1\,\mu(1:n) - \lambda_2\,u(1:n)$

    For $(i=1$ to n){ testFlag = OR(AND(ABS$(\eta(i))\le\varepsilon,\ w(i)\ge-\varepsilon$),
                                 AND$(\eta(i)>\varepsilon,$ ABS$(w(i))\le\varepsilon$)
                   If (.NOT. testFlag){ Next L } }
    Exit N_{out}
  } }

Code 4.3: Pseudo code of the Markowitz() routine.

The VBA code of Markowitz() is given by Code 4.4. For the calculations of A_m, B_m, and C_m, we have used the routine SolveAxb() (see Code 3.4) to first calculate the vectors $\Sigma_m^{-1}\mu_m$ and $\Sigma_m^{-1}u_m$. The matrix multiplications with the transposed vectors u_m^T and μ_m^T can then be performed very easily through the rule $x^Ty = \sum_{i=1}^n x_i\,y_i$ for two $(n\times 1)$ vectors. In addition, the portfolio content **w** in (4.14) can also be calculated immediately using the same results. Notice that the vector $\eta = \partial L/\partial w$ in (4.16) has been determined by directly applying the rule for matrix multiplication and addition as:

$$\eta_i = \sum_{k=1}^n \Sigma_{ik}w_k - \lambda_1\mu_i - \lambda_2u_i,\ \text{for } i = 1,\ 2,\ \ldots,\ n.$$

To exit a nested loop during the checking of non-negative **w** and the KKT condition, we use "GoTo nextL" and label the "Next L" statement in the coding as "nextL." To terminate the entire procedure once the optimal solution has been found, we exit two nested loops using "GoTo exitNout" for which we label the line immediately after "Next Nout" as "exitNout."

We will use the same spreadsheet design in Figures 4.5 and 4.6 for this VBA implementation. The main VBA routine MVO() can be invoked through the "Markowitz" button in the spreadsheet as shown in Figure 4.6. In Code 4.5, we have divided the MVO() routine into three parts handling the data input, the core Markowitz algorithm, and the output. As input, it reads in the total number of risky assets n in cell K15, the expected portfolio return μ_P in cell D18, and the risk-free return μ_0 in cell D17. It also reads in the data arrays $\{\Sigma, \mu, u\}$ according to the size of n with the use of the **OFFSET** function relative to the cells J5, C5, and B5, respectively. As output, it returns the optimal portfolio content and cash position that display in cells F5:F14 and F15, respectively. It should be noted that if n is less than nmax = 10, the additional portfolio contents in F5:F14 will always be zero in the output.

```
Sub Markowitz(n As Integer, mvec() As Double, uvec() As Double, vcmatrix() As Double, mport As Double, _
    riskfree As Double, ByRef wvec() As Double, ByRef w0 As Double)

    Dim Nout As Integer, Nc As Integer
    Dim Iout(1 To Ncmax, 1 To nmax) As Integer
    Dim L As Integer, i As Integer, j As Integer, k As Integer

    Dim mvecm(1 To nmax) As Double
    Dim uvecm(1 To nmax) As Double
    Dim vcmatrixm(1 To nmax, 1 To nmax) As Double
    Dim etavec(1 To nmax) As Double
    Dim tempvec1(1 To nmax) As Double
    Dim tempvec2(1 To nmax) As Double

    Dim Am As Double, Bm As Double, Cm As Double, Dm As Double
    Dim lambda1 As Double, lambda2 As Double
    Dim testFlag As Boolean

    For Nout = 0 To n - 1

        'generate the OUT subsets
        If (Nout = 0) Then
            Nc = 1
        ElseIf (Nout = 1) Then
            Nc = n
            For L = 1 To Nc: Iout(L, 1) = L: Next L
        Else
            Call GetOutSubset(n, Nout, Nc, Iout)
        End If

        For L = 1 To Nc
            'construct the modified arrays
            For i = 1 To n
                mvecm(i) = mvec(i)
                uvecm(i) = uvec(i)
                For j = 1 To n: vcmatrixm(i, j) = vcmatrix(i, j): Next j
            Next i
```

```
     For k = 1 To Nout
       i = Iout(L, k)
       mvecm(i) = 0
       uvecm(i) = 0
       For j = 1 To n
          vcmatrixm(i, j) = 0
          vcmatrixm(j, i) = 0
       Next j
       vcmatrixm(i, i) = 1
     Next k

     'calculate Am, Bm, and Cm
     Call SolveAxb(vcmatrixm, mvecm, tempvec1, n, 1, 1, 1)
     Call SolveAxb(vcmatrixm, uvecm, tempvec2, n, 1, 1, 1)
     Am = 0
     Bm = 0
     Cm = 0
     For i = 1 To n
       Am = Am + uvecm(i) * tempvec1(i)
       Bm = Bm + mvecm(i) * tempvec1(i)
       Cm = Cm + uvecm(i) * tempvec2(i)
     Next i

     'calculate the portfolio content
     Dm = Cm * riskfree ^ 2 - 2 * Am * riskfree + Bm + eps
     lambda1 = (mport - riskfree)/Dm
     lambda2 = -riskfree * (mport - riskfree)/Dm
     For i = 1 To n: wvec(i) = lambda1 * tempvec1(i) + lambda2 * tempvec2(i): Next i
     w0 = 1 - lambda1 * (Am - riskfree * Cm)

     'check that the portfolio content are non-negative
     For i = 1 To n
       If (wvec(i) < -eps) Then GoTo nextL
     Next i

     'checking the KKT condition
     For i = 1 To n
       tempvec1(i) = 0
       For j = 1 To n: tempvec1(i) = tempvec1(i) + vcmatrix(i, j) * wvec(j): Next j
       etavec(i) = tempvec1(i) - lambda1 * mvec(i) - lambda2 * uvec(i)
     Next i

     For i = 1 To n
       testFlag = (Abs(etavec(i)) <= eps And wvec(i) >= - eps)_
       Or (etavec(i) > eps And Abs(wvec(i)) <= eps)
       If (Not testFlag) Then GoTo nextL
     Next i

     GoTo exitNout

nextL: Next L

  Next Nout

exitNout:

End Sub
```

Code 4.4: VBA code of the Markowitz() routine.

```
Option Explicit
Private Const nmax = 10, Ncmax = 252
Private Const eps = 1 * 10 ^ -14

Sub MVO()

    Dim n As Integer
    Dim mvec(1 To nmax) As Double
    Dim uvec(1 To nmax) As Double
    Dim vcmatrix(1 To nmax, 1 To nmax) As Double
    Dim mport As Double
    Dim riskfree As Double
    Dim wvec(1 To nmax) As Double
    Dim w0 As Double
    Dim i As Integer, j As Integer

    n = Range("K15").Value
    mport = Range("D18").Value
    riskfree = Range("D17").Value

    For i = 1 To n
        mvec(i) = Range("C5").Offset(i - 1)
        uvec(i) = Range("B5").Offset(i - 1)
        For j = 1 To n: vcmatrix(i, j) =Range("J5").Offset(j - 1, i - 1):    Next j
    Next i

    Call Markowitz(n, mvec, uvec, vcmatrix, mport, riskfree, wvec, w0)

    For i = 1 To nmax: Range("F5").Offset(i - 1) = wvec(i): Next i
    Range("F15").Value = w0

End Sub
```

Code 4.5: VBA code of the MVO() routine.

REVIEW QUESTIONS

1. Modify the Markowitz algorithm in the current implementation to allow short-selling restrictions to be applied only on a subset of assets A in the portfolio. It should be noted that the optimal $\mathbf{w}$ and w_0 can now be determined through the Kuhn–Tucker conditions as

$$
\begin{array}{rcl}
\partial L/\partial w_0 & = & 0, \\
\partial L/\partial w_i & = & 0 \text{ for } i \notin A, \\
\partial L/\partial w_i & = & 0 \text{ when } w_i \geq 0, \text{ and } \partial L/\partial w_i > 0 \text{ when } w_i = 0 \text{ for } i \in A,
\end{array}
$$

where $\partial L/\partial w_0 = -\lambda_1 \mu_0 - \lambda_2$ and $\partial L/\partial w_i = (\Sigma \mathbf{w} - \lambda_1\boldsymbol{\mu} - \lambda_2\mathbf{u})_i$ as given by equations (4.15) to (4.16).

2. Use SolverSove in VBA to generate the entire efficient frontier of the following MVO problem for a portfolio with n risky assets and cash:

$$Minimize \; \sigma_P^2 = \mathbf{w}^T \Sigma \mathbf{w}$$

$$subject \; to \; \mathbf{w}^T \mu + w_0 \mu_0 = \mu_P, \quad \mathbf{u}^T \mathbf{w} + w_0 = 1,$$

$$b_1 \geq \mathrm{w}_1 \geq a_1, .. \, b_n \geq \mathrm{w}_n \geq a_n$$

The efficient frontier should be plotted in Excel from $\mu_P = \mu_0$ to its maximum extent given the trading limits $[a_1, b_1], \; \ldots, [a_n, b_n]$.

ENDNOTES

1. Robert C. Merton, "An Analytic Deviation of the Efficient Portfolio Frontier," *Journal of Financial and Quantitative Analysis* 7, No. 3 (1972): 1851-1872. We first define the Lagrange function L that incorporates the objective function and the constraints in (4.5) with two multipliers λ_1 and λ_2 as:

$$L = \tfrac{1}{2}\mathbf{w}^T \Sigma \, \mathbf{w} - \lambda_1(\mathbf{w}^T \mu - \mu_P) - \lambda_2(\mathbf{u}^T \mathbf{w} - 1).$$

The optimal $\mathbf{w}$ can be determined through the first order stationary conditions: $\{\partial L/\partial w_1 = 0, \; \ldots, \partial L/\partial w_n = 0\}$ in conjunction with the original constraints.

2. Similarly, we can define the Lagrange function L with two multipliers λ_1 and λ_2 as:

$$L = \tfrac{1}{2}\mathbf{w}^T \Sigma \mathbf{w} - \lambda_1(\mathbf{w}^T \mu + w_0 \mu_0 - \mu_P) - \lambda_2(\mathbf{u}^T \mathbf{w} + w_0 - 1).$$

The optimal $\mathbf{w}$ and w_0 can be determined through the stationary conditions: $\{\partial L/\partial w_0 = 0, \partial L/\partial w_1 = 0, \; \ldots, \partial L/\partial w_n = 0\}$.

3. We can rewrite the optimal risky content in (4.10) as $\mathbf{w} = (1 - w_0) \, \hat{\mathbf{w}}$ where $\hat{\mathbf{w}} = (\Sigma^{-1}\mu - \mu_0\Sigma^{-1}\mathbf{u})/(A - \mu_0 C)$. Along the efficient frontier, we are actually buying or short-selling various units of the so-called market portfolio $\{\hat{w}_1, \; \ldots, \hat{w}_n\}$ together with cash holdings. For $\mu_0 < A/C$, the cash position w_0 can be positive, zero, or negative through borrowing. For $\mu_0 \geq A/C$, the cash position is, however, strictly positive.

4. Define the Lagrange function H with multipliers $\{\lambda_1, \lambda_2, \alpha_1, \; \ldots, \alpha_n\}$ as:

$$H = L - \alpha_1 w_1 - \ldots - \alpha_n w_n,$$

$$where \; L = \frac{1}{2} \; \mathbf{w}^T \Sigma \, \mathbf{w} - \lambda_1(\mathbf{w}^T \mu + w_0 \, \mu_0 - \mu_P) - \lambda_2(\mathbf{u}^T \mathbf{w} + w_0 - 1)$$

With inequality constraints, the optimal $\mathbf{w}$ and w_0 can be determined through the Kuhn–Tucker conditions:

$\partial L / \partial w_0 = 0$, $\partial L / w_i = \alpha_i$, $\alpha_i \geq 0$, $w_i \geq 0$, and $\alpha_i w_i = 0$ for $i = 1, \ldots, n$

that can be rewritten as $\partial L / \partial w_0 = 0$, $\partial L / \partial w_i = 0$ when $w_i \geq 0$, and $\partial L / \partial w_i > 0$ when $w_i = 0$ for $i = 1, \ldots, n$.

5. H.M. Markowitz, G.P. Todd, and W.F. Sharpe, *Mean-Variance Analysis in Portfolio Choice and Capital Markets*, Frank J. Fabozzi Associates, 1987.
6. Refer to mean_variance_opt.xls.

## CHAPTER 5

Newton–Raphson Method

5.1 NEWTON–RAPHSON METHOD FOR SYSTEMS OF EQUATIONS

The use of Excel Solver is quite convenient for finding a solution $\{x_1, \ldots, x_n\}$ for the zero of an objective function where $g(x_1, \ldots, x_n) = 0$. For multiple objective functions with the same variables, however, it is not applicable for Solver to solve simultaneously the zero of a system of equations given by:

$$
\begin{aligned}
g_1(x_1, \ldots, x_n) &= 0 \\
&\cdots \\
g_n(x_1, \ldots, x_n) &= 0.
\end{aligned}
\tag{5.1}
$$

We consider here a powerful numerical procedure known as the Newton–Raphson method[1] capable of handling such a problem. The objective in this chapter is to build a generic VBA routine for the Newton–Raphson procedure that will definitely be useful in the implementation of the financial models to be discussed in forthcoming chapters.

Algebraically, the method is derived from the familiar Taylor series expansion of a function in the neighborhood of a point. Suppose we want to determine the zero of a function with one variable where $g(x^{soln}) = 0$. Consider a trial guess of the solution x^{old} where the error involved ε^{old} is presumably small. The Taylor expansion of the function in the neighborhood of x^{old} can be written as:

$$
g(x^{old} + \varepsilon^{old}) = g(x^{old}) + g'(x^{old}) \varepsilon^{old} + \ldots
$$

where the higher-order terms in the series are unimportant. The entire expression must vanish by definition as $x^{soln} = x^{old} + \varepsilon^{old}$ is the zero of the function. Hence, we can estimate the error in the trial solution as $\varepsilon^{old} \cong - g(x^{old})/g'(x^{old})$ and accordingly update the guess to be:

$$x^{new} = x^{old} - \frac{g(x^{old})}{g'(x^{old})}. \tag{5.2}$$

The error involved in $x^{soln} = x^{new} + \varepsilon^{new}$ after the update will be much smaller as it can be shown that the size of ε^{new} is in quadratic power[2] of ε^{old}. In equation (5.2), it requires the evaluation of both the function and the derivative at the trial guess, and generates an update that is much closer to the solution. Under a defined precision Δx, the derivative can be approximated using the numerical difference given by:

$$g'(x) \cong \frac{g(x + \Delta x) - g(x)}{\Delta x}.$$

The Newton–Raphson procedure should proceed iteratively using (5.2) and stop literally when the improvement has reached the precision limit of $|x^{new} - x^{old}| \leq \Delta x$.

The method can readily be generalized to multiple dimensions such as the system of equations in (5.1). Consider a trial guess of the zero solution $\{x_1^{old}, \ldots, x_n^{old}\}$ with errors $\{\varepsilon_1^{old}, \ldots, \varepsilon_n^{old}\}$. The Taylor expansions of the multivariable functions in the neighborhood of the trial guess can be written as:

$$g_i(x_1^{old} + \varepsilon_1^{old}, \ldots, x_n^{old} + \varepsilon_n^{old}) = g_i(x_1^{old}, \ldots, x_n^{old})$$
$$+ \sum_{j=1}^{n} [\partial g_i(x_1^{old}, \ldots, x_n^{old})/\partial x_j]\varepsilon_j^{old} + \ldots, i = 1, \ldots, n.$$

They must all vanish simultaneously as $\{x_1^{old} + \varepsilon_1^{old}, \ldots, x_n^{old} + \varepsilon_n^{old}\}$ is the zero of the system. Again, we can estimate the errors in the trial solution and update the guess to be:

$$x^{new} = x^{old} - \Omega^{-1}(x_1^{old}, \ldots, x_n^{old})\, g(x_1^{old}, \ldots, x_n^{old}) \tag{5.3}$$

where $x = \{x_1, \ldots, x_n\}$ and $g = \{g_1, \ldots, g_n\}$ are defined to be column vectors in the matrix equation and Ω is a $n \times n$ square matrix given by:

$$\Omega(x_1, \ldots, x_n) = \begin{pmatrix} \partial g_1(x_1, \ldots, x_n)/\partial x_1 & \cdots & \partial g_1(x_1, \ldots, x_n)/\partial x_n \\ \vdots & & \vdots \\ \partial g_n(x_1, \ldots, x_n)/\partial x_1 & \cdots & \partial g_n(x_1, \ldots, x_n)/\partial x_n \end{pmatrix}. \tag{5.4}$$

The partial derivatives in (5.4) can be approximated using the numerical difference under a defined precision Δx as:

$$\frac{\partial}{\partial x_j} g_i(x_1, \ldots, x_n) \cong \frac{g_i(x_1, \ldots x_j + \Delta x, \ldots, x_n) - g_i(x_1, \ldots, x_n)}{\Delta x}. \quad (5.5)$$

Similarly, the Newton–Raphson procedure should proceed iteratively using (5.3) and stop when the improvements for all variables have reached the precision limit of $|x_i^{new} - x_i^{old}| \leq \Delta x$.

5.2 VBA ROUTINE

We want to build a generic VBA routine called NewtonRaphson() that implements the Newton–Raphson procedure as given by equations (5.3), (5.4), and (5.5) in an arbitrary dimension. The objective functions should be defined external to the routine such that it is applicable to different kinds of problems. The pseudo code of NewtonRaphson() is given by Code 5.1. The routine reads in trial values of the variables $\{x_1, \ldots, x_n\}$ together with a designated precision Δx in the solution. It returns the last updated values as the solution of the problem through the iteration procedure bounded by the precision limit. The iteration starts off from the trial values (initiate $x^{old} = x$ with the trial values when $Nitr = 1$) and will continue to update the variables ($x = x^{old} - \Omega^{-1}g$) when the precision limit has not yet been reached (*precflag* = FALSE). To prevent entering a dead loop, we impose an upper limit of $Nitrmax = 1000$ on the maximum number of iterations to be performed. As reference, NewtonRaphson() returns the status of the precision flag at exit to indicate whether it is terminated by the iteration limit where the designated precision has not been met. For cross-checking purposes, the routine also returns the maximum deviation from zero among all the functions as evaluated at the point of exit.

At each update, the iteration requires an *ad hoc* evaluation of both the objective functions and their partial derivatives. This can be done through an external routine called FunctionArray() that defines the kind of problem at hand and returns an array of function values $\{g_1, \ldots, g_n\}$ evaluated at specific input values of $\{x_1, \ldots, x_n\}$. Partial derivatives in the entries of Ω can be estimated by making two consecutive calls to FunctionArray() based on the numerical difference in (5.5). While the double-loop structure with j and i will run through all its entries, the interior loop with k will shift only the appropriate term in the array $\{x_1, \ldots, x_n\}$ by Δx before making a second call to FunctionArray() for changes in function values.

The VBA code of NewtonRaphson() is given by Code 5.2. For the calculation of variable update, we have again used the routine SolveAxb() to calculate the shift $\Omega^{-1}g$. During the iteration, the value of *precflag* under the logical conjunction of an array of conditions can be determined by looping through each of the conditions. The precision limit has been reached (*precflag* = .TRUE.) if there is no violation on either of these conditions. Consider now the use of the NewtonRaphson() routine in the following examples.

EXAMPLE 5.1

Suppose we want to solve simultaneously the zero of a pair of functions ($n = 2$) given by

$$g_1(x_1, x_2) = x_1^2 + x_2^2 - 1$$

$$g_2(x_1, x_2) = x_1 + x_2.$$

Here, the FunctionArray() routine should be able to read in specific values of $\{x_1, x_2\}$ and return the corresponding function values $\{g_1, g_2\}$. The Newton–Raphson solution of this problem will have the following VBA structure.

```
Sub Test()
    Dim x(1 To 2) As Double, n As Integer, prec As Double, precFlag As Boolean,
        maxDev As Double
    n = 2
    x(1) = Range("B2").Value
    x(2) = Range("C2").Value
    prec = Range("D2").Value
    Call NewtonRaphson(n, prec, x, precFlag, maxDev)
    Range("B3:C3") = x
    Range("D3") = precFlag
    Range("E3") = maxDev
End Sub

Sub FunctionArray(n As Integer, x() As Double, ByRef g() As Double)
    g(1) = x(1) ^ 2 + x(2) ^ 2 - 1
    g(2) = x(1) + x(2)
End Sub
```

	A	B	C	D	E
1		x_1	x_2	prec	max dev
2	Trial	1	0	1.00E-12	
3	Last update	0.707106781187	-0.707106781187	TRUE	0.000000000000

EXAMPLE 5.2

A practical example of interest in finance is the estimation of the so-called implied volatility in option pricing where the theoretical Black–Scholes value matches the market price. Taking the volatility parameter σ to be the only variable $(n = 1)$, we want to solve the zero of the following function that represents the difference between, for example, the call option prices based on the Black-Scholes formula and the market.

$$g(\sigma) = SN(d) - Ke^{-rT}N(d - \sigma\sqrt{T}) - c_{market}, \quad d = \frac{\ln(S/K) + (r + \frac{1}{2}\sigma^2)T}{\sigma\sqrt{T}}$$

Here, S is the asset price, r is the risk-free interest rate, and K and T are the strike price and maturity of the option, respectively. The term c_{market} is the market option price with the same strike and maturity. The mathematical function $N(x)$ is the cumulative normal distribution with zero mean and unit standard deviation. In VBA, we can simply use the Excel function **NORMSDIST** for values of $N(x)$. The VBA coding for this routine is given as follows:

```
Sub callImpVol()
    Dim sigma(1 To 1) As Double, n As Integer, prec As Double, precFlag As Boolean, _
        maxDev As Double
    n = 1
    sigma(1) = Range("C7").Value
    prec = Range("C10").Value
    Call NewtonRaphson(n, prec, sigma, precFlag, maxDev)
    Range("C11") = sigma(1)
    Range("C12") = precFlag
    Range("C13") = maxDev
End Sub


Sub FunctionArray(n As Integer, sigma() As Double, ByRef g() As Double)
    Dim assetPrice As Double, exercisePrice As Double, timeMaturity As Double
    Dim riskFree As Double, marketCallPrice As Double, d As Double
    assetPrice = Range("C2").Value
    exercisePrice = Range("C3").Value
    timeMaturity = Range("C4").Value
    riskFree = Range("C5").Value
    marketCallPrice = Range("C6").Value
    d = Log(assetPrice / exercisePrice) + (riskFree + 0.5 * sigma(1) ^ 2) * timeMaturity
    d = d / (sigma(1) * timeMaturity ^ 0.5)
    With Application.WorksheetFunction
        g(1) = assetPrice * .NormSDist(d) - _
            exercisePrice * Exp(-riskFree * timeMaturity) * _
            .NormSDist(d - sigma(1) * timeMaturity ^ 0.5) - marketCallPrice
    End With
End Sub
```

(Continued)

(Continued)

▲	A	B	C	D
1				
2		Asset Price	100.00	
3		Exercise Price	95.00	
4		Time to Maturity	1.00	
5		Riskfree Rate	5.0%	
6		Market Call price	13.00	
7		Historical Volatility	17.0%	
8				
9		Calculate Implied Volatility		
10		Precision	1.00E-08	
11		*Implied Volatility*	18.9490%	
12		*PrecFlag*	TRUE	
13		*Dev.*	1.18378E-14	
14				

NewtonRaphson(n , Δx , x(1:n) , precflag , maxdev)

\# define the maximum number of iterations
   Nitrmax = 1000

\# iterate to a new point when both the precision and iteration limits have not yet been reached
   For(*Nitr* = 1 to *Nitrmax*) {

\# initiate the array of variables for iteration
$$x^{old}(1:n) = x(1:n)$$

\# determine the function values
      call *FunctionArray*(n , $x^{old}(1{:}n)$, $g(1{:}n)$)

\# determine the matrix Ω by making another call to FunctionArray with shifted x

    For (j = 1 to n) { For (k = 1 to n) { $x^{shift}(k) = x^{old}(k) + \Delta x\, \delta_{jk}$ }

      call *FunctionArray*(n , $x^{shift}(1{:}n)$, $g^{shift}(1{:}n)$)

      For (i = 1 to n) { $\Omega(i,j) = [\, g^{shift}(i) - g(i)\,]\,/\,\Delta x$ }
      }

\# iterate and update the column array of variables
   $x(1:n) = x^{old}(1:n) - \Omega^{-1}(1:n, 1:n)\, g(1:n)$

\# check the precision limit and update the precision flag
   precflag (AND($|\, x(1) - x^{old}(1)\,| \le \Delta x$, . . . , $|\, x(n) - x^{old}(n)\,| \le \Delta x$)

    If(*precflag*) then exit *Nitr*
    }

determine at exit the maximum deviation from zero among all the functions
call *FunctionArray*(n , $x(1{:}n)$, $g(1{:}n)$)

$maxdev = \text{MAX}(\, | \, g_1 | \, , \, \ldots \, , | \, g_n | \,)$

Code 5.1: Pseudo code of the NewtonRaphson() routine.

```vba
Sub NewtonRaphson(n As Integer, prec As Double, ByRef x() As Double, ByRef precFlag As
    Boolean, ByRef maxDev As Double)
  Const nItrMax As Integer = 1000
  Dim xOld() As Double: ReDim xOld(1 To n)
  Dim xShift() As Double: ReDim xShift(1 To n)
  Dim gShift() As Double: ReDim gShift(1 To n)
  Dim g() As Double: ReDim g(1 To n)
  Dim omega() As Double: ReDim omega(1 To n, 1 To n)
  Dim Dx() As Double: ReDim Dx(1 To n)

  Dim i As Integer, j As Integer, k As Integer, nItr As Integer
  For nItr = 1 To nItrMax
    'initiate the array of variables and determine the function values
    For i = 1 To n: xOld(i) = x(i): Next i
    Call FunctionArray(n, xOld, g)
    'determine the matrix omega
    For j = 1 To n
      For k = 1 To n: xShift(k) = xOld(k) + prec * IIf(j = k, 1, 0): Next k
      Call FunctionArray(n, xShift, gShift)
      For i = 1 To n: omega(i, j) = (gShift(i) - g(i)) / prec: Next i
    Next j

    'iterate and update the array of variables
    Call SolveAxb(omega, g, Dx, n, 1, 1, 1)
    For i = 1 To n: x(i) = xOld(i) - Dx(i): Next i

    'check the precision limit and update the precision flag
    For i = 1 To n
      If Abs(x(i) - xOld(i)) <= prec Then
        precFlag = True
      Else
        precFlag = False
        Exit For
      End If
    Next i
    If precFlag Then Exit For
  Next nItr
  'determine the maximum deviation at exit
  Call FunctionArray(n, x, g)
  maxDev = 0
  For i = 1 To n
    If Abs(g(i)) > maxDev Then maxDev = Abs(g(i))
  Next i
End Sub
```

Code 5.2: VBA code of the NewtonRaphson() routine.

REVIEW QUESTIONS

1. Use the NewtonRaphson() routine to solve numerically the value of $r_{2\text{-}years}$ in the following equation:

$$\$114.26 = \$5\, e^{-r_{6\text{-}months}\times 0.5} + \$5\, e^{-r_{1\text{-}year}\times 1.0} + \$5\, e^{-\frac{1}{2}\left(r_{1\text{-}year}+r_{2\text{-}years}\right)\times 1.5}$$
$$+ \$105\, e^{-r_{2\text{-}years}\times 2.0}$$

with $r_{6\text{-}months} = 0.0213$ and $r_{1\text{-}year} = 0.0238$.

2. Use the NewtonRaphson() routine to solve numerically the value of λ in the EWMA model in Question 1 when the logarithm of likelihood in Equation (2.5) is maximized $(d\ln(L)/d\lambda = 0)$. How would you choose the trail value of λ to initialize the search?

ENDNOTES

1. W.H. Press, S.A. Teukolsky, W.T. Vetterling, and B.P. Flannery, "Root Finding and Nonlinear Sets of Equations," in *Numerical Recipes in C : The Art of Scientific Computing*, 2nd Edition (Cambridge: Cambridge University Press, 1997), 347–393.

2. From (5.2), we have $\varepsilon^{new} = \varepsilon^{old} + g(x^{soln} - \varepsilon^{old})/g'(x^{soln} - \varepsilon^{old})$. We can expand the terms g and g' around x^{soln} to get $\varepsilon^{new} \approx -\frac{1}{2}\,[g''(x^{soln})/g'(x^{soln})](\varepsilon^{old})^2$.

CHAPTER 6

Yield Curve Construction Using Cubic Spline

6.1 CUBIC SPLINE INTERPOLATION

In this chapter, we describe a generalized bootstrapping method to determine the yield curve given any available data set of bond prices.[1] In the bootstrapping method as discussed in standard texts, zero-coupon rates are extracted iteratively from the net present value expressions of coupon-bearing bond prices for which discount rates for all coupons are presumably determined from previous steps. With insufficient bond data, such intermediate rates could possibly be missing in the bootstrapping sequence causing the entire procedure to cease immediately. Consider, for example, the yield curve construction based on the following sample bond prices as shown in Table 6.1.

TABLE 6.1 Sample bond prices with the bootstrapped zero-coupon rates.

Bond price	Face value	Time to maturity	Semi-annual coupon	Zero-coupon rate
$98.94	$100	6 months	$0	2.13%
$97.65	$100	1 year	$0	2.38%
$114.26	$100	2 years	$5	2.63%

The first two instruments (maturities of six months and one year) are zero-coupon bonds. The corresponding zero-coupon rates of $r_{6\text{-}months} = 2.13\%$ and $r_{1\text{-}year} = 2.38\%$ can be calculated very easily from the bond prices by considering the discount of their face values as:

$$\$98.94 = \$100e^{-r_{6\text{-}months} \times 0.5} \text{ and } \$97.65 = \$100e^{-r_{1\text{-}year} \times 1.0}.$$

The last instrument is a two-year coupon-bearing bond with coupon payments every six months. In the bootstrapping method, the zero rate $r_{2\text{-years}}$ is calculated from the net present value expression of the two-year bond price given by:

$$\$114.26 = \$5e^{-r_{6\text{-months}} \times 0.5} + \$5e^{-r_{1\text{-year}} \times 1.0} + \$5e^{-r_{1.5\text{-years}} \times 1.5} + \$105e^{-r_{2\text{-years}} \times 2.0}.$$

$$(6.1)$$

In equation (6.1), the intermediate zero rate, $r_{1.5\text{-years}}$ for one-and-a-half years, has not yet been determined in the previous procedure. The two-year zero rate cannot be calculated prior to the determination of such a missing rate. Naively, the missing zero rate $r_{1.5\text{-years}}$ can be approximated through linear interpolation between the one-year and two-year zero rates as,

$$r_{1.5\text{-years}} = \tfrac{1}{2}(r_{1\text{-year}} + r_{2\text{-years}}).$$

In this way, the two-year zero rate in equation (6.1) can loosely be estimated as $r_{2\text{-years}} = 2.63\%$. In a generalized method, the same problem can be overcome using cubic spline interpolation instead that estimates all missing rates in the bootstrapping procedure.

Spline is a piecewise smooth function joined together by different segments of polynomials. The polynomials of adjacent segments are joined smoothly at break points, called *knots*, with continuous derivatives. Given n knots $\{(x_1, y_1), (x_2, y_2), \ldots, (x_n, y_n)\}$ as shown in Figure 6.1, interpolation among all these points can be achieved through a spline with $n-1$ polynomials $\{\phi_1, \phi_2, \ldots, \phi_{n-1}\}$. The simplest solution to the interpolating problem would be the spline with linear polynomials. To improve numerical accuracy using higher order polynomials, additional assumptions beside the smoothness conditions are required to uniquely define the coefficients in the polynomials. A common choice would be the spline with cubic polynomials defined through additional linear assumptions at both endpoints of the interpolating interval (known as the natural spline conditions).

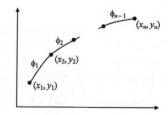

FIGURE 6.1   Cubic spline interpolation with n knots.

In cubic spline interpolation with n knots at $\{(x_1, y_1), (x_2, y_2), \ldots, (x_n, y_n)\}$ where $x_1 < x_2 < \ldots < x_n$, there are $n - 1$ cubic polynomials $\phi_i(x) = a_i + b_i x + c_i x^2 + d_i x^3$ (for $i = 1, 2, \ldots, n - 1$) with a total of $4(n - 1)$ unknown spline coefficients. The polynomials must generate the corresponding knot values to their left and right ends in each segment as:

$$y_i = \phi_i(x_i), \text{ for } i = 1, 2, \ldots, n - 1 \tag{6.2}$$

$$y_{i+1} = \phi_i(x_{i+1}), \text{ for } i = 1, 2, \ldots, n - 1. \tag{6.3}$$

The smoothness conditions are given by the continuities of the polynomials as well as their first and second derivatives, $\phi'_i(x) = b_i + 2c_i x + 3d_i x^2$ and $\phi''_i(x) = 2c_i + 6d_i x$ respectively, at each knot. The polynomials are continuous at each knot according to equations (6.2) and (6.3). The continuities of their first and second derivatives are given by:

$$\phi'_i(x_{i+1}) = \phi'_{i+1}(x_{i+1}), \text{ for } i = 1, 2, \ldots, n - 2 \tag{6.4}$$

$$\phi''_i(x_{i+1}) = \phi''_{i+1}(x_{i+1}), \text{ for } i = 1, 2, \ldots, n - 2. \tag{6.5}$$

There are all together only $4(n-1)-2$ matching conditions as expressed in equations (6.2) to (6.5). The spline coefficients can be uniquely defined through the natural spline conditions that force the spline to be linear outside the interpolating interval. This is given by the vanishing of second derivatives at both end knots as:

$$\phi''_1(x_1) = \phi''_{n-1}(x_n) = 0. \tag{6.6}$$

The matching conditions together with the natural spline conditions can be rewritten in matrix representation as:

$$\begin{pmatrix} y_1 \\ \vdots \\ y_{n-1} \\ y_2 \\ \vdots \\ y_n \\ 0 \\ \vdots \\ \vdots \\ 0 \end{pmatrix} = M \begin{pmatrix} a_1 \\ b_1 \\ c_1 \\ d_1 \\ \vdots \\ \vdots \\ a_{n-1} \\ b_{n-1} \\ c_{n-1} \\ d_{n-1} \end{pmatrix} \tag{6.7}$$

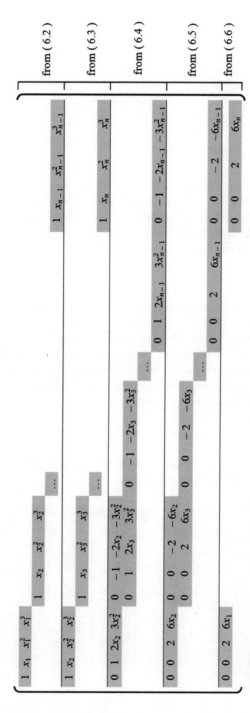

FIGURE 6.2 The square matrix M of size $4(n-1) \times 4(n-1)$. The undepicted entries are all zero.

There are $4(n-1)$ rows in the two column vectors of (6.7) associated with the same number of conditions as expressed in the above equations. The 4 $(n-1) \times 4(n-1)$ square matrix M is shown in Figure 6.2. As indicated in the figure, the highlighted entries can easily be read off from the conditions in (6.2) to (6.6) while all other entries are zero. The spline coefficients on the right side of (6.7) can be determined by inverting the matrix equation with the inverse of matrix M.

EXAMPLE 6.1

Consider the cubic spline interpolation for the zero-coupon rates as extracted previously based on the sample bond prices. In this case, we have $n = 3$ knots located at:

$$x_1 = 0.5 \text{ year}, \; y_1 = 2.13\%$$

$$x_2 = 1.0 \text{ year}, \; y_2 = 2.38\%$$

$$x_3 = 2.0 \text{ years}, \; y_3 = 2.63\%.$$

It requires two cubic polynomials $\phi_1(x)$ and $\phi_2(x)$ in the interpolation. Their coefficients can be determined by solving the matrix equation in (6.7) as:

$$\begin{pmatrix} 2.13 \\ 2.38 \\ 2.38 \\ 2.63 \\ 0 \\ 0 \\ 0 \\ 0 \end{pmatrix} = \begin{pmatrix} 1 & 0.5 & 0.25 & 0.125 & 0 & 0 & 0 & 0 \\ 0 & 0 & 0 & 0 & 1 & 1 & 1 & 1 \\ 1 & 1 & 1 & 1 & 0 & 0 & 0 & 0 \\ 0 & 0 & 0 & 0 & 1 & 2 & 4 & 8 \\ 0 & 1 & 2 & 3 & 0 & -1 & -2 & -3 \\ 0 & 0 & 2 & 6 & 0 & 0 & -2 & -6 \\ 0 & 0 & 2 & 3 & 0 & 0 & 0 & 0 \\ 0 & 0 & 0 & 0 & 0 & 0 & 2 & 12 \end{pmatrix} \begin{pmatrix} a_1 \\ b_1 \\ c_1 \\ d_1 \\ a_2 \\ b_2 \\ c_2 \\ d_2 \end{pmatrix}$$

The cubic spline is then calculated to be:

$$\phi_1(x) = 1.88 + 0.4167x + 0.25x^2 - 0.1667x^3, \text{ for } 0.5 \le x \le 1.0$$

$$\phi_2(x) = 1.63 + 1.1667x - 0.50x^2 + 0.0833x^3, \text{ for } 1.0 \le x \le 2.0.$$

(continued)

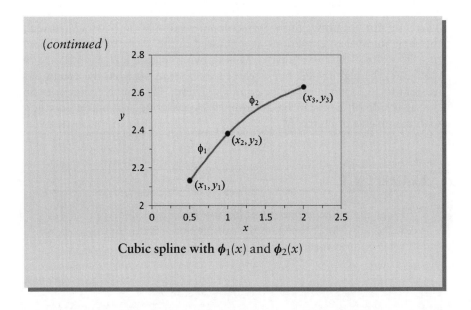

(continued)

Cubic spline with $\phi_1(x)$ and $\phi_2(x)$

We first want to develop a generic VBA routine called CubicSpline() that implements the cubic spline interpolation by solving the coefficients in equation (6.7) given knots. It would be useful in the construction of the yield curve under the problem of missing rates. The pseudo code of CubicSpline() is given by Code 6.1. It reads in the location of n knots at $\{x_1, \ldots, x_n\}$ and $\{y_1, \ldots, y_n\}$, and returns the spline coefficients $\{a_1, \ldots, a_{n-1}\}$, $\{b_1, \ldots, b_{n-1}\}$, $\{c_1, \ldots, c_{n-1}\}$, and $\{d_1, \ldots, d_{n-1}\}$ in the interpolation. The VBA code of CubicSpline() is given by Code 6.2. For the calculation of the spline coefficients, we have again used the routine SolveAxb() to invert the matrix equation in (6.7).

CubicSpline(n, $x(1:n)$, $y(1:n)$, $a(1:n-1)$, $b(1:n-1)$, $c(1:n-1)$, $d(1:n-1)$)

```
# define the column vector R on the left side of equation (6.7)
For ( i = 1 to n − 1 ){R( i ) = y( i )
                       R( n − 1 + i ) = y( i + 1 )
                       R( 2(n − 1) + i ) = 0
                       R( 3(n − 1) + i ) = 0      }

# initialize the entries of matrix M

For ( i = 1 to 4(n − 1) ){  For ( j = 1 to 4(n − 1) ){  M( i , j ) = 0  }  }

# define the entries in the first ( n − 1 ) rows
ptr = 0,                    For ( i = 1 to n − 1 ) {M( ptr + i , 4(i − 1) +1 )= 1
                                                    M( ptr + i , 4(i − 1) +2 )= x( i )
```

$$M(\, ptr + i \,,\, 4(i-1) +3 \,) = x^2(\, i \,)$$
$$M(\, ptr + i \,,\, 4(i-1) +4 \,) = x^3(\, i \,) \quad \}$$

\# define the entries in the second ($n-1$) rows

$ptr = n - 1,$ For ($i = 1$ to $n-1$) { $M(\, ptr + i \,,\, 4(i-1) +1 \,) = 1$

$$M(\, ptr + i \,,\, 4(i-1) +2 \,) = x(\, i+1 \,)$$
$$M(\, ptr + i \,,\, 4(i-1) +3 \,) = x^2(\, i+1 \,)$$
$$M(\, ptr + i \,,\, 4(i-1) +4 \,) = x^3(\, i+1 \,) \quad \}$$

\# define the entries in the following ($n - 2$) rows

$ptr = 2(n - 1),$ For ($i = 1$ to $n-2$) { $M(\, ptr + i \,,\, 4(i-1) +2 \,) = 1$

$$M(\, ptr + i \,,\, 4(i-1) +3 \,) = 2x(\, i+1 \,)$$
$$M(\, ptr + i \,,\, 4(i-1) +4 \,) = 3x^2(\, i+1 \,)$$
$$M(\, ptr + i \,,\, 4(i-1) +6 \,) = -1$$
$$M(\, ptr + i \,,\, 4(i-1) +7 \,) = -2x(\, i+1 \,)$$
$$M(\, ptr + i \,,\, 4(i-1) +8 \,) = -3x^2(\, i+1 \,) \quad \}$$

\# define the entries in the next ($n - 2$) rows

$ptr = 3(n - 1) - 1,$ For ($i = 1$ to $n-2$) { $M(\, ptr + i \,,\, 4(i-1) +3 \,) = 2$

$$M(\, ptr + i \,,\, 4(i-1) +4 \,) = 6x(\, i+1 \,)$$
$$M(\, ptr + i \,,\, 4(i-1) +7 \,) = -2$$
$$M(\, ptr + i \,,\, 4(i-1) +8 \,) = -6x(\, i+1 \,)$$

}

\# define the entries in the last 2 rows

$ptr = 4(n - 1) - 2$

$M(\, ptr + 1 \,,\, 3 \,) = 2,\ M(\, ptr + 1 \,,\, 4 \,) = 6x(\, 1 \,)$

$M(\, ptr + 2 \,,\, 4(n-1) - 1 \,) = 2,\ M(\, ptr + 2 \,,\, 4(n-1) \,) = 6x(\, n \,)$

\# determine the spline coefficients **Q** by solving the matrix equation

$$\mathbf{Q}(\, 1:4(n-1) \,) = \mathbf{M}^{-1}(\, 1:4(n-1) \,,\, 1:4(n-1) \,)\, \mathbf{R}(\, 1:4(n-1) \,)$$

For ($i = 1$ to $n-1$) { $a(\, i \,) = Q(\, 4(i-1) + 1 \,)$

$$b(\, i \,) = Q(\, 4(i-1) + 2 \,)$$
$$c(\, i \,) = Q(\, 4(i-1) + 3 \,)$$
$$d(\, i \,) = Q(\, 4(i-1) + 4 \,) \qquad \}$$

Code 6.1: Pseudo code of the CubicSpline() routine.

```
Sub CubicSpline(n As Integer, x() As Double, y() As Double, ByRef a() As Double, ByRef b()
            As Double, ByRef c() As Double, ByRef d() As Double)

    Dim i As Integer, j As Integer, ptr As Integer
    Dim Mmatrix() As Double: ReDim Mmatrix(1 To 4 * (n - 1), 1 To 4 * (n - 1))
    Dim Rvec() As Double: ReDim Rvec(1 To 4 * (n - 1))
    Dim Qvec() As Double: ReDim Qvec(1 To 4 * (n - 1))

    For i = 1 To (n - 1)
        Rvec(i) = y(i)
        Rvec(n - 1 + i) = y(i + 1)
        Rvec(2 * (n - 1) + i) = 0
        Rvec(3 * (n - 1) + i) = 0
    Next i

    For i = 1 To 4 * (n - 1)
        For j = 1 To 4 * (n - 1): Mmatrix(i, j) = 0: Next j
    Next i
```

```
ptr = 0
For i = 1 To (n - 1)
    Mmatrix(ptr + i, 4 * (i - 1) + 1) = 1
    Mmatrix(ptr + i, 4 * (i - 1) + 2) = x(i)
    Mmatrix(ptr + i, 4 * (i - 1) + 3) = x(i) ^ 2
    Mmatrix(ptr + i, 4 * (i - 1) + 4) = x(i) ^ 3
Next i

ptr = n - 1
For i = 1 To (n - 1)
    Mmatrix(ptr + i, 4 * (i - 1) + 1) = 1
    Mmatrix(ptr + i, 4 * (i - 1) + 2) = x(i + 1)
    Mmatrix(ptr + i, 4 * (i - 1) + 3) = x(i + 1) ^ 2
    Mmatrix(ptr + i, 4 * (i - 1) + 4) = x(i + 1) ^ 3
Next i

ptr = 2 * (n - 1)
For i = 1 To (n - 2)
    Mmatrix(ptr + i, 4 * (i - 1) + 2) = 1
    Mmatrix(ptr + i, 4 * (i - 1) + 3) = 2 * x(i + 1)
    Mmatrix(ptr + i, 4 * (i - 1) + 4) = 3 * x(i + 1) ^ 2
    Mmatrix(ptr + i, 4 * (i - 1) + 6) = -1
    Mmatrix(ptr + i, 4 * (i - 1) + 7) = -2 * x(i + 1)
    Mmatrix(ptr + i, 4 * (i - 1) + 8) = -3 * x(i + 1) ^ 2
Next i

ptr = 3 * (n - 1) - 1
For i = 1 To (n - 2)
    Mmatrix(ptr + i, 4 * (i - 1) + 3) = 2
    Mmatrix(ptr + i, 4 * (i - 1) + 4) = 6 * x(i + 1)
    Mmatrix(ptr + i, 4 * (i - 1) + 7) = -2
    Mmatrix(ptr + i, 4 * (i - 1) + 8) = -6 * x(i + 1)
Next i


ptr = 4 * (n - 1) - 2
Mmatrix(ptr + 1, 3) = 2
Mmatrix(ptr + 1, 4) = 6 * x(1)
Mmatrix(ptr + 2, 4 * (n - 1) - 1) = 2
Mmatrix(ptr + 2, 4 * (n - 1)) = 6 * x(n)

Call SolveAxb(Mmatrix(), Rvec(), Qvec(), 4 * (n - 1), 1, 1, 1)

For i = 1 To (n - 1)
    a(i) = Qvec(4 * (i - 1) + 1)
    b(i) = Qvec(4 * (i - 1) + 2)
    c(i) = Qvec(4 * (i - 1) + 3)
    d(i) = Qvec(4 * (i - 1) + 4)
Next i

End Sub
```

Code 6.2: VBA code of the CubicSpline() routine.

6.2 YIELD CURVE CONSTRUCTION

In example 6.1, we have adopted a two-year zero rate of $r_{2\text{-}years} = 2.63\%$ based on a linear approximation. In this case, the two-year bond price in equation (6.1) will not necessarily be satisfied with the interpolated one-and-a-half year zero rate $r_{1.5\text{-}years} = \phi_2(1.5)$ using the cubic spline. In a generalized method of yield curve construction, $r_{2\text{-}years}$ should be determined such that the resulting cubic spline will provide an interpolated value of $r_{1.5\text{-}years}$ that exactly reproduces the two-year bond price. This can be achieved through a numerical search of $r_{2\text{-}years}$ using the Newton–Raphson procedure over the error on the net present value expression as:

$$\$114.26 = \$5e^{-r_{6\text{-}months} \times 0.5} + \$5e^{-r_{1\text{-}year} \times 1.0} + \$5e^{-\phi_2\left(1.5 | r_{2\text{-}years}\right) \times 1.5} + \$105e^{-r_{2\text{-}years} \times 2.0}$$

$$(6.8)$$

where $\phi_2(x | r_{2\text{-}years})$ denotes the resulting cubic polynomial for a specific value of $r_{2\text{-}years}$. As described in the VBA coding below, we can simply call the NewtonRaphson() routine in chapter 5 with one variable and initiate the search using the value of the nearest zero rate. The error in (6.8) can be calculated based on the following setup in FunctionArray(). Under the precision requirement of 10^{-8}, the two-year zero rate is extracted to be $r_{2\text{-}years} = 2.63125423\%$ with a slight correction from the linear approximation.

```
Sub Searchr2y()
    Dim r2y(1 To 1) As Double, prec As Double, precFlag As Boolean, maxDev As Double
    r2y(1) = 2.38
    prec = 0.00000001
    Call NewtonRaphson(1, prec, r2y, precFlag, maxDev)
    Range("B2").Value = r2y(1)
    Range("B3").Value = precflag
    Range("B4").Value = maxDev
End Sub

Sub FunctionArray(n As Integer, r2y() As Double, ByRef NPVerr() As Double)
    Dim x(1 To 3) As Double, y(1 To 3) As Double
    Dim a(1 To 2) As Double, b(1 To 2) As Double, c(1 To 2) As Double, d(1 To 2) As Double
    x(1) = 0.5
    x(2) = 1.0
    x(3) = 2.0
    y(1) = 2.13
    y(2) = 2.38
    y(3) = r2y(1)
```

```
Call CubicSpline(3, x, y, a, b, c, d)
Dim xm As Double: xm = 1.5
Dim ym As Double: ym = a(2) + b(2) * xm + c(2) * xm ^ 2 + d(2) * xm ^ 3
NPVerr(1) = 114.26 - 5 * Exp(-(y(1) / 100) * x(1)) - 5 * Exp(-(y(2) / 100) * x(2)) - 5 *
            Exp(-(ym / 100) * xm) - 105 * Exp(-(y(3) / 100) * x(3))
End Sub
```

Practically, we perform a yield curve construction based on a set of observed bond prices $\{B_1, B_2, \ldots, B_n\}$ with terms to maturity $\{T_1 < T_2 < \ldots < T_n\}$ and face values $\{L_1, L_2, \ldots, L_n\}$. Associated with each of these bonds, there are fixed coupon payments $\{c_1 = 0, c_2, \ldots, c_n\}$ scheduled sequentially in time at:

$$t_{21}, t_{22}, \ldots \leq T_2, \text{ for bond } B_2$$
$$\cdots \cdots$$
$$t_{n1}, t_{n2}, \ldots \leq T_n, \text{ for bond } B_n.$$

We denote $r(t)$ to be the zero-coupon rate with term to maturity t. The objective is to extract the zero rates $\{r(T_1), \ldots, r(T_n)\}$ according to the observed bond prices. For the construction to be attainable, the first bond B_1 in the data set with the shortest term must be the zero coupon, and all of the above coupon payments must be scheduled on or after T_1. The net present value expressions for each of these bonds are given by:

$$B_1 = L_1 e^{-r(T_1)T_1}$$
$$B_2 = c_2 e^{-r(t_{21})t_{21}} + c_2 e^{-r(t_{22})t_{22}} + \cdots + (c_2 + L_2) e^{-r(T_2)T_2}, T_1 \leq t_{21} < t_{22} < \cdots \leq T_2$$
$$\cdots \cdots$$
$$B_n = c_n e^{-r(t_{n1})t_{n1}} + c_n e^{-r(t_{n2})t_{n2}} + \cdots + (c_n + L_n) e^{-r(T_n)T_n}, T_1 \leq t_{n1} < t_{n2} < \cdots \leq T_n.$$

$$(6.9)$$

In equation (6.9), the bootstrapping procedure starts off from the determination of the shortest zero rate $r(T_1)$ from B_1. However, it is clear that there are missing discount rates for the coupon payments in the immediate determination of $r(T_2)$, and similarly for all others in the following steps, from the coupon-bearing bond prices.

In the generalized method, such a problem can be overcome using cubic spline interpolation with knots at $\{T_1, T_2, \ldots, T_n\}$. Discount rates for coupon payments in (6.9) can be estimated by their interpolated values based on $n-1$ cubic polynomials $\{\phi_1, \phi_2, \ldots, \phi_{n-1}\}$ in the spline as:

$$r(t) = \phi_k(t|r(T_1), \ldots, r(T_n)), \quad T_k < t \leq T_{k+1}. \tag{6.10}$$

In equation (6.10), $\phi_k(t|r(T_1), \ldots, r(T_n))$ denotes the resulting cubic polynomials using (6.7) with specific knot values $\{r(T_1), \ldots, r(T_n)\}$. Thus, we need to determine the zero rates $\{r(T_1), \ldots, r(T_n)\}$ such that the resulting cubic spline will generate interpolated values of coupon discount rates consistent with the bond prices. This is similar to the problem in (6.8) and can also be achieved through a numerical search using the Newton–Raphson method over the errors on the expressions in (6.9). As B_1 is assumed to be a zero-coupon bond, the shortest zero rate $r(T_1)$ can be extracted directly from (6.9) as:

$$r(T_1) = -\frac{1}{T_1}\ln\left(\frac{B_1}{L_1}\right). \tag{6.11}$$

However, it is convenient to include $r(T_1)$ in the Newton–Raphson procedure and formulate a search for the entire set of zero rates with (6.11) taken to be the common initial value. It can be shown that $r(T_1)$ will remain stationary during the search for which the extra loading on the procedure is insignificant.

6.3 EXCEL PLUS VBA IMPLEMENTATION

The errors on the net present value expressions in equation (6.9) can be calculated based on the FunctionArray() routine with pseudo code given by Code 6.3. Given zero rates $\{r(T_1), \ldots, r(T_n)\}$, the routine will return an array of error values $\{g_1, \ldots, g_n\}$ with respect to different expressions in (6.9). Bond data such as bond prices, terms to maturity, face values, coupon payments, number of coupons, and the payment schedules are inputted from Excel and stored as VBA arrays. The layout of the data interface in Excel will be discussed later in this section. For specific values of the zero rates during the search, the corresponding cubic spline is first calculated by calling the CubicSpline() routine. In Code 6.3, $t_c(i, j)$ denotes the time of the j-th coupon payment for the i-th bond. The double loop with labels i and j will run through all coupon payments for the entire set of coupon-bearing bonds. The interpolated value of the discount rate with term $t_c(i, j)$ can be determined according to (6.10) by identifying the relevant segment from T_k to T_{k+1} in the spline such that $T_k < t_c(i, j) \leq T_{k+1}$. The interpolation can then be performed using the cubic polynomial in this segment parameterized by the spline coefficients a_k, b_k, c_k, and d_k. To determine the required value of k, it is straight forward to run k from 1 to $i - 1$ and recall that $t_c(i, j) \leq T_i$ as defined in (6.9). In Code 6.3, we have made efficient use of a pointer ptr that records the location of T_k (setting $ptr = k$) for previous coupon payment. In this way, we can instead run k from ptr to $i - 1$ and start off the pointer from $ptr = 1$ at every initial coupon payment. Once we have identified the appropriate value of k, we should immediately proceed to the next coupon payment with new value of j. It should be noted that the k-loop does not provide the checking for $t_c(i, j)$ at exactly the leftmost knot T_1. We have included such checking and assign the knot value of $r_c(i, j) = r(T_1)$ before the k-loop. As discussed in earlier chapters, the checking should be conducted through the absolute limit $\mid t_c(i, j) - T_1 \mid \leq \varepsilon$ with precision $\varepsilon = 10^{-14}$ to avoid a possible floating point problem. Using the interpolated values of the coupon discount rates, the errors on the net present value expressions in (6.9) can then be calculated very easily in terms of an array $\{g_1, \ldots, g_n\}$.

The numerical search for the zero rates can be conducted very efficiently using the CalZeroRates() routine with pseudo code as depicted in Code 6.4. The number of unknown zero rates n and the designated precision limit of the search $prec$ are first defined in the routine. Data on the shortest zero-coupon bond are also inputted from Excel as the numerical search should be initiated from the value defined in (6.11). The search can be performed by calling the NewtonRaphson() routine that will in turn call the FunctionArray() routine in Code 6.3 for the evaluation of the objective functions $\{g_1, \ldots, g_n\}$. Upon exiting from a successful search, it will return the zero rates $\{r(T_1), \ldots, r(T_n)\}$ for which all error values $\{g_1, \ldots, g_n\}$ have vanished under the designated precision limit with $precflag = \text{TRUE}$ and $maxdev \leq prec$. The returned zero rates together with the precision flag and the maximum deviation should then be outputted into Excel.

Figure 6.3 illustrates the layout of the bond data interface in the Excel spreadsheet.[2] Information on different bonds is arranged in a row-by-row format starting from the ninth row. These include term to maturity (column A), bond price (column C), face value (column D), coupon payment (column E), number of coupons (column F), and payment schedule (column G onward). The VBA code of the FunctionArray() routine is given by Code 6.5. Accordingly, bond data are read off row-by-row from the spreadsheet with the use of the **OFFSET** function relative to the header

	A	B	C	D	E	F	G	H	I	J	K
1											
2	**Bond Data :**										
3											
4	Number of Bonds	8	Calculate	Precision	1.00E-08						
5			Zero Rates	Flag	TRUE						
6				Max. Dev.	5.34E-14						
7											
8	Term to Maturity	Zero Rate	Bond Price	Face Value	Coupon Payment	Number of Coupons	Payment Schedule				
9	0.083	4.448%	99.63	100.00	0.000	0					
10	0.250	4.546%	98.87	100.00	0.000	0					
11	0.500	4.633%	97.71	100.00	0.000	0					
12	1.000	4.783%	95.33	100.00	0.000	0					
13	2.000	4.933%	100.00	100.00	2.495	4	0.500	1.000	1.500	2.000	
14	4.000	5.055%	100.00	100.00	2.555	8	0.500	1.000	1.500	2.000	2.500
15	7.500	5.192%	100.00	100.00	2.620	15	0.500	1.000	1.500	2.000	2.500
16	18.000	4.233%	100.00	100.00	2.250	36	0.500	1.000	1.500	2.000	2.500
17											
18											
19											
20	Scale : yearly										

FIGURE 6.3 Bond data interface in the Excel spreadsheet.

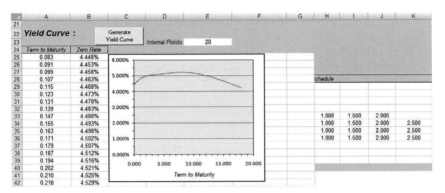

FIGURE 6.4   Constructed yield curve in an Excel spreadsheet.

cells in the eighth row. The VBA code of the main CalZeroRates() routine
is given by Code 6.6. It can be invoked through the "Calculate Zero Rates"
button in Excel. The total number of bonds in the data and the designated
precision of the search are read off from the named cells B4(nbond) and E4
(prec), respectively. Initial values of the zero rates are defined based on the
shortest zero-coupon bond inserted at one row offset from the header row.
Upon exiting from the Newton–Raphson procedure, the returned zero rates
are outputted into the spreadsheet underneath the header "Zero Rate" and
adjacent to the corresponding terms to maturity. As reference, the precision
flag and the maximum deviation of the search are also outputted into cells
E5 and E6, respectively.

As reference, it is useful to generate a smooth yield curve and display in
the spreadsheet the zero rates for intermediate values of the maturity term.
This can be done by calling the CubicSpline() routine with the bootstrapped
zero rates from CalZeroRates() as knot values. The VBA code of the
GenYieldCurve() routine that performs this task is given by Code 6.7.
It can be invoked through the "Generate Yield Curve" button in Excel.
Bootstrapped zero rates and the corresponding terms to maturity are
inputted into VBA through row offset from the header cells B8 and A8,
respectively. They are taken as knots for the CubicSpline() routine in order
to generate the cubic spline approximation of the yield curve. As shown in
Figure 6.4, we have defined in the named cell E23(npoint) the number of
internal points between any two adjacent knots T_i and T_{i+1}. Subsequent
values of the maturity term from the left to right ends are defined through
the double-loop with labels i and j as:

$$term = T_i + j \times (T_{i+1} - T_i)/(npoint + 1), \text{ where } i = 1, \ldots, n - 1$$
$$\text{and } j = 0, \ldots, npoint.$$

In this way, a smooth yield can be generated using the interpolated value $\phi_i(term)$ and outputted into the spreadsheet underneath the header cells A24 and B24. It should be noted that the right-end knot at T_n has not been covered by the double loop. For completeness, it has been appended to the yield curve at the end of Code 6.7.

FunctionArray(n , $r(1:n)$, $g(1:n)$)

```
# input bond data from Excel
Read terms to maturity { T₁, T₂, . . . , Tₙ } as array T(1 : n)
Read bond prices { B₁, B₂, . . . , Bₙ } as array B(1 : n)
Read face values { L₁, L₂, . . . , Lₙ } as array L(1 : n)
Read coupon payments { c₁ = 0, c₂, . . . , cₙ } as array C(1 : n)
Read number of coupon for each bond{ m₁ = 0 , m₂ , . . . , mₙ } as array m(1 : n)
Read coupon payment schedule { { t₂₁, t₂₂, . . . }, . . . , { tₙ₁, tₙ₂, . . . } } as array tc(1 : n , 1 : Max(m) )

# generate the cubic spline given knot values rs at Ts
Call CubicSpline( n , T(1 : n) , r(1 : n) , a(1 : n − 1) , b(1 : n − 1) , c(1 : n − 1) , d(1 : n − 1) )

# interpolate the discount rates rc at all coupon payments tc according to (6.10)
For( i = 2 to n ) {
    ptr = 1
    For( j = 1 to m(i) ) {
        τ = tc(i , j)
        If( | τ − T(1) | ≤ ε ) { rc(i , j) = r(1) , Next j }
        For( k = ptr to i − 1 ) { If( T(k) < τ ≤ T(k + 1) ) Then
                        rc(i , j) = a(k) + b(k) τ + c(k) τ² + d(k) τ³
                        ptr = k
                        Next j
                        Endif    }
            }
        }
# calculate the NPV errors g according to (6.9)

For( i = 1 to n ) { g(i) = B(i) − L(i) e^{−r(i) T(i)}
                For( j = 1 to m(i) ) { g(i) = g(i) − C(i) e^{−rc(i , j) tc(i , j)} }
                }
```

Code 6.3: Pseudo code of the FunctionArray() routine.

CalZeroRates( )

```
# input from EXCEL number of unknown zero rates
Read n

# input from EXCEL the designated precision limit of the numerical search
Read prec

# input from EXCEL data on the shortest zero-coupon bond and initiate the search according to (6.11)
Read T₁, B₁, and L₁
```

$r_{init} = - (1/T_1) \, ln(B_1 / L_1)$
For(i = 1 to n) { $r(i) = r_{init}$ }

\# perform the numerical search for the zero rates using Newton-Raphson procedure
Call *NewtonRaphson*(n , *prec* , r(1 : n) , *precflag* , *maxdev*)

\# output to EXCEL the returned zero rates, precision flag, and maximum deviation
Write r(1 : n), *precflag*, and *maxdev*

Code 6.4: Pseudo code of the CalZeroRates() routine.

```
Option Explicit
Private Const eps = 1 * 10 ^ -14
Private Const mmax = 100


Sub FunctionArray(n As Integer, rzero() As Double, ByRef g() As Double)

  Dim T() As Double: ReDim T(1 To n)
  Dim Bprice() As Double: ReDim Bprice(1 To n)
  Dim par() As Double: ReDim par(1 To n)
  Dim coupon() As Double: ReDim coupon(1 To n)
  Dim m() As Integer: ReDim m(1 To n)
  Dim tc() As Double: ReDim tc(1 To n, 1 To mmax)
  Dim rc() As Double: ReDim rc(1 To n, 1 To mmax)

  Dim i As Integer, j As Integer, k As Integer, ptr As Integer
  Dim tau As Double
  Dim a() As Double: ReDim a(1 To n - 1)
  Dim b() As Double: ReDim b(1 To n - 1)
  Dim c() As Double: ReDim c(1 To n - 1)
  Dim d() As Double: ReDim d(1 To n - 1)

  'input bond data
  For i = 1 To n
    T(i) = Range("A8").Offset(i, 0)
    Bprice(i) = Range("C8").Offset(i, 0)
    par(i) = Range("D8").Offset(i, 0)
    coupon(i) = Range("E8").Offset(i, 0)
    m(i) = Range("F8").Offset(i, 0)
    For j = 1 To m(i)
      tc(i, j) = Range("G8").Offset(i, j - 1)
    Next j
  Next i

  'generate the cubic spline
  Call CubicSpline(n, T, rzero, a, b, c, d)

  'interpolate the coupon discount rates
  For i = 2 To n
    ptr = 1
    For j = 1 To m(i)
      tau = tc(i, j)
```

```
            If (Abs(tau - T(1)) <= eps) Then
               rc(i, j) = rzero(1)
               GoTo nextj
            End If
            For k = ptr To i - 1
               If (tau > T(k) And tau <= T(k + 1)) Then
                  rc(i, j) = a(k) + b(k) * tau + c(k) * tau ^ 2 + d(k) * tau ^ 3
                  ptr = k
                  GoTo nextj
               End If
            Next k
nextj: Next j
   Next i

   'calculate the NPV errors
   For i = 1 To n
      g(i) = Bprice(i) - par(i) * Exp(-rzero(i) * T(i))
      For j = 1 To m(i)
         g(i) = g(i) - coupon(i) * Exp(-rc(i, j) * tc(i, j))
      Next j
   Next i
End Sub
```

Code 6.5: VBA code of the FunctionArray() routine.

```
Sub CalZeroRates()
   Dim n As Integer: n = Range("nbond").Value
   Dim prec As Double: prec = Range("prec").Value

   Dim T As Double: T = Range("A8").Offset(1, 0)
   Dim Bprice As Double: Bprice = Range("C8").Offset(1, 0)
   Dim par As Double: par = Range("D8").Offset(1, 0)
   Dim rinit As Double: rinit = -(1 / T) * Log(Bprice / par)

   Dim i As Integer
   Dim rzero() As Double: ReDim rzero(1 To n)
   Dim precFlag As Boolean
   Dim maxDev As Double

   For i = 1 To n: rzero(i) = rinit: Next i

   Call NewtonRaphson(n, prec, rzero, precFlag, maxDev)

   For i = 1 To n: Range("B8").Offset(i, 0) = rzero(i): Next i
   Range("E5").Value = precFlag
   Range("E6").Value = maxDev

End Sub
```

Code 6.6: VBA code of the CalZeroRates() routine.

```
Sub GenYieldCurve()
  Dim n As Integer: n = Range("nbond").Value
  Dim T() As Double: ReDim T(1 To n)
  Dim rzero() As Double: ReDim rzero(1 To n)
  Dim i As Integer, j As Integer, k As Integer

  Dim a() As Double: ReDim a(1 To n - 1)
  Dim b() As Double: ReDim b(1 To n - 1)
  Dim c() As Double: ReDim c(1 To n - 1)
  Dim d() As Double: ReDim d(1 To n - 1)

  For i = 1 To n
    T(i) = Range("A8").Offset(i, 0)
    rzero(i) = Range("B8").Offset(i, 0)
  Next i

  Call CubicSpline(n, T, rzero, a, b, c, d)

  Dim npoint As Integer: npoint = Range("npoint").Value
  Dim term As Double

  Range("A25:B200").ClearContents

  k = 0
  For i = 1 To n - 1
    For j = 0 To npoint
      k = k + 1
      term = T(i) + j * (T(i + 1) - T(i)) / (npoint + 1)
      Range("A24").Offset(k, 0) = term
      Range("B24").Offset(k, 0) = a(i) + b(i) * term + c(i) * term ^ 2 + d(i) * term ^ 3
    Next j
  Next i

  Range("A24").Offset(k + 1, 0) = T(n)
  Range("B24").Offset(k + 1, 0) = rzero(n)

End Sub
```

Code 6.7: VBA code of the GenYieldCurve() routine.

REVIEW QUESTION

1. Develop a VBA routine that generates the implied volatility surface, with respect to option strike price K and maturity term T, based on the market prices of plain vanilla call options written on the same asset as

$$c(K_1, T_1), \quad c(K_2, T_1), \ldots, \quad c(K_m, T_1)$$
$$c(K_1, T_2), \quad c(K_2, T_2), \ldots, \quad c(K_m, T_2)$$
$$\vdots$$
$$c(K_1, T_n), \quad c(K_2, T_n), \ldots, \quad c(K_m, T_n),$$

n – Number of available option maturity terms

m – Number of available option strike prices

As discussed in Example 5.2, the plain vanilla call option prices can be converted into a set of implied volatilities $\sigma(K_i, T_j)$ utilizing the Black–Scholes pricing formula with current asset price S_0 and risk-free interest rate r. In practice, the implied volatility surface is parameterized as

$$\sigma(K, T) = b_0(T) + b_1(T)\left(\frac{X}{\sqrt{T}}\right) + b_2(T)\left(\frac{X}{\sqrt{T}}\right)^2,$$

$$X = \ln\left(\frac{K}{S_0 e^{rT}}\right) \text{ called moneyness}$$

with coefficients $b_0(T)$, $b_1(T)$, and $b_2(T)$ depending on the maturity term. For each of the maturity term $\{T_1, T_2, \ldots, T_n\}$, the volatility skew ($\sigma$ *versus* K) can be obtained by least-square fitting of the coefficients $b_0(T)$, $b_1(T)$, and $b_2(T)$ to the implied volatilities in the data. Using then the contours of volatility skew, the volatility term structure (σ *versus* T) for arbitrary strike K can be obtained through cubic spline interpolation. In this way, it is possible to estimate the interpolated value of implied volatility $\sigma(K, T)$ for any strike and maturity within $K_1 \le K \le K_m$ and $T_1 \le T \le T_n$, respectively.

ENDNOTES

1. R. Deaves and M. Parlar, "A Generalized Bootstrap Method to Determine the Yield Curve," *Applied Mathematical Finance* 7, No. 4 (2000): 257–270.
2. Refer to yield_curve.xls.

## CHAPTER 7

Binomial Option Pricing Model

7.1 RISK-NEUTRAL OPTION PRICING AND THE BINOMIAL TREE

Options are financial instruments that convey the right, but not the obligation, to enter into a future transaction written on an underlying asset. In the stochastic model, asset price return during the time increment from t to $t + \Delta t$ is assumed to follow a random normal process as:

$$\Delta S_t / S_t = \varepsilon(\mu \Delta t, \ \sigma \sqrt{\Delta t}) \tag{7.1}$$

where μ and σ are the mean rate and volatility of return respectively. For constant and flat interest rate r, the current price of an option written on this asset can be defined based on the present value of its average maturity payoff at time T as:[1]

$$f_0 = e^{-rT} \hat{E}(f_T | S_0). \tag{7.2}$$

In (7.2), we are averaging over all realized maturity payoffs of the option f_T in respect to sample asset prices generated through the so-called risk-neutral process related to (7.1). The option price f_0 is said to be evaluated at the current asset price S_0 that initiates the risk-neutral process. Equation (7.2) is referred to as the risk-neutral option pricing that is proven to be equivalent to the Black–Scholes differential equation. For a traded underlying asset such as stock, it can be shown that the risk-neutral process is simply given by (7.1) with the replacement of the mean rate μ by the interest rate r. The risk-neutral average in (7.2) can only be calculated analytically for options with a simple structure. In general, the calculation would be highly intense for options with an exotic exercising condition.

In Figure 7.1(a), the risk-neutral process of the asset price starts from S_0 and ends with S_T at the option's maturity. The k-th statistical moment of the

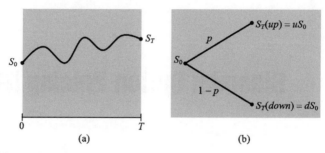

FIGURE 7.1   (a) The risk-neutral process of an asset price, and (b) its one-step binomial tree representation.

maturity price under the risk-neutral process is given by:

$$\hat{E}(S_T^k) = S_0^k\, e^{krT + \frac{1}{2}k(k-1)\sigma^2 T}. \tag{7.3}$$

In the binomial model, we can simplify the calculation of the risk-neutral average in (7.2) by adopting a binomial representation for the price movement in Figure 7.1(a). The simplest model is the one-step binomial tree initiated from S_0 with either an up or down scenario for the maturity price as shown in Figure 7.1(b). In general, it requires three factors in the parameterization: the branching probability p, the up factor u, and the down factor d. They can be determined by matching the statistical moments of the maturity price in (7.4) such that the binomial step will mimic the leading statistical properties of a full stochastic description.

$$p(uS_0)^k + (1-p)(dS_0)^k = S_0^k\, e^{krT + \frac{1}{2}k(k-1)\sigma^2 T}. \tag{7.4}$$

In this way, the risk-neutral average in (7.2) can be estimated to be:

$$\hat{E}(f_T) = p\,f(uS_0, T) + (1-p)\,f(dS_0, T). \tag{7.5}$$

It should be noted that the risk-neutral process itself is parameterized by only two factors, r and σ, in the stochastic model. It is therefore not admissible to find three factors $\{\, p, u, d \,\}$ that satisfy the matching condition (7.4) simultaneously for k equals 1, 2, and 3.

In Cox–Ross–Rubinstein parameterization,[2] we instead define the binomial tree in Figure 7.1(b) with two factors $\{\, p, u, d = 1/u \,\}$ and match (7.4) simultaneously for the first two moments. This gives:

$$p = \frac{e^{rT} - (1/u)}{u - (1/u)} \tag{7.6}$$

$$u = \tfrac{1}{2}(e^{-rT} + e^{(r+\sigma^2)T}) + \tfrac{1}{2}\sqrt{(e^{-rT} + e^{(r+\sigma^2)T})^2 - 4}. \qquad (7.7)$$

For the higher-order moments ($k \geq 3$) in (7.4), it can be shown that the discrepancies are always in the second order of the stochastic factors rT and σ^2T using the parameters p and u as defined above.[3] Thus, the error involved in the estimation in (7.5) will be insignificant if both the sizes of rT and σ^2T are small compared with one. Alternatively, in a more symmetric parameterization by Jarrow and Rudd[4] defined as $\{p = \tfrac{1}{2}, u, d\}$, the binomial factors are calculated in the same way to be:

$$u = e^{rT}(1 + \sqrt{e^{\sigma^2T} - 1}) \qquad (7.8)$$

$$d = e^{rT}(1 - \sqrt{e^{\sigma^2T} - 1}). \qquad (7.9)$$

In this case, the discrepancies for the higher-order moments are shown[5] to be only in the second order of the factor σ^2T.

To improve accuracy, and especially when there are intermediate boundary conditions for the option, it is essential to extend the binomial model into multiple steps of n with equal time intervals of $\Delta t = T/n$ as depicted in Figure 7.2(a). Consider the particular subtree in Figure 7.2(b) that goes from time t to $t + \Delta t$ with the initial asset price of S_t. Here, the binomial factors can be determined by matching the statistical moments of the end price $S_{t + \Delta t}$ under the risk-neutral process and conditional to the initial price as:

$$p(uS_t)^k + (1 - p)(dS_t)^k = S_t^k e^{kr\Delta t + \tfrac{1}{2}k(k-1)\sigma^2\Delta t}. \qquad (7.10)$$

It is obvious from (7.10) that the factors are determined to be independent of the initial price. For constant volatility of return, they are also considered

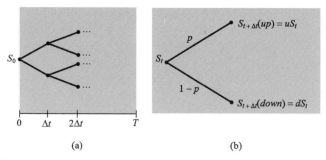

(a)   (b)

FIGURE 7.2   (a) A multiple-step binomial tree of an asset price. (b) A one-step subtree from time t to $t + \Delta t$ with initial asset price S_t.

to be universal for every subtree in the multiple-step representation. In Cox–Ross–Rubinstein or Jarrow-Rudd parameterization, the binomial factors are given by equations (7.6) to (7.9) with time interval T replaced by Δt. The discrepancies in higher-order moments are now in the second order of the smaller quantities $r\Delta t$ and $\sigma^2\Delta t$.

For an n-step binomial model, there are 2^n ways of how S_0 will evolve into the maturity price and pick up a certain sequence of u and d factors along the tree. To evaluate the risk-neutral average in (7.2), we need to keep track of the option's payoff for each of these scenarios in respect to the exercising conditions. This renders the calculation to be highly inefficient for very large n. Since the u and d factors are universal for every subtree, tree nodes are recombining in the way that an up movement followed by a down will have the same asset price as in its reverse order. As shown in Figure 7.3, this makes the number of end nodes to grow in the way as $n + 1$, and the total number of nodes for the entire n-step tree is manageable at $\frac{1}{2}(n + 1)(n + 2)$, a lot less than the scenarios.

At time $t = i\Delta t$, there are $i + 1$ nodes from the top to bottom of the tree with asset prices defined to be $S_{ij} = u^{i-j}d^j S_0$ where j runs from 0 to i. The j-th node is connected to both the j-th and $(j + 1)$-th nodes at a later time $t + \Delta t$ through a subtree. It is then efficient instead to consider an iterative form of risk-neutral pricing with respect to all these subtrees as:

$$f(S_{ij}, t) = e^{-r\Delta t}[\, pf(S_{i+1j}, t + \Delta t) + (1 - p)f(S_{i+1j+1}, t + \Delta t)], \quad j = 0, \ldots, i.$$
$$(7.11)$$

Equation (7.11) allows us to generate the option prices at time t based on the option prices at later time $t + \Delta t$. At option maturity $T = n\Delta t$, there are $n + 1$ nodes with asset prices $S_{nj} = u^{n-j}d^j S_0$ where j runs from 0 to n. We can start the iteration from the maturity payoffs $\psi(S_T)$ of the option and work backward in time toward its current value $f(S_0, 0)$. For exotic options with intermediate boundary conditions, we need to adjust the risk-neutral

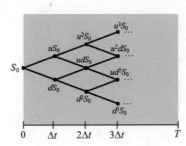

FIGURE 7.3 A multiple-step binomial tree with recombining nodes.

pricings in (7.11) according to the boundary conditions before the next iteration to an earlier time. For example, an American style option can be exercised at any time prior to its maturity based on the same payoff function $\psi(S_{ij})$. We should therefore compare each $f(S_{ij}, t)$ in (7.11) with its intrinsic value and perform the update according to the early exercising condition as:

$$f(S_{ij}, t) = \max\{f(S_{ij}, t), \ \psi(S_{ij})\}. \tag{7.12}$$

7.2 VBA IMPLEMENTATION

The iteration of option prices in (7.11) can be implemented very easily in VBA. We first develop a routine called GenOptionTree() that performs the iteration and generates the option prices at every node in the binomial tree. The pseudo code of GenOptionTree() is given by Code 7.1. It requires the input of option parameters (T, K, S_0, r, σ) and the tree configuration $(n, treetype)$, where *treetype* specifies the use of Cox—Ross—Rubinstein or Jarrow-Rudd parameterization. The routine returns the array of iterated option prices $f_{ij} = f(S_{ij}, i\Delta t)$ as well as the array of asset prices S_{ij} at every tree node with time label i running from 0 to n and node label j running from 0 to i. The iteration starts from the maturity payoffs of the option at end nodes with $i = n$. The payoff condition is defined through an external function payoff(K, S) with strike price K. It works backward in time from $i = n - 1$ to $i = 0$ and applies (7.11) to the subtree of every node in each column. Intermediate boundary conditions are defined using the routine Boundary(K, S, f) that updates the iterated option price immediately after its risk-neutral generation. The VBA code of GenOptionTree() is given by Code 7.2 together with the Payoff() function and Boundary() routine defined specifically for American put options according to (7.12).

Figure 7.4 depicts the spreadsheet design for this VBA implementation.[6] The button labeled "Binomial Pricing" will trigger the main VBA routine called BinomialPricing() with VBA code given by Code 7.3. The option parameters and tree configuration are inputted into this routine through the named cells B4(maturity), B5(strike), B6(assetprice), B7(riskfree), B8 (sigma), B10(treetype), and B11(n). It will call GenOptionTree() for the price arrays and the resulting option price of f_{00} will be outputted to cell B14. The entire option tree will be displayed in the spreadsheet by choosing "Yes" in cell B12. As a reference, the corresponding asset prices will also be displayed adjacent to the option prices. This can be done by running over both the time and node labels for the price arrays, and allocating cells through row and column offsets from the reference cell B17 for j and i,

	A	B	C	D	E	F	G	H	I
1									
2	American Put Option :								
3									
4	Maturity (T) =	1	(year)						
5	Strike (K) =	50							
6	Asset Price (S₀) =	50							
7	Risk-free Rate (r) =	0.05	(per year)						
8	Volatility (σ) =	0.25	(per year)						
9									
10	Binomial Tree Parameterization =	Cox-Ross-Rubinstein							
11	Number of Time Steps (n) =	10							
12	Display Binomial Tree =	Yes							
13									
14	Option Price (f₀) =	3.959	Binomial Pricing						
15									
16	Binomial Tree								
17	Forward Time (year)	0		0.1		0.2		0.3	
18	Option & Asset Prices	3.959	50.000	2.365	54.138	1.197	58.619	0.463	63.470
19				5.670	46.178	3.612	50.000	1.979	54.138
20						7.885	42.649	5.359	46.178
21								10.611	39.389
22									
23									

FIGURE 7.4 Spreadsheet design of binomial option pricing.

respectively. To display the option and asset prices in alternative columns, we have adopted even column offset $2i$ for option prices and odd column offset $2i + 1$ for asset prices. The corresponding forward time on the tree will also be displayed along the header row using even column offset from B17. It should be noted that there are all together 255 columns in this spreadsheet. The number of time steps in B11 should be fewer than 127 when we choose "Yes" in cell B12. It is then necessary to impose a validation check for the cell B11 as:

$$= \text{IF(AND(B12 = "Yes", B11 > = 127), FALSE, TRUE)}$$

under **Data, Validation,** and **Settings** with **Allow** chosen to be **Custom** and to apply the above condition in **Formula.**

GenOptionTree(T, K, S_0, r, σ, n, *treetype*, $S(0:n, 0:n)$, $f(0:n, 0:n)$))

define the size of the time interval

$\Delta t = T/n$

define the tree factors in Cox–Ross–Rubinstein or Jarrow–Rudd parameterization

If(*treetype* = "Cox–Ross–Rubinstein") then

$$u = \frac{1}{2}(e^{-r\Delta t} + e^{(r+\sigma^2)/\Delta t}) + \frac{1}{2}\sqrt{(e^{-r\Delta t} + e^{(r+\sigma^2)\Delta t})^2 - 4}, \quad d = 1/u,$$
$$p = (e^{r\Delta t} - 1/u)/(u - 1/u)$$

Elseif(*treetype* = "Jarrow–Rudd") then

$$u = e^{r\Delta t}(1 + \sqrt{e^{\sigma^2 \Delta t} - 1}), \quad d = e^{r\Delta t}(1 - \sqrt{e^{\sigma^2 \Delta t} - 1}), \ p = \tfrac{1}{2}$$

Endif

setting up the maturity payoffs of the option

For($j = 0$ to n){ $S(n, j) = u^{n-j} d^j S_0$
$f(n, j) = Payoff(K, S(n, j))$ }

iterate the option price backward in time and update according to intermediate boundary condition

For($i = n - 1$ to 0){

For($j = 0$ to i){ $S(i, j) = u^{i-j} d^j S_0$

$f(i, j) = e^{-r\Delta t} [pf(i + 1, j) + (1 - p) f(i + 1, j + 1)]$

Call *Boundary*($K, S(i, j), f(i, j)$) }}

Code 7.1: Pseudo code of the GenOptionTree() routine.

```
Sub GenOptionTree(maturity As Double, strike As Double, assetPrice As Double, riskFree As
            Double, sigma As Double, n As Integer, treetype As Variant, ByRef STree()
            As Double, ByRef fTree() As Double)

Dim St As Double, ft As Double
Dim u As Double, d As Double, p As Double
Dim i As Integer, j As Integer
Dim dtime As Double: dtime = maturity / n

If (treetype = "Cox-Ross-Rubinstein") Then
    u = 0.5 * (Exp(-riskFree * dtime) + Exp((riskFree + sigma ^ 2) * dtime)) _
      + 0.5 * Sqr((Exp(-riskFree * dtime) + Exp((riskFree + sigma ^ 2) * dtime)) ^ 2 - 4)
    d = 1 / u
    p = (Exp(riskFree * dtime) - 1 / u) / (u - 1 / u)
ElseIf (treetype = "Jarrow-Rudd") Then
    u = Exp(riskFree * dtime) * (1 + Sqr(Exp(sigma ^ 2 * dtime) - 1))
    d = Exp(riskFree * dtime) * (1 - Sqr(Exp(sigma ^ 2 * dtime) - 1))
    p = 0.5
End If

For j = 0 To n
    St = u ^ (n - j) * d ^ (j) * assetPrice
    STree(n, j) = St
    fTree(n, j) = Payoff(strike, St)
Next j

For i = n - 1 To 0 Step -1
    For j = 0 To i
        St = u ^ (i - j) * d ^ (j) * assetPrice
        STree(i, j) = St
        ft = Exp(-riskFree * dtime) * (p * fTree(i + 1, j) + (1 - p) * fTree(i + 1, j + 1))
        Call Boundary(strike, St, ft)
        fTree(i, j) = ft
```

```
    Next j
  Next i
  End Sub
```

```
Function Payoff(strike As Double, assetPrice As Double) As Double
  Payoff = Max(strike - assetPrice, 0)
End Function
```

```
Sub Boundary(strike As Double, assetPrice As Double, optionPrice As Double)
  optionPrice = Max(optionPrice, Payoff(strike, assetPrice))
End Sub
```

```
Function Max(x As Double, y As Double) As Double
  If x > y Then Max = x Else Max = y
End Function
```

Code 7.2: VBA code of the GenOptionTree() routine together with the Payoff() function and Boundary() routine defined for an American put option.

```
Sub BinomialPricing()
  Dim maturity As Double: maturity = Range("maturity").Value
  Dim strike As Double: strike = Range("strike").Value
  Dim riskFree As Double: riskFree = Range("riskFree").Value
  Dim sigma As Double: sigma = Range("sigma").Value
  Dim assetPrice As Double: assetPrice = Range("assetPrice").Value
  Dim n As Integer: n = Range("n").Value
  Dim treetype As Variant: treetype = Range("treetype").Text
  Dim fTree() As Double: ReDim fTree(0 To n, 0 To n)
  Dim STree() As Double: ReDim STree(0 To n, 0 To n)
  Dim i As Integer

  Call GenOptionTree(maturity, strike, assetPrice, riskFree, sigma, n, treetype, STree, fTree)
  Range("B14").Value = fTree(0, 0)

  Range("B17:IV144").ClearContents

  If (Range("B12").Text = "Yes") Then
    For i = 0 To n
      Range("B17").Offset(0, 2 * i) = i * (maturity / n)
      For j = 0 To i
        Range("B17").Offset(j + 1, 2 * i) = fTree(i, j)
        Range("B17").Offset(j + 1, 2 * i + 1) = STree(i, j)
      Next j
    Next i
  End If
End Sub
```

Code 7.3: VBA code of the main BinomialPricing() routine.

REVIEW QUESTIONS

1. Modify the GenOptionTree() routine to price a European-style double barrier knock-out call option written on equity with maturity payoff at time T given by

$$f_T = \max\{S_T - K, 0\}, \text{ for } U > S_T > L.$$

   It should be noted that there are substantial errors coming from the location of the two knock-out conditions on a binomial lattice. The convergence is very slow and a large number of time steps are required to obtain a reasonably accurate result.

2. Modify the GenOptionTree() routine to price a one-touch option written on equity. For predetermined upper barrier L above the current asset price S_0, the option gives an agreed upon payout P at hit if the underlying asset reaches or surpasses the barrier level during the life of the option. If the barrier level is not breached prior to expiration at T, the option expires worthless.

3. Modify the GenOptionTree() routine to price an accumulator option written on equity. With accumulator, investor agrees to buy a certain amount N of a stock at a fixed price K over a regular intervals (or settlement dates T_1, T_2, ..., $T_n = T$) for a period T. There is a knock out price L greater than K that terminates the accumulator contract.

ENDNOTES

1. Denotes option price $f_t = f(S_t, t)$ at time t. Using Ito's lemma it can be shown that $e^{-rt}f_t$ is a martingale under risk-neutral preference. This gives $e^{-rt}f_t = \hat{E}(e^{-rs}f_s|S_t)$ for $s > t$, and the conditional expectation is evaluated based on the risk-neutral process of the underlying asset price starting off from S_t.

2. J. Cox, S. Ross, and M. Rubinstein, "Option Pricing: A Simplified Approach," *Journal of Financial Economics* 7, no. 3 (1979): 229-263.

3. In the first order of rT and $\sigma^2 T$, it can be shown using (7.6) and (7.7) that:

$$\Lambda(k) = [u^k - (1/u)^k]/[u - (1/u)] \cong k + (1/6)k(k-1)(k+1)\,\sigma^2 T.$$

   This gives

$$p(u)^k + (1-p)(1/u)^k = e^{rT}\Lambda(k) - \Lambda(k-1) \cong 1 + krT + \tfrac{1}{2}k(k-1)\sigma^2 T.$$

4. R.A. Jarrow and A. Rudd, "Option Pricing," (Homewood, Illinois: Richard D. Irwin, 1983).

5. In this case, we have $p(u)^k + (1-p)(d)^k = \tfrac{1}{2}(u^k + d^k)$ and it is easy to show that $u^k + d^k \cong e^{krT}(2 + k(k-1)\sigma^2 T)$ in the first order of $\sigma^2 T$ using (7.8) and (7.9).

6. Refer to binomialtree_ap.xls.

## CHAPTER 8

The Black–Derman–Toy Model

8.1 THE TERM STRUCTURE MODEL AND THE BLACK–DERMAN–TOY TREE

Analogous to stock options, interest rate derivatives depend on their underlying asset, which is generally the interest rate. The behavior of interest rates for all maturity terms will thus play a crucial role in the corresponding pricing scheme. In a one-factor term structure model, there is only one underlying process known as the *instantaneous short rate* r_t that defines the interest rate at any time t for a very short borrowing term. In this model, the time evolution of the entire yield curve will solely be driven by the behavior of this short-term interest rate. Derivatives can be priced in accordance with the short-rate process under a risk-neutral preference as:

$$f_0 = \hat{E}(e^{-\int_0^T r_t dt} f_T | r_0) \tag{8.1}$$

with a discount factor that cumulates over a generated interest rate path with current value r_0. The option payoff f_T in (8.1) is evaluated according to the realized rate at its maturity. The modern approach to the modeling of stochastic short rate started with the early equilibrium model by Vasicek[1] and evolved into the rigorous no-arbitrage formulation by Heath, Jarrow, and Morton.[2] For numerical pricing of options, however, it is sufficient to have a discrete tree-type model for the risk-neutral short rate that exactly matches the current yield curve and its stochastic properties. In this connection, Black, Derman, and Toy[3] (BDT) have developed a simple binomial model that can be calibrated to fit the current term structures of zero-coupon bond prices and volatilities.

The BDT model has adopted a recombining binomial lattice for the risk-neutral short rate with discrete time interval Δt as shown in Figure 8.1(a).

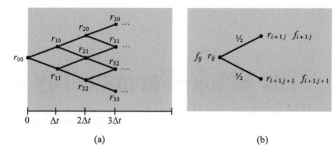

FIGURE 8.1   (a) A BDT binomial model with recombining tree nodes. (b) The risk-neutral pricing of an option along a BDT subtree.

At time $t = i\Delta t$, there are $i+1$ nodes from the top to bottom of the tree with short rates defined to be r_{ij} where j runs from 0 to i. They represent the annualized one-period interest rates for the shortest borrowing term of Δt from time t to $t+\Delta t$. The BDT tree follows the Jarrow and Rudd parameterization with symmetric branching probabilities of $p = \frac{1}{2}$. In general, the up and down factors will depend on time and the corresponding value of the short rate. If we assume a non-stochastic structure for the short-rate volatility, it can be shown that its ratio will only depend on time, and the entire column of short rates at time step i can be parameterized by two factors as:[4]

$$r_{ij} = \alpha_i(\beta_i)^j. \tag{8.2}$$

The BDT tree provides a tool for evaluating the risk-neutral pricing of interest rate options as given by (8.1). Consider the one-step subtree as depicted in Figure 8.1(b), the risk-neutral pricing in (8.1) can be written as:

$$f_{ij} = e^{-r_{ij}\Delta t}\left(\tfrac{1}{2}f_{i+1\,j} + \tfrac{1}{2}f_{i+1\,j+1}\right) \tag{8.3}$$

where $e^{-r_{ij}\Delta t}$ is the discount factor that cumulates over the one-step interest rate path with realized rate r_{ij}. The current price of the option f_{00} can be determined by iterating (8.3) backward in time starting from its maturity payoff $\psi(r_T)$ and along a tree with a longer time horizon.

A short-rate tree with time interval Δt and horizon $T_{tree} = N_{tree}\Delta t$, can be constructed by calibrating the current term structures of zero-coupon bond prices $\{P_0(\tau_1), P_0(\tau_2), \ldots, P_0(\tau_{Ntree+1})\}$ and their volatilities $\{\sigma_0(\tau_2), \ldots, \sigma_0(\tau_{Ntree+1})\}$. The maturity terms of the bonds must coincide with the time structure of the tree for which $\tau_m = m\Delta t$. The size of Δt must be kept very small so as to improve the accuracy and to cope with the intermediate boundary condition for the option. In this respect, the current term structures with arbitrary time intervals can be constructed through cubic spline interpolation as discussed in an earlier chapter. Practically, the size of Δt can be taken as the shortest maturity term available in market bond data in order to maximize precision. For a zero-coupon bond that matures at time τ_m, the forward bond price $P_{ij}(\tau_m)$ at previous tree node (i, j) should satisfy the risk-neutral pricing in (8.3) for the subtree as:

$$P_{ij}(\tau_m) = e^{-r_{ij}\Delta t}\left[\tfrac{1}{2}P_{i+1\,j}(\tau_m) + \tfrac{1}{2}P_{i+1\,j+1}(\tau_m)\right]. \tag{8.4}$$

The current bond price and its volatility can be determined by iterating (8.4) backward in time starting from its maturity at time τ_m with $P_{mj}(\tau_m) = \$1$ for the entire column of tree nodes. The short-rate tree should generate the values consistent with the market term structures such that[5]:

$$P_0(\tau_m) = P_{00}(\tau_m) \tag{8.5}$$

$$\sigma_0(\tau_m) = \frac{1}{2\sqrt{\Delta t}}\ln\left(\frac{P_{11}(\tau_m)}{P_{10}(\tau_m)}\right), \quad m \geq 2. \tag{8.6}$$

It is clear that the current short rate $r_{00} = \alpha_0$ at time step $i = 0$ can be fixed by calibrating $P_{00}(\tau_1)$ from (8.4) with $P_0(\tau_1)$ as in (8.5). This gives:

$$\alpha_0 = -\frac{1}{\Delta t}\ln P_0(\tau_1). \tag{8.7}$$

Knowing r_{00}, the two short rates $r_{10} = \alpha_1$ and $r_{11} = \alpha_1\beta_1$ at time step $i = 1$ can be fixed by calibrating $P_{00}(\tau_2)$, $P_{10}(\tau_2)$, and $P_{11}(\tau_2)$ from (8.4) with $P_0(\tau_2)$ and $\sigma_0(\tau_2)$, as in (8.5) and (8.6), respectively. This can be achieved by implementing the Newton–Raphson procedure for $\{\alpha_1, \beta_1\}$ taking $\{\alpha_0, \beta_0 = 0.5\}$ as their trial values. In (8.2), short rates at time step i are parameterized by only two factors given by $r_{ij} = \alpha_i\,(\beta_i)^{\,j}$. Similarly, they can be fixed by calibrating $P_{00}(\tau_{i+1})$, $P_{10}(\tau_{i+1})$, and $P_{11}(\tau_{i+1})$ from (8.4) with $P_0(\tau_{i+1})$ and $\sigma_0(\tau_{i+1})$ knowing all previous short rates on the tree. In this way, the tree can be constructed through forward induction in time that subsequently matches current bond prices and volatilities with longer maturity terms. A short-rate tree with horizon $T_{tree} = N_{tree}\Delta t$ would require market term structures with maturities $\{\tau_1, \tau_2, \ldots, \tau_{Ntree+1}\}$ as input. The factors $\{\alpha_i, \beta_i\}$ at each stage can be calibrated utilizing the Newton–Raphson procedure with trial values $\{\alpha_{i-1}, \beta_{i-1}\}$ taken from the preceding time step.

A BDT tree can easily be applied to price interest rate derivatives based on the risk-neutral pricing in (8.3). For example, consider a European call option with strike price K and maturity T written on a coupon-bearing bond that matures at later time τ. The bond has a face value of L_{par} and pays regular coupons of value C under the time schedule $\{s_1, s_2, \ldots, s_{n_c}\}$. In this case, we need to construct a BDT tree with a time horizon that covers the entire life of the underlying bond. To maximize the accuracy of the pricing, the chosen size of the time interval Δt must be very close to the shortest maturity term of the bond data, while the BDT tree could also reach τ with discrete time steps. Market term structures with maturities that coincide with such time increments can be constructed through cubic spline interpolation. Strictly speaking, the BDT tree should be constructed up to one time step prior to the maturity of the underlying bond. The total time horizon is thus given by $T_{tree} = \tau - \Delta t$ with $N_{tree} = (\tau/\Delta t) - 1$ steps. For simplicity, suppose the option matures at time step H on the tree for which $T = H\Delta t$. The maturity payoff of the option $\psi(r_{H_j})$ is evaluated according to the realized forward price of the underlying bond on the tree node (H, j) as:

$$f_{H_j} = \max\{K - B_{H_j}(\tau), 0\}, \quad j = 0, 1, \ldots, H. \tag{8.8}$$

The forward bond prices in (8.8) can be determined by iterating (8.3) for the underlying bond that utilizes the BDT tree. The iteration starts off from the bond's maturity at time step N_{tree} with face value L_{par} and works backward to the option's maturity at time step H. The coupon payments can be considered an adjustment to the risk-neutral pricing in (8.3) with respect to the intermediate boundary condition as:

$$B_{ij}(\tau) + \rho_i(s_1, s_2, \ldots, s_{n_c})C. \tag{8.9}$$

The term $\rho_i(s_1, s_2, \ldots, s_{n_c})$ in (8.9) counts the total number of coupons being paid during the time interval $(i - \frac{1}{2})\Delta t < t \leq (i + \frac{1}{2})\Delta t$. Thus, the option payoffs on different tree nodes can readily be evaluated, and the current price of the option f_{00} can be determined by iterating (8.3) backward again for the option from time step H to 0.

8.2 EXCEL PLUS VBA IMPLEMENTATION

We first develop a routine called GenBDTTree() that generates the BDT short-rate tree given current term structures of zero-coupon bond prices and their volatilities. The pseudo code of GenBDTTree() is given by Code 8.1. It requires the input of tree configuration (T_{tree}, N_{tree}) and the market term structures with maturities $\{\tau_1, \tau_2, \ldots, \tau_{Ntree+1}\}$. The routine returns the array of short rates r_{ij} at every node of the BDT tree with time label i runs from 0 to N_{tree} and node label j runs from 0 to i. In GenBDTTree(), the time interval of the tree is defined to be $\Delta t = T_{tree}/N_{tree}$. Together with the input market term structures, they are kept as common data at the module scope that can be accessed by other routines within the module. The routine will generate the factors α and β for each column of short rates through forward-time induction regulated by the time pointer *iptr*. The addressed α_{iptr} and β_{iptr} are determined based on their results at preceding time steps from 0 to $iptr-1$. It is also convenient to declare *iptr*, α, and β as module-level variables rather than passing their updated values through subroutine arguments.

The starting value α_0 is defined in (8.7) and we arbitrarily choose β_0 to be the mid-value 0.5. To generate the entire BDT tree, the time pointer *iptr* would be required to run from 1 to N_{tree}. At each *iptr*, the tree has presumably been constructed up to time step $iptr-1$. The factors α_{iptr} and β_{iptr} are determined by calling a two-dimensional Newton–Raphson procedure as discussed in Chapter 5. It will solve for $x(1)$ and $x(2)$, setting as α_{iptr} and β_{iptr} respectively, such that the discrepancies in (8.5) and (8.6) for maturity term τ_{iptr+1} are both acceptable under the specified precision *prec*. The trial values of $x(1)$ and $x(2)$ in the numerical search are taken to be the results at the preceding time step. The discrepancies, namely $g(1)$ and $g(2)$, are calculated through an external routine Functionarray() that iterates all forward bond prices using (8.4) with maturity values of \$1 at $iptr+1$ and utilizes the trial values at *iptr* together with the results in previous time steps. Here, the values of $P_0(\tau_{iptr+1})$ and $\sigma_0(\tau_{iptr+1})$ on the market term structures as well as the resulting α and β in previous time steps can readily be assessed by virtue of their declaration at the module level. Finally, short rates for the entire BDT tree can easily be generated according to (8.2) once all α and β have been determined.

The VBA code of GenBDTTree() and Functionarray() are given by Code 8.2. Altogether, they are kept under the module called BDTtree[6] and can readily be used to price, for example, the European call option written on a coupon-bearing bond as defined in (8.8). In this respect, we develop a routine called GenBDTBondOptionTree() that performs the iteration and generates the option prices along the BDT tree. The pseudo code of GenBDTBondOptionTree() is given by Code 8.3. It requires the input of option parameters $(T, K, \tau, L_{par}, C, n_c, \{s_1, s_2, \ldots, s_{n_c}\})$ and returns the array of option prices f_{ij} as well as the short rates r_{ij} at every tree node prior to the option maturity with time label i runs from 0 to H and node label j runs from 0 to i. The routine first constructs the market term structures with horizon τ that match the maturity of the underlying bond. These are done through an external procedure called GenTermStructures() capable of generating the term structures with maturities $\{\tau_1, \tau_2, \ldots, \tau_{Nterm} = \tau\}$ where $\tau_m = m\Delta t$.

The size of the time interval Δt has been chosen according to the available bond data as discussed previously. Recall that the BDT tree should be constructed up to one time step prior to the maturity of the bond. We should therefore define the tree configuration to be $N_{tree} = N_{term} - 1$ and $T_{tree} = \tau - \Delta t$. The corresponding BDT tree of short rates can be constructed very easily by calling the GenBDTTree() routine. It is then straightforward to use the short rates on the tree and to generate the forward prices of the underlying bond at option maturity with time label H. For convenience, we should generate the bond prices for the entire BDT tree so that the coding can be easily modified to value exotic options with intermediate boundary conditions that depend on forward bond prices. The forward bond prices $B_H(\tau)$ can be used to evaluate the option payoffs f_{H_j} at maturity, and the option prices f_{ij} at every other tree node can be generated by iterating (8.3) backward in time. The external function CouponCount() counts the number of coupons being paid at each time step in the iteration and updates the risk-neutral pricing as discussed in (8.9). In CouponCount(), we are running through the entire payment schedule $\{s_1, s_2, \ldots, s_{n_c}\}$ in backward order and identifying those payments that appear within the specified time range from t_{low} to t_{up}. It is efficient to exit the procedure by setting $exitFlag = \text{TRUE}$ whenever we see an unmatched payment immediately after a matched case (when $CouponCount > 0$). The VBA code of GenBDTBondOptionTree() is given by Code 8.4.

The VBA code of the GenTermStructures() routine is given by Code 8.5. It takes zero-coupon bond prices and volatilities of available maturities from Excel and generates the required term structures through cubic spline interpolation. It should be noted that the specific horizon should not exceed the longest maturity term of the market bond data. The total number of time steps N_{term} is chosen to be the nearest multiple of the shortest market term in covering the specified horizon. The size of the time interval defined as $\Delta t = (horizon/N_{term})$ will be close to the shortest market term. In fact, it will be greater than the shortest market term as N_{term} is a truncated integer. The cubic spline coefficients can be determined by calling the CubicSpline() routine with market bond data. The output term structures with maturities $\{\Delta t, 2\Delta t, \ldots, N_{term}\Delta t\}$ can then be generated by evaluating the interpolated values using the coefficients based on a similar procedure as discussed in Code 6.5. The routine can also generate the term structures with additional maturities $\{\Delta t, 2\Delta t, \ldots, (N_{term} + N_a)\Delta t\}$ as defined by the integer N_a in the input. However, the total horizon should remain below the longest maturity term of the market bond data.

Zero-Coupon Bond Data :

Number of Bonds =	8							
Maturity Terms =	0.083	0.250	0.500	1.000	2.000	4.000	7.000	18.000	(year)
Prices =	0.9963	0.9887	0.9771	0.9533	0.9055	0.8164	0.6948	0.4667	(par = 1)
Volatilities =	0.08%	0.20%	0.40%	0.70%	1.10%	1.30%	1.40%	1.50%	(per year)

European Bond Call Option :

Option Maturity (T) =	3.00	(year)	Time Steps =	36
Strike (K) =	95.00		Display BDT Tree =	Yes
Bond Maturity (τ) =	4.00	(year)
Bond Par Value (L) =	100.00
Bond Coupon Value (C) =	1.50
Number of Coupons (n_c) =	8
Payment Schedule :	0.50	1.00	1.50	2.00	2.50	3.00	3.50	4.00	(year)

Option Price (f_0) = 3.713   [BDT Pricing]

Black Derman Toy Tree

Forward Time (year)	0.00		0.08		0.17		0.25		0.33		0.42		0.50	
Option Price & Short Rates	3.713	0.044	3.705	0.051	3.700	0.050	3.695	0.054	3.691	0.057	3.689	0.060	3.689	0.062
			3.749	0.041	3.742	0.046	3.736	0.049	3.732	0.052	3.729	0.055	3.727	0.057
					3.782	0.042	3.776	0.044	3.771	0.047	3.767	0.050	3.764	0.052
							3.815	0.040	3.809	0.043	3.804	0.045	3.801	0.048
									3.846	0.038	3.841	0.041	3.837	0.044
											3.877	0.037	3.872	0.040
													3.906	0.037

FIGURE 8.2   Spreadsheet design of Black–Derman–Toy option pricing.

Figure 8.2 depicts the spreadsheet design for this VBA implementation. The market bond data are inputted into the GenTermStructures() routine through the named cell B4(nbond) and the entries in rows 5, 6, and 7. Presumably, these could be obtained utilizing the bootstrapped zero rates from the CalZeroRates() routine as discussed in chapter 6. The button labeled "BDT Pricing" will trigger the main VBA routine called BDTPricing() with the VBA code given by Code 8.6. The option parameters are inputted into this routine through the named cells B12(optionMaturity), B13(strike), B14(bondMaturity), B15(par), B16(coupon), B17(nCoupon), and the entries in row 18. It will call GenBDTBondOptionTree() for the arrays of option prices and short rates. The current option price f_{00} will be outputted to cell B20. By selecting "Yes" in cell E13, the entire option tree will be displayed in the spreadsheet. As a reference, the corresponding short rates will also be displayed adjacent to the option prices. Similar to the procedure discussed in Code 7.3, this can be done by running over both the time and node labels, and allocating cells through row and column offsets from the reference cell B23. Recall that there are all together 255 columns in the spreadsheet. The option maturity in B12 will determine the number of time steps on the tree as displayed in E12 = **INT**(B12/B5). It should be fewer than 127 when we choose "Yes" in E13. It is then necessary to impose a validation check for the cell B12 as:

$$= \text{IF(AND(E13 = "Yes", E12} > = 127), \text{FALSE, TRUE)}$$

under **Data, Validation,** and **Settings.**

define the following module-level variables
Δt, $P_0(1 : Ntreemax + 1)$, $\sigma_0(1 : Ntreemax + 1)$, $iptr$, $\alpha(0 : Ntreemax)$, $\beta(0 : Ntreemax)$

$GenBDTTree(\ T_{tree},\ N_{tree}\ ,\ BondPrice(1 : N_{tree} + 1)\ ,\ BondVol(1 : N_{tree} + 1)\ ,\ r(0 : N_{tree}\ ,\ 0 : N_{tree})\ )$
define the size of the time interval
$\Delta t = T_{tree} / N_{tree}$

# assign the market term structures with maturities $\tau_1, \tau_2, \ldots$, and $\tau_{Ntree + 1}$ to common arrays
For(k = 1 to N_{tree} + 1){ $P_0(k) = BondPrice(k)$, $\sigma_0(k) = BondVol(k)$ }

define α_0 according to (8.7) and choose β_0 to be $\frac{1}{2}$
$\alpha(0) = (-1/\Delta t)\,logP_0(1)$, $\beta(0) = 0.5$

set $x(1)$ and $x(2)$ as α and β, respectively. Use the Newton-Raphson procedure to estimate next $x(1)$
and $x(2)$ taking the last results as trial values.
$x(1) = \alpha(0)$, $x(2) = \beta(0)$
For($iptr$ = 1 to N_{tree}){ Call NewtonRaphson(2, $prec$, $x(1:2)$, $precflag$, $maxdev$)
$\qquad\qquad\qquad\alpha(iptr) = x(1)$, $\beta(iptr) = x(2)$ }

# generate the short-rate tree from the resulting α and β according to (8.2)
For(k = 0 to N_{tree}){ For(j = 0 to k){ $r(k,j) = \alpha(k)\,\beta(k)^j$ } }

$Functionarray(\ n\ ,\ x(1 : n)\ ,\ g(1 : n)\ )$

# define the face values of the zero-coupon bond with maturity at $\tau_{i + 1}$
For(j = 0 to $iptr$ + 1){ $P_{forward}(iptr + 1, j) = 1$ }

iterate (8.4) backward in time and generate all forward bond prices on the tree using the trial values
of $\alpha_i = x(1)$ and $\beta_i = x(2)$ together with known α and β in previous time steps

For(j = 0 to $iptr$){
$\quad P_{forward}(iptr, j) = e^{-x(1)\,x(2)^j\,\Delta t}\,[\frac{1}{2} P_{forward}(iptr + 1, j) + \frac{1}{2} P_{forward}(iptr + 1, j + 1)]$ }

For(k = $iptr$–1 to 0, –1){
$\quad$For(j = 0 to k){ $P_{forward}(k, j) = e^{-\alpha(k)\beta(k)^j\,\Delta t}\,[\frac{1}{2} P_{forward}(k + 1, j) + \frac{1}{2} P_{forward}(k + 1, j + 1)]$ }
$\qquad\qquad$ }

calculate the discrepancies in (8.5) and (8.6)
$g(1) = P_0(iptr + 1) - P_{forward}(0, 0)$

$$g(2) = \sigma_0(iptr + 1) - \frac{1}{2\sqrt{\Delta t}} \ln\left[\frac{P_{forward}(1, 1)}{P_{forward}(1, 0)}\right]$$

Code 8.1: Pseudo code of the GenBDTTree() routine.

```
Option Explicit
Private iptr As Integer
Private dtime As Double
Private alpha(0 To nTreeMax) As Double
Private beta(0 To nTreeMax) As Double
Private P0(1 To nTreeMax + 1) As Double
Private Sigma0(1 To nTreeMax + 1) As Double
```

```
Sub GenBDTTree(Ttree As Double, Ntree As Integer, BondPrice() As Double, BondVol() As Double,
    rshort() As Double)
    Dim x(1 To 2) As Double, prec As Double, precFlag As Boolean, maxDev As Double
    prec = 0.00000001

    Dim k As Integer, j As Integer

    Dim dtime As Double: dtime = Ttree / Ntree

    For k = 1 To Ntree + 1
        P0(k) = BondPrice(k)
        Sigma0(k) = BondVol(k)
    Next k

    alpha(0) = -(1 / dtime) * Log(P0(1))
    beta(0) = 0.5

    x(1) = alpha(0)
    x(2) = beta(0)

    For iptr = 1 To Ntree
        Call NewtonRaphson(2, prec, x, precFlag, maxDev)
        alpha(iptr) = x(1)
        beta(iptr) = x(2)
    Next iptr

    For k = 0 To Ntree
        For j = 0 To k: rshort(k, j) = alpha(k) * beta(k) ^ j: Next j
    Next k
End Sub
```

```
Sub FunctionArray(n As Integer, x() As Double, ByRef g() As Double)
    Dim Pf(0 To nTreeMax + 1, 0 To nTreeMax + 1) As Double
    Dim k As Integer, j As Integer

    For j = 0 To iptr + 1: Pf(iptr + 1, j) = 1: Next j

    For j = 0 To iptr
        Pf(iptr, j) = Exp(-x(1) * x(2) ^ j * dtime) * (Pf(iptr + 1, j) + Pf(iptr + 1, j + 1)) / 2
    Next j

    For k = iptr - 1 To 0 Step -1
        For j = 0 To k
            Pf(k, j) = Exp(-alpha(k) * beta(k) ^ j * dtime) * (Pf(k + 1, j) + Pf(k + 1, j + 1)) / 2
        Next j
    Next k

    g(1) = P0(iptr + 1) - Pf(0, 0)
    g(2) = Sigma0(iptr + 1) - Log(Pf(1, 1) / Pf(1, 0)) / (2 * Sqr(dtime))

End Sub
```

Code 8.2: VBA code of the GenBDTTree() routine together with the Functionarray() routine.

$GenBDTBondOptionTree(T, K, \tau, L_{par}, C, n_c, s(1:n_c), H, r(0:H,0:H), f(0:H,0:H))$

\# generate the market term structures with horizon τ
Call GenTermStructures(τ, 0, N_{term}, Δt, BondPrice($1:N_{term}$), BondVol($1:N_{term}$))

\# define BDT tree configuration
$N_{tree} = N_{term} - 1$, $T_{tree} = \tau - \Delta t$

\# generate the BDT tree with N_{tree} steps and horizon T_{tree}
Call GenBDTTree(T_{tree}, N_{tree}, BondPrice($1:N_{tree}+1$), BondVol($1:N_{tree}+1$), $r(0:N_{tree},0:N_{tree})$)

\# define the time label at option maturity
$H = Int(T / \Delta t)$

\# generate the forward prices of the underlying bond

$\rho = CouponCount((N_{tree}+1-\frac{1}{2})\Delta t, (N_{tree}+1+\frac{1}{2})\Delta t, n_c, s(1:n_c))$
For(j = 0 to N_{tree} + 1) { $B_{forward}(N_{tree}+1, j) = L_{par} + \rho C$ }

For($i = N_{tree}$ to 0, -1) {
 $\rho = CouponCount((i-\frac{1}{2})\Delta t, (i+\frac{1}{2})\Delta t, n_c, s(1:n_c))$
 For(j = 0 to i) { $B_{forward}(i,j) = e^{-r(i,j)\Delta t}[\frac{1}{2}B_{forward}(i+1,j) + \frac{1}{2}B_{forward}(i+1,j+1)] + \rho C$ }
 }

\# generate the option prices

For(j = 0 to H) { $f(H,j) = Payoff(K, B_{forward}(H,j))$ }

For($i = H-1$ to 0, -1) {
 For(j = 0 to i) { $f(i,j) = e^{-r(i,j)\Delta t}[\frac{1}{2}f(i+1,j) + \frac{1}{2}f(i+1,j+1)]$ }
 }

$CouponCount(t_{low}, t_{up}, n_c, s(1:n_c))$

exitFlag = FALSE
CouponCount = 0
For($k = n_c$ to 1, -1) { If ($t_{low} < s(k) \leq t_{up}$) Then
             CouponCount = CouponCount = 1
             Elseif = CouponCount = 0) Then
              exitFlag = TRUE
             Endif
             If(exitFlag) Exit k }

Code 8.3: Pseudo code of the GenBDTBondOptionTree() routine.

```
Sub GenBDTBondOptionTree(optionMaturity As Double, strike As Double, bondMaturity As Double,
           par As Double, coupon As Double, nCoupon As Integer, paymentSchedule()As Double,
           ByRef Hf As Integer, ByRef rShort() As Double,ByRef fTree() As Double)

    Dim bondPrice(1 To nTreeMax + 1) As Double
    Dim bondVol(1 To nTreeMax + 1) As Double
    Dim i As Integer, j As Integer
    Dim Nterm As Integer, dtime As Double

    Call GenTermStructures(bondMaturity, 0, Nterm, dtime, bondPrice, bondVol)

    Dim Ntree As Integer: Ntree = Nterm - 1
    Dim Ttree As Double: Ttree = bondMaturity - dtime

    Call GenBDTTree(Ttree, Ntree, bondPrice, bondVol, rShort)

    Dim Bf() As Double: ReDim Bf(0 To Ntree + 1, 0 To Ntree + 1)

    Hf = Int(optionMaturity / dtime)

    i = Ntree + 1
    Dim rho As Integer
    rho = CouponCount((i - 0.5) * dtime, (i + 0.5) * dtime, nCoupon, paymentSchedule)
    For j = 0 To i: Bf(i, j) = par + rho * coupon: Next j

    For i = Ntree To 0 Step -1
        rho = CouponCount((i - 0.5) * dtime, (i + 0.5) * dtime, nCoupon, paymentSchedule)
        For j = 0 To i
           Bf(i, j) = Exp(-rShort(i, j) * dtime) * (Bf(i + 1, j) + Bf(i + 1, j + 1)) / 2 + rho * coupon
        Next j
    Next i

    For j = 0 To Hf: fTree(Hf, j) = Payoff(strike, Bf(Hf, j)): Next j

    For i = Hf - 1 To 0 Step -1
       For j = 0 To I
          fTree(i, j) = Exp(-rShort(i, j) * dtime) * (fTree(i + 1, j) + fTree(i + 1, j + 1)) / 2
       Next j
    Next i

End Sub
```

```
Function CouponCount(timeLow As Double, timeUp As Double, nCoupon As Integer,
    paymentSchedule() As Double) As Integer
    Dim k As Integer
    Dim exitFlag As Boolean
```

```
exitFlag = False
CouponCount = 0

For k = nCoupon To 1 Step -1
    If (Round(paymentSchedule(k), epsDP) > timeLow And Round(paymentSchedule(k), epsDP) <=
        timeUp) Then
        CouponCount = CouponCount + 1
    ElseIf (CouponCount > 0) Then
        exitFlag = True
    End If
    If (exitFlag) Then Exit For
Next k

End Function
```

Code 8.4: VBA code of the GenBDTBondOptionTree() routine.

```
Sub GenTermStructures(horizon As Double, Na As Integer, ByRef Nterm As Integer, ByRef
    dtime As Double, ByRef bondPrice() As Double, ByRef bondVol() As Double)
    Dim nbond As Integer: nbond = Range("nbond").Value
    Dim bondMaturity() As Double: ReDim bondMaturity(1 To nbond)
    Dim bondPriceData() As Double: ReDim bondPriceData(1 To nbond)
    Dim bondVolData() As Double: ReDim bondVolData(1 To nbond)
    Dim a() As Double: ReDim a(1 To nbond - 1)
    Dim b() As Double: ReDim b(1 To nbond - 1)
    Dim c() As Double: ReDim c(1 To nbond - 1)
    Dim d() As Double: ReDim d(1 To nbond - 1)
    Dim av() As Double: ReDim av(1 To nbond - 1)
    Dim bv() As Double: ReDim bv(1 To nbond - 1)
    Dim cv() As Double: ReDim cv(1 To nbond - 1)
    Dim dv() As Double: ReDim dv(1 To nbond - 1)
    Dim i As Integer, k As Integer

    For i = 1 To nbond
        bondMaturity(i) = Range("A5").Offset(0, i)
        bondPriceData(i) = Range("A6").Offset(0, i)
        bondVolData(i) = Range("A7").Offset(0, i)
    Next i

    Call CubicSpline(nbond, bondMaturity, bondPriceData, a, b, c, d)
    Call CubicSpline(nbond, bondMaturity, bondVolData, av, bv, cv, dv)

    Nterm = Int(horizon / bondMaturity(1))
    dtime = horizon / Nterm

    Dim term As Double
    Dim ptr As Integer

    ptr = 1
    For i = 1 To Nterm + Na
        term = i * dtime
        If (Abs(term - bondMaturity(1)) <= eps) Then
```

```
          bondPrice(i) = bondPriceData(1)
          bondVol(i) = bondVolData(1)
          GoTo Nexti
        End If
        For k = ptr To nbond - 1
          If (term > bondMaturity(k) And term <= bondMaturity(k + 1)) Then
            bondPrice(i) = a(k) + b(k) * term + c(k) * term ^ 2 + d(k) * term ^ 3
            bondVol(i) = av(k) + bv(k) * term + cv(k) * term ^ 2 + dv(k) * term ^ 3
            ptr = k
            GoTo Nexti
          End If
        Next k
      Nexti:   Next i

End Sub
```

Code 8.5: VBA code of the GenTermStructures() routine.

```
Sub BDTPricing()
    Dim i As Integer, j As Integer
    Dim rShort(0 To nTreeMax, 0 To nTreeMax) As Double
    Dim fTree(0 To nTreeMax, 0 To nTreeMax) As Double
    Dim Hf As Integer
    Dim optionMaturity As Double: optionMaturity = Range("optionMaturity").Value
    Dim strike As Double: strike = Range("strike").Value
    Dim bondMaturity As Double: bondMaturity = Range("bondMaturity").Value
    Dim par As Double: par = Range("par").Value
    Dim coupon As Double: coupon = Range("coupon").Value
    Dim nCoupon As Integer: nCoupon = Range("nCoupon").Value
    Dim paymentSchedule() As Double: ReDim paymentSchedule(0 To nCoupon)

    For i = 1 To nCoupon: paymentSchedule(i) = Range("A18").Offset(0, i): Next i

    Call GenBDTBondOptionTree(optionMaturity, strike, bondMaturity, par, coupon, nCoupon,
        paymentSchedule, Hf, rShort, fTree)
    Range("B20").Value = fTree(0, 0)

    Range("B23:IV150").ClearContents

    If (Range("E13").Text = "Yes") Then
      For i = 0 To Hf
        Range("B23").Offset(0, 2 * i) = i * (optionMaturity / Hf)
        For j = 0 To i
          Range("B23").Offset(j + 1, 2 * i) = fTree(i, j)
          Range("B23").Offset(j + 1, 2 * i + 1) = rShort(i, j)
        Next j
      Next i
    End If

End Sub
```

Code 8.6: VBA code of the BDTPricing() routine.

REVIEW QUESTIONS

1. How would you modify the GenBDTBondOptionTree() routine to price an American-style bond option?
2. Develop another VBA routine that can be used to price an interest rate floorlet. A floorlet provides a floor of R_{floor} on LIBOR rate at future time T with borrowing term δ and notional principle M. The floorlet payoff is made at the beginning of the rate period as

$$f_T = \delta M \max\{R_{floor} - L_T(T, \delta),\ 0\}$$

where $L_T(T, \delta)$ is the discrete compounding LIBOR rate as seen at time T for the borrowing period between T and $T + \delta$. It can be related to the forward bond price $P_T(T+\delta)$ with $1 face value as

$$L_T(T, \delta) = (1/\delta)(\$1/P_T(T + \delta) - 1).$$

ENDNOTES

1. O.A. Vasicek, "An Equilibrium Characterization of the Term Structure," *Journal of Financial Economics 5*, No. 2 (1977): 177-188.
2. D. Heath, R. Jarrow, and A. Morton, "Bond Pricing and the Term Structure of Interest Rates; A Discrete Time Approximation," *Journal of Financial and Quantitative Analysis 25*, No. 4 (1990): 419-440.
3. F. Black, E. Derman, and W. Toy, "A One-Factor Model of Interest Rates and Its Application to Treasury Bond Options," *Financial Analysts Journal 46*, No. 1 (1990): 33-39.
4. It can be shown that the variance of $ln(r_{t+\Delta t})$ conditional to r_t is given by $\hat{V}(\ln(r_{t+\Delta t})|r_t) = v_t^2\, \Delta t$, where v_t is the short-rate volatility as seen at time t. Under a binomial representation, the same variance is calculated to be $\frac{1}{4}\ln^2(r_{i+1\,j}/r_{i+1\,j+1})$ conditional to the starting rate of r_{ij}. Thus, the branching rule for r_{ij} should satisfy the condition that:

$$(r_{i+1\,j+1}/r_{i+1\,j}) = (d_{ij}/u_{ij}) = e^{-2v_{ij}\sqrt{\Delta t}}.$$

For non-stochastic short-rate volatility that does not depend on r_{ij}, the factor $\beta_i = e^{-2v_{ij}\sqrt{\Delta t}}$ will depend only on time.
5. Refer to the derivation in Endnote 4 for bond price volatility in (8.6) and note that it is positively defined.
6. Refer to BDTtree_ebc.xls.

## CHAPTER 9

Monte Carlo Option Pricing

9.1 THE MONTE CARLO METHOD

The Monte Carlo method provides numerical solutions to a variety of mathematical problems by performing statistical samplings on a computer. In the risk-neutral pricing of options, we are most interested in evaluating the expected value of a function $g(x)$ under a random variable x as:

$$E(g(x)) = \int_{-\infty}^{+\infty} dx\, g(x)\varphi(x) \tag{9.1}$$

where $\varphi(x)$ is the probability density function of x. In general, it would be difficult to derive an analytical formula for (9.1), and a numerical estimation seems to be the only way out. Monte Carlo simulation provides a simple and flexible numerical method to solve these types of problems.[1] Consider the random sample $\{x_1, x_2, \ldots, x_n\}$ generated based on the probability density function $\varphi(x)$. The estimates of the mean and variance of $g(x)$ are given by:

$$m = \frac{1}{n}\sum_{i=1}^{n} g(x_i) \quad and \quad s^2 = \frac{1}{n-1}\sum_{i=1}^{n} (g(x_i) - m)^2. \tag{9.2}$$

According to the central limit theorem, the random variable defined as:

$$\frac{m - E(g(x))}{\dfrac{s}{\sqrt{n}}} \tag{9.3}$$

tends to follow a standard normal distribution with increasing sample size n and is irrespective of the distribution of $g(x)$. Thus, the sample average m approaches a normal distribution with mean $E(g(x))$ and standard deviation

$(s/\sqrt{n})$. On this basis, the confidence interval in the estimation of $E(g(x))$ can be obtained as:

$$E(g(x)) = m \pm z \frac{s}{\sqrt{n}} \qquad (9.4)$$

with, for example, confidence level of 68.27 percent for $z = 1$. We refer to the term $(s/\sqrt{n})$ in (9.4) as the standard error in the estimation of $E(g(x))$. To reduce the standard error by a factor of ten, the sample size has to be increased one hundredfold. The method is thus computationally inefficient in its fundamental form called the crude Monte Carlo simulation.

There are variance reduction techniques that instead focus on reducing the size of s in the standard error. The common approach is known as the control variate method. It takes the analytic solution of a similar but simpler problem to improve the accuracy in the estimated solution of a complex problem. Suppose that the expected value $E(h(x))$ can be evaluated analytically as H. In relation to the original function $g(x)$, we can introduce a new function given by:

$$\tilde{g}(x) = g(x) - h(x) \qquad (9.5)$$

through the control variate $h(x)$ and rewrite (9.1) as:

$$E(g(x)) = H + \int_{-\infty}^{+\infty} dx\, \tilde{g}(x)\varphi(x). \qquad (9.6)$$

Thus, we can determine the confidence interval in the estimation of $E(g(x))$ based on the estimates of the mean and variance of $\tilde{g}(x)$ instead given by:

$$E(g(x)) = (H + \tilde{m}) \pm z \frac{\tilde{s}}{\sqrt{n}}. \qquad (9.7)$$

It can be shown that the variances of $g(x)$ and $\tilde{g}(x)$ can be related as:

$$var(\tilde{g}(x)) = var(g(x)) + var(h(x)) - 2\,cov(g(x),\, h(x)). \qquad (9.8)$$

If $g(x)$ and $h(x)$ are similar problems, the covariance between them is positive. In (9.8), the variance of $\tilde{g}(x)$ will be less than the variance of $g(x)$ as long as $cov(g(x),\, h(x)) > \frac{1}{2}var(h(x))$. It is therefore possible to reduce the size of the standard error by identifying a highly correlated problem with a known analytic solution.

An alternative approach is known as the antithetic variate method. In the case of a standard normal variable, it makes use of the symmetric property around zero in the density function. Again, we can introduce a new function given by:

$$\hat{g}(x) = \tfrac{1}{2}[g(x) + g(-x)] \tag{9.9}$$

through antithetic variate of the form $-x$. We can rewrite (9.1) using the symmetric property of the standard normal variable x as:

$$E(g(x)) = \int_{-\infty}^{+\infty} dx \, \hat{g}(x)\varphi(x). \tag{9.10}$$

Similarly, we can determine the confidence interval in the estimation of $E(g(x))$ based on the estimates of the mean and variance of $\hat{g}(x)$ given by:

$$E(g(x)) = \hat{m} \pm z \frac{\hat{s}}{\sqrt{n}}. \tag{9.11}$$

The variance of $\hat{g}(x)$ is expected to be smaller than the variance of $g(x)$ as it is already an average quantity of two samples. It can be shown that the two variances can be related as:

$$var(\hat{g}(x)) = \tfrac{1}{2} var(g(x)) + \tfrac{1}{2} cov(g(x),\, g(-x)). \tag{9.12}$$

If the covariance between $g(x)$ and $g(-x)$ is negative, it is always efficient to consider the estimates for $\hat{g}(x)$ rather than doubling the size of independent samples.

Figure 9.1 depicts, for example, the Monte Carlo estimation of the expected value $E(e^x)$ with x taken to be a standard normal variable. In Excel, random samples of $x = \varepsilon(0, 1)$ can be generated very easily by calling the function **NORMSINV(RAND())**. They will be used to evaluate the sample values of $g(x) = e^x$ for which the mean and variance can be estimated. In the figure, we compare the confidence intervals evaluated through the crude simulation with those based on the variance reduction techniques. For the control variate method, we have adopted a highly correlated problem $E(x)$ with a known analytic solution of zero. Thus, we introduce $\tilde{g}(x) = e^x - x$

	A	B	C	D	E
		Random Numbers	Crude Simulation	Control Variate Method	Antithetic Variate Method
1					
2		x	$g(x) = e^x$	$\tilde{g}(x) = e^x - x$	$\hat{g}(x) = \tfrac{1}{2}(e^x + e^{-x})$
3	1	1.049050384	2.854938735	1.805888351	1.602604474
4	2	-1.204751932	0.299766353	1.504518285	1.817848895
5	3	-1.811351962	0.163433032	1.974784994	3.141073571
10001	9999	1.365806708	3.918883171	2.553076463	
10002	10000	-0.96166111	0.382257387	1.343918497	
10003		Mean	1.660	1.651	1.658
10004		Standard Error	0.023	0.017	0.019
10005			(10000 samples)	(10000 samples)	(5000 samples)

FIGURE 9.1 Monte Carlo simulation for $E(e^x)$.

for which $E(e^x) = E(e^x - x)$. For the antithetic variate method, it is clear that the covariance between e^x and e^{-x} is negative. We thus define $\hat{g}(x) = \frac{1}{2}(e^x + e^{-x})$ with $E(e^x) = E(\frac{1}{2}(e^x + e^{-x}))$. In both cases, we have shown that there are significant reductions in the size of the standard errors.

9.2 RISK-NEUTRAL VALUATION

In risk-neutral valuation, the current price of an option can be defined based on the present value of its average maturity payoff at time T as:

$$f_0 = \hat{E}(e^{-rT}f_T|S_0) \qquad (9.13)$$

where r is the constant interest rate. Here, we are averaging over realized maturity payoffs of the option f_T in respect to sample asset prices generated through their risk-neutral process that initiated at current price S_0. In the stochastic model, the asset price return during the time increment from t to $t + \Delta t$ is assumed to follow a random normal process as:

$$\Delta S_t / S_t = \mu \Delta t + \sigma \sqrt{\Delta t}\, \varepsilon(0, 1) \qquad (9.14)$$

where μ and σ are respectively the mean rate and volatility of return. For traded assets such as stocks, the risk-neutral process is simply given by (9.14) with μ replaced by r in the drift term. Practically, it is convenient to consider the asset price movement based on the risk-neutral process. For constant volatility of return, it is shown to follow an iterative equation with arbitrary time duration given by:

$$S_{t+\tau} = S_t exp((r - \tfrac{1}{2}\sigma^2)\tau + \sigma\sqrt{\tau}\,\varepsilon(0, 1)). \qquad (9.15)$$

In particular, we have:

$$S_T = S_0\, exp((r - \tfrac{1}{2}\sigma^2)T + \sigma\sqrt{T}\varepsilon(0, 1)) \qquad (9.16)$$

that generates the maturity price S_T directly from S_0 in a single step. This will be useful when there is no intermediate boundary condition for the option.

As our first example, we consider a European call option written on a non-dividend paying stock with strike price K. It should be noted that an analytic solution, known as the Black–Scholes formula, exists for this option given by:

$$f_0^{BS} = S_0 \, N(d) - K \, e^{-rT} \, N(d - \sigma\sqrt{T}), \quad d = \frac{\ln(S_0/K) + (r + \frac{1}{2}\sigma^2)T}{\sigma\sqrt{T}}. \quad (9.17)$$

Here, we use this simple example to demonstrate the use of the Monte Carlo procedure for option pricing. In this case, the option payoff will depend solely on the underlying asset price at maturity regardless of its intermediate values. We can simply use (9.16) to generate the maturity price of the asset by a single random number ε from $\varepsilon(0, 1)$. The sample maturity price can then be used to evaluate the sample maturity payoff of the option according to the function:

$$f_T(\varepsilon) = \max\{S_T(\varepsilon) - K, 0\}. \quad (9.18)$$

For variance reduction, we can adopt the maturity price S_T itself as the control variate and consider the new function:

$$\tilde{f}_T(\varepsilon) = \max\{S_T(\varepsilon) - K, 0\} - S_T(\varepsilon). \quad (9.19)$$

The control variate has an analytic solution given by $\hat{E}(e^{-rT} S_T | S_0) = S_0$ in which we can rewrite (9.13) as:

$$f_0 = S_0 + \hat{E}(e^{-rT}\tilde{f}_T | S_0). \quad (9.20)$$

Alternatively, we can simply take $-\varepsilon$ as the antithetic variate and introduce the new function:

$$\hat{f}_T(\varepsilon) = \tfrac{1}{2}[\max\{S_T(\varepsilon) - K, 0\} + \max\{S_T(-\varepsilon) - K, 0\}]. \quad (9.21)$$

Figure 9.2 depicts the Monte Carlo results for the current price of the European call option with parameters defined in cells B2:B6. Random samples of ε are first generated in the Excel spreadsheet, and they will be used to generate the sample maturity prices $S_T(\varepsilon)$ as well as their antithetic values $S_T(-\varepsilon)$. Sample values of the functions $f_T(\varepsilon)$, $\tilde{f}_T(\varepsilon)$, and $\hat{f}_T(\varepsilon)$ can then be evaluated, in which their means and variances can be estimated. As shown in the figure, there are significant reductions in the size of the standard errors with the use of the variance reduction techniques. As reference, the Black–Scholes pricing in (9.17) is 12.34 for the European call option parameterized by B2:B6.

An important application of the Monte Carlo method is the pricing of exotic options with intermediate boundary conditions. For example, a

	A	B	C	D	E	F	G
1							
2	$S_0 =$	100					
3	$K =$	100					
4	$T =$	1.00	(years)				
5	$r =$	0.05	(per year)				
6	$\sigma =$	0.25	(per year)				
7					Crude Simulation	Control Variate Method	Antithetic Variate Method
8		ε	$S_T(\varepsilon)$	$S_T(-\varepsilon)$	$e^{-rT}f_T$	$e^{-rT}f_T$	$e^{-rT}f_T$
9	1	1.049050384	132.4470287	78.38696024	30.86456842	-95.12294245	15.43228421
10	2	-1.204751932	75.39433978	137.7042362	0	-71.71731444	17.93268944
11	3	-1.811351962	64.78552479	160.2536987	0	-61.62589746	28.65754558
10007	9999	1.365806708	143.3618513	72.41898647	41.24706888	-95.12294245	
10008	10000	-0.96166111	80.11834936	129.5847962	0	-76.21093135	
10009					$E(e^{-rT}f_T)$	$S_0 + E(e^{-rT}f_T)$	$E(e^{-rT}f_T)$
10010				Mean	12.38	12.20	12.29
10011				Standard Error	0.19	0.11	0.14
10012					(10000 samples)	(10000 samples)	(5000 samples)

FIGURE 9.2 Monte Carlo simulation for the current price of a European call option.

barrier knock-out option will have a maturity payoff depending on whether the underlying asset price has surpassed a predetermined barrier level prior to its maturity. Thus, it is sometimes necessary to generate the entire path of asset prices in discrete time increments $\{t_1, \ldots, t_N = T\}$ during the life of the option. To this end, we can use (9.15) to generate iteratively the risk-neutral asset price at t_{i+1} based on the price at t_i as:

$$S_{t_{i+1}} = S_{t_i} exp((r - \tfrac{1}{2}\sigma^2)(t_{i+1} - t_i) + \sigma\sqrt{t_{i+1} - t_i}\, \varepsilon_{i+1}) \qquad (9.22)$$

and trace out the path by running i from 0 to $N - 1$ with random numbers $\{\varepsilon_1, \ldots, \varepsilon_N\}$ from $\varepsilon(0, 1)$. The sample path can then be used to evaluate the sample option payoff according to some path-dependent conditions. It should be noted that we have defined in the iteration $t_0 = 0$, and the choice of time increments will depend on the boundary conditions of the option.

9.3 VBA IMPLEMENTATION

A crucial part of the Monte Carlo method is the generation of the standard normal random numbers. The procedure starts with a pseudo-random number generator (PRNG) that "randomly" produces a real number between 0 and 1 with uniform probability so that every number will have the same chance of being generated. The numbers generated by PRNG are not truly random in that they are completely determined by an initial *seed* integer. In fact, they are considered to be random only subject to standard statistical tests for randomness.[2] Uniform random numbers can be transformed into standard normal random numbers through the Box-Muller algorithm as:

$$\varepsilon_1 = \sqrt{-2\ln(u_1)}\, cos(2\pi u_2)$$
$$\varepsilon_2 = \sqrt{-2\ln(u_1)}\, sin(2\pi u_2). \qquad (9.23)$$

In (9.23), u_1 and u_2 are two uniform random numbers generated independently by PRNG. They can be transformed into a pair of standard normal random numbers ε_1 and ε_2 that are also independent. A more efficient transformation is to rewrite (9.23) so as to avoid the time-consuming evaluation of trigonometric functions. This is known as the polar rejection algorithm given by:

$$\varepsilon_1 = \sqrt{\frac{-2\ln(w)}{w}}(2u_1 - 1)$$

$$\varepsilon_2 = \sqrt{\frac{-2\ln(w)}{w}}(2u_2 - 1), \qquad \text{if } w = (2u_1 - 1)^2 + (2u_2 - 1)^2 < 1. \tag{9.24}$$

The drawback in (9.24) is that the uniform random numbers inputted should stay inside a unit circle.

In an Excel spreadsheet, PRNG is given by the **RAND()** function that automatically reseeds based on the system clock. The transformation of uniform random numbers into standard normal random numbers is conducted by the **NORMSINV(RAND())** function that takes **RAND()** as input. In VBA implementation, it is highly inefficient to generate random numbers interactively through Excel as the number of calls will be enormous in a Monte Carlo simulation. It is therefore essential to develop a VBA routine that implements for instance the polar rejection algorithm in (9.24). It can be defined through an external function called StdNormNum () that returns a standard normal random number upon each request. The VBA code of this function is given by Code 9.1. In VBA, PRNG is given by the **Rnd()** function in which the generated sequence is completely determined by the default seed value. To prevent using repetitive sequences in Monte Carlo simulation, we can alter the seed based on the system clock by calling **Randomize** once in the main routine. It is important to note that we should not **Randomize** every time we call **Rnd()** as the random behavior can be badly skewed.

In both the Box–Muller and polar rejection algorithms, two usable standard normal random numbers are generated at the same time. In order to obtain maximum efficiency, we should utilize both of them by saving the unused random number for the next request. In Code 9.1, this can be done through two static variables *flagSave* and *snnSave* that retain their latest values after termination of the procedure. The static variable *flagSave* is initialized to 0 at the very first call to the function when *flagSave* is still an empty cell checked by the **IsEmpty** function. When *flagSave* = 0, the function generates two random numbers and returns only the one under *snnUse*. The second random number is saved under *snnSave* with *flagSave* set to 1. The two static variables will retain these values upon the next request where the function simply returns the random number under *snnSave* and resets *flagSave* = 0.

```
Function StdNormNum() As Double
    Dim v1 As Double, v2 As Double, w As Double, fac As Double
    Dim snnUse As Double
    Static flagSave As Integer: If IsEmpty(flagSave) Then flagSave = 0
    Static snnSave As Double
    If (flagSave = 0) Then
newtrial:
        v1 = 2# * Rnd() - 1#
        v2 = 2# * Rnd() - 1#
        w = v1 ^ 2 + v2 ^ 2
        If (w >= 1#) Then GoTo newtrial
        fac = Sqr(-2# * Log(w) / w)
        snnSave = fac * v1
        snnUse = fac * v2
        flagSave = 1
    Else
        snnUse = snnSave
        flagSave = 0
    End If
    StdNormNum = snnUse
End Function
```

Code 9.1: VBA code of the StdNormNum() function.

To generate a very long random sequence, it is advisable to use the standard algorithm for PRNG known as ran0() proposed by Park and Miller[3] instead. This generator has passed all theoretical tests so far and is definitely safer to use despite the fact that it is relatively slower than **Rnd**(). In Code 9.2, we have included the VBA code of ran0() and refer the reader to the original literature (see endnote 3) for a detailed discussion of the algorithm. As in **Rnd**(), the seed value in ran0() should only be initiated once in the main routine. It can be any nonzero integer such as *seed* = 56789 and it must not be altered between successive calls in a random sequence.

```
Public seed As Long

Function ran0() As Double
    Dim IA As Long: IA = 16807
    Dim IM As Long: IM = 2147483647
    Dim IQ As Long: IQ = 127773
    Dim IR As Long: IR = 2836
    Dim MASK As Long: MASK = 123459876
    Dim AM As Double: AM = 1# / IM
    Dim k As Long
```

```
    seed = seed Xor MASK
    k = seed / IQ
    seed = IA * (seed - k * IQ) - IR * k
    If (seed < 0) Then seed = seed + IM
    ran0 = AM * seed
    seed = seed Xor MASK
End Function
```

Code 9.2: VBA code of the ran0() function.

We again consider the pricing of a European call option written on a non-dividend paying stock as discussed in the previous section. Here, it is efficient and convenient to develop VBA routines that separately perform the three different simulation tasks as demonstrated in Figure 9.2. The VBA codes of the McEuropeanCall() routine for crude simulation, the CMcEuropeanCall() routine for control variate method, and the AMcEuropeanCall() routine for antithetic variate method are given by Code 9.3. They all require the input parameters $\{S_0, K, r, \sigma, T, n\}$ and return the estimation of the current option price together with the standard error. In both routines, the random sample of ε is generated by calling the StdNormNum() function, and it will be used to generate sample maturity price $S_T(\varepsilon)$ using (9.16). For the antithetic variate method, the same random number with a negative sign will also be used to generate the antithetic price $S_T(-\varepsilon)$. Sample values of the functions $f_T(\varepsilon)$, $\tilde{f}_T(\varepsilon)$, and $\hat{f}_T(\varepsilon)$ are then evaluated respectively in different routines using (9.18), (9.19), and (9.21). The estimates of the mean and variance of their present values can be obtained by summing up all the sample values and their squares as in (9.2) through a loop that runs from 1 to n. It is also convenient to implement an alternative expression for the variance estimate in (9.2) as:

$$s^2 = \frac{1}{n-1} \sum_{i=1}^{n} g^2(x_i) - \frac{n}{n-1} m^2. \tag{9.25}$$

In both routines, the mean estimate will be returned as the estimation of the current option price. For the control variate method, remember to include the analytic solution of S_0 for the control variate in the mean estimate as discussed in (9.20). The standard error in the estimation can be determined by taking an additional factor of $1/\sqrt{n}$ in the variance estimate. Table 9.1 illustrates the relative performance of the three routines in terms of the sizes of standard errors and computation times. We adopt the same parameterization as in Figure 9.2 and consider one million samples in the Monte Carlo simulation. In this example, the control variate method is shown to be highly effective, while there is only mild improvement for the antithetic variate method.

TABLE 9.1 Relative performance of different Monte Carlo routines for a European call option.

	Crude Simulation	Control Variate Method	Antithetic Variate Method
Mean	12.338	12.334	12.340
Standard Error	0.018	0.011	0.010
Relative CPU Time	1.00	1.02	1.33

As our second example, we consider a European call option written on a stock with expected dividend payments $\{D_1, \ldots, D_N\}$ at $\{t_1, \ldots, t_N = T\}$ prior to its maturity. Assume S_{t_i} represents the asset price right after the dividend D_i has been paid at t_i. We can use (9.22) to first generate the asset price at t_{i+1} using S_{t_i} and then incorporate the price drop due to the payment D_{i+1} as:

$$S_{t_{i+1}} = S_{t_i} exp((r - \tfrac{1}{2}\sigma^2)(t_{i+1} - t_i) + \sigma\sqrt{t_{i+1} - t_i}\,\varepsilon_{i+1}) - D_{i+1}. \qquad (9.26)$$

In this way, the maturity price S_T of the asset can be generated iteratively by running i from 0 to $N - 1$. If at any time the right-hand side (RHS) of (9.26) is less than or equal to zero, the iteration should stop and restart all over again from $i = 0$. The maturity price can be used to evaluate the option pay-off according to the function:

$$f_T(\varepsilon_1, \ldots, \varepsilon_N) = \max\{S_T(\varepsilon_1, \ldots, \varepsilon_N) - K, 0\}. \qquad (9.27)$$

For variance reduction, it is effective to adopt the case of a non-dividend paying stock as the control variate and consider the new function:

$$\tilde{f}_T(\varepsilon_1, \ldots, \varepsilon_N) = \max\{S_T(\varepsilon_1, \ldots, \varepsilon_N) - K, 0\} - \max\{S_T^{(0)}(\varepsilon_1, \ldots, \varepsilon_N) - K, 0\}. \qquad (9.28)$$

The control price $S_T^{(0)}$ at maturity is generated simultaneously with S_T using the same random sequence but with zero dividend payments. The control variate has an analytic solution given by the Black–Scholes formula in (9.17) for which (9.13) can be written as:

$$f_0 = f_0^{BS} + \hat{E}(e^{-rT}\tilde{f}_T|S_0). \qquad (9.29)$$

It is always straightforward to take $-\varepsilon$ as the antithetic variate and generate the antithetic value of S_T using the negative sequence $\{-\varepsilon_1, \ldots, -\varepsilon_N\}$. It is then convenient to introduce the new function:

$$\hat{f}_T(\varepsilon_1,\ldots,\varepsilon_N) = \tfrac{1}{2}[\max\{S_T(\varepsilon_1,\ldots,\varepsilon_N) - K,\, 0\} + \max\{S_T(-\varepsilon_1,\ldots,-\varepsilon_N) - K,\, 0\}]$$

$$(9.30)$$

as the two payoffs are negatively correlated. However, as shown below, the effectiveness of the antithetic variate method in (9.30) is limited.

The pseudo code of the McEuropeanCallDiv() routine for crude simulation is given by Code 9.4. The routine reads in the parameters $\{S_0, K, r, \sigma, n\}$ as well as the details of dividend payments as N, $\{t_1,\ldots,t_N = T\}$, and $\{D_1,\ldots,D_N\}$. To initiate (9.26), the current time $t_0 = 0$ by definition should also be included in the input time array. Similarly, the routine returns the estimation of the current option price together with the standard error. In the inner loop, sample maturity price S_T of the asset is generated iteratively by running i in (9.26) from 0 to $N - 1$. The iteration starts off from S_0 and moves forward by calling the StdNormNum() function successively. It should restart from S_0 at the beginning of the loop if the asset price is less than or equal to zero at any time. Sample payoff f_T in (9.27) and its present value can be evaluated using the asset price immediately after the iteration. The estimates of the mean and variance can be obtained based on the sample sum and squared sum accumulated through the outer loop that runs from sample number 1 to n. The VBA code of the McEuropeanCallDiv() routine is given by Code 9.5.

It is easy to modify the algorithm for crude simulation and include the appropriate procedures for variance reduction. The VBA code of the CMcEuropeanCallDiv() routine for the control variate method is given by Code 9.6. In the inner loop, the iteration of the control price is performed simultaneously with S_T using the same random sequence and the same starting price but with no dividend payment. Again, we should restart both iterations if either one of them is less than or equal to zero. In this way, the sample value of the function $\tilde{f}_T$ in (9.28) can be evaluated based on the iterated prices. In the estimation of the option price, we have also included the Black–Scholes formula given by the function BsEuropeanCall(). The VBA code of the AMcEuropeanCallDiv() routine for the antithetic variate method is also given by Code 9.6. In this case, the antithetic price is generated simultaneously with S_T using, however, the negative sequence. Similarly, the sample value of the function $\hat{f}_T$ in (9.30) can be evaluated based on the prices immediately after the iteration. Table 9.2 illustrates the relative performance of the three routines based on one million simulation samples. We adopt the same parameterization as in Figure 9.2 and consider the dividend payments of $D_{1,2,3,4} = 0.25$ at quarterly time intervals $\{t_1 = 0.25, t_2 = 0.50, t_3 = 0.75, t_4 = 1.00\}$. Again, the control variate method is shown to be much more effective than the antithetic variate method.

TABLE 9.2 Relative performance of different Monte Carlo routines for a European call option written on a dividend paying asset.

	Crude Simulation	Control Variate Method	Antithetic Variate Method
Mean	11.782	11.794	11.802
Standard Error	0.018	0.0005	0.010
Relative CPU Time	1.00	1.31	1.36

```
Sub McEuropeanCall(assetPrice As Double, strike As Double, riskFree As Double, sigma As
      Double, maturity As Double, nsample As Long, ByRef optionPrice As Double,
      ByRef stdErr As Double)
   Dim sum As Double, sum2 As Double, gen As Double
   Dim mean As Double, sd As Double, Ls As Long
   Dim St As Double, fT As Double, pV As Double
   sum = 0
   sum2 = 0
   For Ls = 1 To nsample
      gen = StdNormNum()
      St = assetPrice * Exp((riskFree - 0.5 * sigma ^ 2) * maturity + sigma * Sqr(maturity) * gen)
      fT = CallPayoff(strike, St)
      pV = Exp(-riskFree * maturity) * fT
      sum = sum + pV
      sum2 = sum2 + pV * pV
   Next Ls
   mean = sum / nsample
   sd = Sqr(sum2 / (nsample - 1) - (nsample / (nsample - 1)) * mean ^ 2)
   optionPrice = mean
   stdErr = sd / Sqr(nsample)
End Sub
```

```
Sub CMcEuropeanCall(assetPrice As Double, strike As Double, riskFree As Double, sigma
      As Double, maturity As Double, nsample As Long, ByRef optionPrice As Double,
      ByRef stdErr As Double)
   Dim sum As Double, sum2 As Double, gen As Double
   Dim mean As Double, sd As Double, Ls As Long
   Dim St As Double, fT As Double, pV As Double
   sum = 0
   sum2 = 0
   For Ls = 1 To nsample
      gen = StdNormNum()
      St = assetPrice * Exp((riskFree - 0.5 * sigma ^ 2) * maturity + sigma * Sqr(maturity) * gen)
      fT = CallPayoff(strike, St) - St
      pV = Exp(-riskFree * maturity) * fT
      sum = sum + pV
      sum2 = sum2 + pV * pV
```

```
Next Ls
mean = sum / nsample
sd = Sqr(sum2 / (nsample - 1) - (nsample / (nsample - 1)) * mean ^ 2)
optionPrice = assetPrice + mean
stdErr = sd / Sqr(nsample)
End Sub
```

```
Sub AMcEuropeanCall(assetPrice As Double, strike As Double, riskFree As Double, sigma
      As Double, maturity As Double, nsample As Long, ByRef optionPrice As Double,
      ByRef stdErr As Double)
   Dim sum As Double, sum2 As Double, gen As Double
   Dim mean As Double, sd As Double, Ls As Long
   Dim St As Double, Sta As Double, fT As Double, pV As Double
   sum = 0
   sum2 = 0
   For Ls = 1 To nsample
      gen = StdNormNum()
      St = assetPrice * Exp((riskFree - 0.5 * sigma ^ 2) * maturity + sigma * Sqr(maturity) * gen)
      Sta = assetPrice * Exp((riskFree - 0.5 * sigma ^ 2) * maturity + sigma * Sqr(maturity) *
         (-gen))
      fT = (CallPayoff(strike, St) + CallPayoff(strike, Sta)) / 2
      pV = Exp(-riskFree * maturity) * fT
      sum = sum + pV
      sum2 = sum2 + pV * pV
   Next Ls
   mean = sum / nsample
   sd = Sqr(sum2 / (nsample - 1) - (nsample / (nsample - 1)) * mean ^ 2)
   optionPrice = mean
   stdErr = sd / Sqr(nsample)
End Sub
```

```
Function CallPayoff(strike As Double, assetPrice As Double) As Double
   CallPayoff = Max(assetPrice - strike, 0)
End Function

Function Max(x As Double, y As Double) As Double
   If x > y Then Max = x Else Max = y
End Function
```

Code 9.3: VBA codes of the McEuropeanCall(), CMcEuropeanCall(), and AMcEuropeanCall() routines.

McEuropeanCallDiv(S_0 , K , r , σ , N , $t(0:N)$, $D(1:N)$, n , f_0 , error)

```
# zeroize the sample sum and squared sum
sum = 0 , sum2 = 0
```

For(L_s = 1 to n){

initialize the asset price
   S_t=S_0

# generate the asset price at each dividend date
   For(i = 0 to $N-$ 1){

   $\varepsilon = $ StdNormNum( )
   $S_t = S_t \, exp((r - \frac{1}{2}\sigma^2)[t(i + 1) - t(i)] + \sigma\sqrt{t(i + 1) - t(i)}\varepsilon) - D(i + 1)$

   If($S_t \leq 0$) go back to the statement $S_t = S_0$ and restart all over again   }

evaluate the option payoff function as in (9.27)
   $f_T = $ CallPayoff(K , S_t)
   $PV = e^{-rT}f_T$

accumulate the sample sum and squared sum
   $sum = sum + PV$
   $sum2 = sum2 + PV^2$ }

evaluate the estimates of mean and variance
   $m = sum / n$

$$s = \sqrt{\frac{1}{n-1}sum2 - \frac{n}{n-1}m^2}$$

return the estimation of option price and standard error
   $f_0 = m$
   $error = s / \sqrt{n}$

Code 9.4: Pseudo code of the McEuropeanCallDiv() routine.

```
Sub McEuropeanCallDiv(assetPrice As Double, strike As Double, riskFree As Double,
        sigma As Double, nDiv As Integer, timeDiv() As Double, paymentDiv() As Double,
        nsample As Long, ByRef optionPrice As Double, ByRef stdErr As Double)
    Dim sum As Double, sum2 As Double, gen As Double
    Dim mean As Double, sd As Double, Ls As Long
    Dim St As Double, fT As Double, pV As Double, i As Integer
    sum = 0
    sum2 = 0
    For Ls = 1 To nsample
NewTrial:
    St = assetPrice
    For i = 0 To nDiv - 1
        gen = StdNormNum()
        St = St * Exp((riskFree - 0.5 * sigma ^ 2) * (timeDiv(i + 1) - timeDiv(i)) + sigma *
            Sqr(timeDiv(i + 1) - timeDiv(i)) * gen) - paymentDiv(i + 1)
        If (St <= 0) Then GoTo NewTrial
    Next i
```

```
    fT = CallPayoff(strike, St)
    pV = Exp(-riskFree * timeDiv(nDiv)) * fT
    sum = sum + pV
    sum2 = sum2 + pV * pV
  Next Ls
  mean = sum / nsample
  sd = Sqr(sum2 / (nsample - 1) - (nsample / (nsample - 1)) * mean ^ 2)
  optionPrice = mean
  stdErr = sd / Sqr(nsample)
End Sub
```

Code 9.5: VBA code of the McEuropeanCallDiv() routine.

```
Sub CMcEuropeanCallDiv(assetPrice As Double, strike As Double, riskFree As Double,
        sigma As Double, nDiv As Integer, timeDiv() As Double, paymentDiv() As Double,
        nsample As Long, ByRef optionPrice As Double, ByRef stdErr As Double)
  Dim sum As Double, sum2 As Double, gen As Double
  Dim mean As Double, sd As Double, Ls As Long
  Dim St As Double, St0 As Double, fT As Double, pV As Double, i As Integer
  sum = 0
  sum2 = 0
  For Ls = 1 To nsample
NewTrial:
    St = assetPrice
    St0 = assetPrice
    For i = 0 To nDiv - 1
      gen = StdNormNum()
      St = St * Exp((riskFree - 0.5 * sigma ^ 2) * (timeDiv(i + 1) - timeDiv(i)) + sigma *
          Sqr(timeDiv(i + 1) - timeDiv(i)) * gen) - paymentDiv(i + 1)
      St0 = St0 * Exp((riskFree - 0.5 * sigma ^ 2) * (timeDiv(i + 1) - timeDiv(i)) + sigma *
          Sqr(timeDiv(i + 1) - timeDiv(i)) * gen)
      If (St <= 0 Or St0 <= 0) Then GoTo NewTrial
    Next i
    fT = CallPayoff(strike, St) - CallPayoff(strike, St0)
    pV = Exp(-riskFree * timeDiv(nDiv)) * fT
    sum = sum + pV
    sum2 = sum2 + pV * pV
  Next Ls
  mean = sum / nsample
  sd = Sqr(sum2 / (nsample - 1) - (nsample / (nsample - 1)) * mean ^ 2)
  optionPrice = BsEuropeanCall(assetPrice, strike, riskFree, sigma, timeDiv(nDiv)) + mean
  stdErr = sd / Sqr(nsample)
End Sub
```

```
Sub AMcEuropeanCallDiv(assetPrice As Double, strike As Double, riskFree As Double,
        sigma As Double, nDiv As Integer, timeDiv() As Double, paymentDiv() As Double,
        nsample As Long, ByRef optionPrice As Double, ByRef stdErr As Double)
  Dim sum As Double, sum2 As Double, gen As Double
```

```
Dim mean As Double, sd As Double, Ls As Long
Dim St As Double, Sta As Double, fT As Double, pV As Double, i As Integer
sum = 0
sum2 = 0
For Ls = 1 To nsample
NewTrial:
    St = assetPrice
    Sta = assetPrice
    For i = 0 To nDiv - 1
        gen = StdNormNum()
        St = St * Exp((riskFree - 0.5 * sigma ^ 2) * (timeDiv(i + 1) - timeDiv(i)) + sigma *
            Sqr(timeDiv(i + 1) - timeDiv(i)) * gen) - paymentDiv(i + 1)
        Sta = Sta * Exp((riskFree - 0.5 * sigma ^ 2) * (timeDiv(i + 1) - timeDiv(i)) + sigma *
            Sqr(timeDiv(i + 1) - timeDiv(i)) * (-gen)) - paymentDiv(i + 1)
        If (St <= 0 Or Sta <= 0) Then GoTo NewTrial
    Next i
    fT = (CallPayoff(strike, St) + CallPayoff(strike, Sta)) / 2
    pV = Exp(-riskFree * timeDiv(nDiv)) * fT
    sum = sum + pV
    sum2 = sum2 + pV * pV
Next Ls
mean = sum / nsample
sd = Sqr(sum2 / (nsample - 1) - (nsample / (nsample - 1)) * mean ^ 2)
optionPrice = mean
stdErr = sd / Sqr(nsample)
End Sub
```

```
Function BsEuropeanCall(assetPrice As Double, strike As Double, riskFree As Double,
    sigma As Double, maturity As Double) As Double
    Dim d1 As Double, d2 As Double
    d1 = (Log(assetPrice / strike) + (riskFree + 0.5 * sigma ^ 2) * maturity) / (sigma *
        Sqr(maturity))
    d2 = d1 - sigma * Sqr(maturity)
    With Application.WorksheetFunction
        BsEuropeanCall = assetPrice * .NormSDist(d1) - strike * Exp(-riskFree * maturity) *
        .NormSDist(d2)
    End With
End Function
```

Code 9.6: VBA codes of the CMcEuropeanCallDiv() and
AMcEuropeanCallDiv() routines.

9.4 EXOTIC OPTIONS

In this section, we apply the Monte Carlo method to the pricing of exotic options with path-dependent payoffs at maturity. For example, an Asian call option will have its payoff depending on the average asset price over a set of predetermined forward times $\{t_1, t_2, \ldots, t_N = T\}$ given by:

$$A_T = \frac{1}{N}(S_{t_1} + \ldots + S_{t_N}). \tag{9.31}$$

Again, we can generate iteratively the asset prices at every forward time above by running the index i from 0 to $N - 1$ in (9.22) with random numbers $\{\varepsilon_1, \ldots, \varepsilon_N\}$. The average asset price can be used to evaluate the option payoff according to the function:

$$f_T(\varepsilon_1, \ldots, \varepsilon_N) = \max\{A_T(\varepsilon_1, \ldots, \varepsilon_N) - K, 0\}. \tag{9.32}$$

For variance reduction, it is effective to adopt the case for the geometric average asset price as the control variate and consider the new function:

$$\tilde{f}_T(\varepsilon_1, \ldots, \varepsilon_N) = \max\{A_T(\varepsilon_1, \ldots, \varepsilon_N) - K, 0\} - \max\{G_T(\varepsilon_1, \ldots, \varepsilon_N) - K, 0\}. \tag{9.33}$$

The geometric average asset price is defined as:

$$G_T = \sqrt[N]{S_{t_1} \ldots S_{t_N}}. \tag{9.34}$$

It is easy to show that G_T is lognormally distributed with risk-neutral average given by:

$$\hat{E}(G_T|S_0) = S_0 e^{rv_1 + \frac{1}{2}\sigma^2(v_2 - v_1)}, \quad v_\alpha = \frac{1}{N^\alpha}\sum_{i=1}^{N}(N - i + 1)^\alpha(t_i - t_{i-1}). \tag{9.35}$$

The control variate has an analytic solution given by the Black–Scholes formula as:[4]

$$f_0^{BS} = \hat{E}(G_T|S_0)e^{-rT}N(\rho) - K e^{-rT}N(\rho - \sigma\sqrt{v_2}), \quad \rho = \frac{\ln(\hat{E}(G_T|S_0)/K) + \frac{1}{2}\sigma^2 v_2}{\sigma\sqrt{v_2}}. \tag{9.36}$$

The pseudo code of the CMcArAsianCall() routine for the pricing of an Asian call option is given by Code 9.7. The routine reads in the parameters $\{S_0, K, r, \sigma, n\}$, a set of forward averaging times$\{t_1, \ldots, t_N = T\}$, and N. Similarly, the input time array should also include the current time defined as $t_0 = 0$ to initiate (9.22). Again, the routine returns the estimation of the current option price together with the standard error. In the inner loop, asset prices at every averaging time are generated iteratively for which their arithmetic and geometric averages can be evaluated. It should be noted that the multiplication of a long sequence of prices could possibly overflow the numerical procedure. It is safer to determine the geometric average by summing up the logarithmic prices. Sample payoff $\tilde{f}_T$ in (9.33) and its present value can be evaluated using the iterated average prices. The estimates of the mean and variance can be obtained based on the sample sum and squared sum. We have also included the Black-Scholes formula for the geometric case given by the function BsGeAsianCall(). The VBA code of the CMcArAsianCall() routine is given by Code 9.8. Table 9.3 demonstrates the effectiveness of the use of the geometric average price as a control variate based on one million simulation samples. We adopt the same parameterization as in Figure 9.2 and consider the set of averaging times $\{t_1 = 0.50, t_2 = 0.75, t_3 = 1.00\}$.

As our second example of an exotic option, we consider a double barrier knock-out (DKO) European call option with maturity payoff depending on the breaching condition of the asset price with respect to two predefined barriers $(H > S_0 > L)$. In principle, the intermediate knock-out condition is subjected to continuous asset price movement between time 0 and T. In (9.22), we can adopt an equal time interval of $\Delta t = T/N$ for large N such that the generated prices $\{S_{t_0} = S_0, S_{t_1}, \ldots, S_{t_N} = S_T\}$ at discrete time $t_i = i\Delta t$ will be a good approximation of a continuous path. Thus, we can generate iteratively the asset price movement for the entire life of the option by running i from 0 to $N - 1$ as:

$$S_{t_{i+1}} = S_{t_i} exp((r - \tfrac{1}{2}\sigma^2)\Delta t + \sigma\sqrt{\Delta t}\, \varepsilon_{i+1}) \tag{9.37}$$

with random numbers $\{\varepsilon_1, \ldots, \varepsilon_N\}$. If the asset price hits either one of the barriers at any time prior to the option maturity, the option is immediately knocked-out and the payoff is set to zero or to a constant rebate c payable at the hitting time. Otherwise, it will be evaluated according to the maturity price based on a call-type payoff function as:

$$f_T(\varepsilon_1, \ldots, \varepsilon_N) = \begin{cases} c\, e^{r(T-t_b)}, & \text{if } S_{t_b}(\varepsilon_1, \ldots, \varepsilon_b) \geq H \text{ or } S_{t_b}(\varepsilon_1, \ldots, \varepsilon_b) \leq L \text{ for } t_b \leq T \\ \max\{S_T(\varepsilon_1, \ldots, \varepsilon_N) - K, 0\}, & \text{otherwise} \end{cases}$$

$$\tag{9.38}$$

TABLE 9.3 The relative performance of the CMcArAsianCall() routine as compared with crude simulation.

	Crude Simulation	Control Variate Method
Mean	9.691	9.6787
Standard Error	0.014	0.0004
Relative CPU Time	1.00	1.12

For variance reduction, it is difficult in this case to identify a control variate that works consistently and effectively for a general barrier condition. We have also checked that the antithetic price movement generated through the negative random sequence doesn't work well for the barrier option.

The pseudo code of the McDKOCall() routine for the crude pricing of a DKO European call option is given by Code 9.9. The routine reads in the parameters $\{S_0, K, H, L, c, r, \sigma, N, T, n\}$ and returns the estimation of the option price together with the standard error. Here, the intermediate knock-out condition is examined through an external procedure called DKOBoundary() that assigns *crossflag* = TRUE if the input price has surpassed either one of the barriers H and L. It is essential to first examine the knock-out condition at current time and return the trivial solution $f_0 = 0$ with no estimation error. In the inner loop, sample asset price movement with time interval Δt is generated iteratively using (9.37) starting from its current value S_0. The knock-out condition is checked at every time step by calling DKOBoundary() for the newly iterated price. If *crossflag* = TRUE at any time, the hitting time is tagged as t_h and the iteration should stop immediately. Otherwise, it should continue through the entire loop and exit as the maturity price S_T. In either case, sample payoff f_T in (9.38) can be evaluated according to the flag *crossflag* in conjunction with the hitting time or the maturity price. The VBA code of the McDKOCall() routine is given by Code 9.10.

There are two sources of error in the Monte Carlo pricing of the DKO option. First, the method relies on statistical estimation and the statistical error is governed by the sample size. Second, the statistical estimates are actually referring to the case with discrete time steps. Thus, there is systematic error in the method as we are not estimating the true option price under continuous price movement. The error will depend on the size of Δt in the configuration of the problem. It can be improved by taking smaller time steps, but there is a trade-off between computational time and accuracy. Table 9.4 demonstrates the significance of the size of Δt in the pricing based

TABLE 9.4 The relative performance of the McDKOCall() routine under different time step configurations.

	$\Delta t = 0.1$ ($N = 10$)	$\Delta t = 0.01$ ($N = 100$)	$\Delta t = 0.001$ ($N = 1000$)	$\Delta t = 0.0001$ ($N = 10000$)
Mean	1.2328	0.7533	0.6089	0.5661
Standard Error	0.0035	0.0027	0.0024	0.0023
Relative CPU Time	1.00	7.51	69.61	697.22

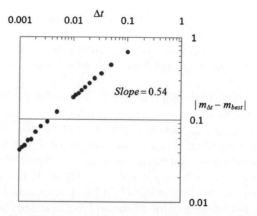

FIGURE 9.3   The plot of systematic error versus Δt for the pricing of the DKO call option.

on one million simulation samples. We adopt the same parameterization as in Figure 9.2 and consider the barrier levels of $H = 120$ and $L = 80$ with zero rebate $c = 0$. It can be seen in the table that the effect is quite critical especially for the mean estimate. We have shown in Figure 9.3 that the systematic error[5] for the mean estimate will only decrease proportionately to the square root of Δt. If the size of Δt is not small enough, the error will be quite substantial.

CMcArAsianCall(S_0 , K , r , σ , N , $t(0:N)$, n , f_0 , *error*)

zeroize the sample sum and squared sum
sum = 0 , *sum2* = 0

For(L_s = 1 to n){

initialize the asset price, sum of price and logarithmic sum of price
   $S_t = S_0$, $\Sigma_S = 0$, $\Sigma_{lnS} = 0$

# generate the asset price at each averaging time
   For(i = 0 to $N-1$){ ε = StdNormNum( )
                    $S_t = S_t \, exp((r - \frac{1}{2}\sigma^2)[t(i+1) - t(i)] + \sigma\sqrt{t(i+1) - t(i)}\varepsilon)$
                    $\Sigma_S = \Sigma_S + S_t$
                    $\Sigma_{lnS} = \Sigma_{lnS} + ln(S_t)$ }

evaluate the arithmetic and geometric average asset prices
   $A_T = \Sigma_S/N$
   $G_T = exp(\Sigma_{lnS}/N)$

evaluate the option payoff function as in (9.33)

$$f_T = CallPayoff(\,K\,,\,A_T\,) - CallPayoff(\,K\,,\,G_T\,)$$
$$PV = e^{-rT}f_T$$

accumulate the sample sum and squared sum

$$sum = sum + PV$$
$$sum2 = sum2 + PV^2 \qquad \}$$

evaluate the estimates of mean and variance

$$m = sum\,/\,n$$

$$s = \sqrt{\tfrac{1}{n-1}\,sum2 - \tfrac{n}{n-1}\,m^2}$$

return the estimation of option price and standard error

$$f_0 = BsGeAsianCall(\,S_0\,,\,K\,,\,r\,,\,\sigma\,,\,N\,,\,t(0:N)\,) + m$$
$$error = s\,/\sqrt{n}$$

Code 9.7: Pseudo code of the CMcArAsianCall() routine.

```
Sub CMcArAsianCall(assetPrice As Double, strike As Double, riskFree As Double,
        sigma As Double, nAvg As Integer, timeAvg() As Double, nsample As Long,
        ByRef optionPrice As Double, ByRef stdErr As Double)
    Dim sum As Double, sum2 As Double, gen As Double
    Dim mean As Double, sd As Double, Ls As Long
    Dim St As Double, fT As Double, pV As Double, i As Integer
    Dim sumPrice As Double, sumLnPrice As Double
    Dim amAvg As Double, gmAvg As Double
    sum = 0
    sum2 = 0
    For Ls = 1 To nsample
        St = assetPrice
        sumPrice = 0
        sumLnPrice = 0
        For i = 0 To nAvg - 1
            gen = StdNormNum()
            St = St * Exp((riskFree - 0.5 * sigma ^ 2) * (timeAvg(i + 1) - timeAvg(i)) + sigma *
                Sqr(timeAvg(i + 1) - timeAvg(i)) * gen)
            sumPrice = sumPrice + St
            sumLnPrice = sumLnPrice + Log(St)
        Next i
        amAvg = sumPrice / nAvg
        gmAvg = Exp(sumLnPrice / nAvg)
        fT = CallPayoff(strike, amAvg) - CallPayoff(strike, gmAvg)
        pV = Exp(-riskFree * timeAvg(nAvg)) * fT
        sum = sum + pV
        sum2 = sum2 + pV * pV
    Next Ls
    mean = sum / nsample
    sd = Sqr(sum2 / (nsample - 1) - (nsample / (nsample - 1)) * mean ^ 2)
    optionPrice = BsGeAsianCall(assetPrice, strike, riskFree, sigma, nAvg, timeAvg) + mean
```

```
    stdErr = sd / Sqr(nsample)
End Sub
```

```
Function BsGeAsianCall(assetPrice As Double, strike As Double, riskFree As Double,
        sigma As Double, nAvg As Integer, timeAvg() As Double) As Double
    Dim meanG As Double
    Dim nu1 As Double, nu2 As Double, i As Integer
    Dim d1 As Double, d2 As Double
    nu1 = 0
    nu2 = 0
    For i = 1 To nAvg
        nu1 = nu1 + (nAvg - i + 1) * (timeAvg(i) - timeAvg(i - 1))
        nu2 = nu2 + (nAvg - i + 1) ^ 2 * (timeAvg(i) - timeAvg(i - 1))
    Next i
    nu1 = nu1 / nAvg
    nu2 = nu2 / nAvg ^ 2
    meanG = assetPrice * Exp(riskFree * nu1 + 0.5 * sigma ^ 2 * (nu2 - nu1))
    d1 = (Log(meanG / strike) + 0.5 * sigma ^ 2 * nu2) / (sigma * Sqr(nu2))
    d2 = d1 - sigma * Sqr(nu2)
    With Application.WorksheetFunction
        BsGeAsianCall = Exp(-riskFree * timeAvg(nAvg)) * (meanG * .NormSDist(d1) - strike *
        .NormSDist(d2))
    End With
End Function
```

Code 9.8: VBA code of the CMcAsianCall() routine.

McDKOCall(S_0 , K , H , L , c , r , σ , N , T , n , f_0 , error)

```
# check the knock-out condition for the current asset price
Call DKOBoundary( H , L , S0 , crossflag )
If( crossflag ) then
    f0 = 0 ,   error = 0
    Exit subroutine
Endif
```

```
# define the size of time interval
Δt = T / N
```

```
# zeroize the sample sum and squared sum
sum = 0 , sum2 = 0
```

For(L_s = 1 to n){

```
# initialize the asset price
    St = S0
# generate the asset price at each intermediate time and check the knock-out condition
    For( i = 0 to N− 1 ){   ε = StdNormNum( )
```
$$S_t = S_t \, exp(\, (\, r - \tfrac{1}{2}\sigma^2) \, \Delta t + \sigma\sqrt{\Delta t}\varepsilon)$$

```
                Call DKOBoundary( H , L , St , crossflag )
                If( crossflag ) then
                    th = iΔt
                    exit i
                Endif                          }
```

\# evaluate the option payoff function as in (9.38)
```
    If( crossflag ) then
        fT = c e^{r( T − tn )}
    Else
        fT = CallPayoff( K , St )
    Endif
```

$$PV = e^{-rT} f_T$$

\# accumulate the sample sum and squared sum
```
    sum = sum + PV
    sum2 = sum2 + PV²          }
```

\# evaluate the estimates of mean and variance
$$m = sum / n$$

$$s = \sqrt{\frac{1}{n-1} sum2 - \frac{n}{n-1} m^2}$$

\# return the estimation of option price and standard error
$$f_0 = m$$
$$error = s / \sqrt{n}$$

Code 9.9: Pseudo code of the McDKOCall() routine.

```
Sub McDKOCall(assetPrice As Double, strike As Double, upperBarrier As Double,
        lowerBarrier As Double, rebate As Double, riskFree As Double, sigma As Double,
        nStep As Integer, maturity As Double, nsample As Long, ByRef optionPrice As Double,
        ByRef stdErr As Double)
    Dim sum As Double, sum2 As Double, gen As Double
    Dim mean As Double, sd As Double, Ls As Long
    Dim St As Double, fT As Double, pV As Double, i As Integer
    Dim crossFlag As Boolean
    Dim timeHit As Double
    Dim dtime As Double: dtime = maturity / nStep

    Call DKOBoundary(upperBarrier, lowerBarrier, assetPrice, crossFlag)
    If (crossFlag) Then
        optionPrice = 0
        stdErr = 0
        Exit Sub
    End If
    sum = 0
```

```
    sum2 = 0
    For Ls = 1 To nsample
      St = assetPrice
      For i = 0 To nStep - 1
        gen = StdNormNum()
        St = St * Exp((riskFree - 0.5 * sigma ^ 2) * dtime + sigma * Sqr(dtime) * gen)
        Call DKOBoundary(upperBarrier, lowerBarrier, St, crossFlag)
        If (crossFlag) Then
          timeHit = i * dtime
          Exit For
        End If
      Next i
      If (crossFlag) Then
        fT = rebate * Exp(riskFree * (maturity - timeHit))
      Else
        fT = CallPayoff(strike, St)
      End If
      pV = Exp(-riskFree * maturity) * fT
      sum = sum + pV
      sum2 = sum2 + pV * pV
    Next Ls
    mean = sum / nsample
    sd = Sqr(sum2 / (nsample - 1) - (nsample / (nsample - 1)) * mean ^ 2)
    optionPrice = mean
    stdErr = sd / Sqr(nsample)
End Sub
```

```
Sub DKOBoundary(upperBarrier As Double, lowerBarrier As Double, assetPrice As Double,
    ByRef crossFlag As Boolean)
  If (assetPrice >= upperBarrier Or assetPrice <= lowerBarrier) Then
    crossFlag = True
  Else
    crossFlag = False
  End If
End Sub
```

Code 9.10: VBA codes of the McDKOCall() and DKOBoundary() routines.

9.5 AMERICAN OPTIONS

One of the most important problems in option pricing is the valuation of American-style options with early exercising features. For example, an American put option can be exercised at any time prior to its maturity with its intrinsic value evaluated according to the payoff function $\psi(S) = max\{K - S, 0\}$. At time t with underlying asset price S_t, the fair value of an American put option can be defined based on the risk-neutral expectation of its discounted payoff as:

$$F(S_t, t) = \hat{E}(e^{-r(\tau_s - t)} \, \psi(S_{\tau_s}) | S_t) \qquad (9.39)$$

where τ_s is the first exercising time along a random asset price movement starting off from S_t. It can occur at option's maturity or at any earlier time when the intrinsic value is greater than the fair value at that point. Similarly, it is optimal to exercise the option early at time t based on the criteria as:

$$\psi(S_t) \geq F(S_t, t). \qquad (9.40)$$

The price of the American put option should also include this feature and is given by:

$$f(S_t, t) = \max\{F(S_t, t), \, \psi(S_t)\}. \qquad (9.41)$$

The equality condition in (9.40) can serve to define a critical price $S_c(t)$ at time t for which the early exercising criteria will be satisfied[6] whenever $S_t \leq S_c(t)$. In this way, the criteria can be implemented very easily by checking the asset price with respect to a critical price. It should be noted that the fair value $F(S_t, t)$ can only be evaluated when all critical prices, or a boundary, at forward time of t have been determined. This means that critical price $S_c(t)$ can only be determined through backward iteration starting off from the option's maturity with $S_c(T) = K$. To determine the current price of the American put option, we need to first generate the entire critical boundary prior to its maturity and then evaluate the risk-neutral expectation as:

$$f_0 = \max\{\hat{E}(e^{-r\tau_s} \psi(S_{\tau_s}) | S_0), \, \psi(S_0)\}. \qquad (9.42)$$

Again, we can adopt equal time interval of $\Delta t = T/N$ for large N and consider the discrete time steps $t_i = i\Delta t$ for the entire life of the option with i runs from 0 to N. At time t_i, consider $S_{t_i} = x$ and suppose the critical boundary at forward time is given by $\{S_c(t_{i+1}), \ldots, S_c(t_N) = K\}$. The fair value of the American put option can be estimated by Monte Carlo simulation as:

$$F(S_{t_i} = x, \, t_i) = \hat{E}(e^{-r(\tau_s - t_i)} \, \psi(S_{\tau_s}) | S_{t_i} = x). \qquad (9.43)$$

In (9.43), we can generate iteratively the asset price movement for the remaining life of the option by running j in (9.44) from i to $N - 1$ starting from $S_{t_i} = x$.

$$S_{t_{j+1}} = S_{t_j} \exp((r - \tfrac{1}{2}\sigma^2)\Delta t + \sigma\sqrt{\Delta t}\,\varepsilon_j) \qquad (9.44)$$

If the generated price $S_{t_{j+1}} \leq S_c(t_{j+1})$ at any forward time prior to the option's maturity, the option should be exercised immediately and $\tau_s = t_{j+1}$ in (9.43). Otherwise, it will be exercised at maturity for positive payoff and $\tau_s = T$. The critical price $S_c(t_i)$ at time t_i can be determined by identifying the value of x for which the mean estimate in (9.43) matches the intrinsic value. This is the same as solving the root of the function given by:

$$y(x) = F(x, t_i) - \psi(x) \tag{9.45}$$

where $y(x)$ is subjected to the standard error in the estimation of $F(x, t_i)$. It can be done by performing a linear regression for $y(x) \approx \beta x + \alpha$ in the neighborhood[7] of its trial value $x = S_c(t_{i+1})$ with $x_{root} \approx - \alpha/\beta$. It is essential for the size of $y(x_{root})$ to be less than the standard error in $F(x, t_i)$. Otherwise, a new x_{root} should be determined through another linear regression around the old one until $y(x_{root})$ becomes zero within the statistical error. In this way, the entire critical boundary can be determined by iterating the above procedure for all t_i in a backward scheme starting from t_{N-1} to t_0 with $S_c(t_N) = K$.

We first develop a routine called FvAmericanPut() capable of estimating the fair value of an American put option at forward time based on Monte Carlo simulation. The pseudo code of FvAmericanPut() is given by Code 9.11. It reads in the parameters $\{x, K, r, \sigma, N, T, n\}$, a time pointer i for the reference forward time t_i, and the critical prices $\{S_c(t_{i+1}), \ldots, S_c(t_N)\}$ thereafter. The routine returns the Monte Carlo estimation of the fair value together with the standard error. In the inner loop, asset price movement between t_i and T is generated iteratively using (9.44) with time interval of Δt. At each time step, the early exercising criteria is examined through an external procedure called APBoundary() that assigns *exerciseflag* = TRUE if the iterated asset price is less than the critical price. If *exerciseflag* = TRUE at any time, the iteration should terminate immediately with stopping time taken to be the updated τ_s in the loop. Otherwise, it should continue until the option matures at which $\tau_s = T$. The discounted payoff in (9.43) can then be evaluated using the stopping time and the terminal asset price in the iteration. The VBA code of FvAmericanPut() is given by Code 9.12.

We then develop a routine called McAmericanPut() that performs the backward iteration based on the FvAmericanPut() routine. The pseudo code of McAmericanPut() is given by Code 9.13. It reads in the parameters $\{S_0, K, r, \sigma, N, T, n\}$ and returns the estimation of the option price together with the standard error. In the backward iteration, we can generate the critical boundary by running the time pointer i in FvAmericanPut() backward from $N - 1$ to 0 with $S_c(t_N) = K$ being the starting value. At time t_i in the loop, the critical prices from t_{i+1} to t_N are presumably calculated in previous steps. It is then straightforward to estimate $F(x, t_i)$ in (9.45) by calling FvAmericanPut(), and the main task is to determine the root of $y(x)$ that corresponds to the critical price $S_c(t_i)$ at time t_i. We adopt $S_c(t_{i+1})$ as the trial value of the root and consider a linear regression for $y(x)$ in the neighborhood of this value. In the inner loop, we generate $h = 100$ data points for the regression with values of x that spread across a small region of $\delta = 1$ percent below the trial value. The linear regression can be performed through an external routine called Regn() and it should be noted that the errors in $y(x)$ are roughly constant.[8] The resulting α and β would provide a good approximation for x_{root} and the corresponding $y(x_{root})$ should be calculated by calling FvAmericanPut(). In the IF statement, it is important to check explicitly that $y(x_{root})$ is zero within the standard error in the estimation. If so, we can assign x_{root} to be the critical price $S_c(t_i)$. Otherwise, it can be used to update the trial value and the regression should be repeated starting from the line labeled "NewTrialValue." The VBA code of McAmericanPut() is given by Code 9.14.

Once we have determined the critical boundary in the backward iteration, the current price of the American put option can be estimated by calling FvAmericanPut() with S_0 and comparing the fair value with the intrinsic value according to (9.42). The systematic error here would depend on the accuracy of the critical boundary determined under discrete time interval. Figure 9.4 illustrates the deviation in the critical boundaries determined based on, for example, $\Delta t = 0.1$ and $\Delta t = 0.001$. Table 9.5 demonstrates the overall significance of the size of Δt in the pricing of the American put option. We adopt the same parameterization as in Figure 9.2 and consider again one million samples in the simulation. It has been show in Figure 9.5 that the systematic error for the mean estimate will only decrease proportionately to the linear order of Δt. Thus, the error will be less substantial here than in the pricing of a DKO option.

TABLE 9.5 The relative performance of the McAmericanPut() routine under different time step configurations.

	$\Delta t = 0.1$ $(N = 10)$	$\Delta t = 0.01$ $(N = 100)$	$\Delta t = 0.001$ $(N = 1000)$
Mean	7.909	7.982	7.985
Standard Error	0.009	0.009	0.009
Relative CPU Time	1.00	26.76	752.62

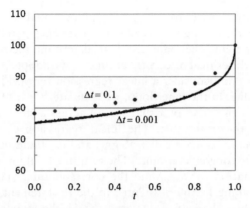

FIGURE 9.4   Critical boundary of the American put option.

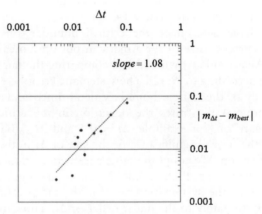

FIGURE 9.5   The plot of systematic error versus Δt for the pricing of the American put option.

FvAmericanPut(x , K , r , σ , N , T , i , $S_c(i +1 : N)$, n ,   F , error)

\# define the size of time interval and the reference forward time
$\Delta t = T / N$, $t_i = i\Delta t$

\# zeroize the sample sum and squared sum
sum = 0 , *sum2* = 0

For(L_s = 1 to *n*){
\# initialize the asset price
   $S_t = x$

\# generate the asset price at each time step, check early exercising criteria, and update
the latest time

For($j = i$ to $N-1$){ ε = StdNormNum( )

$$S_t = S_t \, exp((\, r - \tfrac{1}{2}\sigma^2)\,\Delta t + \sigma\sqrt{\Delta t}\varepsilon)$$

Call *APBoundary*(S_t , S_c(j + 1) , *exerciseflag*)

τ_s ((j + 1)Δt

If(*exerciseflag*) exit j }

\# evaluate the discounted payoff in (9.43)

$$PV = e^{-r(\,\tau_s - t_i\,)} PutPayoff(\, K \,, S_t\,)$$

\# accumulate the sample sum and squared sum

sum = *sum* + *PV*

sum2 = *sum2* + *PV*^{2} }

\# evaluate the estimates of mean and variance

m = *sum* / *n*

$$s = \sqrt{\frac{1}{n-1}\, sum2 - \frac{n}{n-1}\, m^2}$$

\# return the estimation of option price and standard error

F = *m*

error = $s / \sqrt{n}$

Code 9.11: Pseudo code of the FvAmericanPut() routine.

```
Sub FvAmericanPut(assetPrice As Double, strike As Double, riskFree As Double,
        sigma As Double, nStep As Integer, maturity As Double, iptr As Integer,
        Scritical() As Double, nsample As Long, ByRef fairValue As Double,
        ByRef stdErr As Double)
  Dim sum As Double, sum2 As Double, gen As Double
  Dim mean As Double, sd As Double, Ls As Long
  Dim St As Double, pV As Double, j As Integer
  Dim exerciseFlag As Boolean
  Dim timeStop As Double
  Dim dtime As Double: dtime = maturity / nStep
  Dim timeRef As Double: timeRef = iptr * dtime
  sum = 0
  sum2 = 0
  For Ls = 1 To nsample
    St = assetPrice
    For j = iptr To nStep - 1
      gen = StdNormNum()
      St = St * Exp((riskFree - 0.5 * sigma ^ 2) * dtime + sigma * Sqr(dtime) * gen)
      timeStop = (j + 1) * dtime
      Call APBoundary(St, Scritical(j + 1), exerciseFlag)
      If (exerciseFlag) Then Exit For
```

```
    Next j
    pV = Exp(-riskFree * (timeStop - timeRef)) * PutPayoff(strike, St)
    sum = sum + pV
    sum2 = sum2 + pV * pV
  Next Ls
  mean = sum / nsample
  sd = Sqr(sum2 / (nsample - 1) - (nsample / (nsample - 1)) * mean ^ 2)
  fairValue = mean
  stdErr = sd / Sqr(nsample)
End Sub
```

```
Sub APBoundary(assetPrice As Double, criticalPrice As Double, exerciseFlag As Boolean)
  If (assetPrice <= criticalPrice) Then
    exerciseFlag = True
  Else
    exerciseFlag = False
  End If
End Sub
```

```
Function PutPayoff(strike As Double, assetPrice As Double) As Double
  PutPayoff = Max(strike - assetPrice, 0)
End Function
```

Code 9.12: VBA code of the FvAmericanPut() routine.

$McAmericanPut(S_0 , K , r , \sigma , N , T , n , f_0 , error)$

define the configuration of the linear regression
$h = 100 , \delta = 0.01$

define the critical price at option's maturity
$S_c(N) = K$

generate the critical boundary
$For(i = N - 1 \text{ to } 0, -1) \{$

define the trial value for the root of (9.45)
$\quad x_{root} = S_c(i + 1)$

$NewTrialValue : inc = \delta x_{root} / h$

generate plotting points for (9.45) in the neighborhood of the trial value
$\quad For(k = 1 \text{ to } h) \{ \quad X_{fit}(k) = x_{root} - k \, inc$
$\qquad\qquad\qquad Call\ FvAmericanPut(X_{fit}(k) , K , r , \sigma , N , T , i , S_c(i + 1 : N) , n , \quad F , error)$
$\qquad\qquad\qquad Y_{fit}(k) = F - PutPayoff(K , X_{fit}(k)) \qquad \}$

\# perform a linear regression for (9.45) and obtain an approximation for its root
 Call Regn($X_{fit}($ 1 : h) , $Y_{fit}($ 1 : h) , h , β , α)
 $x_{root} = -\,\alpha\,\beta$

\# check the validity of the approximated root and, if necessary, use it as a new trial value.
 Call *FvAmericanPut*(x_{root} , K , r , σ , N , T , i , $S_c(i + 1 : N)$, n , F , *error*)
 If($|\ F{-}PutPayoff(\ K\ ,\ x_{root}\ )\ | > error$) Then GoTo   NewTrialValue

\# assign the valid root of (9.45) as the critical price
 $S_c(i) = x_{root}$ }

\# knowing the critical boundary, evaluate the option price and standard error according to (9.42)
Call *FvAmericanPut*(S_0 , K , r , σ , N , T , i , $S_c(0 : N)$, n , F , *error*)
$f_0 = max($ F , $PutPayoff(\ K\ ,\ S_0\ )$))

Code 9.13: Pseudo code of the McAmericanPut() routine.

```
Sub McAmericanPut(assetPrice As Double, strike As Double, riskFree As Double,
        sigma As Double, nStep As Integer, maturity As Double, nsample As Long,
        ByRef optionPrice As Double, ByRef stdErr As Double)
    Dim Scritical() As Double: ReDim Scritical(0 To nStep)
    Dim iptr As Integer, k As Integer
    Dim nFit As Integer: nFit = 100
    Dim delta As Double: delta = 0.01
    Dim inc As Double
    Dim xroot As Double, fairValue As Double
    Dim xFit() As Double: ReDim xFit(1 To nFit)
    Dim yFit() As Double: ReDim yFit(1 To nFit)
    Dim slope As Double, intercept As Double
    Scritical(nStep) = strike
    For iptr = nStep - 1 To 0 Step -1
        xroot = Scritical(iptr + 1)
NewTrialValue: inc = delta * xroot / nFit
        For k = 1 To nFit
            xFit(k) = xroot - k * inc
            Call FvAmericanPut(xFit(k), strike, riskFree, sigma, nStep, maturity, iptr, Scritical,
                nsample, fairValue, stdErr)
            yFit(k) = fairValue - PutPayoff(strike, xFit(k))
        Next k
        Call Regn(xFit, yFit, nFit, slope, intercept)
        xroot = -intercept / slope
        Call FvAmericanPut(xroot, strike, riskFree, sigma, nStep, maturity, iptr, Scritical,
            nsample, fairValue, stdErr)
        If (Abs(fairValue - PutPayoff(strike, xroot)) > stdErr) Then GoTo NewTrialValue
        Scritical(iptr) = xroot
        Range("A1").Offset(nStep - 1 - iptr, 0) = iptr * (maturity / nStep)
```

```
    Range("B1").Offset(nStep - 1 - iptr, 0) = xroot
    Application.StatusBar = "Done simulation i : " & iptr
Next iptr
Call FvAmericanPut(assetPrice, strike, riskFree, sigma, nStep, maturity, 0, Scritical,
    nsample, fairValue, stdErr)
    optionPrice = Max(fairValue, PutPayoff(strike, assetPrice))
End Sub
```

```
Sub Regn(xFit() As Double, yFit() As Double, nFit As Integer, ByRef slope As Double,
    ByRef intercept As Double)
Dim avgX As Double, avgY As Double, avgX2 As Double, avgY2 As Double, avgXY
    As Double
Dim i As Integer
avgX = 0
avgY = 0
avgX2 = 0
avgY2 = 0
avgXY = 0
For i = 1 To nFit
    avgX = avgX + xFit(i)
    avgY = avgY + yFit(i)
    avgX2 = avgX2 + xFit(i) ^ 2
    avgY2 = avgY2 + yFit(i) ^ 2
    avgXY = avgXY + xFit(i) * yFit(i)
Next i
avgX = avgX / nFit
avgY = avgY / nFit
avgX2 = avgX2 / nFit
avgY2 = avgY2 / nFit
avgXY = avgXY / nFit
slope = (avgXY - avgX * avgY) / (avgX2 - avgX ^ 2)
intercept = (avgX2 * avgY - avgX * avgXY) / (avgX2 - avgX ^ 2)
End Sub
```

Code 9.14: VBA code of the McAmericanPut() routine.

REVIEW QUESTIONS

1. A lookback call option written on equity has the maturity payoff at time T given by

$$c_T = S_T - K, \ K = \min\{D_T, S_{min}\}.$$

The strike price K of the option is the minimum asset price that has achieved when looking back from the maturity time to its issue time. Here, D_T is the minimum price achieved from current time $t = 0$ up to option's maturity, and S_{min} is the historical minimum price achieved from issue time up to current time. Use Monte-Carlo simulation to price a lookback call option and use a European call option with S_{min} being the strike price as control variate in the simulation.

2. Repeat the pricing of a one-touch option in Question (7.2) using Monte Carlo simulation. Use antithetic variate as variance reduction technique in the simulation.

3. In the Cox–Ingersoll–Ross model, the risk-neutral process of short rate is given by

$$\Delta r_t = a(b - r_t)\Delta t + \sigma\sqrt{r_t}\sqrt{\Delta t}\varepsilon(0, 1)$$

where a, b, σ, and r_0 are constant parameters. Interest rate derivatives are considered to be function over this stochastic variable for which current value of derivatives can be determined through risk-neutral expectation of discounted payoff at maturity. Use Monte Carlo simulation to estimate the risk-neutral pricing of pure discount bond with maturity at T given by

$$P_0(T) = \hat{E}\left(\exp\left(-\int_0^T r_t \, dt\right) \$1 | r_0\right)$$

where $\{a, b, \sigma, r_0\}$ are taken to be input parameters. As control variate in the simulation, consider the analytic solution from the Vasicek model written as

$$P_0(T) = (\$1)\exp\left\{\frac{(B(T) - T)(a^2 b - \frac{1}{2}\sigma^2)}{a^2} - \frac{\sigma^2 B(T)^2}{4a}\right\}e^{-B(T)r_0}, \ B(T) = \frac{1 - e^{-aT}}{a}$$

In this model, short rate follows instead the risk-neutral process given by

$$\Delta r_t = a(b - r_t)\Delta t + \sigma\sqrt{\Delta t}\,\varepsilon(0, 1)$$

with the same parameters.

ENDNOTES

1. P. P. Boyle, "Options: A Monte Carlo Approach," *Journal of Financial Economics* 4, No. 3 (1977): 323-338.

2. W.H. Press, S.A. Teukolsky, W.T. Vetterling, and B.P. Flannery, "Random Numbers," in *Numerical Recipes in C : The Art of Scientific Computing*, 2nd Edition (Cambridge: Cambridge University Press, 1997), 274-328.

3. Ibid.

4. A. Kemna and A. Vorst, "A Pricing Method for Options Based on Average Asset Values," *Journal of Banking and Finance* 14, No. 1 (1990): 113-129.

5. Consider the systematic error given by $| m_{\Delta t} - m_{true} | \approx a(\Delta t)^b$ where a and b are constants. As m_{true} is not known *a priori*, we can choose m_{best} to be the best estimate in Table 9.4 and write:

$$log_{10}|m_{\Delta t} - m_{best}| = b\, log_{10}\Delta t + log_{10}a + log_{10}|1 - \delta|,$$

$$\delta = (m_{best} - m_{true})/(m_{\Delta t} - m_{true}).$$

In the region where Δt is not too small, the term δ is negligible and b can be estimated by the slope of the plot $log_{10}| m_{\Delta t} - m_{best} |$ *versus* $log_{10}\Delta t$ in Figure 9.3. It can be shown that $b \approx 0.5$ in the linear fitting.

6. This is true as both $\psi(S_t)$ and $F(S_t, t)$ are decreasing function with S_t. Also, $\psi(S_t)$ vanishes for large S_t.

7. Avoid taking the out-of-money region of the option by virtue of the linear approximation for (9.45).

8. In the fitting of a set of h data points (x_k, y_k) to a straight line $y = \beta x + \alpha$ where y is subjected to a constant measurement error, the best fit parameters in the linear model are given by:

$$\beta = (\langle xy \rangle - \langle x \rangle \langle y \rangle)/\Delta, \quad \alpha = (\langle x^2 \rangle \langle y \rangle - \langle x \rangle \langle xy \rangle)/\Delta, \quad \Delta = \langle x^2 \rangle - \langle x \rangle^2.$$

The estimation errors of α and β are both in the order of $1/\sqrt{h}$. Thus, the size of h must be sufficiently large to ensure stability in the iteration of the critical boundary.

CHAPTER 10

Portfolio Value-at-Risk

10.1 PORTFOLIO RISK SIMULATION

Value-at-Risk (*VaR*) is a single number summarizing the uncertainty in the future value of a financial asset. It is an extrapolation into the future based on the assumption that the *future will behave statistically the same as the past*. In the random walk regime, we have adopted a statistical description of what should have happened in the past. Thus, we can only predict what might happen in the future based on the same principle, making the future asset value statistically uncertain. In this chapter, we describe the two approaches for calculating the *VaR* measure of a financial asset based on historical data. In general, we define *VaR* as the asset value in the worst case scenario under certain confidence level. For example, there is a 95 percent chance that the future asset value will be greater than its 95 percent *VaR* number.[1] Suppose, $\{q(1), q(2), \ldots, q(100)\}$ are the daily price returns of an asset for the last 100 days. Under the random walk assumption, asset price returns are considered to be independent and identically distributed. Tomorrow's return q_0 is a random quantity that follows the same statistical distribution inferred from the historical sequence. In this sense, the historical returns are taken to be random samples of q_0 with a 95 percent *VaR* simply given by the fifth lowest return. This is known as the historical simulation that generates the *VaR* measure directly from historical data. An alternative approach is called the Monte Carlo simulation that adopts a random normal process for the price returns with mean and standard deviation estimated from the data. In this case, random samples of q_0 are generated from the random normal drawing with 95 percent *VaR* given by the return at exactly the 5 percent left-tail probability of normal distribution.

In Monte Carlo simulation, asset price return over the time horizon T is assumed to follow a random normal process given by:[2]

$$q = \varepsilon(\mu_T, \sigma_T) \tag{10.1}$$

143

where μ_T and σ_T are estimated from its historical returns $\{q(1), q(2), \ldots, q(n_d)\}$ with the same time horizon. Random samples of future asset return $\{\hat{q}_0(1), \hat{q}_0(2), \ldots, \hat{q}_0(n_s)\}$ for the following period of T are generated through (10.1) that embodies the statistical mean and standard deviation as observed in the past. For a portfolio constructed based on this single asset, the mark-to-market value of the portfolio $\Phi(S_t, t)$ can be evaluated given the asset price together with the reference time. The corresponding random samples of future portfolio return $\{\hat{Q}_0(1), \hat{Q}_0(2), \ldots, \hat{Q}_0(n_s)\}$ over T can be generated based on the changes in its mark-to-market values according to the sample asset returns as:[3]

$$\hat{Q}_0(L) = \frac{\Phi(\hat{S}_T(L), T) - \Phi(S_0, 0)}{\Phi(S_0, 0)} \tag{10.2}$$

where S_0 is the current asset price and $\hat{S}_T(L) = S_0(1 + \hat{q}_0(L))$ is the future asset price at T with respect to a sample return. The portfolio VaR can then be determined through the sample mean Γ_T and standard deviation Σ_T of the portfolio returns. In particular, the 95 percent VaR of the portfolio over the time horizon T is given by $\Gamma_T - 1.645\Sigma_T$.

It is easy to use (10.1) and extend the VaR measure over a longer time horizon $T_h = hT$ that is a multiple of T. Random sequences of future asset returns for consecutive periods of T can be generated through (10.1) as $\{\{\hat{q}_0(L), \hat{q}_{T_1}(L), \ldots, \hat{q}_{T_{h-1}}(L)\}, L = 1, 2, \ldots, n_s\}$. The future asset price at T_h can be evaluated with respect to a return sequence as:

$$\hat{S}_{T_h}(L) = S_0(1 + \hat{q}_0(L))(1 + \hat{q}_{T_1}(L)) \ldots (1 + \hat{q}_{T_{h-1}}(L)). \tag{10.3}$$

Random samples of the portfolio return over the time horizon T_h can be generated using (10.2) with mean Γ_{T_h} and standard deviation Σ_{T_h}, and the 95 percent portfolio VaR is determined to be $\Gamma_{T_h} - 1.645\Sigma_{T_h}$.

EXAMPLE 10.1

Consider the following historical set of $n_d = 1000$ daily price returns of the Hang Seng Index (HSI) during the period from June 9, 2004 to June 5, 2008.[4] Suppose it is June 5, 2008 with a daily closing of the index $S_0 = 24,255.29$ and the risk-free interest rate $r = 5$ percent per year.

(I) Use Monte Carlo simulation to determine the one-day 95 percent VaR of a portfolio containing one European call option written on the index with *Strike* = 24,500, *Maturity* = 0.25 year, and *Volatility* = 25 percent per year.

1. As shown in Figure 10.1, the time horizon of the simulation is $T = 1$ day.
2. Historical mean and standard deviation of the HSI daily price return are estimated based on the data set in C3:C1002 to be $\mu_T = 0.0767$ percent and $\sigma_T = 1.3514$ percent.
3. Random samples of the HSI daily price return $\{\hat{q}_0(1), \hat{q}_0(2), \ldots, \hat{q}_0(n_s = 5,000)\}$ are generated in D3:D5002 through the random normal number generator $\varepsilon(\mu_T = 0.0767$ percent, $\sigma_T = 1.3514$ percent).
4. The corresponding index values $\{\hat{S}_T(1), \hat{S}_T(2), \ldots, \hat{S}_T(5,000)\}$ at one-day horizon are determined in E3:E5002 according to $\hat{S}_T(L) = S_0(1 + \hat{q}_0(L))$.
5. The current mark-to-market value of the portfolio is evaluated in I10 using the Black—Scholes call pricing as:

$$\Phi(S_0, 0) = BSCallPrice(S_0, Strike, r, Volatility, Maturity)$$
$$= 1,237.34.$$

6. Mark-to-market values of the portfolio at one-day horizon are also evaluated in F3:F5002 as:

$$\Phi(\hat{S}_T(L), T) = BSCallPrice(\hat{S}_T(L), Strike, r, Volatility, Maturity - T)$$

with sample portfolio returns calculated in G3:G5002 using (10.2). The mean and standard deviation of the portfolio returns at the one-day horizon can then be estimated as $\Gamma_T = 0.7870$ percent and $\Sigma_T = 14.4039$ percent using these samples. The one-day 95 percent *VaR* of the portfolio is given by the left-tail value $\Gamma_T - 1.645 \, \Sigma_T = -22.91$ percent.

(II) Determine now the five-day 95 percent *VaR* of the same portfolio.
1. As shown in Figure 10.2, the time horizon of the simulation is $T_5 = 5$ days.
2. In row 3, for example, a random sequence of the HSI daily returns $\{\hat{q}_0(1), \hat{q}_{T_1}(1), \hat{q}_{T_2}(1), \hat{q}_{T_3}(1), \hat{q}_{T_4}(1)\}$ for five consecutive days is generated in A3:E3 using the same random normal

(Continued)

(Continued)

	A	B	C	D	E	F	G	H	I	J
1	Date	Close	Returns	Sample Returns	Sample Index Values	Sample MTM Portfolio Prices	Sample Portfolio Returns			
2	8-Jun-04	12344.16						Horizon T	1	(days)
3	9-Jun-04	12339.94	-0.000342	-0.003635	24167.11	1179.38	-0.046836	Historical mean μ_τ	0.0767%	(per day)
4	10-Jun-04	12422.87	0.006720	0.007724	24442.63	1327.76	0.073077	Historical s.d. σ_τ	1.3514%	(per day)
5	11-Jun-04	12396.39	-0.002132	-0.021168	23741.87	970.22	-0.215881	Current Asset Price	24255.29	
6	14-Jun-04	12076.57	-0.025799	-0.003661	24166.48	1179.06	-0.047100			
7	15-Jun-04	12050.69	-0.002143	-0.016160	23863.32	1027.48	-0.169605	Strike	24500	
8	16-Jun-04	12161.78	0.009219	0.003977	24351.76	1277.71	0.032633	Maturity	0.25	(years)
9	17-Jun-04	12082.86	-0.006489	0.013087	24572.71	1401.25	0.132476	Volatility	25.00%	(per year)
10	18-Jun-04	11855.55	-0.018813	-0.018858	23797.88	996.38	-0.194738	Risk-free Rate	5.00%	(per year)
11	21-Jun-04	11845.59	-0.000840	0.002808	24323.40	1262.32	0.020194			
12	23-Jun-04	11849.77	0.000353	0.017513	24680.07	1463.56	0.182629	Current MTM portfolio price	1237.34	
13	24-Jun-04	12163.68	0.026491	0.004187	24356.85	1280.49	0.034875	Sample portfolio returns :		
14	25-Jun-04	12185.52	0.001796	-0.004749	24140.10	1165.38	-0.058157	Mean Γ_T	0.7870%	(per day)
15	28-Jun-04	12194.6	0.000745	-0.000688	24238.59	1216.91	-0.016504	Standard Deviation Σ_T	14.4039%	(per day)
1002	5-Jun-08	24255.29	0.005474	-0.039333	23301.26	779.19	-0.370272	1-day 95% VaR	-22.91%	
1003				0.012519	24558.94	1393.37	0.126105			
5002				-0.004566	24144.54	1167.67	-0.056302			
5003										

FIGURE 10.1 Monte Carlo simulation of a single-asset portfolio with a one-day horizon.

	A	B	C	D	E	F	G	H	I	J	K
1	Sample Sequences of Daily Returns for 5 Consecutive Days					Sample Index Values	Sample MTM Portfolio Prices	Sample Portfolio Returns			
2									*Horizon* T_5	5	(days)
3	0.004253	-0.011032	0.002796	0.012861	-0.001972	24419.50	1267.49	0.024373	*Current MTM portfolio price*	1237.34	
4	-0.009376	0.027782	-0.001978	0.006365	0.009761	25045.57	1638.48	0.324199	*Sample portfolio returns :*		
5	-0.004152	-0.007341	-0.025835	-0.018406	0.015986	23294.42	734.41	-0.406455	*Mean* Γ_{T5}	1.7636%	(per 5 day)
6	0.012030	0.003986	0.018499	-0.005548	-0.017110	24534.50	1331.77	0.076324	*Standard Deviation* Σ_{T5}	32.6659%	(per 5 day)
7	-0.002479	-0.006008	0.000603	-0.008700	-0.008530	23651.45	884.57	-0.285098	*5-day 95% VaR*	-51.97%	
8	0.005861	0.000985	-0.015501	0.009096	0.000729	24279.30	1191.55	-0.037007			
9	0.017243	0.002635	-0.005903	-0.014825	0.014185	24571.61	1352.89	0.093391			
5002	-0.005763	-0.014784	0.014648	-0.031198	-0.003334	23269.82	724.72	-0.414291			
5003											

FIGURE 10.2 Monte Carlo simulation of the single-asset portfolio with a five-day horizon.

(Continued)

(Continued)
number generator as above. The corresponding index value at
the five-day horizon is determined in F3 according to:

$$\hat{S}_{T_s}(1) = S_0(1 + 0.004253)(1 - 0.011032)(1 + 0.002796)$$
$$(1 + 0.012861)(1 - 0.001972).$$

3. The mark-to-market value of the portfolio at five-day horizon
is evaluated in G3 as:

$$\Phi(\hat{S}_{T_s}(1), T_5) = BSCallPrice(\hat{S}_{T_s}(1), Strike, r, Volatility,$$
$$Maturity - T_5)$$

with portfolio return calculated in H3 using (10.2) again.
There are all together 5000 sample return sequences being
generated in row 3 to row 5002. The mean and standard deviation of portfolio returns at five-day horizon are estimated to
be $\Gamma_{T_s} = 1.7636$ percent and $\Sigma_{T_s} = 32.6659$ percent, and the
five-day 95 percent *VaR* is given by $\Gamma_{T_s} - 1.645\,\Sigma_{T_s} = -51.97$
percent.

In historical simulation, historical returns $\{q(1), q(2), \ldots, q(n_d)\}$
themselves are taken as the random samples of asset return
$\{\tilde{q}_0(1) = q(1), \tilde{q}_0(2) = q(2), \ldots, \tilde{q}_0(n_s) = q(n_s)\}$ for the following period of
T. In principle, the adopted samples will exhibit all statistical properties as
observed in the past. However, the drawback of using historical simulation
is that it can only generate a finite amount of samples for which $n_s \leq n_d$.
Random samples of portfolio return $\{\tilde{Q}_0(1), \tilde{Q}_0(2), \ldots, \tilde{Q}_0(n_s)\}$ over the
same horizon can be generated based on the changes in its mark-to-market
values according to (10.2) with asset price at T taken to be $\tilde{S}_T(L) = S_0(1 +
\tilde{q}_0(L))$ with respect to a sample return. The portfolio *VaR* can be deter-
mined through the left-tail value of its probability distribution. The tail
pointer corresponding to a $p\%$ confidence is given by $I_V = (1 - 0.01p)n_s$,
and the $p\%$ *VaR* measure is defined to be the (I_V)-th lowest portfolio return
in the generated sample set.

We can also extend the *VaR* measure over a longer time horizon T_h
based on the same historical data set. Random sequences of asset returns for
consecutive periods of T can be generated through non-overlapping

sequences of historical returns in $\{q(1), q(2), \ldots, q(n_d)\}$ as:

$$\{\underbrace{q(1), \ldots q(h)}_{L=1}, \quad \underbrace{q(h+1), \ldots, q(2h)}_{L=2}, \ldots,$$

$$\underbrace{q((n_s - 1)h + 1), \ldots, q(n_s h)}_{L=n_s}, \ldots, q(n_d)\}$$

such that:

$$\{\tilde{q}_0(L) = q((L-1)h + 1), \tilde{q}_{T_1}(L) = q((L-1)h + 2), \ldots, \tag{10.4}$$
$$\tilde{q}_{T_{h-1}}(L) = q(Lh)\}, \, L = 1, 2, \ldots, n_s$$

with sample size $n_s \leq (n_d/h)$. Similarly, future asset price at T_h can be evaluated with respect to a return sequence as:

$$\tilde{S}_{T_h}(L) = S_0(1 + \tilde{q}_0(L))(1 + \tilde{q}_{T_1}(L)) \ldots (1 + \tilde{q}_{T_{h-1}}(L)). \tag{10.5}$$

Random samples of portfolio return over T_h can be generated using (10.2) with the *VaR* measure again determined through its probability tail.

EXAMPLE 10.1 (CONTINUED)

(III) Use historical simulation to determine the one-day 95 percent *VaR* of the call option portfolio.
1. As shown in Figure 10.3, the time horizon of the simulation is $T = 1$ day.
2. Historical returns in C3:C1002 are taken directly as the random samples of HSI daily price return $\{\tilde{q}_0(1), \tilde{q}_0(2), \ldots, \tilde{q}_0(n_s = 1000)\}$ depicted in D3:D1002. It is clear that the maximum sample size is limited to be $n_s = n_d = 1000$.
3. The same number of random portfolio returns are generated in G3:G1002 following the same procedure as adopted previously.
4. The left-tail pointer corresponding to a 95 percent confidence is given by $I_V = (1 - 0.95) \times 1,000 = 50$, and the one-day 95 percent VaR of the portfolio is determined to be -22.41 percent using the Excel function **SMALL**(G3:G1002, I_V).

(IV) Now determine the five-day 95 percent *VaR* of the portfolio.
1. As shown in Figure 10.4, the time horizon of the simulation is $T_5 = 5$ days.

(Continued)

	A	B	C	D	E	F	G		H	I	J
1	Date	Close	Returns	Sample Returns	Sample Index Values	Sample MTM Portfolio Prices	Sample Portfolio Returns				
2	8-Jun-04	12344.16									
3	9-Jun-04	12339.94	-0.000342	-0.000342	24247.00	1221.37	-0.012901		Horizon T	1	(days)
4	10-Jun-04	12422.87	0.006720	0.006720	24418.30	1314.25	0.062161		Current MTM portfolio price	1237.34	
5	11-Jun-04	12396.39	-0.002132	-0.002132	24203.59	1198.45	-0.031426		n_s	1000	
6	14-Jun-04	12076.57	-0.025799	-0.025799	23629.52	919.02	-0.257258		I_V	50	
7	15-Jun-04	12050.69	-0.002143	-0.002143	24203.31	1198.31	-0.031544		1-day 95% VaR	-22.41%	
8	16-Jun-04	12161.78	0.009219	0.009219	24478.89	1348.02	0.089455				
9	17-Jun-04	12082.86	-0.006489	-0.006489	24097.89	1143.69	-0.075686				
10	18-Jun-04	11855.55	-0.018813	-0.018813	23798.98	996.90	-0.194317				
11	21-Jun-04	11845.59	-0.000840	-0.000840	24234.91	1214.97	-0.018079				
1001	4-Jun-08	24123.25	-0.010359	-0.010359	24004.03	1096.30	-0.113983				
1002	5-Jun-08	24255.29	0.005474	0.005474	24388.05	1297.57	0.048682				
1003											

FIGURE 10.3 Historical simulation of the single-asset portfolio with a one-day horizon.

	D	E	F	G	H	I	J	K		L	M	N
1	Sample Sequences of Daily Returns for 5 Consecutive Days					Sample Index Values	Sample MTM Portfolio Prices	Sample Portfolio Returns				
2										Horizon T_5	5	(days)
3	-0.000342	0.006720	-0.002132	-0.025799	-0.002143	23678.64	896.74	-0.275267		Current MTM portfolio price	1237.34	
4	0.009219	-0.006489	-0.018813	-0.000840	0.000353	23850.88	976.16	-0.211077		n_s	200	
5	0.026491	0.001796	0.000745	-0.006421	0.013985	25147.70	1703.76	0.376959		I_v	10	
6	-0.005341	0.002617	0.002609	0.002945	-0.016275	23927.56	1012.85	-0.181428		5-day 95% VaR	-46.72%	
7	0.006808	-0.000922	-0.009243	-0.012046	0.000551	23894.38	996.87	-0.194342				
8	0.010033	0.008935	-0.003560	0.022393	-0.006043	25028.90	1627.94	0.315683				
201	-0.013139	-0.023742	0.006413	-0.001340	0.305546	23616.90	869.27	-0.297468				
202	0.006116	0.012157	-0.018348	-0.010359	0.305474	24127.27	1112.22	-0.101120				
1001												
1002												
1003												

FIGURE 10.4 Historical simulation of the single-asset portfolio with a five-day horizon.

(*Continued*)

(*Continued*)

2. Random sequences of HSI daily returns for five consecutive days are generated through non-overlapping sequences of historical returns in C3:C1002. For example, $\{\tilde{q}_0(1), \tilde{q}_{T_1}(1),$ $\tilde{q}_{T_2}(1), \tilde{q}_{T_3}(1), \tilde{q}_{T_4}(1)\}$ in D3:H3 are taken from C3:C7, while $\{\tilde{q}_0(2), \tilde{q}_{T_1}(2), \tilde{q}_{T_2}(2), \tilde{q}_{T_3}(2), \tilde{q}_{T_4}(2)\}$ in D8:H8 are taken from C8:C12, and so on. This can be achieved by taking row and column offsets from C3 and assigning them to the cells with the sample sequences of daily returns as:

$$\text{OFFSET}(\$C\$3, (\text{ROW}() - \text{ROW}(\$C\$3)) * 5 + \text{COLUMN}() - \text{COLUMN}(\$C\$3) - 1, 0).$$

3. The maximum sample size is now limited to $n_s = Int(n_d / h) = 200$.

4. Random samples of portfolio returns are generated in K3:K202 as before.

5. The left-tail pointer corresponding to a 95 percent confidence is given by $I_V = (1 - 0.95) \times 200 = 10$, and the one-day 95 percent VaR of the portfolio is determined to be -46.72 percent using the Excel function **SMALL(K3:G202, I_V)**.

10.2 MONTE CARLO SIMULATION FOR MULTIPLE-ASSET PORTFOLIOS

For a portfolio with multiple assets, price return over the time horizon T is defined as the change in its mark-to-market value according to the asset price returns in the portfolio content. In Monte Carlo simulation, random samples of future asset returns $\{\hat{q}_{i,0}(1), \hat{q}_{i,0}(2), \ldots, \hat{q}_{i,0}(n_s)\}$ over the period T are generated for all underlying assets with label $i = 1, 2, \ldots, n$. Random samples of portfolio price return $\{\hat{Q}_0(1), \hat{Q}_0(2), \ldots, \hat{Q}_0(n_s)\}$ can be generated based on the sample asset returns as:

$$\hat{Q}_0(L) = \frac{\Phi(\hat{S}_{1,T}(L), \hat{S}_{2,T}(L), \ldots, \hat{S}_{n,T}(L), T) - \Phi(S_{1,0}, S_{2,0}, \ldots, S_{n,0}, 0)}{\Phi(S_{1,0}, S_{2,0}, \ldots, S_{n,0}, 0)}, \quad (10.6)$$
$$L = 1, 2, \ldots, n_s$$

where $\hat{S}_{i,T}(L) = S_{i,0}(1 + \hat{q}_{i,0}(L))$ is the future price of asset i at time T with respect to a sample return. In the real market, it has been observed that asset price returns can be significantly correlated. The existence of such a correlation causes the contribution of risk coming from different assets to be diversified in the portfolio.

It is essential to extend (10.1) for the random generation of multiple asset price returns with defined means and variance-covariance among assets. We first construct a set of correlated random normal numbers $\{\omega_1, \omega_2, \ldots, \omega_n\}$ based on an independent set $\{\varepsilon_1, \varepsilon_2, \ldots, \varepsilon_n\}$ generated from $\varepsilon(0,1)$. We consider the linear combination for every ω_i as:

$$\omega_i = \sum_{k=1}^{n} \alpha_{ik}\varepsilon_k \tag{10.7}$$

with mean $E(\omega_i) = 0$ and variance-covariance $\rho_{ij} = E(\omega_i\omega_j) = \sum_{k=1}^{n} \alpha_{ik}\alpha_{jk}$. Since ρ_{ij} are positively defined and symmetric, it can be shown through Cholesky decomposition that α is a lower triangular matrix with strictly positive diagonal entries. This implies a simpler structure for (10.7) given by:

$$
\begin{aligned}
\omega_1 &= \alpha_{11}\varepsilon_1 \\
\omega_2 &= \alpha_{21}\varepsilon_1 + \alpha_{22}\varepsilon_2 \\
&\cdots \cdots \cdots \\
\omega_n &= \alpha_{n1}\varepsilon_1 + \alpha_{n2}\varepsilon_2 + \ldots + \alpha_{nn}\varepsilon_n
\end{aligned} \tag{10.8}
$$

with

$$\rho_{ij} = \alpha_{i1}\alpha_{j1} + \alpha_{i2}\alpha_{j2} + \ldots + \alpha_{ij}\alpha_{jj}, \text{ for } i \geq j. \tag{10.9}$$

It is then easy to adopt the so-called Cholesky algorithm and determine all α_{ij} in (10.8) iteratively using (10.9) by running i from 1 to n as:

$$\rho_{11} = \alpha_{11}\alpha_{11},\ \alpha_{11}^2 = \rho_{11}$$

$$\rho_{21} = \alpha_{21}\alpha_{11},\ \alpha_{21} = \frac{\rho_{21}}{\alpha_{11}} = \rho_{21}$$

$$\rho_{22} = \alpha_{21}\alpha_{21} + \alpha_{22}\alpha_{22},\ \alpha_{22}^2 = \rho_{22} - \alpha_{21}^2 = \rho_{22} - \rho_{21}^2$$

$$\rho_{31} = \alpha_{31}\alpha_{11},\ \alpha_{31} = \frac{\rho_{31}}{\alpha_{11}} = \rho_{31}$$

$$\rho_{32} = \alpha_{31}\alpha_{21} + \alpha_{32}\alpha_{22},\ \alpha_{32} = \frac{(\rho_{32} - \alpha_{31}\alpha_{21})}{\alpha_{22}} = \frac{(\rho_{32} - \rho_{31}\rho_{21})}{\sqrt{1 - \rho_{21}^2}}$$

$$\rho_{33} = \alpha_{31}\alpha_{31} + \alpha_{32}\alpha_{32} + \alpha_{33}\alpha_{33},$$

$$\alpha_{33}^2 = \rho_{33} - \alpha_{31}^2 - \alpha_{32}^2$$

$$= \rho_{33} - \frac{\rho_{31}(\rho_{31} - \rho_{32}\rho_{21}) + \rho_{32}(\rho_{32} - \rho_{31}\rho_{21})}{(1 - \rho_{21}^2)}$$

. . . and so on.

Equivalently, the algorithm can also be performed through the following equations[5] where α_{ij} are determined iteratively by running i from 1 to n.

$$\alpha_{ij} = \frac{\rho_{ij} - \sum_{k=1}^{j-1} \alpha_{ik}\alpha_{jk}}{\alpha_{jj}}, \quad \text{for } j = 1, 2, \ldots, i-1 \tag{10.10}$$

$$\alpha_{ii} = \sqrt{\rho_{ii} - \sum_{k=1}^{i-1} \alpha_{ik}^2} \tag{10.11}$$

It should be noted that the iteration starts off from the diagonal entry $\alpha_{11} = \sqrt{\rho_{11}}$ in (10.11). For $i > 1$, the off-diagonal entries are determined iteratively by running j from 1 to $i-1$ in (10.10) prior to the determination of the diagonal entry in (10.11). For multiple asset price returns over the time horizon T with means $\{\mu_{1,T}, \mu_{2,T}, \ldots, \mu_{n,T}\}$ and variance-covariance $\sigma_{ij,T}$ among assets, we first generate the random set $\{\omega_1, \omega_2, \ldots, \omega_n\}$ using (10.8) with $\rho_{ij} = \sigma_{ij,T}/(\sigma_{i,T}\,\sigma_{j,T})$, where $\sigma_{i,T} = \sqrt{\sigma_{ii,T}}$. We then rescale ω_i to become $\hat{q}_{i,0}$ according to its mean and standard deviation as:

$$\hat{q}_{i,0} = \mu_{i,T} + \alpha_{i,T}\,\omega_i, \quad \text{for } i = 1, 2, \ldots, n \tag{10.12}$$

such that the conditions $E(\hat{q}_{i,0}) = \mu_{i,T}$ and $E[(\hat{q}_{i,0} - \mu_{i,T})(\hat{q}_{j,0} - \mu_{j,T})] = \sigma_{ij,T}$ are explicitly satisfied. It is convenient to develop a generic VBA routine called Cholesky() capable of generating a set of correlated random normal numbers given their means and variance-covariance. The pseudo code of Cholesky() is given in Code 10.1. For our purpose, it reads in $\{n, \sigma_{ij,T}, \mu_{i,T}\}$ and returns an array of correlated asset price returns $\{\hat{q}_{1,0}, \hat{q}_{2,0}, \ldots, \hat{q}_{n,0}\}$. The VBA code of the Cholesky() routine is given in Code 10.2.

```
Cholesky( n , σ(1 : n , 1 : n) , μ(1 : n) , q(1 : n) )

# define the correlation coefficients
For( i = 1 to n ){ For( j = 1 to i ){  ρ( i , j ) = σ( i , j )/√(σ(i,i)σ(j,j))  } }

# determine α iteratively through (10.10) and (10.11)
For( i = 1 to n ){
   For( j = 1 to i – 1 ){ Σα = 0
                  For( k = 1 to j – 1 ){ Σα = Σα + α( i , k ) α( j , k ) }
                  α( i , j ) = [ ρ( i , j ) – Σα ]/α( j , j )          }
   Σα = 0
   For( k = 1 to i – 1 ){ Σα = Σα + α( i , k ) α( i , k ) }
   α( i , i ) = √(ρ(i,i) – Σα)                              }

# generate an independent sequence of ε from ε( 0 , 1 )
For( i = 1 to n ){ ε(i) = StdNormNum( ) }
```

construct a correlated sequence of q using (10.8) and (10.12)

For(i = 1 to n){ $q(i)$ = 0

$\quad\quad\quad\quad$ For(j = 1 to i){ $q(i)$ = $q(i)$ + $\alpha(i,j)\,\varepsilon(j)$ }

$\quad\quad\quad\quad$ $q(i) = \mu(i) + \sqrt{\sigma(i,i)}\,q(i)$ $\quad\quad\quad\quad\quad\quad\quad\quad\quad$ }

Code 10.1: Pseudo code of the Cholesky() routine.

```
Sub Cholesky(n As Integer, vc() As Double, mean() As Double, ByRef qvec() As Double)
    Dim rho() As Double: ReDim rho(1 To n, 1 To n)
    Dim alpha() As Double: ReDim alpha(1 To n, 1 To n)
    Dim gen() As Double: ReDim genvec(1 To n)
    Dim i As Integer, j As Integer, k As Integer
    Dim alphasum As Double

    For i = 1 To n For j = 1 To i: rho(i, j) = vc(i, j)/Sqr(vc(i, i) * vc(j, j)): Next j: Next i

    For i = 1 To n
      For j = 1 To i − 1
        alphasum = 0
        For k = 1 To j − 1: alphasum = alphasum + alpha(i, k) * alpha(j, k): Next k
        alpha(i, j) = (rho(i, j) − alphasum)/alpha(j, j)
      Next j
      alphasum = 0
      For k = 1 To i − 1: alphasum = alphasum + alpha(i, k) * alpha(i, k): Next k
      alpha(i, i) = Sqr(rho(i, i) − alphasum)
    Next i

    For i = 1 To n: genvec(i) = StdNormNum(): Next i

    For i = 1 To n
      qvec(i) = 0
      For j = 1 To i: qvec(i) = qvec(i) + alpha(i, j) * genvec(j): Next j
      qvec(i) = mean(i) + Sqr(vc(i, i)) * qvec(i)
    Next i
End Sub
```

Code 10.2: VBA code of the Cholesky() routine.

EXAMPLE 10.2

Consider the following historical set of $n_d = 1000$ daily price returns of the Hang Seng Index (HSI) and the Hong Kong Shanghai Banking Corporation (HSBC) during the period from June 9, 2004 to June 5, 2008.[6] Suppose it is currently June 5, 2008, with daily closings of $S_{HSI,0} = 24{,}255.29$ and $S_{HSBC,0} = 131.30$, and the risk-free interest rate is $r = 5$ percent per year.

(Continued)

(*Continued*)

(I) Use Monte Carlo simulation to determine the one-day 95 percent *VaR* of a portfolio containing the following assets:
- One European call option written on the HSI index with *Strike*1 = 24,500, *Maturity*1 = 0.25 year, and *Volatility*1 = 25 percent per year.
- One European put option written on 100 shares of HSBC stock with *Strike*2 = 130, *Maturity*2 = 0.50 year, and *Volatility*2 = 30 percent per year.

1. As shown in Figure 10.5, the time horizon of the simulation is $T = 1$ day.
2. The historical means and variance-covariance of daily price returns in L6:M6 and L4:M5, respectively, are estimated based on the synchronized data sets in C3:C1002 and E3:E1002.
3. Random samples of $n_s = 5000$ correlated daily price returns $\hat{q}_{HSI,0}(L)$ and $\hat{q}_{HSBC,0}(L)$ are generated by calling the Cholesky() routine in VBA as

```
Sub genMC1day()
    Dim mean(1 To 2) As Double, vc(1 To 2, 1 To 2) As Double
    Dim q(1 To 2) As Double, assetPriceListNow(1 To 2) As Double
    Dim Ls As Long, i As Integer
    mean(1) = Range("MC1day!L6").Value
    mean(2) = Range("MC1day!M6").Value
    vc(1, 1) = Range("MC1day!L4").Value
    vc(1, 2) = Range("MC1day!M4").Value
    vc(2, 1) = Range("MC1day!L5").Value
    vc(2, 2) = Range("MC1day!M5").Value
    assetPriceListNow(1) = Range("MC1day!L7").Value
    assetPriceListNow(2) = Range("MC1day!M7").Value
    seed = 56789
    For Ls = 1 To 5000
        Call Cholesky(2, vc, mean, q)
        For i = 1 To 2: Range("MC1day!F3").Offset(Ls - 1, i - 1) =
        assetPriceListNow(i) *(1 + q(i)): Next i
    Next Ls
End Sub
```

4. The corresponding future asset prices $\hat{S}_{HSI,T}(L)$ and $\hat{S}_{HSBC,T}(L)$ at the one-day horizon are determined in F3:F5002 and G3:G5002, respectively, according to $\hat{S}_{i,T}(L) = S_{i,0}(1 + \hat{q}_{i,0}(L))$.

Date	HSI Close	HSI Returns	HSBC Close	HSBC Returns	Sample HSI Prices	Sample HSBC Prices	Sample MTM Portfolio Prices	Sample Portfolio Returns
8-Jun-04	12344.16		118.50					
9-Jun-04	12339.94	-0.000342	118.00	-0.004219	24254.73	132.33	2061.88	-0.025851
10-Jun-04	12422.87	0.006720	119.00	0.008475	23929.29	130.52	1967.01	-0.070675
11-Jun-04	12396.39	-0.002132	118.00	-0.008403	23843.93	131.98	1868.13	-0.117392
14-Jun-04	12076.57	-0.025799	116.00	-0.016945	24350.82	131.82	2133.41	0.007344
15-Jun-04	12050.69	-0.002143	115.50	-0.004310	24770.96	133.63	2305.90	0.089435
16-Jun-04	12161.78	0.009219	116.50	0.008658	24321.22	131.87	2115.26	-0.000637
17-Jun-04	12082.86	-0.006489	116.00	-0.004292	24233.54	130.66	2116.04	-0.000262
18-Jun-04	11855.55	-0.018813	114.50	-0.012931	23821.45	130.52	1915.10	-0.095201
21-Jun-04	11845.59	-0.000840	115.00	0.004367	23746.72	129.03	1941.18	-0.082877
23-Jun-04	11849.77	0.000353	114.00	-0.008696	23597.02	129.62	1849.08	-0.126391
24-Jun-04	12163.68	0.026491	116.50	0.021930	23978.24	129.95	2014.38	-0.048295
25-Jun-04	12185.52	0.001796	116.50	0.000000	24119.91	130.48	2064.04	-0.024831
28-Jun-04	12194.6	0.000745	117.00	0.004292	24123.14	130.97	2045.88	-0.033411
29-Jun-04	12116.3	-0.006421	116.00	-0.008547	25149.33	134.07	2525.40	0.193140
30-Jun-04	12285.75	0.013985	117.50	0.012931	24355.58	132.62	2105.37	-0.005305
2-Jul-04	12220.13	-0.005341	116.00	-0.012766	23893.07	129.16	2005.72	-0.052384
5-Jun-08	24255.29	0.005474	131.30	0.009224	24158.84	131.30	2051.49	-0.030760
					24363.36	131.83	2139.68	0.010907
					23613.91	128.53	1902.82	-0.101002

Parameters:

		HSI	HSBC	
Horizon T		1		(days)
Historical variance-covariance $\sigma_{ij,T}$	HSI	0.000182	0.000112	(per day)
	HSBC	0.000112	0.000106	(per day)
Historical mean μ_T		0.0767%	0.0155%	(per day)
Current Asset Price		24255.29	131.30	
Strike		24500	130	
Maturity		0.25	0.5	(years)
Volatility		25.00%	30.00%	(per year)
Risk-free Rate		5.00%		(per year)
Current MTM portfolio price		2116.60		
Sample portfolio returns :				
Mean Γ_T		0.1665%		(per day)
Standard Deviation Σ_T		6.4869%		(per day)
1-day 95% VaR		-10.51%		

FIGURE 10.5 Monte Carlo simulation of a multiple-asset portfolio with a one-day horizon.

(*Continued*)

(Continued)

5. The current mark-to-market value of the portfolio is evaluated in L12 using the Black–Scholes call and put pricings as:

$$
\begin{aligned}
\Phi(S_{\text{HSI},0}, S_{\text{HSBC},0}, 0) &= BSCallPrice(S_{\text{HSI},0}, Strike1, r, \\
&\quad Volatility1, Maturity1) \\
&\quad +100 \times BSPutPrice(S_{\text{HSBC}, 0}, Strike2, \\
&\quad r, Volatility2, Maturity2) \\
&= 2116.60.
\end{aligned}
$$

6. The mark-to-market values of the portfolio at the one-day horizon are also evaluated in H3:H5002 as:

$$
\begin{aligned}
\Phi(\hat{S}_{\text{HSI},T}(L), \hat{S}_{\text{HSBC},T}(L), T) &= BSCallPrice(\hat{S}_{\text{HSI},T}(L), \\
Strike1, r, Volatility1, Maturity1 - T) \\
+ 100 \times BSPutPrice(\hat{S}_{\text{HSBC},T}(L), Strike2, r, \\
Volatility2, Maturity2 - T)
\end{aligned}
$$

with sample portfolio returns calculated in I3:I5002 using (10.6). The mean and standard deviation of the portfolio returns at the one-day horizon can then be estimated as $\Gamma_T = 0.1566$ percent and $\Sigma_T = 6.4869$ percent using these samples. The one-day 95 percent *VaR* of the portfolio is given by the left-tail value $\Gamma_T - 1.645\, \Sigma_T = -10.51$ percent.

It is easy to extend the *VaR* measure over a longer time horizon $T_h = hT$. Random sequences of multiple asset price returns for consecutive periods of T can be generated by calling the Cholesky() routine repeatedly for every time step as:

$$
\begin{aligned}
&\{\, \hat{q}_{1,0}(L)\,,\, \hat{q}_{1,T_1}(L)\,,\, \ldots\,,\, \hat{q}_{1,T_{h-1}}(L) \,\} \\
&\{\, \hat{q}_{2,0}(L)\,,\, \hat{q}_{2,T_1}(L)\,,\, \ldots\,,\, \hat{q}_{2,T_{h-1}}(L) \,\} \\
&\quad\vdots \qquad\quad \vdots \qquad\qquad\quad \vdots \\
&\{\, \hat{q}_{n,0}(L)\,,\, \hat{q}_{n,T_1}(L)\,,\, \ldots\,,\, \hat{q}_{n,T_{h-1}}(L) \,\} \qquad L = 1, 2, \ldots, n_s. \\
&\quad\uparrow \qquad\quad \uparrow \qquad\qquad\qquad \uparrow \\
&\text{Cholesky( )} \quad \text{Cholesky( )} \qquad\qquad \text{Cholesky( )}
\end{aligned}
$$

Future asset prices at T_h can be evaluated iteratively with respect to the return sequences as:

$$\hat{S}_{i,T_h}(L) = S_{i,0}(1 + \hat{q}_{i,0}(L))(1 + \hat{q}_{i,T_1}(L)) \dots (1 + \hat{q}_{i,T_{h-1}}(L)) \qquad (10.13)$$

and the procedure can be implemented very easily based on the pseudo code given by:

```
For( L = 1 to n_s ){
          For( i = 1 to n ){ Ŝ(i) = S_{i,0}}
          For( m = 0 to h – 1 ){ Call Cholesky( n, σ(1: n, 1: n), μ(1: n),q̂(1: n) )
                    For( i = 1 to n ){ Ŝ(i) = Ŝ(i)(1 + q̂(i))   }   }
     }
```

EXAMPLE 10.2 (CONTINUED)

(II) Use Monte Carlo simulation to determine the five-day 95 percent *VaR* of the same option portfolio.

	A	B	C	D	E	F	G
1	Sample HSI Prices	Sample HSBC Prices	Sample MTM Portfolio Prices	Sample Portfolio Returns			
2					Horizon T_s	5	(days)
3	24117.63	135.09	1831.83	-0.134540	Current MTM portfolio price	2116.60	
4	22729.36	126.54	1600.66	-0.243756	Sample portfolio returns :		
5	24690.27	132.85	2226.47	0.051907	Mean Γ_{T_s}	0.6907%	(per 5 day)
6	23845.36	126.66	2036.34	-0.037917	Standard Deviation Σ_{T_s}	15.3368%	(per 5 day)
7	24759.16	133.98	2225.94	0.051657	5-day 95% VaR	-24.54%	
8	23838.34	130.21	1878.18	-0.112640			
9	24301.43	132.13	2035.49	-0.038321			
5002	25350.32	134.86	2569.68	0.214062			
5003							

FIGURE 10.6 Monte Carlo simulation of the multiple-asset portfolio with a five-day horizon.

1. As shown in Figure 10.6, the time horizon of the simulation is $T_5 = 5$ days.
2. Random samples of $n_s = 5,000$ future asset prices $\hat{S}_{\text{HSI},T_s}(L)$ and $\hat{S}_{\text{HSBC},T_s}(L)$ at the five-day horizon are generated in A3:A5002 and B3:B5002, respectively, using the VBA code according to (10.13) as:

```
Sub genMC5day()
    Dim mean(1 To 2) As Double, vc(1 To 2, 1 To 2) As Double
    Dim q(1 To 2) As Double, assetPriceListNow(1 To 2) As Double, assetPriceList
        (1 To 2) As Double
```

(Continued)

(*Continued*)

```
Dim Ls As Long, m As Integer, i As Integer
mean(1) = Range("MC1day!L6").Value
mean(2) = Range("MC1day!M6").Value
vc(1, 1) = Range("MC1day!L4").Value
vc(1, 2) = Range("MC1day!M4").Value
vc(2, 1) = Range("MC1day!L5").Value
vc(2, 2) = Range("MC1day!M5").Value
assetPriceListNow(1) = Range("MC1day!L7").Value
assetPriceListNow(2) = Range("MC1day!M7").Value
seed = 56789
For Ls = 1 To 5000
  For i = 1 To 2: assetPriceList(i) = assetPriceListNow(i): Next i
  For m = 0 To 4
    Call Cholesky(2, vc, mean, q)
    For i = 1 To 2: assetPriceList(i) = assetPriceList(i) * (1 + q(i)): Next i
  Next m
  For i = 1 To 2: Range("MC5day!A3").Offset(Ls - 1, i - 1) = assetPriceList(i):
  Next i
Next Ls
End Sub
```

3. Mark-to-market values of the portfolio at the five-day horizon are also evaluated in C3:C5002 as:

$$\Phi(\hat{S}_{HSI,T_s}(L), \hat{S}_{HSBC,T_s}(L)T_5)$$

$$= BSCallPrice(\hat{S}_{HSI,T_s}(L), Strike1, r, Volatility1, Maturity1 - T_5)$$

$$+100 \times BSPutPrice(\hat{S}_{HSBC,T_s}(L)Strike2, r, Volatility2, Maturity2 - T_5)$$

with sample portfolio returns calculated in D3:D5002. The mean and standard deviation of the portfolio returns at the five-day horizon are estimated to be $\Gamma_{T_s} = 0.6907$ percent and $\Sigma_{T_s} = 13.3368$ percent. The five-day 95 percent *VaR* of the portfolio is given by $\Gamma_{T_s} - 1.645 \, \Sigma_{T_s} = -24.54$ percent.

10.3 HISTORICAL SIMULATION FOR MULTIPLE-ASSET PORTFOLIOS

In historical simulation, historical price returns for multiple assets are taken directly as random samples of correlated asset returns for the following period of T. In this manner, we can generate the sample returns as:

$$\tilde{q}_{i,0}(L) = q_i(L), \quad \text{for } i = 1, 2, \ldots, n \tag{10.14}$$

by reading off synchronized price returns from the historical data set given by:

$$
\begin{array}{cccccc}
\{ \; q_1(1), & q_1(2) & , & \cdots & , \; q_1(n_s) & , & \cdots & , \; q_1(n_d) \; \} \\
\{ \; q_2(1), & q_2(2) & , & \cdots & , \; q_2(n_s) & , & \cdots & , \; q_2(n_d) \; \} \\
\vdots & \vdots & & & \vdots & & & \\
\{ \; q_n(1), & q_n(2) & , & \cdots & , \; q_n(n_s) & , & \cdots & , \; q_n(n_d) \; \} \\
\uparrow & \uparrow & & & \uparrow & & & \\
L = 1 & L = 2 & & & L = n_s & & &
\end{array}
$$

Future asset prices at T can then be evaluated as $\tilde{S}_{i,T}(L) = S_{i,0}(1 + \tilde{q}_{i,0}(L))$ with respect to the sample returns. In principle, the adopted samples will exhibit all statistical properties as observed in the past including the correlation among different assets.

For a longer time horizon T_h, random sequences of multiple asset returns for consecutive periods of T can be generated through non-overlapping sequences of historical returns as:

$$
\tilde{q}_{i,T_m}(L) = q_i((L-1)h + m + 1), \text{ for } i = 1, 2, \ldots, n \\
m = 0, 1, \ldots, h - 1 \tag{10.15}
$$

$$
\begin{array}{cccc}
\{ \; q_1(1), \ldots, q_1(h); & q_1(h+1), \ldots, q_1(2h); & \ldots & q_1((n_s-1)h+1), \ldots, q_1(n_s h); & \ldots & , q_1(n_d) \; \} \\
\{ \; q_2(1), \ldots, q_2(h); & q_2(h+1), \ldots, q_2(2h); & \ldots & q_2((n_s-1)h+1), \ldots, q_2(n_s h); & \ldots & , q_2(n_d) \; \} \\
\vdots & \vdots & & \vdots & & \\
\{ \; q_n(1), \ldots, q_n(h); & q_n(h+1), \ldots, q_n(2h); & \ldots & q_n((n_s-1)h+1), \ldots, q_n(n_s h); & \ldots & , q_n(n_d) \; \} \\
\uparrow & \uparrow & & \uparrow & & \\
L = 1 & L = 2 & & L = n_s & &
\end{array}
$$

Again, the maximum sample size is limited to $n_s \leq (n_d/h)$. The future asset prices at T_h can be evaluated with respect to the return sequence as:

$$\tilde{S}_{i,T_h}(L) = S_{i,0}(1 + \tilde{q}_{i,0}(L))(1 + \tilde{q}_{i,T_1}(L)) \ldots (1 + \tilde{q}_{i,T_{h-1}}(L)) \tag{10.16}$$

that can be implemented through the pseudo code given by:

```
For( L = 1 to n_s ){
        For( i = 1 to n ){ S̃(i) = S_{i,0}
                For( m = 0 to h − 1 ){ q̃(i) = q( (L − 1)h + m + 1)
                        S̃(i) = S̃(i)(1 + q̃(i) )} }
        }
```

EXAMPLE 10.3

(I) Use historical simulation to determine the one-day 95 percent *VaR* of the same option portfolio in Example 10.2.

1. As shown in Figure 10.7, the time horizon of the simulation is $T = 1$ day.

2. Historical returns in C3:C1002 and E3:E1002 are taken as the random samples of daily price returns $\tilde{q}_{HSI,0}(L)$ and $\tilde{q}_{HSBC,0}(L)$, respectively. The sample size is limited to $n_s = n_d = 1000$.

3. Future asset prices $\tilde{S}_{HSI,T}(L)$ and $\tilde{S}_{HSBC,T}(L)$ at the one-day horizon are determined in F3:F1002 and G3:G1002, respectively, according to $\tilde{S}_{i,T}(L) = S_{i,0}(1 + \tilde{q}_{i,0}(L))$.

4. The same number of random portfolio returns are generated in I3:I1002.

5. The left-tail pointer corresponding to a 95 percent confidence is given by $I_V = (1 − 0.95) \times 1,000 = 50$, and the one-day 95 percent *VaR* of the portfolio is determined to be $−10.17$ percent.

(II) Now determine the five-day 95 percent *VaR* of the portfolio.

1. As shown in Figure 10.8, the time horizon of the simulation is $T_5 = 5$ days.

2. Random samples of $n_s = Int(n_d/h) = 200$ future asset prices $\tilde{S}_{HSI,T_5}(L)$ and $\tilde{S}_{HSBC,T_5}(L)$ at the five-day horizon are generated in A3:A202 and B3:B202, respectively, using the VBA code according to (10.16) as:

```
Sub genHS5day()
    Dim nd As Integer: nd = Range("HS1day!K4").Value
    Dim ns As Integer: ns = Int(nd / 5)
```

FIGURE 10.7 Historical simulation of the multiple-asset portfolio with a one-day horizon.

	A	B	C	D	E	F	G	H	I	J	K	L
1	Date	HSI Close	HSI Returns	HSBC Close	HSBC Returns	Sample HSI Prices	Sample HSBC Prices	Sample MTM Portfolio Prices	Sample Portfolio Returns			
2	8-Jun-04	12344.16		118.50							Horizon T	1 (days)
3	9-Jun-04	12339.94	-0.000342	118.00	-0.004219	24247.00	130.75	2119.68	0.001458		Current MTM portfolio price	2116.60
4	10-Jun-04	12422.87	0.006720	119.00	0.008475	24418.30	132.41	2147.61	0.014652		n_d	1000
5	11-Jun-04	12396.39	-0.002132	118.00	-0.008403	24203.59	130.20	2119.02	0.001143		n_s	1000
6	14-Jun-04	12076.57	-0.025799	116.00	-0.016549	23629.52	129.07	1886.37	-0.108773		l_v	50
7	15-Jun-04	12050.69	-0.002143	115.50	-0.004310	24203.31	130.73	2097.10	-0.009214		1-day 95% VaR	-10.17%
8	16-Jun-04	12161.78	0.009219	116.50	0.008658	24478.89	132.44	2180.47	0.030178			
9	17-Jun-04	12082.86	-0.006489	116.00	-0.004292	24097.89	130.74	2042.38	-0.035065			
10	18-Jun-04	11855.55	-0.018813	114.50	-0.012931	23798.98	129.60	1942.03	-0.082476			
11	21-Jun-04	11845.59	-0.000840	115.00	0.004367	24234.91	131.87	2068.93	-0.022523			
1001	4-Jun-08	24123.25	-0.010359	130.10	-0.002301	24004.03	131.00	1984.55	-0.062388			
1002	5-Jun-08	24255.29	0.005474	131.30	0.009224	24388.05	132.51	2127.22	0.005018			
1003												

FIGURE 10.8 Historical simulation of the multiple-asset portfolio with a five-day horizon.

	A	B	C	D	E	F	G
1	Sample HSI Prices	Sample HSBC Prices	Sample MTM Portfolio Prices	Sample Portfolio Returns			
2							
3	23678.64	127.98	1900.09	-0.102290		Horizon T_5	5 (days)
4	23850.88	129.59	1909.78	-0.097713		Current MTM portfolio price	2116.60
5	25147.70	135.33	2420.13	0.143407		n_d	1000
6	23927.56	128.51	1992.93	-0.058429		n_s	200
7	23894.38	130.73	1883.89	-0.109945		l_v	10
8	25028.90	132.45	2447.88	0.156615		5-day 95% VaR	-18.56%
201	23616.90	130.41	1769.40	-0.164038			
202	24127.27	131.40	1972.54	-0.068062			
1001							
1002							
1003							

(Continued)

(Continued)

```
Dim qHistory() As Double: ReDim qHistory(1 To 2, 1 To nd)
Dim assetPriceListNow(1 To 2) As Double, assetPriceList(1 To 2) As Double
Dim Ls As Long, m As Integer, j As Integer
For j = 1 To nd
  qHistory(1, j) = Range("HS1day!C3").Offset(j - 1, 0)
  qHistory(2, j) = Range("HS1day!E3").Offset(j - 1, 0)
Next j
assetPriceListNow(1) = Range("MC1day!L7").Value
assetPriceListNow(2) = Range("MC1day!M7").Value
For Ls = 1 To ns
  For i = 1 To 2
    assetPriceList(i) = assetPriceListNow(i)
    For m = 0 To 4
    assetPriceList(i) = assetPriceList(i) * (1 + qHistory(i, (Ls - 1) * 5 + m + 1))
    Next m
  Next i
  Range("HS5day!A3").Offset(Ls - 1, 0) = assetPriceList(1)
  Range("HS5day!B3").Offset(Ls - 1, 0) = assetPriceList(2)
  Next Ls
End Sub
```

3. The same number of random portfolio returns is generated in D3:D002.
4. The left-tail pointer corresponding to a 95 percent confidence is given by $I_V = (1 - 0.95) \times 200 = 10$, and the five-day 95 percent VaR of the portfolio is determined to be -18.56 percent.

10.4 VBA IMPLEMENTATION OF PORTFOLIO RISK SIMULATION

In this section, we consider the implementation of portfolio risk simulation using Excel and VBA. To ensure flexibility and expandability, the implementation is effectively modularized and follows the system architecture as laid out in Figure 10.9. It contains the following modules that perform different tasks in the risk simulation.

Market Data—it provides the current and historical closing prices of all spot assets that could possibly be included in the portfolio.

Trade Data—it defines the portfolio contents and details for each trading contract.

FIGURE 10.9 System architecture of portfolio risk simulation.

Valuation Library—it serves as a function library that provides the pricing formulae for different types of instruments.

Risk Engine—it works as the simulation core that generates sample asset prices driven by the historical data in **Market Data**, and then evaluates sample portfolio values according to the portfolio contents in **Trade Data** with reference to the pricing functions in the **Valuation Library**.

Reporting—it manages the output from the **Risk Engine** and generates the risk report to be displayed.

(1) Market Data

Figure 10.10 depicts the layout of the worksheet "MarketData" with the historical daily closing prices of 20 major stocks on the Hong Kong Stock Exchange during the period from June 8, 2004 to June 5, 2008.[7] The worksheet works as the database for the **Market Data** module that drives the simulation. The cell A1 defines the time horizon T, in number of days, of the historical data. Sequences of closing prices are recorded one column per asset starting from column B onward with the corresponding timestamp given by column A. The top two cells in each column contain, respectively, the ticker symbol of the asset and its denominated currency. The database can be updated by appending new closing prices to the last row of the worksheet. It is also scalable to include more spot assets by adding new columns of historical prices.

	A	B	C	D	E	F	G	H	I	J	K	L	M	N	O	P
1	1.00	hsi.hk	0001.hk	0002.hk	0004.hk	0005.hk	0008.hk	0011.hk	0013.hk	0016.hk	0066.hk	0144.hk	0291.hk	0293.hk	0386.hk	0857.hk
2		HKD	HKD	HKD	HKD	HKD	HKD	HKD	HKD	HKD	HKD	HKD	HKD	HKD	HKD	HKD
3	8-Jun-04	12344.16	59.25	42.1	21.45	118.5	5.35	101	52.5	65.5	11.75	10.45	9.75	14.5	2.95	3.7
4	9-Jun-04	12339.94	59.25	42	21.6	118	5.35	101	52.75	65.5	11.8	10.75	10	14.5	2.95	3.65
5	10-Jun-04	12422.87	59.75	42.3	21.8	119	5.75	101	53.25	65.75	11.85	10.85	10	14.75	2.97	3.7
6	11-Jun-04	12396.39	60	42.4	21.9	118	5.6	100	53.5	65.5	11.85	10.6	9.95	14.6	3.05	3.7
7	14-Jun-04	12076.57	57.75	41.7	21.45	116	5.35	99.25	51.75	63.75	11.3	10.25	9.35	14.25	2.9	3.62
8	15-Jun-04	12050.69	57.5	41.8	21.2	115.5	5.4	99	51.75	63.5	11.4	10.2	9.7	14.35	2.85	3.58
9	16-Jun-04	12161.78	57.5	42.4	21.4	116.5	5.45	99.5	52.25	63.75	11.55	9.85	9.55	14.6	2.85	3.55
10	17-Jun-04	12082.86	56.75	42.4	21.3	116	5.35	99.5	52	63.25	11.75	9.5	9.35	14.35	2.78	3.47
1002	4-Jun-08	24123.25	122.9	66.05	38.4	130.1	4.78	160.6	84	125.4	26.75	33.6	25.55	16.82	7.81	10.84
1003	5-Jun-08	24255.29	125	67.7	39	131.3	4.76	162	83.6	126.4	27.4	34.5	25.3	16.8	8.02	10.86
1004																

FIGURE 10.10 The layout of the worksheet "MarketData" with historical closing prices.

The worksheet works in conjunction with an interface routine called getMarketData() as given by Code 10.3. The routine grabs the following essential information from the worksheet in order to facilitate the risk simulation in **Risk Engine**.

- Time horizon of the historical data (T)
- Total number of assets in the database (n)
- Data length of the historical prices (n_d)
- Ticker symbols of the assets
- Denominated currencies of the assets
- Historical means of the assets for Monte Carlo simulation $(\mu_{i,T})$
- Historical variance-covariance of the assets for Monte Carlo simulation $(\sigma_{ij,T})$
- Historical price returns of the assets for historical simulation $(q_i(1), q_i(2), \ldots, q_i(n_d))$
- Current prices of the assets $(S_{i,0})$.

The size parameters n and n_d can be determined very easily by counting the number of nonblank cells in row 1 and column A of the worksheet, respectively. Ticker symbols and currencies can be read off from the first two rows of the worksheet while current asset prices can be taken from the last row. They are returned to the main program as a one-dimensional array with asset label $(i = 1, 2, \ldots, n)$. Historical price returns are evaluated based on the closing prices, and they are collected inside a two-dimensional array with asset label $(i = 1, 2, \ldots, n)$ as well as time label $(L_d = 1, 2, \ldots, n_d)$. Historical means and variance-covariance of the assets are calculated in a straightforward way using the historical data. They are stored in different arrays with a single asset label for the means $(i = 1, 2, \ldots, n)$ and with double asset labels $(i, j = 1, 2, \ldots, n)$ for the variance-covariance.

```
Sub getMarketData(ByRef T As Double, ByRef n As Integer, ByRef nd As Integer,
                  ByRef tickerSymbol() As Variant, ByRef currencyDenom() As Variant,
                  ByRef mean() As Double, ByRef vc() As Double,
                  ByRef qHistory() As Double, ByRef assetPriceListNow() As Double)
Dim i As Integer, j As Integer, Ld As Integer
T = Range("MarketData!A1").Value
n = Worksheets("MarketData").Range("1:1").Cells.SpecialCells(xlCellTypeConstants).
    Count - 1
nd = Worksheets("MarketData").Range("A:A").Cells.SpecialCells(xlCellTypeConstants).
    Count - 1

For i = 1 To n: tickerSymbol(i) = Range("MarketData!A1").Offset(0, i): Next i
For i = 1 To n: currencyDenom(i) = Range("MarketData!A2").Offset(0, i): Next i

Dim assetPriceData() As Double: ReDim assetPriceData(1 To n, 1 To nd)
For i = 1 To n
  For Ld = 1 To nd: assetPriceData(i, Ld) = Range("MarketData!A2").Offset(Ld, i):
  Next Ld
Next i

For i = 1 To n
  assetPriceListNow(i) = assetPriceData(i, nd)
  For Ld = 1 To nd - 1: qHistory(i, Ld) = (assetPriceData(i, Ld + 1) - assetPriceData(i, Ld))/
  assetPriceData(i, Ld): Next Ld
Next i
nd = nd - 1

Dim sumi As Double, sumj As Double, sumij As Double
For i = 1 To n
  For j = 1 To i
    sumi = 0
    sumj = 0
    sumij = 0
    For Ld = 1 To nd
      sumi = sumi + qHistory(i, Ld)
      sumj = sumj + qHistory(j, Ld)
      sumij = sumij + qHistory(i, Ld) * qHistory(j, Ld)
    Next Ld
    mean(i) = sumi/nd
    vc(i, j) = sumij/(nd - 1) - (sumi/nd) * (sumj/nd) * nd/(nd - 1)
    vc(j, i) = vc(i, j)
  Next j
Next i

End Sub
```

Code 10.3: VBA code of the getMarketData() routine.

	A	B	C	D	E	F	G	H
1		HKD	USD	RMB	EUR	GBP	JPY	
2	Exchange Rate	1.0000	7.7500	1.1364	10.3873	11.7251	0.07834	
3	Annualized Interest Rate	1.5000%	0.2500%	5.5800%	1.2500%	0.5000%	0.1000%	
4								
5								
6								

FIGURE 10.11   The layout of the worksheet "CurrencyData" with currency rates.

In this implementation, we focus on the simulation of portfolio risk due to the random behavior of asset prices. The exchange rates and risk-free interest rates for different currencies are considered to be static parameters in the simulation. Figure 10.11 depicts the layout of the worksheet "Currency-Data" that keeps the latest currency information. It serves as a database for the **Market Data** module in dealing with instruments denominated in foreign currencies. The worksheet works in conjunction with a routine called getCurrencyData() in Code 10.4 that collects the following currency rates from the worksheet:

■ Currency symbols
■ Exchange rates of the currencies to HKD
■ Annualized risk-free interest rates of the currencies.

```
Sub getCurrencyData(ByRef nCurrency As Integer, ByRef currencySymbol() As Variant,
                ByRef currencyRateList() As Double, ByRef riskFreeList() As Double)

    Dim i As Integer
    nCurrency = Worksheets("CurrencyData").Range("1:1").Cells.SpecialCells
      (xlCellTypeConstants).Count

    For i = 1 To nCurrency: currencySymbol(i) = Range("CurrencyData!A1").Offset(0, i): Next i
    For i = 1 To nCurrency: currencyRateList(i) = Range("CurrencyData!A2").Offset(0, i): Next i
    For i = 1 To nCurrency: riskFreeList(i) = Range("CurrencyData!A3").Offset(0, i): Next i

End Sub
```

Code 10.4: VBA code of the getCurrencyData() routine.

(2) Valuation Library

The role of the **Valuation Library** module in risk simulation is to enable *ad hoc* valuation of financial derivatives given sample asset prices. It provides some ready-to-use pricing formulae of derivatives written as VBA functions that furnish the calculation of the market-to-market portfolio value. We have included in this implementation a VBA module called "Valuation Library" that includes the pricing functions for different instruments such as:

Instruments	VBA Functions	Function Parameters
Spot asset:	SpotPrice()	asset price
European option:		
Call	BSCallPrice()	asset price, strike, risk-free
Put	BSPutPrice()	rate, volatility, maturity
Futures:	FuturesContractPrice()	asset price, delivery price, risk-free rate, maturity
Single barrier option:		
Up-and-in call	UpInCallPrice()	asset price, strike, upper barrier,
Up-and-out call	UpOutCallPrice()	risk-free rate, volatility, maturity
Up-and-in put	UpInPutPrice()	
Up-and-out put	UpOutPutPrice()	
Down-and-in call	DownInCallPrice()	asset price, strike, lower barrier,
Down-and-out call	DownOutCallPrice()	risk-free rate, volatility, maturity
Down-and-in put	DownInPutPrice()	
Down-and-out put	DownOutPutPrice()	
Asian option:		
Geometric call	AsianGeCallPrice()	asset price, strike, risk-free rate,
Geometric put	AsianGePutPrice()	volatility, number of maturities, array of maturities

In the simulation, the VBA functions above can be used to price different types of contracts in the portfolio given sample asset prices together with the trading details specified in the **Trade Data** module.

(3) Trade Data

The **Trade Data** module is a database that records the contents of the portfolio and also the trading details for each contract. It works in conjunction with an interface routine called calContractValue() that serves to define the data model in relation to the parameters in the pricing of a derivative contract. In general, a derivative contract can be specified through its attributes defined in **Trade Data** as:

Contract type: (*contractType* as Text)

contractType—{ "Spot", "European Call", "European Put", "Futures"
"Up-and-In Call", "Up-and-Out Call", "Up-and-In Put", "Up-and-Out Put" "
Down-and-In Call", "Down-and-Out Call", "Down-and-In Put",
"Down-and-Out Put"
"Asian Geometric Call", "Asian Geometric Put" }

Contract size : (*contractSize*(1: 2) as array of Double)

    contractSize(1)—total trading units of the contract
    contractSize(2)—exchange ratio to underlying asset

Asset price : (*assetPrice* as Double)

    assetPrice—underlying asset price

Strike price : (*strikeArray*(1: 3) as array of Double)

    strikeArray(1)—strike price of option or delivery price of futures
    strikeArray(2)—upper barrier price of option
    strikeArray(3)—lower barrier price of option

Maturity : (*maturityArray*( ) as array of Double with dynamical size)

    maturityArray(1)—last maturity in years of the contract
    maturityArray(2)—second last maturity in years of the contract[8]

Volatility : (*volatility* as Double)

    volatility—annualized volatility of the underlying asset

Currency exchange rate : (*currencyRate* as Double)

    currencyRate—exchange rate for the denominated currency of the contract

Interest rate : (*riskFree* as Double)

    riskFree—annualized risk-free interest rate for the denominated currency of the contract

The VBA code of calContractValue() that incorporates such data conversion is given by Code 10.5. It returns the mark-to-market value of a particular contract in the portfolio by encoding its attributes from **Trade Data** and then referring to the corresponding pricing function in **Valuation Library**. It should be noted that the scope of the data model can be expanded to include more instrument types by enlarging the sizes of the attribute arrays. For instance, a basket option can be included very easily by expanding *assetPrice* and *volatility* into arrays of double to cater for multiple underlying assets.

```
Sub calContractValue(contractType As Variant, contractSize() As Double,
        assetPrice As Double, strikeArray() As Double, maturityArray() As Double,
        volatility As Double, currencyRate As Double, riskFree As Double,
        ByRef contractValue)
If (contractType = "Spot") Then
  contractValue = SpotPrice(assetPrice)
```

```
ElseIf (contractType = "European Call") Then
    contractValue = BSCallPrice(assetPrice, strikeArray(1), riskFree, volatility, maturityArray(1))
ElseIf (contractType = "European Put") Then
    contractValue = BSPutPrice(assetPrice, strikeArray(1), riskFree, volatility, maturityArray(1))
ElseIf (contractType = "Futures") Then
    contractValue = FuturesContractPrice(assetPrice, strikeArray(1), riskFree, maturityArray(1))
ElseIf (contractType = "Up-and-In Call") Then
    contractValue = UpInCallPrice(assetPrice, strikeArray(1), strikeArray(2), riskFree, volatility,
        maturityArray(1))
ElseIf (contractType = "Up-and-Out Call") Then
    contractValue = UpOutCallPrice(assetPrice, strikeArray(1), strikeArray(2), riskFree,
        volatility, maturityArray(1))
ElseIf (contractType = "Up-and-In Put") Then
    contractValue = UpInPutPrice(assetPrice, strikeArray(1), strikeArray(2), riskFree, volatility,
        maturityArray(1))
ElseIf (contractType = "Up-and-Out Put") Then
    contractValue = UpOutPutPrice(assetPrice, strikeArray(1), strikeArray(2), riskFree,
        volatility, maturityArray(1))
ElseIf (contractType = "Down-and-In Call") Then
    contractValue = DownInCallPrice(assetPrice, strikeArray(1), strikeArray(3), riskFree,
        volatility, maturityArray(1))
ElseIf (contractType = "Down-and-Out Call") Then
    contractValue = DownOutCallPrice(assetPrice, strikeArray(1), strikeArray(3), riskFree,
        volatility, maturityArray(1))
ElseIf (contractType = "Down-and-In Put") Then
    contractValue = DownInPutPrice(assetPrice, strikeArray(1), strikeArray(3), riskFree,
        volatility, maturityArray(1))
ElseIf (contractType = "Down-and-Out Put") Then
    contractValue = DownOutPutPrice(assetPrice, strikeArray(1), strikeArray(3), riskFree,
        volatility, maturityArray(1))
ElseIf (contractType = "Asian Geometric Call") Then
    contractValue = AsianGeCallPrice(assetPrice, strikeArray(1), riskFree, volatility,
        maturityArray)
ElseIf (contractType = "Asian Geometric Put") Then
    contractValue = AsianGePutPrice(assetPrice, strikeArray(1), riskFree, volatility,
        maturityArray)
End If

contractValue = currencyRate * contractSize(1) * contractSize(2) * contractValue

End Sub
```

Code 10.5: VBA code of the calContractValue() routine.

Figure 10.12 depicts the layout of the worksheet "TradeData" that can be used as an interface to insert the trading details for each contract in the portfolio. In each row, the entries in Column B to Column L record the attributes for each contract as discussed above. The ticker symbol in

	A	B	C	D	E	F	G	H	I	J	K	L	M
1	Label	Type	Size (1)	Size (2)	Ticker	Strike (1)	Strike (2)	Strike (3)	Maturity (1)	Maturity (2)	Maturity (3)	Volatility	
2	1	European Call	1	1	hsi.hk	24500.00			0.25			0.25	
3	2	European Put	1	300	0005.hk	130.00			0.50			0.30	
4	3	Spot	500	1	0005.hk								
5	4	Up-and-In Call	-1	500	0857.hk	11.00	13.00		1.00			0.45	
6	5	Spot	500	1	0857.hk								
7	6	Down-and-In Call	1	600	0941.hk	114.00		108.00	0.75			0.40	
8	7	Asian Geometric Call	1	300	0001.hk	130.00			0.50	0.75	1.00	0.20	
9													
10													

FIGURE 10.12   The layout of the worksheet "TradeData" with trading details.

Column E will be used later on to capture the corresponding sample asset price from the simulation. It will also be used to identify the denominated currency for the adopted interest rate as well as the exchange rate for the domestic currency. The routine getTradeData() in Code 10.6 collects all these attributes for a particular contract from the worksheet with reference to the trade label defined in Column A.

```
Sub getTradeData(tradeLabel As Integer, ByRef contractType As Variant,
        ByRef contractSize() As Double, ByRef contractTickerSymbol As Variant,
        ByRef strikeArray() As Double, ByRef maturityArray() As Double, ByRef
        volatility As Double)

    Dim i As Integer
    contractType = Range("TradeData!B1").Offset(tradeLabel, 0)
    For i = 1 To 2: contractSize(i) = Range("TradeData!C1").Offset(tradeLabel, i - 1): Next i
    contractTickerSymbol = Range("TradeData!E1").Offset(tradeLabel, 0)
    For i = 1 To 3: strikeArray(i) = Range("TradeData!F1").Offset(tradeLabel, i - 1): Next i
    For i = 1 To 3: maturityArray(i) = Range("TradeData!I1").Offset(tradeLabel, i - 1): Next i
    volatility = Range("TradeData!L1").Offset(tradeLabel, 0)

End Sub
```

Code 10.6: VBA code of the getTradeData() routine.

It is straightforward to evaluate the current mark-to-market value of a particular contract by first calling getTradeData() for the trading details and then using calContractValue for the valuation. During the course of evaluation, it will require capturing the current price and identifying the currency rates for the underlying asset from **Market Data**. The following VBA procedure will perform such task for the contract with *tradeLabel* = 1, for example, given market and currency information.

```
tradeLabel = 1
Call getTradeData(tradeLabel, contractType, contractSize, contractTickerSymbol, strikeArray,
        maturityArray, volatility)

For i = 1 To n
  If (contractTickerSymbol = tickerSymbol(i)) Then
```

```
    assetLabel = i
    Exit For
  End If
Next i
assetPrice = assetPriceListNow(assetLabel)

For i = 1 To nCurrency
  If (currencyDenom(assetLabel) = currencySymbol(i)) Then
    currencyRate = currencyRateList(i)
    riskFree = riskFreeList(i)
    Exit For
  End If
Next i

Call calContractValue(contractType, contractSize, assetPrice, strikeArray, maturityArray,
  volatility, currencyRate, riskFree, contractValue)
```

The VBA function portValue() as shown in Code 10.7 extends the mark-to-market procedure to the case of a portfolio consisting of numerous contracts. It works as the function Φ in (10.6) that evaluates the mark-to-market value of the portfolio according to the list of asset prices $\{S_{1,0}, S_{2,0}, \ldots, S_{n,0}\}$ at current time with $refTime = 0$. The function also requires the inputs of market and currency information as:

- Total number of assets in the database
- Ticker symbols of the assets
- Denominated currencies of the assets
- Total number of currencies in the database
- Currency symbols
- Exchange rates of the currencies
- Annualized risk-free interest rates of the currencies.

It repeatedly implements the above mark-to-market procedure one contract at a time and accumulates the contract value to the portfolio. The looping stops when there is a blank line in "TradeData" indicating the end of the portfolio content. The mark-to-market procedure can also be extended to forward time $refTime = T$ using random asset prices $\{\hat{S}_{1,T}(L), \hat{S}_{2,T}(L), \ldots, \hat{S}_{n,T}(L)\}$. In this case, the reference forward time will be used to adjust all relevant maturities acquired from "TradeData." It should be noted that irrelevant maturity will always be zero if it reads an undefined blank cell in the worksheet.

```
Function portValue(assetPriceList() As Double, refTime As Double, n As Integer,
        tickerSymbol() As Variant, currencyDenom() As Variant, nCurrency As Integer,
        currencySymbol() As Variant, currencyRateList() As Double,
        riskFreeList() As Double) As Double
```

```vba
Dim tradeLabel As Integer: tradeLabel = 0
Dim contractType As Variant
Dim contractSize(1 To attSizemax) As Double
Dim contractTickerSymbol As Variant
Dim strikeArray(1 To attSizemax) As Double
Dim maturityArray(1 To attSizemax) As Double
Dim volatility As Double

Dim i As Integer
Dim assetPrice As Double
Dim currencyRate As Double
Dim riskfree As Double
Dim assetlabel As Integer
Dim contractValue As Double

portValue = 0
nextContract: tradeLabel = tradeLabel + 1
  Call getTradeData(tradeLabel, contractType, contractSize, contractTickerSymbol,
    strikeArray, maturityArray, volatility)
  If (contractType = "") Then Exit Function

  For i = 1 To n
    If (contractTickerSymbol = tickerSymbol(i)) Then
      assetlabel = i
      Exit For
    End If
  Next i
  assetPrice = assetPriceList(assetlabel)

  For i = 1 To nCurrency
    If (currencyDenom(assetlabel) = currencySymbol(i)) Then
      currencyRate = currencyRateList(i)
      riskfree = riskFreeList(i)
      Exit For
    End If
  Next i

  i = 1
  Do While maturityArray(i) > 0
    maturityArray(i) = maturityArray(i) - refTime
    i = i + 1
  Loop

  Call calContractValue(contractType, contractSize, assetPrice, strikeArray, maturityArray,
  volatility, currencyRate, riskfree, contractValue)
  portValue = portValue + contractValue
  GoTo nextContract

End Function
```

Code 10.7: VBA code of the portValue() function.

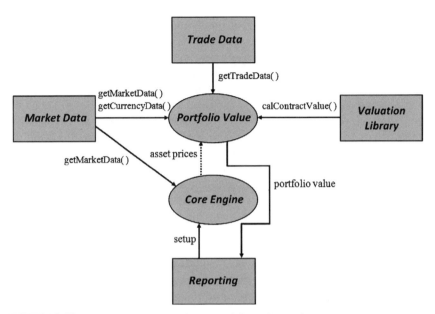

FIGURE 10.13 A schematic view of the portfolio risk simulation.

(4) Risk Engine

The **Risk Engine** module is considered to be the central part of the portfolio risk simulation. It simulates the uncertainty in the future portfolio value by generating random samples of future asset prices. Figure 10.13 illustrates a schematic view of the risk simulation performed by the **Risk Engine** module. It contains two major components, namely the portValue() function together with a core engine. As discussed above, the evaluation of the current mark-to-market portfolio value can be conducted by feeding the portValue() function with market and currency information from **Market Data**. The portValue() function will then evaluate the current portfolio value according to the portfolio contents as recorded in **Trade Data**. The reference forward time is set as *refTime* = 0 and derivative contracts are valued with reference to the **Valuation Library**. The top part of the VBA routine riskEngine() in Code 10.8 implements the mark-to-market procedure at current time.

In the same module, the core engine first acquires the essential market information from **Market Data** and then generates random samples of future asset prices for all assets in the database. For Monte Carlo simulation, the random generation is driven by the historical means and variance-covariance of the assets through the Cholesky algorithm. This refers back to the genMC5day() routine in section 10.2 with a slight modification to cater for the arbitrary number of assets and time steps. In this method, the core engine is given by the routine MCSim() in Code 10.9 capable of generating one set of random asset prices $\{\tilde{S}_{1,T_h}(L), \tilde{S}_{2,T_h}(L), \ldots, \tilde{S}_{n,T_h}(L)\}$ for every single call to the routine. For historical simulation, the random generation is driven by historical asset price returns. In this case, the core engine is given by the routine HistSim() in Code 10.9 that is similar to the genHS5day() routine in section 10.3. Again, it generates one set of historical asset prices $\{\tilde{S}_{1,T_h}(L), \tilde{S}_{2,T_h}(L), \ldots, \tilde{S}_{n,T_h}(L)\}$ for every single call taking the sample number L as a reference pointer in the historical data sequence.

The simulation time horizon should be in multiple steps h of the time horizon T as defined in **Market Data.** The simulation setup such as type of simulation {*Monte Carlo, Historical*}, number of time steps h, and sample size n_s are all specified in the **Reporting** module. Remember that the sample size is limited to $n_s \le Int(n_d / h)$ for historical simulation. The bottom part of riskEngine() performs the portfolio risk simulation by feeding the portValue() function with random samples of asset prices at a specified time horizon. The portValue() function will evaluate the corresponding mark-to-market portfolio values and divert these random samples to the database in the **Reporting** module. The time horizon T in **Market Data** is defined in number of days. It should be converted into a yearly scale through the day count factor $dayCount = 260$ representing the number of trading days in one year. Thus, the reference forward time should be quoted as $refTime = hT/ dayCount$ in the mark-to-market procedure. It is also useful to display the progress of the simulation through the status bar after the completion of every 100 samples.

```
Option Explicit
Public Const nmax = 100
Public Const ndmax = 3000
Public Const attSizemax = 10
Public Const nlocationmax = 100
Public Const dayCount = 260
```

```
Sub riskEngine()

    Dim T As Double
    Dim n As Integer, nd As Integer
    Dim tickerSymbol(1 To nmax) As Variant
    Dim currencyDenom(1 To nmax) As Variant
    Dim mean(1 To nmax) As Double
    Dim vc(1 To nmax, 1 To nmax) As Double
    Dim qHistory(1 To nmax, 1 To ndmax) As Double
    Dim assetPriceListNow(1 To nmax) As Double
    Dim nCurrency As Integer
```

```
    Dim currencySymbol(1 To nmax) As Variant
    Dim currencyRateList(1 To nmax) As Double
    Dim riskFreeList(1 To nmax) As Double

' evaluate the current mark-to-market portfolio value

    Call getMarketData(T, n, nd, tickerSymbol, currencyDenom, mean, vc, qHistory,
        assetPriceListNow)
    Call getCurrencyData(nCurrency, currencySymbol, currencyRateList, riskFreeList)

    Dim refTime As Double
    Dim currentValue As Double

    Range("ReportingData!A:A").ClearContents
    refTime = 0
    currentValue = portValue(assetPriceListNow, refTime, n, tickerSymbol, currencyDenom,
        nCurrency, currencySymbol, currencyRateList, riskFreeList)
    Range("ReportingData!A1") = currentValue

' generate sample mark-to-market portfolio values at forward time

    Dim simType As Variant: simType = Range("Reporting!simType").Text
    Dim hstep As Integer: hstep = Range("Reporting!hstep").Value
    Dim ns As Long: ns = Range("Reporting!ns").Value
    If (simType = "Historical" And ns > Int(nd/hstep)) Then ns = Int(nd/hstep)

    Dim assetPriceList(1 To nmax) As Double
    Dim sampleValue As Double
    Dim Ls As Long

    For Ls = 1 To ns
        If (simType = "Monte Carlo") Then
            Call MCSim(n, mean, vc, assetPriceListNow, hstep, assetPriceList)
        ElseIf (simType = "Historical") Then
            Call HistSim(n, qHistory, assetPriceListNow, hstep, Ls, nd, assetPriceList)
        End If
        refTime = hstep * T/dayCount
        sampleValue = portValue(assetPriceList, refTime, n, tickerSymbol, currencyDenom,
            nCurrency, currencySymbol, currencyRateList, riskFreeList)
        Range("ReportingData!A2").Offset(Ls - 1, 0) = sampleValue
        If (Ls Mod 100) = 0 Then Application.StatusBar = "Done simulation sample " & Ls
    Next Ls

End Sub
```

Code 10.8: VBA code of the riskEngine() routine.

```
Sub MCSim(n As Integer, mean() As Double, vc() As Double, assetPriceListNow() As Double,
    hstep As Integer, ByRef assetPriceList() As Double)
    Dim i As Integer, m As Integer
```

```
Dim qvec() As Double: ReDim qvec(1 To n)
For i = 1 To n: assetPriceList(i) = assetPriceListNow(i): Next i
For m = 0 To hstep - 1
  Call Cholesky(n, vc, mean, qvec)
For i = 1 To n: assetPriceList(i) = assetPriceList(i) * (1 + qvec(i)): Next i
Next m
End Sub
```

```
Sub HistSim(n As Integer, qHistory() As Double, assetPriceListNow() As Double, hstep
    As Integer, Ls As Long, nd As Integer, ByRef assetPriceList() As Double)
  Dim i As Integer, m As Integer
  Dim qvec() As Double: ReDim qvec(1 To n)
  Do While Ls > Int(nd/hstep): Ls = Ls - Int(nd/hstep): Loop
  For i = 1 To n: assetPriceList(i) = assetPriceListNow(i): Next i
  For m = 0 To hstep - 1
    For i = 1 To n: assetPriceList(i) = assetPriceList(i) * (1 + qHistory(i, (Ls - 1) * hstep + m + 1)): Next i
  Next m
End Sub
```

Code 10.9: VBA code of the MCSim() and HistSim() routines.

Reporting

The **Reporting** module is a user-defined interface that analyzes the outputs from **Risk Engine**. In general, it contains a reporting interface together with a database. In this implementation, the worksheet "ReportingData" works as the database that keeps all raw outputs from the simulation. The worksheet "Reporting" demonstrates, for example, a minimal layout of the reporting interface as depicted in Figure 10.14. It defines the simulation

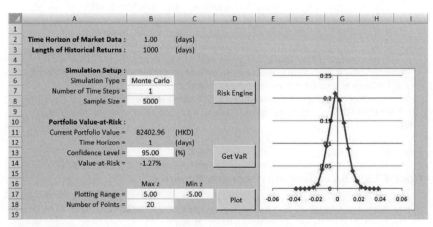

FIGURE 10.14 The layout of the worksheet "Reporting."

setup in B6:B8 (named as simType, hstep, and ns) and displays the portfolio *VaR* in B14 by extracting the relevant information from the database through a reporting tool called getVaR(). The confidence level of the *VaR* number is defined in B13 (confLevel). The VBA code of getVaR() is given by Code 10.10. The reporting interface can also be expanded to include more reporting tools such as a graphic routine that plots the probability distribution of the future portfolio return. The VBA code of this routine is given by Code 10.11.

```vba
Sub getVaR()
    Dim ns As Integer: ns = Worksheets("ReportingData").Range("A:A").Cells.SpecialCells
        (xlCellTypeConstants).Count - 1
    Dim currentValue As Double: currentValue = Range("ReportingData!A1").Value
    Dim sampleValue As Double
    Dim sampleReturn() As Double: ReDim sampleReturn(1 To ns)
    Dim i As Integer
    For i = 1 To ns
        sampleValue = Range("ReportingData!A2").Offset(i - 1, 0)
        sampleReturn(i) = (sampleValue - currentValue)/Abs(currentValue)
    Next i

    Dim simType As Variant: simType = Range("Reporting!simType").Text
    Dim confLevel As Double: confLevel = Range("Reporting!confLevel").Value
    If (simType = "Monte Carlo") Then
        With WorksheetFunction
            Range("Reporting!B14") = .Average(sampleReturn) - .NormSInv(confLevel/100) *
            .StDev(sampleReturn)
        End With
    ElseIf (simType = "Historical") Then
        Range("Reporting!B14") = Application.WorksheetFunction.Small(sampleReturn,
        Int((1 - confLevel/100) * ns))
    End If

End Sub
```

Code 10.10: VBA code of the getVaR() routine.

```vba
Sub genPlot()
    Dim ns As Integer: ns = Worksheets("ReportingData").Range("A:A").Cells.SpecialCells
        (xlCellTypeConstants).Count - 1
    Dim currentValue As Double: currentValue = Range("ReportingData!A1").Value
    Dim sampleValue As Double
    Dim sampleReturn() As Double: ReDim sampleReturn(1 To ns)

    Dim i As Integer
    For i = 1 To ns
        sampleValue = Range("ReportingData!A2").Offset(i - 1, 0)
```

```
    sampleReturn(i) = (sampleValue - currentValue)/Abs(currentValue)
  Next i

  Dim meanReturn As Double: meanReturn = WorksheetFunction.Average(sampleReturn)
  Dim sdReturn As Double: sdReturn = WorksheetFunction.StDev(sampleReturn)

  Dim zMax As Double: zMax = Range("Reporting!zMax")
  Dim zMin As Double: zMin = Range("Reporting!zMin")
  Dim npoint As Integer: npoint = Range("Reporting!npoint")
  Dim inc As Double: inc = (zMax - zMin)/(npoint - 1)

  Dim upper As Double, lower As Double
  Dim j As Integer, sum As Integer

  For j = 1 To npoint
    Range("Reporting!M1").Offset( j - 1, 0) = meanReturn + (zMin + ( j - 1) * inc) * sdReturn
    upper = meanReturn + (zMin + ( j - 1 + 0.5) * inc) * sdReturn
    lower = meanReturn + (zMin + ( j - 1 - 0.5) * inc) * sdReturn
    sum = 0
    For i = 1 To ns
      If sampleReturn(i) >= lower And sampleReturn(i) < upper Then sum = sum + 1
    Next i
    Range("Reporting!N1").Offset( j - 1, 0) = sum * 1#/ns
  Next j
  Charts.Add
  ActiveChart.ChartType = xlXYScatterLines
  ActiveChart.SetSourceData Source:=Sheets("Reporting").Range("M1:N100")
  ActiveChart.Location Where:=xlLocationAsObject, Name:="Reporting"

End Sub
```

Code 10.11: VBA code of the genPlot() routine.

10.5 DRILL DOWN OF PORTFOLIO RISK

It is useful to separate the total portfolio risk into different components with respect to the corporate hierarchy. In this way, the risk contribution from each contract owner can be clearly identified and the risk diversification within the hierarchy will also be transparent. Suppose, the corporate hierarchy can be defined as:

$$\text{Corporate} \rightarrow \text{Divisions} \rightarrow \text{Trading Desks} \rightarrow \text{Traders}.$$

The contract owners are the individual traders. Each of them holds a sub-portfolio that is presumably well diversified among different contracts. The trading desk, on the other hand, holds a larger sub-portfolio combining all contracts from its traders, and the risk diversification now appears among

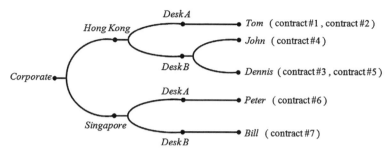

FIGURE 10.15 The Corporate hierarchy inserted in Figure 10.16.

different traders. This works all the way up to the single corporate portfolio at the top of the hierarchy where the risk diversification is considered to be an aggregated effect from many sub-portfolios. Thus, the risk separation enables an important feature of drilling down to the components of the portfolio risk at different locations in the hierarchy.

The risk separation can be achieved by extending the attributes of each contract in **Trade Data** to include the owner's location in the hierarchy. Suppose, for example, that the contracts as inserted in worksheet "Trade-Data" are held by different traders under the corporate hierarchy as shown in Figure 10.15. Figure 10.16 depicts the extended layout of the worksheet "TradeData" that records the trading details as well as the owner's location for each contract.

A drill-down location of interest in the risk separation can be defined using any array of characters such as (*Hong Kong: A: Tom*) that aims, for example, at the sub-portfolio held by *Tom* in *Desk A* of the *Hong Kong* division. It can also be defined at a higher level such as (*Hong Kong: A*) that

Label	Type	Size (1)	Size (2)	Ticker	Strike (1)	Strike (2)	Strike (3)	Maturity (1)	Maturity (2)	Maturity (3)	Volatility
1	European Call	1	1	hsi.hk	24500.00			0.25			0.25
2	European Put	1	300	0005.hk	130.00			0.50			0.30
3	Spot	500	1	0005.hk							
4	Up-and-In Call	-1	500	0857.hk	11.00	13.00		1.00			0.45
5	Spot	500	1	0857.hk							
6	Down-and-In Call	1	600	0941.hk	114.00		108.00	0.75			0.40
7	Asian Geometric Call	1	300	0001.hk	130.00			0.50	0.75	1.00	0.20

Label	Division	Desk	Trader
1	Hong Kong	A	Tom
2	Hong Kong	A	Tom
3	Hong Kong	B	Dennis
4	Hong Kong	B	John
5	Hong Kong	B	Dennis
6	Singapore	A	Peter
7	Singapore	B	Bill

FIGURE 10.16 The extended layout of the worksheet "TradeData" with trading details and owner's location.

aims at a larger sub-portfolio held by *Desk A* in the same division. Thus, the depth of a drill-down location is determined by the first time we see a blank in the array. The VBA function subPortValue() as shown in Code 10.12 extends the mark-to-market procedure to the case of a sub-portfolio specified by a drill-down array. It differs from the portValue() function by adding a routine called checkDrill() that filters out irrelevant contracts. As shown in Code 10.13, the routine checkDrill() returns a flag that confirms whether the owner's location for a particular contract belongs to a drill-down. Hence, the sub-portfolio value is only accumulated from those relevant contracts under the drill-down location.

The full corporate hierarchy is defined in the extended layout of worksheet "Reporting" as shown in Figure 10.17. The array of characters from each row inside the box D23:H33 represents a possible drill-down location in the hierarchy. Altogether, there are *nlocation* = 11 locations in the corporate hierarchy as depicted in B22 (nlocation). The routine getHierarchy() in Code 10.14 collects all these drill-down locations into a two-dimensional character array with two indices given by:

hierarchy(*lptr* = 1, 1) = Hong Kong
hierarchy(*lptr* = 2, 1) = Singapore
hierarchy(*lptr* = 3, 1) = Hong Kong, hierarchy(*lptr* = 3, 2) = A

$$\cdots \cdots \cdots \cdots$$

hierarchy(*lptr* = 11, 1) = Singapore, hierarchy(*lptr* = 11, 2) = B, hierarchy(*lptr* = 11, 3) = Bill

The routine riskEngineDrill() in Code 10.15 modifies the routine riskEngine () in Code 10.8 so as to perform the risk separation. It reads off the corporate hierarchy through getHierarchy() and evaluates the mark-to-market sub-portfolio values for every drill-down locations labeled by *lptr*. The sample sub-portfolio values are again diverted to the worksheet

	A	B	C	D	E	F	G	H	I
20									
21	Corporate Hierarchy :			Drill Down					
22	Number of Locations =	11							
23	Value-at-Risk =	-1.50%	(%)	Hong Kong					
24		-7.58%	(%)	Singapore					
25		-4.38%	(%)	Hong Kong	A				
26		-1.65%	(%)	Hong Kong	B				
27		-13.32%	(%)	Singapore	A				
28		-26.55%	(%)	Singapore	B				
29		-4.38%	(%)	Hong Kong	A	Tom			
30		-13.45%	(%)	Hong Kong	B	John			
31		-1.74%	(%)	Hong Kong	B	Dennis			
32		-13.32%	(%)	Singapore	A	Peter			
33		-26.55%	(%)	Singapore	B	Bill			
34									

FIGURE 10.17   The extended layout of the worksheet "Reporting" with full corporate hierarchy.

"ReportingData" and organized in different columns with respect to *lptr*. The *VaR* numbers at different drill-down locations are determined by calling a routine named getVaRDrill(). The routine getVaRDrill() in Code 10.16 is very similar to getVaR() in Code 10.10 except it looks at the column specified by the pointer *lptr*.

```
Function subPortValue(assetPriceList() As Double, refTime As Double, n As Integer,
        tickerSymbol() As Variant, currencyDenom() As Variant, nCurrency As Integer,
        currencySymbol() As Variant, currencyRateList() As Double,
        riskFreeList() As Double, drillDown() As Variant) As Double
Dim tradeLabel As Integer: tradeLabel = 0
Dim contractType As Variant
Dim contractSize(1 To attSizemax) As Double
Dim contractTickerSymbol As Variant
Dim strikeArray(1 To attSizemax) As Double
Dim maturityArray(1 To attSizemax) As Double
Dim volatility As Double

Dim i As Integer
Dim assetPrice As Double
Dim currencyRate As Double
Dim riskfree As Double
Dim assetlabel As Integer
Dim contractValue As Double
Dim flag As Boolean

subPortValue = 0
nextContract:   tradeLabel = tradeLabel + 1
Call getTradeData(tradeLabel, contractType, contractSize, contractTickerSymbol,
        strikeArray, maturityArray, volatility)
If (contractType = "") Then Exit Function
Call checkDrill(tradeLabel, drillDown, flag)
If (Not flag) Then GoTo nextContract

For i = 1 To n
   If (contractTickerSymbol = tickerSymbol(i)) Then
      assetlabel = i
      Exit For
   End If
Next i
assetPrice = assetPriceList(assetlabel)

For i = 1 To nCurrency
   If (currencyDenom(assetlabel) = currencySymbol(i)) Then
      currencyRate = currencyRateList(i)
      riskfree = riskFreeList(i)
      Exit For
   End If
Next i
```

```
i = 1
Do While maturityArray(i) > 0
   maturityArray(i) = maturityArray(i) - refTime
   i = i + 1
Loop

   Call calContractValue(contractType, contractSize, assetPrice, strikeArray, maturityArray,
         volatility, currencyRate, riskfree, contractValue)
   subPortValue = subPortValue + contractValue
   GoTo nextContract

End Function
```

Code 10.12: VBA code of the subPortValue() function.

```
Sub checkDrill(tradeLabel As Integer, drillDown() As Variant, ByRef flag As Boolean)

   Dim i As Integer
   For i = 1 To 3
      If (drillDown(i) = "") Then GoTo exiti
      If (drillDown(i) < > Range("TradeData!refOffsetCell").Offset(tradeLabel, i - 1)) Then
         flag = False
         Exit Sub
      End If
   Next i
exiti:   flag = True

End Sub
```

Code 10.13: VBA code of the checkDrill() routine.

```
Sub getHierarchy(ByRef nlocation As Integer, ByRef hierarchy() As Variant)

   Dim lptr As Integer, i As Integer
   nlocation = Range("reporting!nlocation").Value
   For lptr = 1 To nlocation
      For i = 1 To attSizemax: hierarchy(lptr, i) = Range("Reporting!D23").Offset(lptr - 1, i - 1).
         Text: Next i
   Next lptr

End Sub
```

Code 10.14: VBA code of the getHierarchy() routine.

```
Sub riskEngineDrill()

   Dim T As Double
   Dim n As Integer, nd As Integer
   Dim tickerSymbol(1 To nmax) As Variant
   Dim currencyDenom(1 To nmax) As Variant
```

```
    Dim mean(1 To nmax) As Double
    Dim vc(1 To nmax, 1 To nmax) As Double
    Dim qHistory(1 To nmax, 1 To ndmax) As Double
    Dim assetPriceListNow(1 To nmax) As Double

    Dim nCurrency As Integer
    Dim currencySymbol(1 To nmax) As Variant
    Dim currencyRateList(1 To nmax) As Double
    Dim riskFreeList(1 To nmax) As Double

    Dim hierarchy(1 To nlocationmax, 1 To attSizemax)
    Dim drillDown(1 To attSizemax) As Variant
    Dim nlocation As Integer, lptr As Integer, i As Integer

    Call getHierarchy(nlocation, hierarchy)

' evaluate the current mark-to-market portfolio value

    Call getMarketData(T, n, nd, tickerSymbol, currencyDenom, mean, vc, qHistory,
        assetPriceListNow)
    Call getCurrencyData(nCurrency, currencySymbol, currencyRateList, riskFreeList)

    Dim refTime As Double
    Dim currentValue As Double

    For lptr = 1 To nlocation
        For i = 1 To attSizemax: drillDown(i) = hierarchy(lptr, i): Next i
        Range("ReportingData!A:A").Offset(0, lptr).ClearContents
        refTime = 0
        currentValue = subPortValue(assetPriceListNow, refTime, n, tickerSymbol, currencyDe-
nom, nCurrency, currencySymbol, currencyRateList, riskFreeList, drillDown)
        Range("ReportingData!A1").Offset(0, lptr) = currentValue
    Next lptr

' generate sample mark-to-market portfolio values at forward time

    Dim simType As Variant: simType = Range("Reporting!simType").Text
    Dim hstep As Integer: hstep = Range("Reporting!hstep").Value
    Dim ns As Long: ns = Range("Reporting!ns").Value
    If (simType = "Historical" And ns > Int(nd / hstep)) Then ns = Int(nd / hstep)

    Dim assetPriceList(1 To nmax) As Double
    Dim sampleValue As Double
    Dim Ls As Long

    For Ls = 1 To ns
        If (simType = "Monte Carlo") Then
            Call MCSim(n, mean, vc, assetPriceListNow, hstep, assetPriceList)
        ElseIf (simType = "Historical") Then
            Call HistSim(n, qHistory, assetPriceListNow, hstep, Ls, nd, assetPriceList)
        End If
```

```
    For lptr = 1 To nlocation
        For i = 1 To attSizemax: drillDown(i) = hierarchy(lptr, i): Next i
        refTime = hstep * T / dayCount
        sampleValue = subPortValue(assetPriceList, refTime, n, tickerSymbol, currencyDenom,
            nCurrency, currencySymbol, currencyRateList, riskFreeList, drillDown)
        Range("ReportingData!A2").Offset(Ls - 1, lptr) = sampleValue
        Next lptr
    If (Ls Mod 100) = 0 Then Application.StatusBar = "Done simulation sample " & Ls
    Next Ls

    For lptr = 1 To nlocation: Call getVaRDrill(lptr): Next lptr

End Sub
```

Code 10.15: VBA code of the riskEngineDrill() routine.

```
Sub getVaRDrill(lptr As Integer)

    Dim ns As Integer: ns = Worksheets("ReportingData").Range("A:A").Cells.SpecialCells
        (xlCellTypeConstants).Count - 1
    Dim currentValue As Double: currentValue = Range("ReportingData!A1").Offset(0, lptr).
        Value
    Dim sampleValue As Double
    Dim sampleReturn() As Double: ReDim sampleReturn(1 To ns)

    Dim i As Integer
    For i = 1 To ns
        sampleValue = Range("ReportingData!A2").Offset(i - 1, lptr)
        sampleReturn(i) = (sampleValue - currentValue) / Abs(currentValue)
    Next i

    Dim simType As Variant: simType = Range("Reporting!simType").Text
    Dim confLevel As Double: confLevel = Range("Reporting!confLevel").Value
    If (simType = "Monte Carlo") Then
        With WorksheetFunction
            Range("Reporting!B23").Offset(lptr - 1, 0) = .Average(sampleReturn) - .NormSInv
                (confLevel / 100) * .StDev(sampleReturn)
        End With
    ElseIf (simType = "Historical") Then
        Range("Reporting!B23").Offset(lptr - 1, 0) = Application.WorksheetFunction.Small
            (sampleReturn, Int((1 - confLevel / 100) * ns))
    End If
End Sub
```

Code 10.16: VBA code of the getVaRDrill() routine.

REVIEW QUESTION

1. How would you include exchange rate risk in the portfolio risk simulation?

ENDNOTES

1. The $p\%$ *VaR* corresponds to the value at $(100 - p)\%$ tail on the left side of the probability distribution.
2. We define asset price return at time t over the time horizon T as $q_t = (S_{t+T} - S_t)/S_t$.
3. Strictly speaking, it should be taken as $Q = (\Phi_{new} - \Phi_{old})/|\Phi_{old}|$ since portfolio value can be negative.
4. Refer to HSI_Historical_daily.xls.
5. W.H. Press, S.A. Teukolsky, W.T. Vetterling, and B.P. Flannery, "Solution of Linear Algebraic Equations," in *Numerical Recipes in C : The Art of Scientific Computing*, 2nd Edition, (Cambridge: Cambridge University Press, 1997), 32–104.
6. Refer to HSI_HSBC_Historical_daily.xls
7. Refer to risk.xls
8. Consider, for example, a one-year Asian option with averaging times at 6 months, 9 months, and 1 year. In this case, we set *maturityArray*(1) = 1 year, *maturityArray*(2) = 0.75 year, and *maturityArray*(3) = 0.50 year.

## CHAPTER 11

The Hull–White Model

11.1 HULL–WHITE TRINOMIAL TREE

In this chapter, we extend the numerical procedures discussed in Chapter 8 and consider a generalized formulation of a stochastic interest rate. This is known as the Hull–White model[1] of instantaneous short rate constructed under the no arbitrage assumption. A particular form of the model is referred to as the extended Vasicek model in which risk-neutral short rate r_t as seen at time t is assumed to follow a mean reverting stochastic process given by:

$$\Delta r_t = \phi(r_t,\, t)\Delta t + \sigma\sqrt{\Delta t}\varepsilon(0,\, 1),\ \ \phi(r_t,\, t) = \theta(t) - ar_t. \qquad (11.1)$$

It has adopted a non-stochastic volatility structure for zero-coupon bond price $P_t(T)$, as seen at time t with maturity at T, as:[2]

$$\sigma_t(T) = \frac{\sigma}{a}\left[1 - e^{-a(T-t)}\right] \qquad (11.2)$$

with two parameters σ and a. The function $\theta(t)$ in (11.1) can be related to the current yield curve as:

$$\theta(t) = 2R_0'(t) + tR_0''(t) + a[R_0(t) + tR_0'(t)] + \frac{\sigma^2}{2a}(1 - e^{-2at}) \qquad (11.3)$$

where $R_0(t)$ is the current interest rate with maturity term t. In its simple form, the risk-neutral short rate process can be constructed based on the current yield curve together with a two-factor parameterization of the bond price volatilities in (11.2).

The Black–Scholes differential equation for derivative $f(r_t,\, t)$ written on short rate can be solved by iterating the explicit finite difference equation[3] backward in time along a two-dimensional grid with sizes Δr

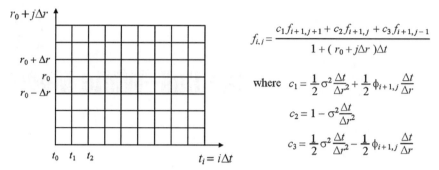

$$f_{i,j} = \frac{c_1 f_{i+1,j+1} + c_2 f_{i+1,j} + c_3 f_{i+1,j-1}}{1 + (r_0 + j\Delta r)\Delta t}$$

where $\quad c_1 = \frac{1}{2}\sigma^2 \frac{\Delta t}{\Delta r^2} + \frac{1}{2}\phi_{i+1,j}\frac{\Delta t}{\Delta r}$

$$c_2 = 1 - \sigma^2 \frac{\Delta t}{\Delta r^2}$$

$$c_3 = \frac{1}{2}\sigma^2 \frac{\Delta t}{\Delta r^2} - \frac{1}{2}\phi_{i+1,j}\frac{\Delta t}{\Delta r}$$

FIGURE 11.1 A two-dimensional grid for the explicit finite difference equation.

and Δt as shown in Figure 11.1. In the figure, we have denoted $f_{i,j}$ and $\phi_{i,j}$ as the values of $f(r_t, t)$ and $\phi(r_t, t)$, respectively, at node (i,j) on the grid. It is important to ensure the convergence of the estimated value to its true value as Δt and $\Delta r \rightarrow 0$. A sufficient condition for convergence of the iteration is that the coefficients $\{c_1, c_2, c_3\}$ are all positive in this limit. This can be satisfied if both $\sigma^2\Delta t/\Delta r^2 < 1$ and $|\phi(r_t, t)|\Delta r < \sigma^2$. Thus, it is necessary for the drift $\phi(r_t, t)$ to be a bounded function, and the ratio $\Delta t/\Delta r^2$ should remain finite and less than $1/\sigma^2$ as Δt and $\Delta r \rightarrow 0$. In (11.1), the drift $\phi(r_t, t)$ in the Hull–White model is not bounded. It follows that the convergence of the explicit finite difference method cannot be ensured.

It can be shown that the explicit finite difference method is equivalent to a trinomial tree approach that utilizes the risk-neutral pricing with movement of risk-neutral short rate on the same grid. To overcome the convergence problem, we may consider a general formulation of a trinomial tree with branching process from node (i,j) to one of $(i + 1, k + 1)$, $(i + 1, k)$, or $(i + 1, k - 1)$ for some middle value of k as shown in Figure 11.2. The branching probabilities $\{p_{i,j}^u, p_{i,j}^m, p_{i,j}^d\}$ at node (i,j) can be determined by

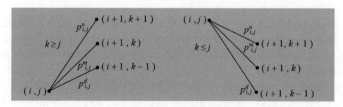

FIGURE 11.2 A trinomial tree with generalized branching process on the grid.

matching the first and second moments of Δr_t given by (11.1). This gives:

$$p_{i,j}^u = \frac{1}{2}\sigma^2 \frac{\Delta t}{\Delta r^2} + \frac{1}{2}\eta + \frac{1}{2}\eta^2$$

$$p_{i,j}^m = 1 - \sigma^2 \frac{\Delta t}{\Delta r^2} - \eta^2 \tag{11.4}$$

$$p_{i,j}^d = \frac{1}{2}\sigma^2 \frac{\Delta t}{\Delta r^2} - \frac{1}{2}\eta + \frac{1}{2}\eta^2, \quad \eta = j - k + \phi_{i,j}\frac{\Delta t}{\Delta r}.$$

Convergence requires the branching probabilities in (11.4) to be positive as Δt and $\Delta r \to 0$. This can be satisfied if we impose the constraint such that $0.25 < \sigma^2 \Delta t/\Delta r^2 < 0.75$ and fix k to be the nearest integer to $j + \phi_{i,j}\,\Delta t/\Delta r$. This means that if Δr is chosen within the range of $\sigma\sqrt{(4/3)\Delta t}$ to $\sigma\sqrt{4\Delta t}$, it is always possible to find a k such that the branching probabilities are all positive. An optimal choice of Δr as suggested by Hull and White in endnote 3 is that $\Delta r = \sigma\sqrt{3\Delta t}$. It then follows that the chosen value of k will always be finite even though $\phi(r_t, t)$ is not bounded in the model. The current value of derivative can be determined by iterating backward along the tree through risk-neutral pricing as:

$$f_{i,j} = e^{-(r_0 + j\Delta r)\Delta t}(p_{i,j}^u f_{i+1,k+1} + p_{i,j}^m f_{i+1,k} + p_{i,j}^d f_{i+1,k-1}). \tag{11.5}$$

The generalized trinomial tree can be considered a modification of the explicit finite difference method to ensure convergence of the iteration.

The risk-neutral drift $\phi(r_t, t)$ in (11.1) can be evaluated at each node on the trinomial tree given the current yield curve together with the parameters σ and a for the bond price volatilities. However, it is clear that the terms $R_0'(t)$ and $R_0''(t)$ in (11.3) cannot be calculated accurately under a finite set of zero rates. In a numerical approach, it is sufficient to construct a tree that is consistent with the current yield curve. The time-dependent function $\theta(t)$ in (11.3) can be calibrated at every time step $t_i = i\Delta t$ on the tree using zero rates $R_0(t_i)$ with maturity terms that coincide with the tree structure. Accordingly, the risk-neutral drift $\phi(r_t, t)$ at every tree node can be evaluated as:

$$\phi_{i,j} = \theta(t_i) - a(r_0 + j\Delta r) \tag{11.6}$$

Define $Q(i,j)$ as the current value of a security that pays \$1 at node (i,j) and zero elsewhere. The value of $Q(i,j)$ for every tree node can be generated using the relationship given by:

$$Q(i+1, h) = \sum_{j=L(i)}^{U(i)} Q(i,j)\,prob(i,j,h)e^{-(r_0 + j\Delta r)\Delta t}. \tag{11.7}$$

where $L(i)$ and $U(i)$ denote the labels of the bottom and top nodes, respectively, at time i. The term $prob(i, j, h)$ is the probability in going from node

(i,j) to node $(i + 1, h)$. For any given j, it is clear that $prob(i, j, h)$ is zero for all h except when h equals one of the $\{k + 1, k, k - 1\}$ for which it becomes the three branching probabilities $\{p_{i,j}^u, p_{i,j}^m, p_{i,j}^d\}$ in (11.4). A trinomial tree is said to be consistent with the current yield curve if the values of $Q(i,j)$ satisfy the condition:

$$e^{-R_0(t_i)t_i} = \sum_{j=L(i)}^{U(i)} Q(i,j). \tag{11.8}$$

At every time step, the function $\theta(t_i)$ can be calibrated to the zero rates using the above condition to give:[4]

$$\theta(t_i) = \frac{1}{\Delta t^2} R_0(t_{i+2})(t_{i+2}) + \frac{1}{2}\sigma^2 \Delta t$$
$$+ \frac{1}{\Delta t^2} \ln\left(\sum_{j=L(i)}^{U(i)} Q(i,j)e^{-2(r_0+j\Delta r)\Delta t + a(r_0+j\Delta r)\Delta t^2}\right). \tag{11.9}$$

A trinomial tree for the short rate in (11.1) with time interval Δt and horizon $T_{tree} = N_{tree}\Delta t$ can be constructed by calibrating with the current term structure of zero rates $\{R_0(t_1), R_0(t_2), \ldots, R_0(t_{N_{tree}+1})\}$ where $t_i = i\Delta t$. Equations (11.4), (11.6), (11.7), and (11.9) can be used iteratively to construct the trinomial tree with initial conditions $L(0) = U(0) = 0$, $Q(0, 0) = 1$, and $r_0 = R_0(t_1)$. Suppose at any time t_i that we have already determined $L(i)$, $U(i)$, and $Q(i,j)$ for all j from $L(i)$ to $U(i)$.

1. Determine $\theta(t_i)$ from (11.9) using $R_0(t_{i+2})$ and then evaluate $\phi_{i,j}$ from (11.6) for all j.
2. For all j, determine the branching probabilities $\{p_{i,j}^u, p_{i,j}^m, p_{i,j}^d\}$ from (11.4) with the value of k in the middle branch taken to be:[5]

$$k_{i,j} = j + \text{CINT}(\phi_{i,j}\Delta t/\Delta r)$$

where the function $\text{CINT}(x)$ returns the nearest integer to the real argument x.

3. Use $k_{i,L(i)}$ and $k_{i,U(i)}$ to update $L(i + 1) = k_{i,L(i)} - 1$ and $U(i + 1) = k_{i,U(i)} + 1$.
4. Except at $t_{Ntree-1}$, update also $Q(i + 1, h)$ from (11.7) for all h from $L(i + 1)$ to $U(i + 1)$.

To generate a trinomial tree with time interval Δt and horizon $T_{tree} = N_{tree}\Delta t$, we should repeat steps (1) to (4) for t_i from t_0 to $t_{N_{tree}-1}$. It would require the current term structure of zero rates $\{R_0(t_1), R_0(t_2), \ldots, R_0(t_{N_{tree}+1})\}$ according to (11.9).

EXAMPLE 11.1

Consider a two-step trinomial tree for the Hull–White model with yearly time interval $\Delta t = 1.00$ and $N_{tree} = 2$. We assume that the bond price volatility structure is parameterized using (11.2) with factors $\sigma = 0.01$ and $a = 0.1$. The trinomial tree can be constructed using zero rates with maturity terms that coincide with the tree structure as given by Table 11.1.

TABLE 11.1 The current term structure of zero rates.

Maturity Terms (years)	Bond Prices $P_0(t_i)$ ($1 par value)	Zero Rates $R_0(t_i)$ (annual)
$t_1 = 1.00$	$0.9533	4.783%
$t_2 = 2.00$	$0.9055	4.963%
$t_3 = 3.00$	$0.8525	5.319%

In the table, zero rates are calculated from the zero-coupon bond prices with a $1 par value as:

$$R_0(t_i) = -(1/t_i)\ln(P_0(t_i)/\$1).$$

Choose $\Delta r = \sigma\sqrt{3\Delta t} = 0.01732$ and assign $r_0 = R_0(t_1) = 0.04783$.

When $i = 0$, we have $L(0) = U(0) = 0$, and $Q(0, 0) = 1$. We can first evaluate $\theta(t_0)$ as:

$$\theta(t_0) = (1/\Delta t^2)R_0(t_2)t_2 + \tfrac{1}{2}\sigma^2\Delta t + (1/\Delta t^2)\ln(Q(0,0)e^{-2r_0\Delta t + a r_0\Delta t^2})$$
$$= 0.00843.$$

For $j = L(0) = U(0) = 0$, the branching probabilities at node $(0, 0)$ can be determined as:

$$\phi_{0,0} = \theta(t_0) - a r_0 = 0.00365$$

$$k_{0,0} = 0 + \text{CINT}(\phi_{0,0}\Delta t/\Delta r) = 0$$

$$p_{0,0}^u = \tfrac{1}{2}\sigma^2\Delta t/\Delta r^2 + \tfrac{1}{2}(0 - 0 + \phi_{0,0}\Delta t/\Delta r) + \tfrac{1}{2}(0 - 0 + \phi_{0,0}\Delta t/\Delta r)^2$$
$$= 0.2942$$

$$p_{0,0}^m = 1 - \sigma^2\Delta t/\Delta r^2 - (0 - 0 + \phi_{0,0}\Delta t/\Delta r)^2 = 0.6223$$

$$p_{0,0}^d = 1 - p_{0,0}^u - p_{0,0}^m = 0.0835$$

(continued)

(*continued*)

Then update $L(1) = k_{0,L(0)} - 1 = -1$, $U(1) = k_{0,U(0)} + 1 = 1$

$Q(1, 1) = Q(0, 0)prob(0, 0, 1)e^{-r_0\Delta t} = Q(0, 0)p_{0,0}^u e^{-r_0\Delta t} = 0.2805$

$Q(1, 0) = Q(0, 0)prob(0, 0, 0)e^{-r_0\Delta t} = Q(0, 0)p_{0,0}^m e^{-r_0\Delta t} = 0.5932$

$Q(1, -1) = Q(0, 0)prob(0, 0, -1)e^{-r_0\Delta t} = Q(0, 0)p_{0,0}^d e^{-r_0\Delta t} = 0.0796$

When $i = 1$, we can evaluate $\theta(t_1)$ using the updated values of $L(1)$, $U(1)$, and $Q(1, j)$ as:

$$\theta(t_1) = (1/\Delta t^2)R_0(t_3)t_3 + \tfrac{1}{2}\sigma^2\Delta t$$
$$+ (1/\Delta t^2)\ln(Q(1, -1)e^{-2(r_0-\Delta r)\Delta t + a(r_0-\Delta r)\Delta t^2}$$
$$+ Q(1, 0)e^{-2r_0\Delta t + a r_0\Delta t^2} + Q(1, 1)e^{-2(r_0+\Delta r)\Delta t + a(r_0+\Delta r)\Delta t^2})$$
$$= 0.01416$$

For $j = L(1)$ to $j = U(1)$, the branching probabilities at nodes $(1, -1)$, $(1, 0)$, and $(1, 1)$ can be determined as:

$j = -1$: $\phi_{1,-1} = \phi(t_1) - a(r_0 - \Delta r) = 0.0111$

$\quad k_{1,-1} = -1 + \text{CINT}(\phi_{1,-1}\Delta t/\Delta r) = 0$

$\quad p_{1,-1}^u = \tfrac{1}{2}\sigma^2\Delta t/\Delta r^2 + \tfrac{1}{2}(-1 - 0 + \phi_{1,-1}\Delta t/\Delta r)$
$\quad\quad + \tfrac{1}{2}(-1 - 0 + \phi_{1,-1}\Delta t/\Delta r)^2$
$\quad\quad = 0.0516$

$\quad p_{1,-1}^m = 1 - \sigma^2\Delta t/\Delta r^2 - (-1 - 0 + \phi_{1,-1}\Delta t/\Delta r)^2 = 0.5380$

$\quad p_{1,-1}^d = 1 - p_{1,-1}^u - p_{1,-1}^m = 0.4104$

$j = 0$: $\phi_{1,0} = \theta(t_1) - a r_0 = 0.00938$

$\quad k_{1,0} = 0 + \text{CINT}(\phi_{1,0}\Delta t/\Delta r) = 1$

$\quad p_{1,0}^u = \tfrac{1}{2}\sigma^2\Delta t/\Delta r^2 + \tfrac{1}{2}(0 - 1 + \phi_{1,0}\Delta t/\Delta r)$
$\quad\quad + \tfrac{1}{2}(0 - 1 + \phi_{1,0}\Delta t/\Delta r)^2$
$\quad\quad = 0.0425$

$\quad p_{1,0}^m = 1 - \sigma^2\Delta t/\Delta r^2 - (0 - 1 + \phi_{1,0}\Delta t/\Delta r)^2 = 0.4563$

$\quad p_{1,0}^d = 1 - p_{1,0}^u - p_{1,0}^m = 0.5012$

$j = 1$: $\phi_{1,1} = \theta(t_1) - a(r_0 + \Delta r) = 0.00764$

$\quad k_{1,1} = 1 + \text{CINT}(\phi_{1,1}\Delta t/\Delta r) = 1$

$\quad p_{1,1}^u = \tfrac{1}{2}\sigma^2\Delta t/\Delta r^2 + \tfrac{1}{2}(1 - 1 + \phi_{1,1}\Delta t/\Delta r)$
$\quad\quad + \tfrac{1}{2}(1 - 1 + \phi_{1,1}\Delta t/\Delta r)^2$
$\quad\quad = 0.4847$

$\quad p_{1,1}^m = 1 - \sigma^2\Delta t/\Delta r^2 - (1 - 1 + \phi_{1,1}\Delta t/\Delta r)^2 = 0.4719$

$\quad p_{1,1}^d = 1 - p_{1,1}^u - p_{1,1}^m = 0.0434$

Then update $L(2) = k_{1,L(1)} - 1 = -1$ and $U(2) = k_{1,U(1)} + 1 = 2$. As t_1 already reaches $t_{N_{tree}-1}$, there is no need to update Q for t_2. The two-step trinomial tree is constructed as shown in Figure 11.3.

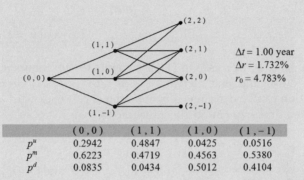

	$(0,0)$	$(1,1)$	$(1,0)$	$(1,-1)$
p^u	0.2942	0.4847	0.0425	0.0516
p^m	0.6223	0.4719	0.4563	0.5380
p^d	0.0835	0.0434	0.5012	0.4104

FIGURE 11.3 The two-step trinomial tree constructed using the zero rates in Table 11.1.

A Hull–White trinomial tree can easily be applied to price interest rate derivatives based on the risk-neutral pricing in (11.5). Consider again a European call option with strike price K and maturity T written on a coupon-bearing bond that matures at later time τ. The bond has a face value of L_{par} and pays regular coupons of value C under the time schedule $\{s_1, s_2, \ldots, s_{n_c}\}$. Similar to the discussion in section 8.2, we need to construct a trinomial tree with a time horizon that covers the entire life of the underlying bond. The size of the time interval Δt must be chosen very close to the shortest maturity term of the available bond prices while it could also reach τ with discrete time steps. Again, market term structures with maturities that coincide with such time increments can be constructed through cubic spline interpolation. In this case, the trinomial tree should be constructed up to the maturity of the underlying bond. The total time horizon is thus given by $T_{tree} = \tau$ with $N_{tree} = \tau/\Delta t$ time steps.[6] Suppose the option matures at time step H on the tree for which $T = H\Delta t$. The maturity payoff of the option $\psi(r_{Hj})$ is evaluated according to the forward price of the underlying bond on the tree node (H, j) given by:

$$f_{H,j} = \max\{K - B_{Hj}(\tau), 0\}, \quad j = L(H), \ldots, U(H). \tag{11.10}$$

The forward bond prices in (11.10) can be determined by iterating (11.5) for the underlying bond utilizing the branching probabilities and short rates on the trinomial tree. The iteration starts off from the bond's maturity at time step N_{tree} with face value L_{par} and works backward to the option's maturity at time step H as:

$$B_{i,j}(\tau) = e^{-(r_0+j\Delta r)\Delta t}(p_{i,j}^u B_{i+1,k+1}(\tau) + p_{i,j}^m B_{i+1,k}(\tau) + p_{i,j}^d B_{i+1,k-1}(\tau))$$
$$+ \rho_i(s_1, s_2, \ldots, s_{n_c})C, \quad j = L(i), \ldots, U(i) \text{ and } k = k_{i,j}. \tag{11.11}$$

The term $\rho_i(s_1, s_2, \ldots, s_{n_c})$ in (11.11) counts the total number of coupon payments during the time interval $(i - \frac{1}{2})\Delta t < t \leq (i + \frac{1}{2})\Delta t$. The current price of the option can be determined by iterating (11.5) backward again for the option from time step H to 0 along the tree as:

$$f_{i,j} = e^{-(r_0+j\Delta r)\Delta t}(p_{i,j}^u f_{i+1,k+1} + p_{i,j}^m f_{i+1,k} + p_{i,j}^d f_{i+1,k-1}),$$
$$j = L(i), \ldots, U(i) \text{ and } k = k_{i,j} \tag{11.12}$$

where time label i is running from $H - 1$ to 0.

11.2 EXCEL PLUS VBA IMPLEMENTATION

We first develop a routine called GenHullWhiteTree() that generates the Hull–White trinomial tree for the short rate in (11.1) given current term structures of bond prices and their volatilities. The pseudo code of GenHull-WhiteTree() is given by Code 11.1. It requires the input of tree configuration (T_{tree}, N_{tree}), current zero-coupon bond prices $P_0(t_i)$ with maturities $\{t_1, t_2, \ldots, t_{N_{tree}+1}\}$, and the parameters σ and a for their volatilities. The routine returns the labels of the bottom and top nodes $L(i)$ and $U(i)$, respectively, at every time step of the tree with i runs from 0 to N_{tree}. It also returns the branching probabilities $\{p_{i,j}^u, p_{i,j}^m, p_{i,j}^d\}$ and the corresponding values of $k_{i,j}$ at every tree node with time label i runs from 0 to $N_{tree} - 1$ and node label j runs from $L(i)$ to $U(i)$. For completeness, short rates $r_{i,j} = r_0 + j\Delta r$ at every node are also returned with i runs from 0 to N_{tree} and j runs again from $L(i)$ to $U(i)$. The time interval of the tree is defined to be $\Delta t = T_{tree}/N_{tree}$, and the rate interval is optimally chosen as $\Delta r = \sigma\sqrt{3\Delta t}$. The zero rates $R_0(t_i)$ with maturities $\{t_1, t_2, \ldots, t_{N_{tree}+1}\}$ are first calculated from the zero-coupon bond prices. The initial values of the arrays $(L(0), U(0), Q(0,0), r_{0,0})$ are defined at t_0 with the use of $R_0(t_1)$ prior to the iteration. It will run from t_0 to $t_{N_{tree}-1}$ taking the zero rates and the volatility parameters as calibration data. At time t_i, the arrays $(L(i), U(i), Q(i,j), r_{ij})$ should presumably be determined up to the same time. Together with the zero rate $R_0(t_{i+2})$ and the volatility parameters, there is enough information to determine the arrays $\{p_{i,j}^u, p_{i,j}^m, p_{i,j}^d, k_{i,j}\}$ at time t_i following the procedures (1) and (2) in section 11.1. Subsequently, the arrays $(L(i), U(i), Q(i,j), r_{ij})$ are updated to time t_{i+1} through (3) and (4) before the iteration proceeds to t_{i+1}. It should be noted that the last update for $Q(i,j)$ at $t_{N_{tree}-1}$ is not necessary in the construction. In (11.7), the term $prob(i, j, h)$ is nonzero only when h equals one of the $\{k_{i,j} + 1, k_{i,j}, k_{i,j} + 1\}$. Thus, it can be implemented very easily using an "If" condition and identifying the corresponding branching probabilities at node (i,j).

The VBA code of GenHullWhiteTree() is given by Code 11.2. It is kept under the module called HWtree[7] and can be used to price the European call option written on a coupon-bearing bond. Similar to the implementation in the BDT tree, we develop a routine called GenHWBondOptionTree() capable of generating the option prices along the Hull–White trinomial tree. The pseudo code of GenHWBondOptionTree() is given by Code 11.3. The routine requires the same input of option parameters $(T, K, \tau, L_{par}, C, n_c, \{s_1, s_2, \ldots, s_{n_c}\})$. It returns the number of time steps H to option maturity together with the bottom and top-node labels $L(i)$ and $U(i)$ at each step. It also returns the option prices $f_{i,j}$ as well as the short rates $r_{i,j}$ at every tree node prior to the option maturity with time label i runs from 0 to H and node label j runs from $L(i)$ to $U(i)$. The routine first constructs the term structures of bond prices and volatilities with maturities $\{t_1, t_2, \ldots, t_{N_{term}+1}\}$, where $t_i = i\Delta t$, using the GenTermStructures() routine in Code 8.5. The size of the time interval Δt is taken to be the closest to the shortest market term where $t_{N_{term}} = N_{term} \Delta t$ exactly matches the maturity of the underlying bond τ. The trinomial tree should be constructed up to the maturity of the underlying bond. Thus, we define the tree configuration to be $N_{tree} = N_{term}$ and $T_{tree} = \tau$. In the current implementation, the term structure of volatilities is not required as it is parameterized by (11.2) in the model. Instead, the parameters σ and a are directly inputted from the Excel worksheet. The corresponding trinomial tree of short rates can be constructed very easily by calling the GenHullWhiteTree() routine. It is then straightforward to use (11.11) and generate the forward prices of the underlying bond for the entire trinomial tree. As discussed in (8.9) and Code 8.3, the external function CouponCount() counts the number of coupons being paid at each time step in the iteration and updates the risk-neutral pricing. In particular, the forward bond prices $B_{H,j}(\tau)$ can be used to evaluate the option payoffs $f_{H,j}$ at maturity and the option prices $f_{i,j}$ at every other tree node can be generated by iterating (11.12) backward in time. The VBA code of GenHWBondOptionTree() is given by Code 11.4.

Figure 11.4 depicts the spreadsheet design for this VBA implementation. For the input of market bond data and option parameters, we have adopted the same design as in the implementation for the BDT tree in

Zero-Coupon Bond Data :

Number of Bonds =	8								
Maturity Terms =	0.083	0.250	0.500	1.000	2.000	4.000	7.000	18.000	(year)
Prices =	0.9963	0.9887	0.9771	0.9533	0.9055	0.8164	0.6948	0.4667	(par = 1)
Volatilities =	0.08%	0.20%	0.40%	0.70%	1.05%	1.26%	1.40%	1.50%	(per year)

European Bond Call Option :

Hull-White Parameterization
σ	0.0091
a	0.6337
Squared-Error Sum	9.52E-07

Option Maturity (T) =	3.00	(year)	Time Steps =	36
Strike (K) =	95.00		Display BDT Tree =	Yes
Bond Maturity (τ) =	4.00	(year)		
Bond Par Value (L) =	100.00			
Bond Coupon Value (C) =	1.50			
Number of Coupons (n_x) =	8			

Payment Schedule :	0.50	1.00	1.50	2.00	2.50	3.00	3.50	4.00	(year)

Option Price (f_0) = 3.713   Hull-White Pricing

Hull-White Trinomial Tree

Forward Time (year) / Short Rate	0.00	0.08	0.17	0.25	0.33	0.42	0.50	0.58	0.67	0.75	0.83	0.92	1.00
0.099													2.857
0.095												2.968	2.960
0.090											3.070	3.058	3.043
0.086										3.163	3.156	3.148	3.138
0.081									3.248	3.247	3.244	3.239	3.233
0.076								3.326	3.329	3.331	3.332	3.331	3.329
0.072							3.397	3.404	3.411	3.416	3.421	3.424	3.426
0.067						3.463	3.473	3.484	3.493	3.503	3.511	3.518	3.525
0.063					3.523	3.537	3.550	3.564	3.577	3.590	3.602	3.613	3.624
0.058				3.578	3.595	3.611	3.628	3.645	3.661	3.678	3.694	3.709	3.724
0.054			3.630	3.648	3.667	3.686	3.706	3.727	3.747	3.767	3.787	3.806	3.826
0.049		3.680	3.697	3.718	3.740	3.763	3.786	3.809	3.833	3.857	3.880	3.904	3.928
0.044	3.713	3.746	3.766	3.789	3.814	3.840	3.866	3.893	3.920	3.947	3.975	4.003	4.032
0.040		3.812	3.835	3.861	3.889	3.917	3.947	3.977	4.008	4.039	4.071	4.103	4.136
0.035			3.905	3.934	3.964	3.996	4.029	4.062	4.097	4.132	4.168	4.204	4.242
0.031				4.007	4.041	4.075	4.111	4.149	4.187	4.226	4.266	4.306	4.348
0.026					4.118	4.156	4.195	4.236	4.277	4.320	4.364	4.410	4.456
0.022						4.237	4.279	4.324	4.369	4.416	4.464	4.514	4.565
0.017							4.365	4.412	4.462	4.513	4.565	4.619	4.675
0.013								4.502	4.555	4.610	4.667	4.725	4.786

FIGURE 11.4   Spreadsheet design of Hull–White option pricing.

Figure 8.2. The Hull–White parameters σ and a for the volatility structure are given by the named cells K10(hwsigma) and K11(hwa), respectively. They are estimated through least squares fitting of (11.2) to the volatility data in B7:L7. Given σ and a, the sums of squared error in the fitting are calculated through an external routine ErrSum2(). Their best fit values can be estimated using Solver by minimizing the squared-error sum under the non-negative constraints for the parameters. The market bond data are inputted into the GenTermStructures() routine through the named cell B4 (nbond) and the entries in rows 5, 6, and 7. The button labeled "Hull–White Pricing" will trigger the main VBA routine called HWPricing() with the VBA code given by Code 11.5. The option parameters are inputted into this routine through the named cells B12(optionMaturity), B13(strike), B14 (bondMaturity), B15(par), B16(coupon), B17(nCoupon), and the entries in row 18. It will call GenHWBondOptionTree() for the arrays of option prices and short rates. The current option price $f_{0,0}$ will be outputted to cell B20. By selecting "Yes" in cell E13, the entire option tree will be displayed in the spreadsheet. It should be noted that the row number for the zero offset of the trinomial tree can be fixed based on its largest top node label "*zeroptr.*" As a reference, the corresponding short rates will also be displayed in column B from B24 onward.

$GenHullWhiteTree(\ T_{tree},\ N_{tree}\ ,\ BondPrice(\ 1:N_{tree}+1\ ),\sigma\ ,\ a\ ,\ k(\ 0:N_{tree}-1\ ,\ L:U\ ),$
$\qquad\qquad p^u(\ 0:N_{tree}-1\ ,\ L:U\ ),\ p^m(\ 0:N_{tree}-1\ ,\ L:U\ ),\ p^d(\ 0:N_{tree}-1\ ,\ L:U\ ),$
$\qquad\qquad L(\ 0:N_{tree}\ ),\ U(\ 0:N_{tree}\ ),\ r(\ 0:N_{tree}\ ,\ L:U\ )\ )$

```
# define the size of Δt and the optimal choice of Δr
```
$\Delta t = T_{tree}\ /\ N_{tree}\ ,\quad \Delta r = \sigma\sqrt{3\Delta t}$

```
# convert the zero-coupon bond prices to zero rates with maturities t₁, t₂, . . . , and t_{N_tree+1}
```
$For(\ i=1\ to\ N_{tree}+1\ )\{\ \ R(i)=-\log(\ BondPrice(i)\ )/(i\Delta t)\ \ \}$

```
# define the initial values of { L , U , Q , r } at t₀
```
$L(0)=0\ ,\ U(0)=0\ ,\ Q(\ 0\ ,0\ )=1\ ,\ r(\ 0\ ,0\ )=R(1)$

$For(\ i=0\ to\ N_{tree}-1\ )\{$

```
    # At time step i in the following loop, { L , U , Q , r } have presumably been determined up to tᵢ
    # determine θ at tᵢ
```
$\qquad Q_{sum}=0$
$\qquad For(\ j=L(i)\ to\ U(i)\ )\{\ \ Q_{sum}=Q_{sum}+Q(\ i\ ,j\ )\exp(\ -2\ r(\ i\ ,j\ )\ \Delta t + a r(\ i\ ,j\ )\ \Delta t^2\ )\ \ \}$
$\qquad \theta = (1/\Delta t)\ (\ i+2\ )\ R(\ i+2\ )+\tfrac{1}{2}\sigma^2\Delta t+(1/\Delta t^2)\ \ln(\ Q_{sum}\ )$

```
    # determine { p^u, p^m , p^d , k } for all nodes at tᵢ
```
$\qquad For(\ j=L(i)\ to\ U(i)\ )\{\ \ \phi = \theta - a r(\ i\ ,j\ )$
$\qquad\qquad k(\ i\ ,j\ )=j+CINT(\ \phi\ (\Delta t/\Delta r)\ )$
$\qquad\qquad \eta = j - k(\ i\ ,j\ )+\phi\ (\Delta t/\Delta r)$
$\qquad\qquad p^u(\ i\ ,j\ )=\tfrac{1}{2}\sigma^2(\Delta t/\Delta r^2)+\tfrac{1}{2}\eta+\tfrac{1}{2}\eta^2$
$\qquad\qquad p^m(\ i\ ,j\ )=1-\sigma^2(\Delta t/\Delta r^2)-\eta^2$
$\qquad\qquad p^d(\ i\ ,j\ )=1-p^u(\ i\ ,j\ )-p^m(\ i\ ,j\ )\ \ \}$

```
    # update { L , U , Q , r } to t_{i+1}
```
$\qquad\qquad L(i+1)=k(\ i\ ,L(i)\ )-1$
$\qquad\qquad U(i+1)=k(\ i\ ,U(i)\ )+1$
$\qquad\qquad For(\ h=L(i+1)\ to\ U(i+1)\ )\{$
$\qquad\qquad\qquad r(\ i+1\ ,h\ )=r(\ 0\ ,0\ )+h\Delta r$
$\qquad\qquad\qquad If\ (\ i=N_{tree}-1\ )\ then\ Next\ h$
$\qquad\qquad\qquad Q_{sum}=0$
$\qquad\qquad\qquad For(\ j=L(i)\ to\ U(i)\ )\{$
$\qquad\qquad\qquad\qquad If\ (\ h=k(\ i\ ,j\ )+1\ )\ then$
$\qquad\qquad\qquad\qquad Q_{sum}=Q_{sum}+Q(\ i\ ,j\ )\ p^u(\ i\ ,j\ )\exp(\ -r(\ i\ ,j\ )\Delta t\ )$
$\qquad\qquad\qquad\qquad Elseif\ (\ h=k(\ i\ ,j\ )\ )\ then$
$\qquad\qquad\qquad\qquad Q_{sum}=Q_{sum}+Q(\ i\ ,j\ )\ p^m(\ i\ ,j\ )\exp(\ -r(\ i\ ,j\ )\Delta t\ )$
$\qquad\qquad\qquad\qquad Elseif\ (\ h=k(\ i\ ,j\ )-1\ )\ then$
$\qquad\qquad\qquad\qquad Q_{sum}=Q_{sum}+Q(\ i\ ,j\ )\ p^d(\ i\ ,j\ )\exp(\ -r(\ i\ ,j\ )\Delta t\ )$
$\qquad\qquad\qquad\qquad Endif\ \ \}$
$\qquad\qquad\qquad Q(\ i+1\ ,h\ )=Q_{sum}\qquad \}$
$\qquad\qquad \}$

Code 11.1: Pseudo code of the GenHullWhiteTree() routine.

```
Sub GenHullWhiteTree(Ttree As Double, Ntree As Integer, bondPrice() As Double, sigma As
    Double, a As Double, ByRef kmat() As Integer, ByRef pu() As Double,
```

```
        ByRef pm() As Double, ByRef pd() As Double, ByRef Lower() As Integer,
        ByRef Upper() As Integer, ByRef rshort() As Double)
Dim dtime As Double: dtime = Ttree / Ntree
Dim dr As Double: dr = sigma * Sqr(3 * dtime)
Dim i As Integer, j As Integer, h As Integer
Dim Qsum As Double, theta As Double, phi As Double, eta As Double
Dim Q() As Double: ReDim Q(0 To Ntree, - 5 * Ntree To 5 * Ntree)
Dim zeroRate() As Double: ReDim zeroRate(1 To Ntree + 1)

For i = 1 To Ntree + 1:   zeroRate(i) = -Log(bondPrice(i)) / (i * dtime): Next i

Lower(0) = 0
Upper(0) = 0
Q(0, 0) = 1
rshort(0, 0) = zeroRate(1)
For i = 0 To Ntree - 1
  Qsum = 0
  For j = Lower(i) To Upper(i)
    Qsum = Qsum + Q(i, j) * Exp(- 2 * rshort(i, j) * dtime + a * rshort(i, j) * dtime ^ 2)
  Next j
  theta = (i + 2) * zeroRate(i + 2) / dtime + 0.5 * sigma ^ 2 * dtime + Log(Qsum) / dtime ^ 2

  For j = Lower(i) To Upper(i)
    phi = theta - a * rshort(i, j)
    kmat(i, j) = j + CInt(phi * (dtime / dr))
    eta = j - kmat(i, j) + phi * (dtime / dr)
    pu(i, j) = 0.5 * sigma ^ 2 * (dtime / dr ^ 2) + 0.5 * eta + 0.5 * eta ^ 2
    pm(i, j) = 1 - sigma ^ 2 * (dtime / dr ^ 2) - eta ^ 2
    pd(i, j) = 1 - pu(i, j) - pm(i, j)
  Next j
  Lower(i + 1) = kmat(i, Lower(i)) - 1
  Upper(i + 1) = kmat(i, Upper(i)) + 1

  For h = Lower(i + 1) To Upper(i + 1)
    rshort(i + 1, h) = rshort(0, 0) + h * dr
    If (i = Ntree - 1) Then GoTo Nexth
    Qsum = 0
    For j = Lower(i) To Upper(i)
      If (h = kmat(i, j) + 1) Then
        Qsum = Qsum + Q(i, j) * pu(i, j) * Exp(- rshort(i, j) * dtime)
      ElseIf (h = kmat(i, j)) Then
        Qsum = Qsum + Q(i, j) * pm(i, j) * Exp(- rshort(i, j) * dtime)
      ElseIf (h = kmat(i, j) - 1) Then
        Qsum = Qsum + Q(i, j) * pd(i, j) * Exp(- rshort(i, j) * dtime)
      End If
    Next j
    Q(i + 1, h) = Qsum
  Nexth: Next h
Next i

End Sub
```

Code 11.2: VBA code of the GenHullWhiteTree() routine.

$GenHWBondOptionTree(\ T\,,K\,,\tau\,,L_{par}\,,C\,,n_c\,,s(\ 1:n_c\ )\,,H\,,L(\ 0:H\ )\,,U(\ 0:H\ )\,,$
$\qquad\qquad\qquad r(\ 0:H,0:H\ )\,,\ f(\ 0:H,0:H\ )\ )$

generate the market term structures with horizon $\tau+\Delta t$
Call GenTermStructures$(\ \tau\,,1\,,N_{term}\,,\Delta t\,,BondPrice(\ 1:N_{term}+1\ )\,,BondVol(\ 1:N_{term}+1\ )\ )$

input from EXCEL the parameters σ and a
Read σ and a

define BDT tree configuration
$N_{tree}=N_{term}\ ,\ T_{tree}=\tau$

generate the Hull-White tree with N_{tree} steps and horizon T_{tree}
Call GenHullWhiteTree$(\ T_{tree}\,,N_{tree}\,,BondPrice(\ 1:N_{tree}+1\ )\,,\sigma\,,a\,,k(\ 0:N_{tree}-1\,,L:U\ )\,,$
$\qquad\qquad p^u(\ 0:N_{tree}-1\,,L:U\ )\,,p^m(\ 0:N_{tree}-1\,,L:U\ )\,,p^d(\ 0:N_{tree}-1\,,L:U\ )\,,$
$\qquad\qquad L(\ 0:N_{tree}\ )\,,U(\ 0:N_{tree}\ )\,,r(\ 0:N_{tree}\,,L:U\ )\ )$

define the time label at option maturity
$H=\text{Int}(\ T\,/\,\Delta t\ )$

generate the forward prices of the underlying bond

$\rho=CouponCount(\ (\ N_{tree}-\tfrac{1}{2}\ )\Delta t\,,(\ N_{tree}+\tfrac{1}{2}\ )\Delta t\,,n_c\,,s(\ 1:n_c\ )\ )$
For$(\ j=L(N_{tree}\ )$ to $U(N_{tree}\ )\ )\{\ B_{forward}(\ N_{tree}\,,j\ )=L_{par}+\rho C\ \}$

For$(\ i=N_{tree}-1$ to $0\,,-1\ )\{$
$\quad \rho=CouponCount(\ (\ i-\tfrac{1}{2}\ )\Delta t\,,(\ i+\tfrac{1}{2}\ )\Delta t\,,n_c\,,s(\ 1:n_c\ )\ )$
$\quad$For$(\ j=L(i)$ to $U(i)\ )\{\ B_{forward}(\ i\,,j\ )=e^{-r(i\,,j)\,\Delta t}[\ p^u(\ i\,,j\ )\,B_{forward}(\ i+1\,,k(\ i\,,j\ )+1)$
$\qquad\qquad\qquad\qquad\qquad\qquad\qquad\qquad\qquad +p^m(\ i\,,j\ )\,B_{forward}(\ i+1\,,k(\ i\,,j\ ))$
$\qquad\qquad\qquad\qquad\qquad\qquad\qquad\qquad\qquad +p^d(\ i\,,j\ )\,B_{forward}(\ i+1\,,k(\ i\,,j\ )-1)\ ]+\rho C\}$
$\qquad\qquad\}$

generate the option prices

For$(\ j=L(H)$ to $U(H)\ )\{\ f(\ H\,,j\ )=Payoff(\ K\,,B_{forward}(\ H\,,j\ )\ )\ \}$

For$(\ i=H-1$ to $0\,,-1\ )\{$
$\quad$For$(\ j=L(i)$ to $U(i)\ )\{\ f(\ i\,,j\ )=e^{-r(i\,,j)\,\Delta t}[\ p^u(\ i\,,j\ )\,f(\ i+1\,,k(\ i\,,j\ )+1)$
$\qquad\qquad\qquad\qquad\qquad\qquad\qquad\qquad +p^m(\ i\,,j\ )\,f(\ i+1\,,k(\ i\,,j\ ))$
$\qquad\qquad\qquad\qquad\qquad\qquad\qquad\qquad +p^d(\ i\,,j\ )\,f(\ i+1\,,k(\ i\,,j\ )-1)]\ \}$
$\qquad\qquad\}$

Code 11.3: Pseudo code of the GenHWBondOptionTree() routine.

```
Sub GenHWBondOptionTree(optionMaturity As Double, strike As Double,
        bondMaturity As Double, par As Double, coupon As Double, nCoupon As Integer,
        paymentSchedule() As Double, ByRef Hf As Integer, ByRef Lower() As Integer,
        ByRef Upper() As Integer, ByRef rshort() As Double, ByRef fTree() As Double)
    Dim bondPrice(1 To nTreeMax + 1) As Double
    Dim bondVol(1 To nTreeMax + 1) As Double
    Dim i As Integer, j As Integer, k As Integer
```

```
Dim Nterm As Integer, dtime As Double

Call GenTermStructures(bondMaturity, 1, Nterm, dtime, bondPrice, bondVol)

Dim sigma As Double: sigma = Range("hwsigma").Value
Dim a As Double: a = Range("hwa").Value

Dim Ntree As Integer: Ntree = Nterm
Dim Ttree As Double: Ttree = bondMaturity
Dim kmat() As Integer: ReDim kmat(0 To Ntree - 1, - 5 * Ntree To 5 * Ntree)
Dim pu() As Double: ReDim pu(0 To Ntree - 1, - 5 * Ntree To 5 * Ntree)
Dim pm() As Double: ReDim pm(0 To Ntree - 1, - 5 * Ntree To 5 * Ntree)
Dim pd() As Double: ReDim pd(0 To Ntree - 1, - 5 * Ntree To 5 * Ntree)
Dim Bf() As Double: ReDim Bf(0 To Ntree, - 5 * Ntree To 5 * Ntree)

Call GenHullWhiteTree(Ttree, Ntree, bondPrice, sigma, a, kmat, pu, pm, pd, Lower, Upper,
    rshort)

Hf = Int(optionMaturity / dtime)

i = Ntree
Dim rho As Integer
rho = CouponCount((i - 0.5) * dtime, (i + 0.5) * dtime, nCoupon, paymentSchedule)
For j = Lower(i) To Upper(i): Bf(i, j) = par + rho * coupon: Next j

For i = Ntree - 1 To 0 Step - 1
    rho = CouponCount((i - 0.5) * dtime, (i + 0.5) * dtime, nCoupon, paymentSchedule)
    For j = Lower(i) To Upper(i)
        k = kmat(i, j)
        Bf(i, j) = Exp(-rshort(i, j) * dtime) * (pu(i, j) * Bf(i + 1, k + 1) + pm(i, j) * Bf(i + 1, k) + pd(i, j)
        * Bf(i + 1, k - 1)) + rho * coupon
    Next j
Next i

For j = Lower(Hf) To Upper(Hf): fTree(Hf, j) = Payoff(strike, Bf(Hf, j)): Next j

For i = Hf - 1 To 0 Step -1
    For j = Lower(i) To Upper(i)
        k = kmat(i, j)
        fTree(i, j) = Exp(-rshort(i, j) * dtime) * (pu(i, j) * fTree(i + 1, k + 1) + pm(i, j) * fTree(i + 1, k)
        + pd(i, j) * fTree(i + 1, k - 1))
    Next j
Next i
End Sub
```

Code 11.4: VBA code of the GenHWBondOptionTree() routine.

```
Sub HWPricing()
    Dim i As Integer, j As Integer
    Dim rshort(0 To nTreeMax, − 5 * nTreeMax To 5 * nTreeMax) As Double
```

```
Dim fTree(0 To nTreeMax, − 5 * nTreeMax To 5 * nTreeMax) As Double
Dim Lower(0 To nTreeMax) As Integer
Dim Upper(0 To nTreeMax) As Integer
Dim Hf As Integer, zeroptr As Integer

Dim optionMaturity As Double: optionMaturity = Range("optionMaturity").Value
Dim strike As Double: strike = Range("strike").Value
Dim bondMaturity As Double: bondMaturity = Range("bondMaturity").Value
Dim par As Double: par = Range("par").Value
Dim coupon As Double: coupon = Range("coupon").Value
Dim nCoupon As Integer: nCoupon = Range("nCoupon").Value
Dim paymentSchedule() As Double: ReDim paymentSchedule(0 To nCoupon)

For i = 1 To nCoupon: paymentSchedule(i) = Range("A18").Offset(0, i): Next i

Call GenHWBondOptionTree(optionMaturity, strike, bondMaturity, par, coupon, nCoupon,
    paymentSchedule, Hf, Lower(), Upper(), rshort(), fTree())

Range("B20").Value = fTree(0, 0)

Range("B23:IV150").ClearContents

zeroptr = 0
For i = 0 To Hf
    If (Upper(i) > Upper(zeroptr)) Then zeroptr = i
Next i

If (Range("E13").Text = "Yes") Then
    For i = 0 To Hf
        Range("B23").Offset(0, i + 1) = i * (optionMaturity / Hf)
        For j = Lower(i) To Upper(i)
            Range("B23").Offset(Upper(zeroptr) - j + 1, i + 1) = fTree(i, j)
            Range("B23").Offset(Upper(zeroptr) - j + 1, 0) = rshort(i, j)
        Next j
    Next i
End If

End Sub
```

Code 11.5: VBA code of the HWPricing() routine.

11.3 THE GENERAL HULL–WHITE MODEL

In this section, we consider a general Hull–White model for the risk-neutral short rate that involves two time-dependent functions in the drift term given by:

$$\Delta r_t = \phi(r_t,\, t)\Delta t + \sigma\sqrt{\Delta t}\varepsilon(0,\, 1),\; \phi(r_t,\, t) = \theta(t) - \psi(t)r_t. \qquad (11.13)$$

In this model, the volatility function in endnote 2 is again taken to be a constant factor σ. It can be shown that the functions $\theta(t)$ and $\psi(t)$ can be related to the current yield curve and the current bond price volatility structure.[8] Thus, the risk-neutral short rate process in (11.13) can be constructed using the two market term structures. The extension to construct a trinomial tree that is consistent with yield and volatility data requires a change to the geometry of the trinomial tree. The tree is made binomial during the first time step $t_1 = \Delta t$ with equal probabilities for the up and down scenarios, and is reverting to trinomial thereafter as shown in Figure 11.5. This is analogous to the case of a BDT tree for which the forward zero-coupon bond prices $P_{1,U}(\tau)$ and $P_{1,D}(\tau)$, with maturity at $\tau > t_1$, on the binomial tree can be related to the market term structures as:[9]

$$P_{1,U}(\tau) = \frac{2e^{r_0\Delta t}e^{-R_0(\tau)\tau}}{1 + exp(2\sigma_0(\tau)\sqrt{\Delta t})}, \quad P_{1,D}(\tau) = \frac{2e^{r_0\Delta t}e^{-R_0(\tau)\tau}}{1 + exp(-2\sigma_0(\tau)\sqrt{\Delta t})}. \quad (11.14)$$

The trinomial tree from t_1 onward to $t_{N_{tree}}$ can be constructed using a procedure similar to that in Section 11.1 by calibrating with the forward zero rates at the binomial nodes $(1, U)$ and $(1, D)$. The zero rates $\{R_{1,U}(t_2), R_{1,U}(t_3), \ldots, R_{1,U}(t_{N_{tree}+1})\}$ and $\{R_{1,D}(t_2), R_{1,D}(t_3), \ldots, R_{1,D}(t_{N_{tree}+1})\}$ can be determined from (11.14) as:

$$R_{1,j}(t_i) = -\frac{1}{t_i - t_1}\ln P_{1,j}(t_i), \quad J = D, U \quad (11.15)$$

using the market term structures $\{R_0(t_1), R_0(t_2), \ldots, R_0(t_{N_{tree}+1})\}$ and $\{\sigma_0(t_1), \sigma_0(t_2), \ldots, \sigma_0(t_{N_{tree}+1})\}$. The short rates at the leading binomial nodes are given by $r_0 = R_0(t_1)$, $r_{1,U} = R_{1,U}(t_2)$, and $r_{1,D} = R_{1,D}(t_2)$. For $t_i \geq t_2$, the trinomial nodes are equally spaced with $r_{i,j} = r_0 + j\Delta r$ where again $\Delta r = \sigma\sqrt{3\Delta t}$, and the factor σ is estimated to be $\sigma = \sigma_0'(0) = (1/\Delta t)\sigma_0(t_1)$ as $\sigma_0(0) = 0$. It should be noted that $r_{1,U}$ and $r_{1,D}$ are not necessarily fitted into a trinomial lattice with grid size Δr. In fact, it can be shown that[10] the size of the interval between $r_{1,U}$ and $r_{1,D}$ is approximately given by $(4/\sqrt{3})\Delta r$. The branching process from t_1 to t_2 requires a slight modification in describing

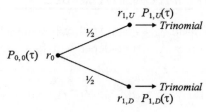

FIGURE 11.5 The leading binomial step in a Hull–White tree.

the transitions from $r_{1,U}$ and $r_{1,D}$ into the trinomial lattice. The branching probabilities at nodes $(1, U)$ and $(1, D)$ are given by:

$$p_{1,j}^u = \frac{1}{2}\sigma^2 \frac{\Delta t}{\Delta r^2} + \frac{1}{2}\zeta + \frac{1}{2}\zeta^2$$

$$p_{1,j}^m = 1 - \sigma^2 \frac{\Delta t}{\Delta r^2} - \zeta^2 \qquad (11.16)$$

$$p_{1,j}^d = \frac{1}{2}\sigma^2 \frac{\Delta t}{\Delta r^2} - \frac{1}{2}\zeta + \frac{1}{2}\zeta^2, \quad \zeta = \frac{(r_{1,j} - r_0)}{\Delta r} - k + \phi_{1,j}\frac{\Delta t}{\Delta r}, \quad j = D, U$$

with the values of k in the middle branches taken to be:

$$k_{1,j} = \text{CINT}\left(\frac{(r_{1,j} - r_0)}{\Delta r} + \phi_{1,j}\frac{\Delta t}{\Delta r}\right), \quad j = D, U. \qquad (11.17)$$

The node label at time t_1 is running over the binomial cases $L(1) = D$ and $U(1) = U$. At time t_2, it can be shown that the branching rule will never skip any internal point between $k_{1,D} + 1$ and $k_{1,U} - 1$ on the lattice.[11] The node label at t_2 is then running from $L(2) = k_{1,L(1)} - 1$ to $U(2) = k_{1,U(1)}+1$.

The risk-neutral drift $\phi(r_t, t)$ at every tree node can be evaluated as:

$$\phi_{i,j} = \theta(t_i) - \psi(t_i)r_{i,j}. \qquad (11.18)$$

The time-dependent functions $\theta(t)$ and $\psi(t)$ in (11.18) can be calibrated at every time step on the tree except t_0 using the forward zero rates at nodes $(1, U)$ and $(1, D)$.

Define:

$Q_U(i,j)$ as the value of a security as seen at node $(1, U)$ that pays \$1 at node (i,j) and zero elsewhere.

$Q_D(i,j)$ as the value of a security as seen at node $(1, D)$ that pays \$1 at node (i,j) and zero elsewhere.

The values of $Q_U(i,j)$ and $Q_D(i,j)$ for every tree node can be generated using the relationship given by:

$$Q_U(i+1, h) = \sum_{j=L(i)}^{U(i)} Q_U(i, j)prob(i, j, h)e^{-r_{i,j}\Delta t} \qquad (11.19)$$

$$Q_D(i+1, h) = \sum_{j=L(i)}^{U(i)} Q_D(i, j)prob(i, j, h)e^{-r_{i,j}\Delta t} \qquad (11.20)$$

The initial conditions for $Q_U(i,j)$ and $Q_D(i,j)$ in (11.19) and (11.20) are given by $Q_U(1, U) = 1$, $Q_U(1, D) = 0$, $Q_D(1, D) = 1$, and $Q_D(1, U) = 0$. At every time step, the functions $\theta(t_i)$ and $\psi(t_i)$ can be calibrated to the forward zero rates as:[12]

$$\theta(t_i) = \frac{1}{2}\sigma^2 \Delta t + \frac{1}{\Delta t^2}\ln\left(\frac{B_D(i)A_U(i) - B_U(i)A_D(i)}{A_U(i)e^{-R_{1,D}(t_{i+2})(t_{i+2}-t_1)} - A_D(i)e^{-R_{1,U}(t_{i+2})(t_{i+2}-t_1)}}\right)$$

(11.21)

$$\psi(t_i) = \frac{1}{\Delta t^2}\frac{B_D(i)e^{-R_{1,U}(t_{i+2})(t_{i+2}-t_1)} - B_U(i)e^{-R_{1,D}(t_{i+2})(t_{i+2}-t_1)}}{A_U(i)e^{-R_{1,D}(t_{i+2})(t_{i+2}-t_1)} - A_D(i)e^{-R_{1,U}(t_{i+2})(t_{i+2}-t_1)}}$$

(11.22)

where

$$A_U(i) = \sum_{j=L(i)}^{U(i)} Q_U(i,j)e^{-2r_{i,j}\Delta t}r_{i,j} \quad \text{and} \quad B_U(i) = \sum_{j=L(i)}^{U(i)} Q_U(i,j)e^{-2r_{i,j}\Delta t}$$

$$A_D(i) = \sum_{j=L(i)}^{U(i)} Q_D(i,j)e^{-2r_{i,j}\Delta t}r_{i,j} \quad \text{and} \quad B_D(i) = \sum_{j=L(i)}^{U(i)} Q_D(i,j)e^{-2r_{i,j}\Delta t}.$$

At time t_1, we can determine $\theta(t_1)$ and $\psi(t_1)$ from above using the forward rates $R_{1,U}(t_3)$ and $R_{1,D}(t_3)$ together with the initial conditions. The risk-neutral drifts $\phi_{1,U}$ and $\phi_{1,D}$ at the binomial nodes can then be evaluated from (11.18) with the corresponding short rates $r_{1,U}$ and $r_{1,D}$, respectively. The branching rules $k_{1,U}$, $k_{1,D}$, $\{p_1^u{}_{,U}, p_1^m{}_{,U}, p_1^d{}_{,U}\}$, and $\{p_{1,D}^u, p_{1,D}^m, p_{1,D}^d\}$ from the binomial nodes back to the trinomial tree can be determined using (11.16) and (11.17). To proceed, we need to first update the labels of the bottom and top nodes at t_2 as $L(2) = k_{1,D} - 1$ and $U(2) = k_{1,U} + 1$. We also need to update $Q_U(2, h)$ and $Q_D(2, h)$ from (11.19) and (11.20) for all h from $L(2)$ to $U(2)$. Steps (1) to (4) below will be repeated for t_i running from t_2 to $t_{N_{tree}-1}$. Suppose at any time $t_i \geq t_2$ that we have already determined $L(i)$, $U(i)$, $Q_U(i,j)$, and $Q_U(i,j)$ for all j from $L(i)$ to $U(i)$.

1. Determine $\theta(t_i)$ and $\psi(t_i)$ from (11.21) and (11.22) using $R_{1,U}(t_{i+2})$ and $R_{1,D}(t_{i+2})$. Then, evaluate $\phi_{i,j}$ from (11.18) for all j.
2. For all j, determine the branching probabilities $\{p_{i,j}^u, p_{i,j}^m, p_{i,j}^d\}$ from (11.4) with the value of k in the middle branch taken to be $k_{i,j} = j + \text{CINT}(\phi_{i,j}\,\Delta t/\Delta r)$.
3. Use $k_{i,L(i)}$ and $k_{i,U(i)}$ to update $L(i + 1) = k_{i,L(i)} - 1$ and $U(i + 1) = k_{i,U(i)} + 1$.
4. Except at $t_{N_{tree}-1}$, update also $Q_U(i + 1, h)$ and $Q_D(i + 1, h)$ from (11.19) and (11.20) for all h from $L(i + 1)$ to $U(i + 1)$.

Again, the current value of an interest rate option can be determined by iterating backward the risk-neutral pricing of the option starting from its maturity to the binomial nodes $(1, U)$ and $(1, D)$ along the trinomial tree as in (11.12), and then carrying on the iteration to node $(0, 0)$ along the binomial tree as:

$$f_{0,0} = e^{-r_0 \Delta t}(\tfrac{1}{2}f_{1,U} + \tfrac{1}{2}f_{1,D}). \tag{11.23}$$

EXAMPLE 11.2

Consider a three-step tree for the general Hull–White model with yearly time interval $\Delta t = 1.00$ and $N_{tree} = 3$. It can be constructed using the market term structures with maturity terms that coincide with the tree structure given by Table 11.2.

TABLE 11.2 The current term structures of zero rates and bond price volatilities.

Maturity Terms (years)	Bond Prices $P_0(t_i)$ ($1 par value)	Zero Rates $R_0(t_i)$ (annual)	Volatilities $\sigma_0(t_i)$ (annual)
$t_1 = 1.00$	$0.9533	4.783%	0.76%
$t_2 = 2.00$	$0.9055	4.963%	1.12%
$t_3 = 3.00$	$0.8525	5.319%	1.32%
$t_4 = 4.00$	$0.8015	5.532%	1.43%

Take $r_0 = R_0(t_1) = 0.04783$ and $\sigma = (1/\Delta t)\sigma_0(t_1) = 0.0076$. Evaluate the forward zero rates at the binomial nodes $(1, U)$ and $(1, D)$ as:

$$\{R_{1,U}(t_2) = 6.271\%, R_{1,U}(t_3) = 6.252\%, R_{1,U}(t_4) = 6.262\%\}$$
$$\{R_{1,D}(t_2) = 4.031\%, R_{1,D}(t_3) = 4.932\%, R_{1,D}(t_4) = 5.308\%\}$$

Choose $\Delta r = \sigma\sqrt{3\Delta t} = 0.01316$. Assign $r_{1,U} = R_{1,U}(t_2) = 0.06271$ and $r_{1,D} = R_{1,D}(t_2) = 0.04031$.

When $i = 1$, we have the initial conditions $L(1) = D$, $U(1) = U$, $Q_U(1, U) = 1$, $Q_U(1, D) = 0$, $Q_D(1, D) = 1$, and $Q_D(1, U) = 0$. We can first evaluate $\theta(t_1)$ and $\psi(t_1)$ as:

$$A_U(1) = Q_U(1, U)e^{-2r_{1,U}\Delta t}r_{1,U} = 0.0553, \quad B_U(1) = Q_U(1, U)e^{-2r_{1,U}\Delta t} = 0.8821$$
$$A_D(1) = Q_D(1, D)e^{-2r_{1,D}\Delta t}r_{1,D} = 0.0372, \quad B_D(1) = Q_D(1, D)e^{-2r_{1,D}\Delta t} = 0.9226$$

(continued)

(*continued*)

These give $\theta(t_1) = 0.0520$ and $\psi(t_1) = 0.8577$ with the use of the zero rates $R_{1,U}(t_3) = 0.06252$ and $R_{1,D}(t_3) = 0.04932$. The branching rules at nodes $(1, U)$ and $(1, D)$ can be determined as:

$$j = D : \phi_{1,D} = \theta(t_1) - \psi(t_1)r_{1,D} = 0.0175$$

$$k_{1,D} = \text{CINT}((r_{1,D} - r_0)/\Delta r + \phi_{1,D}\Delta t/\Delta r) = 1$$

$$\zeta = (r_{1,D} - r_0)/\Delta r - k_{1,D} + \phi_{1,D}\Delta t/\Delta r = -0.2435$$

$$p_{1,D}^u = \tfrac{1}{2}\sigma^2\Delta t/\Delta r^2 + \tfrac{1}{2}\zeta + \tfrac{1}{2}\zeta^2 = 0.0746$$

$$p_{1,D}^m = 1 - \sigma^2\Delta t/\Delta r^2 - \zeta^2 = 0.6074$$

$$p_{1,D}^d = 1 - p_{1,D}^u - p_{1,D}^m = 0.3180$$

$$j = U : \phi_{1,U} = \theta(t_1) - \psi(t_1)r_{1,U} = -0.00173$$

$$k_{1,U} = \text{CINT}((r_{1,U} - r_0)/\Delta r + \phi_{1,U}\Delta t/\Delta r) = 1$$

$$\zeta = (r_{1,U} - r_0)/\Delta r - k_{1,U}\Delta t/\Delta r = -0.00139$$

$$p_{1,U}^u = \tfrac{1}{2}\sigma^2\Delta t/\Delta r^2 + \tfrac{1}{2}\zeta + \tfrac{1}{2}\zeta^2 = 0.1660$$

$$p_{1,U}^m = 1 - \sigma^2\Delta t/\Delta r^2 - \zeta^2 = 0.6667$$

$$p_{1,U}^d = 1 - p_{1,D}^u - p_{1,D}^m = 0.1673$$

Then update $L(2) = k_{1,D} - 1 = 0, \quad U(2) = k_{1,U} + 1 = 2$

$$Q_U(2,2) = Q_U(1,U)prob(1,U,2)e^{-r_{1,U}\Delta t} = p_{1,U}^u e^{-r_{1,U}\Delta t} = 0.1559$$

$$Q_U(2,1) = Q_U(1,U)prob(1,U,1)e^{-r_{1,U}\Delta t} = p_{1,U}^m e^{-r_{1,U}\Delta t} = 0.6261$$

$$Q_U(2,0) = Q_U(1,U)prob(1,U,0)e^{-r_{1,U}\Delta t} = p_{1,U}^d e^{-r_{1,U}\Delta t} = 0.1572$$

$$Q_D(2,2) = Q_D(1,D)prob(1,D,2)e^{-r_{1,D}\Delta t} = p_{1,D}^u e^{-r_{1,D}\Delta t} = 0.0716$$

$$Q_D(2,1) = Q_D(1,D)prob(1,D,1)e^{-r_{1,D}\Delta t} = p_{1,D}^m e^{-r_{1,D}\Delta t} = 0.5834$$

$$Q_D(2,0) = Q_D(1,D)prob(1,D,0)e^{-r_{1,D}\Delta t} = p_{1,D}^d e^{-r_{1,D}\Delta t} = 0.3055$$

When $i = 2$, we can evaluate $\theta(t_2)$ and $\psi(t_2)$ using the updated values of $L(2)$, $U(2)$, $Q_U(2, j)$, and $Q_D(2, j)$ as (recall that $r_{2,j} = r_0 + j\Delta r$ on the trinomial lattice):

$$A_U(2) = Q_U(2,2)e^{-2r_{2,2}\Delta t}r_{2,2} + Q_U(2,1)e^{-2r_{2,1}\Delta t}r_{2,1}$$
$$+ Q_U(2,0)e^{-2r_{2,0}\Delta t}r_{2,0} = 0.0506$$

$$B_U(2) = Q_U(2,2)e^{-2r_{2,2}\Delta t} + Q_U(2,1)e^{-2r_{2,1}\Delta t} + Q_U(2,0)e^{-2r_{2,0}\Delta t} = 0.8315$$

$$A_D(2) = Q_D(2,2)e^{-2r_{2,2}\Delta t}r_{2,2} + Q_D(2,1)e^{-2r_{2,1}\Delta t}r_{2,1}$$
$$+ Q_D(2,0)e^{-2r_{2,0}\Delta t}r_{2,0} = 0.0494$$

$$B_D(2) = Q_D(2,2)e^{-2r_{2,2}\Delta t} + Q_D(2,1)e^{-2r_{2,1}\Delta t} + Q_D(2,0)e^{-2r_{2,0}\Delta t} = 0.8558$$

These give $\theta(t_2) = 0.00670$ and $\psi(t_2) = 0.0552$ with the use of the zero rates $R_{1,U}(t_4) = 0.06262$ and $R_{1,D}(t_4) = 0.05308$. The branching rules at nodes (2, 0), (2, 1), and (2, 2) can be determined as:

$j = 0:$ $\phi_{2,0} = \theta(t_2) - \psi(t_2)r_{2,0} = 0.00406$
$$k_{2,0} = 0 + \text{CINT}(\phi_{2,0}\Delta t/\Delta r) = 0$$
$$\eta = 0 - k_{2,0} + \phi_{2,0}\Delta t/\Delta r = 0.3083$$
$$p_{2,0}^u = \tfrac{1}{2}\sigma^2\Delta t/\Delta r^2 + \tfrac{1}{2}\eta + \tfrac{1}{2}\eta^2 = 0.3683$$
$$p_{2,0}^m = 1 - \sigma^2\Delta t/\Delta r^2 - \eta^2 = 0.5716$$
$$p_{2,0}^d = 1 - p_{1,D}^u - p_{1,D}^m = 0.0601$$

$j = 1:$ $\phi_{2,1} = \theta(t_2) - \psi(t_2)r_{2,1} = 0.00333$
$$k_{2,1} = 1 + \text{CINT}(\phi_{2,1}\Delta t/\Delta r) = 1$$
$$\eta = 1 - k_{2,1} + \phi_{2,1}\Delta t/\Delta r = 0.2531$$
$$p_{2,1}^u = \tfrac{1}{2}\sigma^2\Delta t/\Delta r^2 + \tfrac{1}{2}\eta + \tfrac{1}{2}\eta^2 = 0.3252$$
$$p_{2,1}^m = 1 - \sigma^2\Delta t/\Delta r^2 - \eta^2 = 0.6026$$
$$p_{2,1}^d = 1 - p_{1,D}^u - p_{1,D}^m = 0.0722$$

$j = 2:$ $\phi_{2,2} = \theta(t_2) - \psi(t_2)r_{2,2} = 0.00260$
$$k_{2,2} = 2 + \text{CINT}(\phi_{2,2}\Delta t/\Delta r) = 2$$
$$\eta = 2 - k_{2,2} + \phi_{2,2}\Delta t/\Delta r = 0.1979$$
$$p_{2,2}^u = \tfrac{1}{2}\Delta t/\Delta r^2 + \tfrac{1}{2}\eta + \tfrac{1}{2}\eta^2 = 0.2852$$
$$p_{2,2}^m = 1 - \sigma^2\Delta t/\Delta r^2 - \eta^2 = 0.6275$$
$$p_{2,2}^d = 1 - p_{1,D}^u - p_{1,D}^m = 0.0873$$

Then update $L(3) = k_{2,L(2)} - 1 = -1$ and $U(3) = k_{2,U(2)} + 1 = 3$.

(*continued*)

(continued)

As t_2 already reaches $t_{N_{tree}-1}$, there is no need to update Q_U and Q_D for t_3. The three-step Hull–White tree is constructed as shown in Figure 11.6.

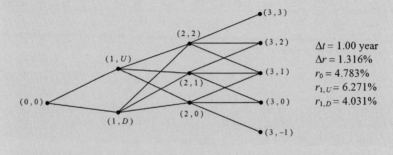

$\Delta t = 1.00$ year
$\Delta r = 1.316\%$
$r_0 = 4.783\%$
$r_{1,U} = 6.271\%$
$r_{1,D} = 4.031\%$

	$(0,0)$	$(1,U)$	$(1,D)$	$(2,2)$	$(2,1)$	$(2,0)$
p^u	0.5	0.1660	0.0746	0.2852	0.3252	0.3683
p^m	–	0.6667	0.6074	0.6275	0.6026	0.5716
p^d	0.5	0.1673	0.3180	0.0873	0.0722	0.0601

FIGURE 11.6 The three-step Hull–White tree constructed using the zero rates and volatilities in Table 11.2.

11.4 IMPLEMENTATION OF THE GENERAL HULL–WHITE MODEL

Again, we first develop a routine called GenHullWhiteTree2() that generates the Hull–White tree for the short rate in (11.13) given current term structures of bond prices and their volatilities. The pseudo code of GenHull-WhiteTree2() is given by Code 11.6. The routine requires the input of tree configuration (T_{tree}, N_{tree}), current zero-coupon bond prices $P_0(t_i)$, and their volatilities $\sigma_0(t_i)$ with maturities $\{t_1, t_2, \ldots, t_{N_{tree}+1}\}$. Similar to GenHull-WhiteTree() in Code 11.1, it returns the bottom and top-node labels $L(i)$ and $U(i)$, branching probabilities $\{p_{i,j}^u, p_{i,j}^m, p_{i,j}^d\}$, middle branch labels $k_{i,j}$, and short rates $r_{i,j}$ at every node. As before, the time interval of the tree is defined to be $\Delta t = T_{tree}/N_{tree}$ and the rate interval is optimally chosen as $\Delta r = \sigma\sqrt{3\Delta t}$ with $\sigma = (1/\Delta t)\sigma_0(t_1)$ in the general model. The current zero rates $R_0(t_i)$ with maturities $\{t_1, t_2, \ldots, t_{N_{tree}+1}\}$ are first calculated from the zero-coupon bond prices. The short rate $r_{0,0}$ on the tree is defined as $R_0(t_1)$; the forward zero rates $R_{1,U}(t_i)$ and $R_{1,D}(t_i)$ with different maturities can be evaluated from (11.14) and (11.15) using the corresponding values of $R_0(t_i)$ and $\sigma_0(t_i)$. In the general model, the iteration will run from t_1 to $t_{N_{tree}-1}$ taking the forward zero rates as calibration data. For completeness, the values of $(L(0), U(0), p_{0,0}^u, p_{0,0}^m, p_{0,0}^d)$ are trivially assigned at t_0 and it is clear that $k_{0,0}$ is irrelevant for the leading binomial nodes. The initial values of the arrays $(L(1), U(1), Q_U(1, j), Q_D(1, j), r_{1,j})$ at t_1 are defined prior to the iteration with the use of the forward rates $R_{1,U}(t_2)$ and $R_{1,D}(t_2)$ for the two short rates. For convenience, we have assigned the node labels for the U and D cases as $j = 1$ and $j = 0$, respectively.

At time t_i in the iteration, the arrays $(L(i), U(i), Q_U(i,j), Q_D(i,j), r_{ij})$ should presumably be determined up to the same time. Together with the forward zero rates $R_{1,U}(t_i)$ and $R_{1,D}(t_i)$, there is enough information to determine the arrays $\{p_{i,j}^u, p_{i,j}^m, p_{i,j}^d, k_{i,j}\}$ following the procedures (1) to (2) in Section 11.3. Subsequently, the arrays $(L(i), U(i), Q_U(i,j), Q_D(i,j), r_{ij})$ are updated to time t_{i+1} through procedures (3) to (4) before the iteration proceeds to t_{i+1}. It should be noted that the determination of $\{p_{1,j}^u, p_{1,j}^m, p_{1,j}^d, k_{1,j}\}$ in (11.16) and (11.17) can be integrated into the same loop structure in the iteration. This can be achieved by taking $k_{i,j}$ and η to be:

$$k_{i,j} = \text{CINT}((r_{i,j} - r_0)/\Delta r + \phi_{i,j}\Delta t/\Delta r) \rightarrow j + \text{CINT}(\phi_{i,j}\Delta t/\Delta r) \quad \text{when } i \geq 2$$

$$\eta = (r_{i,j} - r_0)/\Delta r - k_{i,j} + \phi_{i,j}\Delta t/\Delta r \rightarrow j - k_{i,j} + \phi_{i,j}\Delta t/\Delta r \quad \text{when } i \geq 2$$

that return the original expressions as $(r_{i,j} - r_0)/\Delta r = j$ on the trinomial lattice, and become (11.16) and (11.17) when $i = 1$.

The VBA code of GenHullWhiteTree2() is given by Code 11.7. It is also kept under the module called HWtree and can be used to price the European call option written on a coupon-bearing bond. Again, we develop a routine called GenHWBondOptionTree2() capable of generating the option prices along the general Hull–White tree. It is similar to GenHWBondOptionTree() in Code 11.3 except it will call GenHullWhiteTree2() taking bond price volatilities directly as input. Also, the backward iteration of option prices for the last binomial step ($i = 0$) follows (11.23) with branching probabilities $p_{0,0}^u = p_{0,0}^d = \frac{1}{2}$ instead. The VBA code of GenHWBondOptionTree2() is given by Code 11.8. Figure 11.7 depicts the modified spreadsheet design that includes the choice of tree type in the named cell F20(treetype). It specifies the use of the extended-Vasicek model ("Ext Vasicek") or the general Hull–White model ("General HW") in the pricing. In the new HWPricing() routine as given by Code 11.9, the choice of *treetype* will be taken as a decision flag to call either GenHWBondOptionTree() or GenHWBondOptionTree2() in the pricing. The current option price $f_{0,0}$ will be outputted to cell B20. By selecting "Yes" in cell E13, the entire option tree will be displayed in the spreadsheet. It should be noted that the option prices $f_{1,U}$ and $f_{1,D}$ on the binomial nodes will

Zero-Coupon Bond Data :

Number of Bonds =	8								
Maturity Terms =	0.083	0.250	0.500	1.000	2.000	4.000	7.000	18.000	(year)
Prices =	0.9963	0.9887	0.9771	0.9533	0.9055	0.8164	0.6948	0.4667	(par = 1)
Volatilities =	0.08%	0.20%	0.40%	0.70%	1.05%	1.26%	1.40%	1.50%	(per year)

European Bond Call Option :

Hull-White Parameterization

σ	0.0091
a	0.6337
Squared-Error Sum	9.52E-07

Option Maturity (T) =	3.00	(year)	Time Steps = 36
Strike (K) =	95.00		Display BDT Tree = Yes
Bond Maturity (τ) =	4.00	(year)	
Bond Par Value (L) =	100.00		
Bond Coupon Value (C) =	1.50		
Number of Coupons (n_c) =	8		
Payment Schedule :	0.50 1.00 1.50 2.00 2.50 3.00 3.50 4.00	(year)	
Option Price (f_0) =	3.713	Hull-White Pricing Tree Type General HW	

Hull-White Trinomial Tree

Forward Time (year)

A	B (0.00)	0.08	0.17	0.25	0.33	0.42	0.50	0.58	0.67	0.75	0.83	0.92	1.00
	0.107												
	0.102												3.163
	0.097											3.231	3.226
	0.093										3.299	3.294	3.293
	0.088									3.365	3.360	3.358	3.360
	0.083								3.427	3.424	3.422	3.423	3.427
	0.078								3.483	3.483	3.484	3.488	3.494
	0.073						3.533	3.536	3.539	3.543	3.547	3.554	3.563
	0.069					3.574	3.583	3.590	3.596	3.603	3.611	3.620	3.631
	0.064				3.603	3.622	3.634	3.644	3.654	3.664	3.675	3.687	3.701
	0.059			3.624	3.651	3.671	3.685	3.698	3.712	3.725	3.740	3.755	3.771
	0.054		3.646	3.676	3.699	3.720	3.737	3.753	3.770	3.787	3.805	3.823	3.842
0.0506	0.049	3.700	3.703	3.727	3.749	3.769	3.789	3.809	3.829	3.850	3.871	3.892	3.913
0.0410	0.044	3.713	3.761	3.779	3.798	3.818	3.841	3.865	3.889	3.913	3.938	3.962	3.985	
	0.040		3.819	3.832	3.848	3.869	3.894	3.921	3.949	3.977	4.005	4.032	4.058
	0.035			3.885	3.899	3.919	3.947	3.978	4.010	4.042	4.073	4.103	4.132
	0.030				3.949	3.970	4.001	4.036	4.071	4.107	4.142	4.175	4.206
	0.025					4.022	4.056	4.094	4.133	4.172	4.211	4.247	4.281
	0.020						4.110	4.152	4.195	4.238	4.281	4.320	4.356
	0.016											4.394	4.433
	0.011												4.510
	0.006												

(Option Price & Short Rates)

FIGURE 11.7 The modified spreadsheet design of Hull–White option pricing.

be displayed according to their node labels $j = 1$ and $j = 0$, respectively. As before, the short rates on the trinomial tree will be displayed in column B, and for completeness the two short rates $r_{1,U}$ and $r_{1,D}$ will also be shown in column A.

```
GenHullWhiteTree2( Ttree, Ntree , BondPrice( 1 : Ntree + 1 ), BondVol( 1 : Ntree + 1 ),
     k( 0 : Ntree − 1, L : U ), pᵘ( 0 : Ntree − 1, L : U ), pᵐ( 0 : Ntree − 1, L : U ),
     pᵈ( 0 : Ntree − 1, L : U ), L( 0 : Ntree ), U( 0 : Ntree ), r( 0 : Ntree, L : U ) )
```

define the sizes of Δt, σ, and the optimal choice of Δr

$$\Delta t = T_{tree} / N_{tree}, \quad \sigma = (1/\Delta t)\, BondVol(1), \quad \Delta r = \sigma\sqrt{3\Delta t}$$

convert the zero-coupon bond prices to zero rates with maturities $t_1, t_2, \ldots$, and $t_{N_{tree} + 1}$

For($i = 1$ to $N_{tree} + 1$){ $R(i) = -\log(BondPrice(i))/(i\Delta t)$ }

define the value of r_0

$r(0, 0) = R(1)$

evaluate the forward zero rates at the binomial nodes

$$\text{For}(i = 2 \text{ to } N_{tree} + 1)\left\{ R_U(i) = -\frac{1}{(i-1)\Delta t}\ln\left(\frac{2e^{r(0,0)\Delta t}\,e^{-R(i)(i\Delta t)}}{1 + \exp(2BondVol(i)\sqrt{\Delta t})}\right)\right.$$

$$R_D(i) = -\frac{1}{(i-1)\Delta t} \ln\left(\frac{2e^{r(0,0)\Delta t}e^{-R(i)(i\Delta t)}}{1 + \exp(2BondVol(i)\sqrt{\Delta t})}\right)\Big\}$$

\# define L, U, p^u, p^m, and p^d at t_0 for completeness ($k(\,0\,,0\,)$ is irrelevant)
$L(0) = 0$, $U(0) = 0$, $p^u(\,0\,,0\,) = 0.5$, $p^m(\,0\,,0\,) = 0$, $p^d(\,0\,,0\,) = 0.5$

\# define the initial values of $\{\,L\,,\,U\,,\,Q_U\,,\,Q_D\,,\,r\,\}$ at t_1
$L(1) = 0$, $U(1) = 1$, $Q_U(\,1\,,0\,) = 0$, $Q_U(\,1\,,1\,) = 1$, $Q_D(\,1\,,0\,) = 1$, $Q_D(\,1\,,1\,) = 0$
$r(\,1\,,0\,) = R_D(2)$, $r(\,1\,,1\,) = R_U(2)$

For(i = 1 to $N_{tree} - 1$) {

\# At time step i in the following loop, $\{\,L\,,\,U\,,\,Q_U\,,\,Q_D\,,\,r\,\}$ have presumably been
determined up to t_i

\# determine θ and ψ at t_i
$\quad A_U = 0$, $B_U = 0$, $A_D = 0$, $B_D = 0$
$\quad$For($j = L(i)$ to $U(i)$) {$\quad A_U = A_U + Q_U(\,i\,,j\,)\exp(-2\,r(\,i\,,j\,)\,\Delta t)\,r(\,i\,,j\,)$
$\qquad\qquad\qquad\qquad\quad B_U = B_U + Q_U(\,i\,,j\,)\exp(-2\,r(\,i\,,j\,)\,\Delta t)$
$\qquad\qquad\qquad\qquad\quad A_D = A_D + Q_D(\,i\,,j\,)\exp(-2\,r(\,i\,,j\,)\,\Delta t)\,r(\,i\,,j\,)$
$\qquad\qquad\qquad\qquad\quad B_D = B_D + Q_D(\,i\,,j\,)\exp(-2\,r(\,i\,,j\,)\,\Delta t)$ }

$$\psi = \frac{1}{\Delta t^2}\frac{B_D\exp(-R_U(i+2)(i+1)\Delta t) - B_U\exp(-R_D(i+2)(i+1)\Delta t)}{A_U\exp(-R_D(i+2)(i+1)\Delta t) - A_D\exp(-R_U(i+2)(i+1)\Delta t)}$$

$$\theta = \tfrac{1}{2}\sigma^2\Delta t + \frac{1}{\Delta t^2}\ln\left(\frac{B_D A_U - B_U A_D}{\begin{array}{c}A_U\exp(-R_D(i+2)(i+1)\Delta t)\\ -A_D\exp(-R_U(i+2)(i+1)\Delta t)\end{array}}\right)$$

\# determine $\{\,p^u, p^m\,, p^d\,, k\,\}$ for all nodes at t_i

$\quad$For($j = L(i)$ to $U(i)$) { $\phi = \theta - \psi r(\,i\,,j\,)$
$\qquad\qquad\qquad\qquad k(\,i\,,j\,) = \text{CINT}(\,(\,r(\,i\,,j\,) - r(\,0\,,0\,)\,)/\Delta r + \phi\,(\Delta t/\Delta r)\,)$
$\qquad\qquad\qquad\qquad \eta = (\,r(\,i\,,j\,) - r(\,0\,,0\,)\,)/\Delta r - k(\,i\,,j\,) + \phi\,(\Delta t/\Delta r)$
$\qquad\qquad\qquad\qquad p^u(\,i\,,j\,) = \tfrac{1}{2}\sigma^2(\Delta t/\Delta r^2) + \tfrac{1}{2}\eta + \tfrac{1}{2}\eta^2$
$\qquad\qquad\qquad\qquad p^m(\,i\,,j\,) = 1 - \sigma^2(\Delta t/\Delta r^2) - \eta^2$
$\qquad\qquad\qquad\qquad p^d(\,i\,,j\,) = 1 - p^u(\,i\,,j\,) - p^m(\,i\,,j\,)$ }

\# update $\{\,L\,,\,U\,,\,Q_U\,,\,Q_D\,,\,r\,\}$ to t_{i+1}
$\quad L(i+1) = k(\,i\,,L(i)\,) - 1$
$\quad U(i+1) = k(\,i\,,U(i)\,) + 1$
$\quad$For($h = L(i+1)$ to $U(i+1)$) {
$\qquad\qquad r(\,i+1\,,h\,) = r(\,0\,,0\,) + h\Delta r$
$\qquad\qquad$If ($i = N_{tree} - 1$) then Next h
$\qquad\qquad Q^U_{sum} = 0$
$\qquad\qquad Q^D_{sum} = 0$
$\qquad\qquad$For($j = L(i)$ to $U(i)$) {If ($h = k(\,i\,,j\,) + 1$) then
$\qquad\qquad\qquad\qquad Q^U_{sum} = Q^U_{sum} + Q_U(\,i\,,j\,)\,p^u(\,i\,,j\,)\exp(-r(\,i\,,j\,)\Delta t\,)$
$\qquad\qquad\qquad\qquad Q^D_{sum} = Q^D_{sum} + Q_D(\,i\,,j\,)\,p^u(\,i\,,j\,)\exp(-r(\,i\,,j\,)\Delta t\,)$

$$\text{Elseif } (\, h = k(\, i \, , j \,) \,) \text{ then}$$
$$Q^{U}_{sum} = Q^{U}_{sum} + Q_{U}(\, i \, , j \,) \, p^{m}(\, i \, , j \,) \exp(- \, r(\, i \, , j \,) \, \Delta t \,)$$
$$Q^{D}_{sum} = Q^{D}_{sum} + Q_{D}(\, i \, , j \,) \, p^{m}(\, i \, , j \,) \exp(- \, r(\, i \, , j \,) \, \Delta t \,)$$
$$\text{Elseif } (\, h = k(\, i \, , j \,) - 1 \,) \text{ then}$$
$$Q^{U}_{sum} = Q^{U}_{sum} + Q_{U}(\, i \, , j \,) \, p^{d}(\, i \, , j \,) \exp(- \, r(\, i \, , j \,) \, \Delta t \,)$$
$$Q^{D}_{sum} = Q^{D}_{sum} + Q_{D}(\, i \, , j \,) \, p^{d}(\, i \, , j \,) \exp(- \, r(\, i \, , j \,) \, \Delta t \,)$$
$$\text{Endif} \quad \}$$

$$Q_{U}(\, i + 1 \, , h \,) = Q^{U}_{sum}$$
$$Q_{D}(\, i + 1 \, , h \,) = Q^{D}_{sum} \quad \}$$
$$\}$$

Code 11.6: Pseudo code of the GenHullWhiteTree2( ) routine.

```
Sub GenHullWhiteTree2(Ttree As Double, Ntree As Integer, bondPrice() As Double,
        bondVol() As Double, ByRef kmat() As Integer, ByRef pu() As Double,
        ByRef pm() As Double, ByRef pd() As Double, ByRef Lower() As Integer,
        ByRef Upper() As Integer, ByRef rshort() As Double)
    Dim dtime As Double: dtime = Ttree / Ntree
    Dim sigma As Double: sigma = bondVol(1) / dtime
    Dim dr As Double: dr = sigma * Sqr(3 * dtime)
    Dim i As Integer, j As Integer, h As Integer
    Dim AU As Double, BU As Double, AD As Double, BD As Double
    Dim theta As Double, psi As Double, phi As Double, eta As Double, QUsum As Double,
        QDsum As Double
    Dim zeroRate() As Double: ReDim zeroRate(1 To Ntree + 1)
    Dim QU() As Double: ReDim QU(1 To Ntree, - 5 * Ntree To 5 * Ntree)
    Dim QD() As Double: ReDim QD(1 To Ntree, - 5 * Ntree To 5 * Ntree)
    Dim RU() As Double: ReDim RU(2 To Ntree + 1)
    Dim RD() As Double: ReDim RD(2 To Ntree + 1)

    For i = 1 To Ntree + 1:   zeroRate(i) = - Log(bondPrice(i)) / (i * dtime): Next i

    rshort(0, 0) = zeroRate(1)

    For i = 2 To Ntree + 1
        RU(i) = - Log(2 * Exp(rshort(0, 0) * dtime) * Exp(-zeroRate(i) * i * dtime) / (1 + Exp(2 *
            bondVol(i) * Sqr(dtime)))) / ((i - 1) * dtime)
        RD(i) = - Log(2 * Exp(rshort(0, 0) * dtime) * Exp(-zeroRate(i) * i * dtime) / (1 + Exp(- 2 *
            bondVol(i) * Sqr(dtime)))) / ((i - 1) * dtime)
    Next i

    Lower(0) = 0
    Upper(0) = 0
    pu(0, 0) = 0.5
    pm(0, 0) = 0
    pd(0, 0) = 0.5
    Lower(1) = 0
    Upper(1) = 1
```

```
QU(1, 0) = 0
QU(1, 1) = 1
QD(1, 0) = 1
QD(1, 1) = 0
rshort(1, 0) = RD(2)
rshort(1, 1) = RU(2)

For i = 1 To Ntree - 1

   AU = 0
   BU = 0
   AD = 0
   BD = 0
   For j = Lower(i) To Upper(i)
      AU = AU + QU(i, j) * Exp(- 2 * rshort(i, j) * dtime) * rshort(i, j)
      BU = BU + QU(i, j) * Exp(- 2 * rshort(i, j) * dtime)
      AD = AD + QD(i, j) * Exp(- 2 * rshort(i, j) * dtime) * rshort(i, j)
      BD = BD + QD(i, j) * Exp(- 2 * rshort(i, j) * dtime)
   Next j
   psi = (1 / dtime ^ 2) *(BD * Exp(- RU(i + 2) *(i + 1) * dtime) - BU *Exp(-RD(i + 2) *(i + 1) *
         dtime)) / (AU * Exp(- RD(i + 2) * (i + 1) * dtime) - AD * Exp(- RU(i + 2) * (i + 1) *
         dtime))
   theta = 0.5 * sigma ^ 2 * dtime + (1 / dtime ^ 2) * Log((BD * AU - BU * AD) _
            / (AU * Exp(-RD(i + 2) * (i + 1) * dtime) - AD * Exp(- RU(i + 2) * (i + 1) * dtime)))

   For j = Lower(i) To Upper(i)
      phi = theta - psi * rshort(i, j)
      kmat(i, j) = CInt((rshort(i, j) - rshort(0, 0)) / dr + phi * (dtime / dr))
      eta = (rshort(i, j) - rshort(0, 0)) / dr - kmat(i, j) + phi * (dtime / dr)
      pu(i, j) = 0.5 * sigma ^ 2 * (dtime / dr ^ 2) + 0.5 * eta + 0.5 * eta ^ 2
      pm(i, j) = 1 - sigma ^ 2 * (dtime / dr ^ 2) - eta ^ 2
      pd(i, j) = 1 - pu(i, j) - pm(i, j)
   Next j

   Lower(i + 1) = kmat(i, Lower(I)) - 1
   Upper(i + 1) = kmat(i, Upper(i)) + 1

   For h = Lower(i + 1) To Upper(i + 1)
      rshort(i + 1, h) = rshort(0, 0) + h * dr
      If (i = Ntree - 1) Then GoTo Nexth
      QUsum = 0
      QDsum = 0
      For j = Lower(i) To Upper(i)
         If (h = kmat(i, j) + 1) Then
            QUsum = QUsum + QU(i, j) * pu(i, j) * Exp(- rshort(i, j) * dtime)
            QDsum = QDsum + QD(i, j) * pu(i, j) * Exp(- rshort(i, j) * dtime)
         ElseIf (h = kmat(i, j)) Then
            QUsum = QUsum + QU(i, j) * pm(i, j) * Exp(- rshort(i, j) * dtime)
            QDsum = QDsum + QD(i, j) * pm(i, j) * Exp(-rshort(i, j) * dtime)
         ElseIf (h = kmat(i, j) - 1) Then
```

```
                QUsum = QUsum + QU(i, j) * pd(i, j) * Exp(-rshort(i, j) * dtime)
                QDsum = QDsum + QD(i, j) * pd(i, j) * Exp(-rshort(i, j) * dtime)
            End If
        Next j
        QU(i + 1, h) = QUsum
        QD(i + 1, h) = QDsum
    Nexth: Next h
    Next i
End Sub
```

Code 11.7: VBA code of the GenHullWhiteTree2() routine.

```
Sub GenHWBondOptionTree2(optionMaturity As Double, strike As Double, bondMaturity
    As Double, par As Double, coupon As Double, nCoupon As Integer,
    paymentSchedule() As Double, ByRef Hf As Integer, ByRef Lower() As Integer,
    ByRef Upper() As Integer, ByRef rshort() As Double, ByRef fTree() As Double)
Dim bondPrice(1 To nTreeMax + 1) As Double
Dim bondVol(1 To nTreeMax + 1) As Double
Dim i As Integer, j As Integer, k As Integer
Dim Nterm As Integer, dtime As Double

Call GenTermStructures(bondMaturity, 1, Nterm, dtime, bondPrice, bondVol)

Dim Ntree As Integer: Ntree = Nterm
Dim Ttree As Double: Ttree = bondMaturity

Dim kmat() As Integer: ReDim kmat(0 To Ntree - 1, -5 * Ntree To 5 * Ntree)
Dim pu() As Double: ReDim pu(0 To Ntree - 1, -5 * Ntree To 5 * Ntree)
Dim pm() As Double: ReDim pm(0 To Ntree - 1, -5 * Ntree To 5 * Ntree)
Dim pd() As Double: ReDim pd(0 To Ntree - 1, -5 * Ntree To 5 * Ntree)
Dim Bf() As Double: ReDim Bf(0 To Ntree, -5 * Ntree To 5 * Ntree)

Call GenHullWhiteTree2(Ttree, Ntree, bondPrice, bondVol, kmat, pu, pm, pd, Lower, Upper,
    rshort)

Hf = Int(optionMaturity / dtime)

i = Ntree
Dim rho As Integer
rho = CouponCount((i - 0.5) * dtime, (i + 0.5) * dtime, nCoupon, paymentSchedule)
For j = Lower(i) To Upper(i): Bf(i, j) = par + rho * coupon: Next j

For i = Ntree - 1 To 0 Step -1
    rho = CouponCount((i - 0.5) * dtime, (i + 0.5) * dtime, nCoupon, paymentSchedule)
    For j = Lower(i) To Upper(i)
        k = kmat(i, j)
        Bf(i, j) = Exp(- rshort(i, j) * dtime) * (pu(i, j) * Bf(i + 1, k + 1) + pm(i, j) * Bf(i + 1, k) + pd(i, j) *
        Bf(i + 1, k - 1)) + rho * coupon
    Next j
Next i
```

```
For j = Lower(Hf) To Upper(Hf): fTree(Hf, j) = Payoff(strike, Bf(Hf, j)): Next j

For i = Hf - 1 To 1 Step -1
    For j = Lower(i) To Upper(i)
        k = kmat(i, j)
        fTree(i, j) = Exp(-rshort(i, j) * dtime) * (pu(i, j) * fTree(i + 1, k + 1) + pm(i, j) * fTree(i + 1,
        k) +  pd(i, j) * fTree(i + 1, k - 1))
    Next j
Next i


fTree(0, 0) = Exp(-rshort(0, 0) * dtime) * (pu(0, 0) * fTree(1, 1) + pd(0, 0) * fTree(1, 0))


End Sub
```

Code 11.8: VBA code of the GenHWBondOptionTree2() routine.

```
Sub HWPricing()
    Dim i As Integer, j As Integer
    Dim rshort(0 To nTreeMax, -5 * nTreeMax To 5 * nTreeMax) As Double
    Dim fTree(0 To nTreeMax, -5 * nTreeMax To 5 * nTreeMax) As Double
    Dim Lower(0 To nTreeMax) As Integer
    Dim Upper(0 To nTreeMax) As Integer
    Dim Hf As Integer, zeroptr As Integer

    Dim optionMaturity As Double: optionMaturity = Range("optionMaturity").Value
    Dim strike As Double: strike = Range("strike").Value
    Dim bondMaturity As Double: bondMaturity = Range("bondMaturity").Value
    Dim par As Double: par = Range("par").Value
    Dim coupon As Double: coupon = Range("coupon").Value
    Dim nCoupon As Integer: nCoupon = Range("nCoupon").Value
    Dim paymentSchedule() As Double: ReDim paymentSchedule(0 To nCoupon)

    For i = 1 To nCoupon: paymentSchedule(i) = Range("A18").Offset(0, i): Next i

    Dim treetype As Variant: treetype = Range("treetype").Text
    If (treetype = "Ext Vasicek") Then
        Call GenHWBondOptionTree(optionMaturity, strike, bondMaturity, par, coupon, nCoupon,
            paymentSchedule, Hf, Lower(), Upper(), rshort(), fTree())
    ElseIf (treetype = "General HW") Then
        Call GenHWBondOptionTree2(optionMaturity, strike, bondMaturity, par, coupon,
        nCoupon, paymentSchedule, Hf, Lower(), Upper(), rshort(), fTree())
    End If

    Range("B20").Value = fTree(0, 0)

    Range("B23:IV150").ClearContents
    Range("A25:A150").ClearContents
    zeroptr = 0
    For i = 0 To Hf
        If (Upper(i) > Upper(zeroptr)) Then zeroptr = i
    Next i
```

```
If (Range("E13").Text = "Yes") Then

   If (treetype = "Ext Vasicek") Then
      For i = 0 To Hf
         Range("B23").Offset(0, i + 1) = i * (optionMaturity / Hf)
         For j = Lower(i) To Upper(i)
            Range("B23").Offset(Upper(zeroptr) - j + 1, i + 1) = fTree(i, j)
            Range("B23").Offset(Upper(zeroptr) - j + 1, 0) = rshort(i, j)
         Next j
      Next i
   ElseIf (treetype = "General HW") Then
      For i = 0 To Hf
         Range("B23").Offset(0, i + 1) = i * (optionMaturity / Hf)
         For j = Lower(i) To Upper(i)
            If (i = 1) Then
               Dim dr As Double: dr = rshort(2, Lower(2) + 1) - rshort(2, Lower(2))
               Range("B23").Offset(Upper(zeroptr) - Int((rshort(1, j) - rshort(0, 0)) / dr)
               + 1, 2) = fTree(1, j)
               Range("B23").Offset(Upper(zeroptr) - Int((rshort(1, j) - rshort(0, 0)) / dr)
               + 1, -1) =  rshort(1, j)
            Else
               Range("B23").Offset(Upper(zeroptr) - j + 1, i + 1) = fTree(i, j)
               Range("B23").Offset(Upper(zeroptr) - j + 1, 0) = rshort(i, j)
            End If
         Next j
      Next i
   End If

End If

End Sub
```

Code 11.9: VBA code of the new HWPricing() routine.

REVIEW QUESTION

1. Given current bond prices and volatilities with different maturities as,

Maturity (years)	Current Bond Prices (par = $1)	Current Bond Price Vol (%)
0.5	$0.9830	0.08
1.0	$0.9625	0.20
1.5	$0.9392	0.40
2.0	$0.9137	0.70
2.5	$0.8867	1.05
3.0	$0.8585	1.26
3.5	$0.8358	1.40
4.0	$0.8127	1.50

Use VBA to implement the construction of the general Hull-White trinomial tree and determine the current value of a three-year caplet written on a 6-month LIBOR with caplet rate of 4.5 percent and notion principal of $10,000.

An interest rate caplet provides a ceiling of R_{cap} on LIBOR rate at future time T with borrowing term δ and notional principle M. The caplet payoff is made at the beginning of the rate period as

$$f_T = \delta M \max\{L_T(T, \delta) - R_{cap}, 0\}$$

where $L_T(T,\delta)$ is the discrete compounding LIBOR rate as seen at time T for the borrowing period between T and $T + \delta$.

ENDNOTES

1. J. Hull and A. White, "One-Factor Interest-Rate Models and the Valuation of Interest-Rate Derivative Securities," *Journal of Financial and Quantitative Analysis* 28, No. 2 (1993): 235–254.

2. In general, if bond price volatility is non-stochastic and has adopted the functional form as:

$$\sigma_t(T) = g(t)[h(T) - h(t)]$$

it can be shown that the risk-neutral short rate is then a Markov process given by:

$$\Delta r_t = [\theta(t) - \psi(t)r_t]\Delta t + v(t)\sqrt{\Delta t}\varepsilon(0, 1)$$

where $\psi(t) = -h''(t)/h'(t)$,
$\theta(t) = 2R_0'(t) + tR_0''(t) + \psi(t)[R_0(t) + tR_0'(t)] + h'(t)^2\int_0^t g(u)^2\, du$,
and $v(t) = g(t)h'(t)$.

3. J. Hull and A. White, "Valuing Derivative Securities Using the Explicit Finite difference Method," *Journal of Financial and Quantitative Analysis* 25, No. 1 (1990): 87–100.

4. It is easy to rewrite (11.8) as:

$$
\begin{aligned}
e^{-R_0(t_{i+2})t_{i+2}} &= \sum_{j=L(i),\dots,U(i)} Q(i,j)e^{-(r_0+j\Delta r)\Delta t}\hat{E}(exp(-r_{t_{i+1}}\Delta t)|r_{t_i} = r_0 + j\Delta r)\\
&= \sum_{j=L(i),\dots,U(i)} Q(i,j)e^{-(r_0+j\Delta r)\Delta t}e^{-(r_0+j\Delta r)\Delta t - [\theta(t_i)-a(r_0+j\Delta r)-\frac{1}{2}\sigma^2\Delta t]\Delta t^2}\\
&= e^{-\theta(t_i)\Delta t^2 + \frac{1}{2}\sigma^2\Delta t^3}\sum_{j=L(i),\dots,U(i)} Q(i,j)e^{-2(r_0+j\Delta r)\Delta t + a(r_0+j\Delta r)\Delta t^2}.
\end{aligned}
$$

The time-dependent function $\theta(t_i)$ is factorized out of summation operation over j to become (11.9).

5. It can be shown that $k_{i,\,j-1} + 1 = j + \text{CINT}(\phi_{i,j}\,\Delta t/\Delta r + a\Delta t) \geq k_{i,\,j}$. Thus, the branching rule will never skip any internal points on the lattice.

6. Recall that branching probabilities are determined up to the time label $N_{tree} - 1$ on the trinomial tree.

7. Refer to HWtree_ebc.xls.

8. From Endnote 2, current bond price volatility is given by $\sigma_0(T) = g(0)[h(T) - h(0)]$. Suppose the volatility function $v(t) = g(t)h'(t) = \sigma$, it is then straight forward to show that $\sigma = \sigma_0'(0)$,

$$\psi(t) = -\sigma_0''(t)/\sigma_0'(t) \text{ and}$$
$$\theta(t) = 2R_0'(t) + tR_0''(t) + \psi(t)[R_0(t) + tR_0'(t)] + \sigma^2 \int_0^t [\sigma_0'(t)/\sigma_0'(u)]^2 du.$$

9. From (8.5) and (8.6), we have $e^{-R_0(\tau)\tau} = P_{0,0}(\tau)$ and $\sigma_0(\tau)\sqrt{\Delta t} = \frac{1}{2}\ln[P_{1,D}(\tau)/P_{1,U}(\tau)]$ for the bond prices on the binomial tree. The expressions for $P_{1,U}(\tau)$ and $P_{1,D}(\tau)$ in (11.14) can be obtained by imposing the risk-neutral pricing $P_{0,0}(\tau) = e^{-r_0\Delta t}\left[\frac{1}{2}P_{1,U}(\tau) + \frac{1}{2}P_{1,D}(\tau)\right]$.

10. It is easy to check that $\sigma_0(t_2) = (\sigma/h'(0))[h(t_2) - h(0)] \approx 2\sigma\Delta t$. From (11.14) and (11.15), the interval size between $r_{1,U}$ and $r_{1,D}$ can be estimated as:

$$r_{1,U} - r_{1,D} = (1/\Delta t)(2\sigma_0(t_2)\sqrt{\Delta t} + \ldots) \approx 4\sigma\sqrt{\Delta t} \text{ or } (4/\sqrt{3})\Delta r.$$

11. From (11.17), we can rewrite $k_{1,D}$ as:

$$k_{1,D} = \text{CINT}((r_{1,U} - r_0)/\Delta r + \phi_{1,U}(\Delta t/\Delta r) - (r_{1,U} - r_{1,D})/\Delta r$$
$$+ \psi(t_1)(r_{1,U} - r_{1,D})(\Delta t/\Delta r))$$
$$\geq k_{1,U} - 3$$

where $\psi(t) > 0$ for the mean reverting process and with the use of   Endnote 10.

12. Refer to Endnote node 4. For $(1, U)$ we have:

$$e^{-R_{1,U}(t_{i+2})(t_{i+2}-t_1)}$$
$$= \sum_{j=L(i),\ldots,U(i)} Q_U(i,j)e^{-r_{i,j}\Delta t}\hat{E}(\exp(-r_{t_{i+1}}\Delta t)|r_{t_i}=r_{i,j})$$
$$= \sum_{j=L(i),\ldots,U(i)} Q_U(i,j)e^{-r_{i,j}\Delta t}e^{-r_{i,j}\Delta t - [\theta(t_i)-\psi(t_i)r_{i,j}-\frac{1}{2}\sigma^2\Delta t]\Delta t^2}$$
$$= e^{-\theta(t_i)\Delta t^2 + \frac{1}{2}\sigma^2\Delta t^3} \sum_{j=L(i),\ldots,U(i)} Q_U(i,j)e^{-2r_{i,j}\Delta t}(1+\psi(t_i)r_{i,j}\Delta t^2+\cdots)$$
$$= e^{-\theta(t_i)\Delta t^2 + \frac{1}{2}\sigma^2\Delta t^3}\Big(\sum_{j=L(i),\ldots,U(i)} Q_U(i,j)e^{-2r_{i,j}\Delta t}$$
$$+ \psi(t_i)\Delta t^2 \sum_{j=L(i),\ldots,U(i)} Q_U(i,j)e^{-2r_{i,j}\Delta t}r_{i,j} + \cdots\Big)$$

In the Taylor expansion, the time-dependent function $\psi(t_i)$ is factorized out of the summation operation over j. There exists a similar expression for node $(1, D)$ with $R_{1,D}(t_{i+2})$, and $Q_D(i,j)$ in the equation instead. Together, these give (11.21) and (11.22) by solving two linear equations.

## CHAPTER 12

CreditMetrics Model

12.1 THE CREDITMETRICS MODEL

CreditMetrics was published by J.P. Morgan in 1997. It is a scheme to address market risk due to changes in fixed income value. Its methodology is based not only on the probability of defaults, but also on the probability of upgrades and downgrades in credit quality within a given time horizon. More importantly, the risk is evaluated on a portfolio basis, rather than on an individual asset basis. Thus, the correlation of credit quality among firms is the key element in the model as diversification benefits or concentration risks can be assessed across the portfolio. Since there is much material to be discussed within the CreditMetrics framework,[1] the core of this chapter concentrates on:

1. Individual (Segregate) Asset Valuation Framework
2. Monte Carlo Simulation in Detail.

12.2 INDIVIDUAL (SEGREGATE) ASSET VALUATION FRAMEWORK

For an individual bond, risk comes not only when its obligor defaults, but also when its credit rating is upgraded or downgraded by credit rating agencies such as Standard and Poor's, Moody's, and Fitch. Therefore, it is critical to approximate the chance of migrating from one credit rating to any possible credit quality state within a given horizon. A default scenario is just one of several credit quality states. In general, the probabilities of credit rating migration for each credit rating are summarized in a transition matrix. Throughout this chapter, a time horizon of one year is used so the transition matrix is commonly called a one-year transition matrix as shown in Figure 12.1.[2]

	A	B	C	D	E	F	G	H	I	J
1										
2	Initial				Year End Rating					
3	Rating	AAA	AA	A	BBB	BB	B	CCC	Default	
4	AAA	90.81	8.33	0.68	0.06	0.12	0	0	0	
5	AA	0.7	90.65	7.79	0.64	0.06	0.14	0.02	0	
6	A	0.09	2.27	91.05	5.52	0.74	0.26	0.01	0.06	
7	BBB	0.02	0.33	5.95	86.93	5.3	1.17	0.12	0.18	
8	BB	0.03	0.14	0.67	7.73	80.53	8.84	1	1.06	
9	B	0	0.11	0.24	0.43	6.48	83.47	4.07	5.2	
10	CCC	0.22	0	0.22	1.3	2.38	11.24	64.85	19.79	
11										

FIGURE 12.1 One-year transition matrix in percentages.
Source: Standard & Poor's *CreditWeek*, 1996.

Based on the structural model developed by Robert C. Merton,[3] the CreditMetrics model relates changes in asset value to changes in credit ratings. It is apparent that the asset value of an obligor determines its ability to pay its debt owners. If the asset value falls underneath the debt value in the future, the obligor will go into default. Since default is just one of the scenarios in the transition matrix, a series of asset values are required in order to decide a credit rating of an obligor in the future.

The CreditMetrics model proposes that the change in asset value of an obligor is directly related to its credit rating migration. The model assumes the changes in asset value are normally distributed and parameterized by mean μ and standard deviation σ. With this parameterization of the asset value process, a link is established between the asset return thresholds and the transition probabilities. Since there are asset return thresholds, Z_{Def}, Z_{CCC}, Z_{BB}, Z_{AA}, and so on such that when r, an asset return, is less than Z_{Def}, then the obligor is in default. When r is between Z_{Def} and Z_{CCC}, then the credit rating of the obligor is set to CCC and so on until r is between Z_{AA} and Z_{AAA}, then the credit rating of the obligor is set to AAA. With the assumption that r is normally distributed, the probability of each credit event is stated as:

$$Prob(Default) = Prob(r < Z_{Def}) = N\left(\frac{Z_{Def}}{\sigma}\right) \qquad (12.1)$$

$$Prob(CCC) = Prob(Z_{Def} < r < Z_{CCC}) = N\left(\frac{Z_{CCC}}{\sigma}\right) - N\left(\frac{Z_{Def}}{\sigma}\right) \quad (12.2)$$

and continues until:

$$Prob(AAA) = Prob(Z_{AA} < r < Z_{AAA}) = 1 - N\left(\frac{Z_{AA}}{\sigma}\right). \qquad (12.3)$$

Once all the asset return thresholds are calculated, the transition probabilities and the values of the asset return threshold can be aligned for each
credit rating. Let's use a senior unsecured bond with a credit rating of single
A, coupon of 5 percent, and maturity of four years to illustrate the concept.
From Figure 12.1, the probability of a single A rated obligor to migrate to
default is 0.06 percent. Then $N(Z_{Def}/\sigma)$ has to equal 0.06 percent using
(12.1). Therefore:

$$Z_{Def} = N^{-1}(0.06\%) \times \sigma = -3.24\sigma$$

where $N^{-1}(p)$ yields the level below a standard normal distributed variable
with probability p. In Excel, it is given by the **NORMSINV()** function.
Utilizing this method, Z_{CCC} to Z_{AA} can be calculated respectively. For
instance, the probability of the same obligor to migrate to CCC is 0.01
percent. Using (12.2), we have:

$$N\left(\frac{Z_{CCC}}{\sigma}\right) = Prob(CCC) + Prob(Default) = 0.01\% + 0.06\% = 0.07\%$$
$$Z_{CCC} = N^{-1}(0.07\%) \times \sigma = -3.19\sigma.$$

The transition probabilities and asset return thresholds for the single A
rated obligor are summarized in Table 12.1.

The next step is to calculate the bond value corresponding to each
credit rating migration within a given time horizon. A one-year horizon is
chosen in order to match the one-year transition matrix. Moreover, one
year forward zero curves for each credit rating category are obtained to
perform a present value bond evaluation as shown in Figure 12.2.

Let's re-evaluate the senior unsecured bond with credit rating of single
A, coupon of 5 percent, and maturity of four years at the end of one year
assuming the credit rating has not changed.

$$BV = \$5 + \frac{\$5}{(1+0.0372)} + \frac{\$5}{(1+0.0432)^2} + \frac{\$105}{(1+0.0493)^3} = \$105.30$$

$$(12.4)$$

TABLE 12.1 Transition probabilities and asset return thresholds for a single A
rated obligor.

				Threshold				
	Z_{AAA}	Z_{AA}	Z_A	Z_{BBB}	Z_{BB}	Z_B	Z_{CCC}	Z_{Def}
Probability	0.09%	2.27%	91.05%	5.52%	0.74%	0.26%	0.01%	0.06%
Threshold value	–	3.12σ	1.98σ	-1.51σ	-2.30σ	-2.72σ	-3.19σ	-3.24σ

	A	B	C	D	E	F
15	Credit	Year				
16	Rating	Year 1	Year 2	Year 3	Year 4	
17	AAA	3.60	4.17	4.73	5.12	
18	AA	3.65	4.22	4.78	5.17	
19	A	3.72	4.32	4.93	5.32	
20	BBB	4.10	4.67	5.25	5.63	
21	BB	5.55	6.02	6.78	7.27	
22	B	6.05	7.02	8.03	8.52	
23	CCC	15.05	15.02	14.03	13.52	
24						

FIGURE 12.2 Arbitrary instance of one year forward zero curves for each credit rating.

The remaining bond values for other credit ratings are calculated respectively. Table 12.2 below shows the possible values at the end of one year. In regard to the default value for a senior unsecured bond, a recovery rate of 51.13 percent is used. This static value is used for illustrative purposes and it will be elaborated on during the implementation of the Monte Carlo simulation approach in Section 12.3.

At this stage, the mean μ and the standard deviation σ of the above bond can be calculated by applying a probability-weighted approach using the data in Table 12.2. Thus, the stand-alone risk can be deduced. However, it is preferable not to calculate the stand-alone risk at this stage because:

1. When using the Monte Carlo method to simulate the portfolio values, each of the underlying bond values is simulated first before aggregating to the overall portfolio values. Therefore, it is preferred to estimate the stand-alone risk of each bond from the simulation approach rather than the analytical approach.
2. In case of a default scenario, it is recommended to use a random number instead of a static number for the recovery rate. This will be discussed further in the next section.

TABLE 12.2 List of bond values of a single A bond in one year.

	AAA	AA	A	BBB	BB	B	CCC	Default
			Year End Rating					
Probability	0.09%	2.27%	91.05%	5.52%	0.74%	0.26%	0.01%	0.06%
Bond value ($)	105.84	105.70	105.30	104.43	100.43	97.36	83.94	51.13

	C	D	E	F	G	H	I	J
1								
2				Portfolio Data				
3		Identifer	Rating	Seniority	Coupon	Maturity (years)	Holdings ($)	
4		3598A8	AA	Senior Unsecured	4.50%	5	4,000,000	
5		5987Y2	A	Senior Unsecured	5.00%	4	3,000,000	
6		6899T3	B	Senior	7.00%	5	2,000,000	
7		8934M7	CCC	Subordinated	10.00%	3	1,000,000	
8								

FIGURE 12.3   Basic characteristics of the sample portfolio of four bonds.

12.3 MONTE CARLO SIMULATION IN DETAIL

The computation of asset return thresholds and one year forward values have established the building block for applying the Monte Carlo simulation to a portfolio level. Let's use a sample portfolio of four bonds detailed in Figure 12.3.

Based on the methodology of calculating the asset return threshold for the single A obligor, the asset return threshold[4] of each obligor within the portfolio is summarized in Table 12.3 below.

With the aim of describing how the asset values of the four obligors move jointly, it is assumed that the asset returns for each firm are normally distributed and the correlation for each pair of firms are specified.[5] When estimating asset return correlations, there are various alternatives to estimate them. The CreditMetrics model uses the correlation between obligors' equity returns as a proxy for the correlation of asset returns. Specifically, an obligor's volatility of the weighted index along with its country-industry pairs is used to compute the correlations. Once the correlation matrix is defined, generating random scenarios for the asset return of the four obligors is a matter of generating correlated, normally distributed variates. Cholesky

TABLE 12.3   Asset return thresholds (in units of σ) of the sample portfolio of four obligors.

				Threshold			
	Z_{AA}	Z_A	Z_{BBB}	Z_{BB}	Z_B	Z_{CCC}	Z_{Def}
AA Obligor	2.46	−1.36	−2.38	−2.85	−2.95	−3.54	−6.36
A Obligor	3.12	1.98	−1.51	−2.30	−2.72	−3.19	−3.24
B Obligor	8.16	3.06	2.70	2.42	1.46	−1.32	−1.63
CCC Obligor	2.85	2.85	2.62	2.11	1.74	1.02	−0.85

factorization, singular value decomposition, and so on are just a number of methods to accomplish this.

The next step is to generate random variables in order to create different scenarios for standardized asset returns. For each scenario, a new "state of the world"[6] is revealed. Since each obligor is mapped to a new credit rating, this new credit rating can directly map to a new bond value in a way similar to Table 12.2.

For default scenarios, the valuation is somewhat different. When an obligor is in default, its recovery rate does not follow a deterministic process. Instead, it follows a stochastic process, so the recovery rate presents a huge amount of variation. To model this variation, the mean and standard deviation of the recovery rate are collected for each obligor's seniority; then, a random recovery rate is generated according to a beta distribution[7] with these two input parameters.

Let's use the sample portfolio to calculate the possible portfolio values with a horizon of one year. As shown in Table 12.4, the sample portfolio with five correlated random scenarios is used with the purpose of illustrating the same concept. It is important to keep in mind that the value is the same in scenarios with the same credit rating, except for default scenarios. The recovery value is different in each default scenario because each default scenario requires a randomly generated recovery rate.[8]

So far, five scenarios of future possible portfolio values have been generated. Once the simulation is extended to 10,000 scenarios, a number of descriptive statistics can be concluded. Some of the main descriptive statistics are:

1. the mean
2. the standard deviation
3. the 5th percentile
4. the 1st percentile.

Once the stand-alone risk of each bond can be derived from the simulation process, the marginal risk of each bond can also be derived. A marginal risk is the difference between the standard deviation of the portfolio and the standard deviation of the portfolio excluding the specific bond. First, each bond's individual (stand-alone) standard deviation of value is estimated excluding other bonds in the portfolio. Second, the individual percent standard deviation is computed, which is just the individual standard deviation expressed as a percentage of the mean value for the given bond. Third, each bond's marginal standard deviation is computed. Last, this number is expressed in percent terms, providing the percent marginal standard deviation.

TABLE 12.4   Mapping among return scenarios, rating scenarios and valuation scenarios.

	Asset Return Thresholds			
Scenario	*AA* Obligor	*A* Obligor	*B* Obligor	*CCC* Obligor
1	1.20864	0.31811	− 0.39797	− 0.89260
2	− 0.98732	0.25956	− 0.71610	1.12732
3	− 1.50742	− 2.08923	0.15314	0.18177
4	− 0.09141	− 1.06525	− 1.46234	− 1.56301
5	− 0.25611	0.99727	0.93067	− 0.55134

	New Credit Ratings			
	AA Obligor	*A* Obligor	*B* Obligor	*CCC* Obligor
1	AA	A	B	Def
2	AA	A	B	B
3	A	BBB	B	CCC
4	AA	A	CCC	Def
5	AA	A	B	CCC

	Asset Values				
	AA Obligor	*A* Obligor	*B* Obligor	*CCC* Obligor	Portfolio
1	$4,092,567	$3,158,992	$2,048,324	$381,938	$9,681,821
2	$4,092,567	$3,158,992	$2,048,324	$1,154,719	$10,454,602
3	$4,072,039	$3,132,750	$2,048,324	$1,018,388	$10,271,501
4	$4,092,567	$3,158,992	$1,750,549	$436,871	$9,438,979
5	$4,092,567	$3,158,992	$2,048,324	$1,018,388	$10,318,270

12.4 EXCEL AND VBA IMPLEMENTATION

Before applying the Monte Carlo simulation approach to fully evaluate the future possible portfolio values in one year's time, there are many initial steps to be taken. Based on the one-year transition matrix from Figure 12.1, the asset return threshold matrix can be derived. Each credit rating has its own threshold values and they are combined to form the matrix in Figure 12.4.

In the following VBA routine called calAssetThreshold(), Z_{Def} is computed first. Then Z_{Def} is used in order to compute Z_{CCC} to Z_{AA} respectively. The routine returns the threshold matrix as depicted in Figure 12.4 with two labels ($L_{InitRating}$, $L_{Threshold}$). The first label $L_{InitRating}$ is running from 1 to 7 referring to the initial ratings from *AAA* to *CCC*. The second label

	K	L	M	N	O	P	Q	R	S
1									
2	Credit				Threshold				
3	Rating	Z_{AA}	Z_A	Z_{BBB}	Z_{BB}	Z_B	Z_{CCC}	Z_{Def}	
4	AAA	-1.33	-2.38	-2.91	-3.04	-6.19	-6.25	-6.36	
5	AA	2.46	-1.36	-2.38	-2.85	-2.95	-3.54	-6.36	
6	A	3.12	1.98	-1.51	-2.30	-2.72	-3.19	-3.24	
7	BBB	3.54	2.70	1.53	-1.49	-2.18	-2.75	-2.91	
8	BB	3.43	2.93	2.39	1.37	-1.23	-2.04	-2.30	
9	B	8.16	3.06	2.70	2.42	1.46	-1.32	-1.63	
10	CCC	2.85	2.85	2.62	2.11	1.74	1.02	-0.85	
11									

FIGURE 12.4 Asset return threshold matrix (in units of σ).

$L_{Threshold}$ is also running from 1 to 7 referring to the threshold values from Z_{AA} to Z_{Def}.

```
Sub calAssetThreshold(ByRef assetThresholdMatrix() As Double)

    Dim tranMatrix(1 To 7, 1 To 8) As Double
    Dim LInitRating As Integer
    Dim LEndRating As Integer
    Dim LThreshold As Integer
    Dim k As Integer
    Dim tempProb As Double

'reading in the one year transition matrix

    For LInitRating = 1 To 7
      For LEndRating = 1 To 8
        tranMatrix(LInitRating, LEndRating) = Worksheets("Reference").Range("B4").
          Offset(LInitRating - 1, LEndRating - 1).Value / 100
      Next LEndRating
    Next LInitRating

'evaluating the asset return threshold matrix

    For LInitRating = 1 To 7
      For LThreshold = 7 To 1 Step -1
        tempProb = 0
        For k = 7 To LThreshold Step -1
          tempProb = tempProb + WorksheetFunction.Max(tranMatrix(LInitRating, k + 1),
            0.0000000001) `1E-10 is used to avoid zero
        Next k
        assetThresholdMatrix(LInitRating, LThreshold) = WorksheetFunction.NormSInv
          (tempProb)
      Next LThreshold
    Next LInitRating

End Sub
```

	C	D	E	J	K	L	M	N	O	P	Q	R	S
1													
2		**Portfolio Data**						**Year End Rating and Values**					
3		Identifer	Rating		AAA	AA	A	BBB	BB	B	CCC	Default	
4		3598A8	AA		102.49	102.31	101.80	100.73	95.39	91.59	77.77		
5		5987Y2	A		105.84	105.70	105.30	104.43	100.43	97.36	83.94		
6		6899T3	B		113.93	113.74	113.20	112.07	106.42	102.42	87.53		
7		8934M7	CCC		121.02	120.92	120.72	120.01	117.34	115.47	101.84		
8													

FIGURE 12.5 List of bond values of AA bond, single A bond, single B bond, and CCC bond in one year.

Recall the sample portfolio from Figure 12.3, the VBA routine, calForwardBondValues(), is called to compute the year-end values of each bond for each credit rating based on the same logic from Equation (12.4). The result is summarized in Figure 12.5. The default values are missing (and temporarily assigned to be zero) because the random recovery rate needs to be generated each time the asset threshold value falls below its respective value of Z_{Def}. The label $L_{EndRating}$ runs eight times (from 1 to 8) referring to the credit ratings from *AAA* to *Default*.

```
Sub calForwardBondValues(couponRate As Double, yearToMaturity As Integer,
    oneYearForwardBondValues() As Double)

    Dim oneYearForwardCurves(1 To 7, 1 To 4) As Double
    Dim LEndRating As Integer
    Dim LYear As Integer
    Dim k As Integer
    Dim sum As Double

'reading in the one year forward zero curve for different year end non-default ratings

    For LEndRating = 1 To 7
        For LYear = 1 To 4
            oneYearForwardCurves(LEndRating, LYear) = Worksheets("Reference").Range
                ("B17").Offset(LEndRating - 1, LYear - 1).Value / 100
        Next LYear
    Next LEndRating

'evaluating the one year bond values for different year end ratings

    For LEndRating = 1 To 7
        sum = couponRate * 100
        For k = 1 To yearToMaturity - 1
            sum = sum + couponRate * 100 / ((1 + oneYearForwardCurves(LEndRating, k)) ^ k)
            If k = yearToMaturity - 1 Then
                sum = sum + 100 / ((1 + oneYearForwardCurves(LEndRating, k)) ^ k)
            End If
        Next k
```

```
oneYearForwardBondValues(LEndRating) = sum
Next LEndRating

oneYearForwardBondValues(8) = 0

End Sub
```

In addition to the computation of the year-end values for each bond under different credit ratings, the asset return threshold for each bond in the portfolio also has to be set up. A "Select Case" statement is used to perform this task.

```
Select Case portHldg(LBond, 2)
  Case "AAA"
    LInitRating = 1
  Case "AA"
    LInitRating = 2
  Case "A"
    LInitRating = 3
  Case "BBB"
    LInitRating = 4
  Case "BB"
    LInitRating = 5
  Case "B"
    LInitRating = 6
  Case "CCC"
    LInitRating = 7
End Select
For LThreshold = 1 To 7
  portAssetThreshold(LBond, LThreshold) = assetThresholdMatrix(LInitRating, LThreshold)
Next LThreshold
```

Let's suppose the correlation of the sample portfolio has been arbitrarily estimated.[9] Then the Cholesky decomposition is applied to produce a lower triangular matrix with strictly positive diagonal entries. After that, an array of random variables is created, and is multiplied by the Cholesky decomposed matrix in order to generate an array of correlated random variables. A list of functions is designed to facilitate this calculation and their VBA codes are given by Code 12.1:

CholeskyDecom()

invStdNorRandomArray()

corInvStdNorRandomArray().

The next step is to compare each correlated random variable with its asset threshold value, and thus to map to its respective bond values. This is performed through the VBA routine called simPortValue() as given by Code 12.2. In the case of default, a predefined function, randomInvBetaDist(), is called to randomly produce a recovery value based on the seniority of the specific bond.[10] The VBA codes of the randomInvBetaDist() function is also given by Code 12.1. Again, a "For Loop" is used to compute the asset values of the bonds and the portfolio.

The stand-alone risk is simply the standard deviation of the simulated asset values for each individual bond. It can be determined through the procedure given by:

```
For LBond = 1 To nbond
  Worksheets("OutputResult").Range("D4").Offset(LBond - 1, 0) = portHldg(LBond, 1)
  Worksheets("OutputResult").Range("E4").Offset(LBond - 1, 0) = portHldg(LBond, 2)
  For Ls = 1 To numOfIterations
    tempArray(Ls) = simulatedPortValue(Ls, LBond)
  Next Ls
  mean = WorksheetFunction.Average(tempArray)
  stdev = WorksheetFunction.stdev(tempArray)
  Worksheets("OutputResult").Range("F4").Offset(LBond - 1, 0) = stdev
  If mean <> 0 Then
    Worksheets("OutputResult").Range("G4").Offset(LBond - 1, 0) = stdev / mean
  End If
Next LBond
```

On the other hand, the overall portfolio risk can be determined in both dollar and percentage terms as:

```
For Ls = 1 To numOfIterations
  tempArray(Ls) = 0
  For LBond = 1 To nbond
    tempArray(Ls) = tempArray(Ls) + simulatedPortValue(Ls, LBond)
  Next LBond
Next Ls

mean = WorksheetFunction.Average(tempArray)
stdev = WorksheetFunction.stdev(tempArray)
Worksheets("OutputResult").Range("B4").Value = mean
Worksheets("OutputResult").Range("B5").Value = stdev
Worksheets("OutputResult").Range("B6").Value = stdev / mean
Worksheets("OutputResult").Range("B7").Value = WorksheetFunction.Percentile(tempArray,
  0.05)
Worksheets("OutputResult").Range("B8").Value = WorksheetFunction.Percentile(tempArray,
  0.01)
```

In terms of calculating the marginal risk of each bond, the holding of each bond is set to be zero, respectively. A full evaluation of the portfolio standard deviation is calculated from the above procedure. Hence the marginal risk is the difference between the resulting portfolio standard deviation and the original portfolio standard deviation.

```
For Lptr = 1 To nbond
  tempsave = portHldg(Lptr, 6)
  portHldg(Lptr, 6) = 0
  Call simPortValue(numOfIterations, corRandomArray, nbond, portHldg,
  portAssetThreshold, oneYearForwardPortValues, simulatedPortValue)

  For Ls = 1 To numOfIterations
    tempArray(Ls) = 0
    For LBond = 1 To nbond
      tempArray(Ls) = tempArray(Ls) + simulatedPortValue(Ls, LBond)
    Next LBond
  Next Ls
  stdev = WorksheetFunction.stdev(tempArray)
  Worksheets("OutputResult").Range("H4").Offset(Lptr - 1, 0) = Worksheets("OutputResult").
    Range("B5").Value - stdev
  Worksheets("OutputResult").Range("I4").Offset(Lptr - 1, 0) = (Worksheets("OutputResult").
    Range("B5").Value - stdev) / Worksheets("OutputResult").Range("B4").Value
  portHldg(Lptr, 6) = tempsave
Next Lptr
```

The final result is summarized in Figure 12.6. The VBA routine called creditEngine(), which implements all of the above procedures, is given by Code 12.3.

On a separate note, the sample portfolio consists of four bonds, but the program can easily handle more than four bonds as long as "Number of bonds," "Correlation matrix range," and the actual correlation matrix are specified correctly as shown in Figure 12.7.

	A	B	C	D	E	F	G	H	I	J
1										
2	Number of iterations =	10000				Stand Alone Risk		Marginal Risk		
3				Identifer	Rating	(S)	(%)	(S)	(%)	
4	Overall Mean Value =	10,126,841		3598A8	AA	23,940	0.59%	-3,975	-0.04%	
5	Overall Standard Deviation (S) =	443,956		5987Y2	A	45,840	1.45%	4,210	0.04%	
6	Overall Standard Deviation (%) =	4.38%		6899T3	B	312,799	15.84%	140,010	1.38%	
7	The 5th Percentile =	9,316,721		8934M7	CCC	302,145	33.31%	122,681	1.21%	
8	The 1th Percentile =	8,441,103								
9										
10		Credit Engine								
11										
12										

FIGURE 12.6 Output of portfolio risk, stand-alone risk, and marginal risk of the bond portfolio.

	A	B	T	U	V	W	X	Y
1								
2	Number of bonds	4			**Correlation Matrix**			
3				3598A8	5987Y2	6899T3	8928B7	
4			3598A8	1	0.16	0.08	0.02	
5	Correlation Range	U4:X7	5987Y2	0.16	1	0.34	0.12	
6			6899T3	0.08	0.34	1	0.06	
7			8928B7	0.02	0.12	0.06	1	
8								

FIGURE 12.7 Specification of correlation matrix, its range, and number of bonds.

```
Function CholeskyDecom(ByRef sigma As Object)

    Dim n As Integer: n = sigma.Columns.Count
    Dim X As Double
    Dim a() As Double: ReDim a(1 To n, 1 To n)
    Dim M() As Double: ReDim M(1 To n, 1 To n)
    Dim i As Integer, j As Integer, k As Integer

    For i = 1 To n
      For j = 1 To n
        a(i, j) = sigma.Cells(i, j).Value
        M(i, j) = 0
      Next j
    Next i

    For i = 1 To n
      For j = i To n
        X = a(i, j)
        For k = 1 To (i - 1)
          X = X - M(i, k) * M(j, k)
        Next k
        If j = i Then
          M(i, i) = Sqr(X)
        Else
          M(j, i) = X / M(i, i)
        End If
      Next j
    Next i

    CholeskyDecom = M

End Function
```

```
Function invStdNorRandomArray(numOfRows As Integer, numOfColumns As Integer)
    Dim i As Integer, j As Integer
    Dim anArray() As Double: ReDim anArray(1 To numOfRows, 1 To numOfColumns)
```

```vba
For i = 1 To numOfRows
  For j = 1 To numOfColumns
    anArray(i, j) = StdNormNum()
  Next j
Next i
invStdNorRandomArray = anArray
End Function
```

```vba
Function corInvStdNorRandomArray(ByRef randomArray() As Double, ByRef choleskyMatrix
    () As Double)
  Dim i As Integer, j As Integer, k As Integer
  Dim numOfRows As Integer: numOfRows = UBound(randomArray, 1)
  Dim numOfColumns As Integer: numOfColumns = UBound(randomArray, 2)
  Dim anArray() As Double: ReDim anArray(1 To numOfRows, 1 To numOfColumns)
  For i = 1 To numOfRows
    For j = 1 To numOfColumns
      anArray(i, j) = 0
      For k = 1 To numOfColumns
        anArray(i, j) = anArray(i, j) + randomArray(i, k) * choleskyMatrix(j, k)
      Next k
    Next j
  Next i
  corInvStdNorRandomArray = anArray
End Function
```

```vba
Function randomInvBetaDist(mean As Double, stdDev As Double) As Double
  randomInvBetaDist = WorksheetFunction.BetaInv(Rnd(), mean * (mean * (1 - mean) /
    (stdDev ^ 2) - 1), (1 - mean) * (mean * (1 - mean) / (stdDev ^ 2) - 1))
End Function
```

Code 12.1: VBA codes of user functions.

```vba
Sub simPortValue(numOfIterations As Integer, corRandomArray() As Double, nbond As
    Integer, portHldg() As Variant, portAssetThreshold() As Double,
    oneYearForwardPortValues() As Double, ByRef simulatedPortValue() As Double)

  Dim Ls As Integer
  Dim LBond As Integer
  Dim LEndRating As Integer
  Dim recoveryMean As Double
  Dim recoveryStdDev As Double

  For Ls = 1 To numOfIterations
    For LBond = 1 To nbond
```

```
If corRandomArray(Ls, LBond) > portAssetThreshold(LBond, 1) Then
    LEndRating = 1
ElseIf corRandomArray(Ls, LBond) > portAssetThreshold(LBond, 2) Then
    LEndRating = 2
ElseIf corRandomArray(Ls, LBond) > portAssetThreshold(LBond, 3) Then
    LEndRating = 3
ElseIf corRandomArray(Ls, LBond) > portAssetThreshold(LBond, 4) Then
    LEndRating = 4
ElseIf corRandomArray(Ls, LBond) > portAssetThreshold(LBond, 5) Then
    LEndRating = 5
ElseIf corRandomArray(Ls, LBond) > portAssetThreshold(LBond, 6) Then
    LEndRating = 6
ElseIf corRandomArray(Ls, LBond) > portAssetThreshold(LBond, 7) Then
    LEndRating = 7
Else
    LEndRating = 8
End If


If LEndRating <> 8 Then
    simulatedPortValue(Ls, LBond) = oneYearForwardPortValues(LBond, LEndRating) /
        100 * portHldg(LBond, 6)
Else
    Select Case portHldg(LBond, 3)
        Case "Senior Secured"
            recoveryMean = 0.538
            recoveryStdDev = 0.2686
            simulatedPortValue(Ls, LBond) = randomInvBetaDist(recoveryMean,
                recoveryStdDev) * portHldg(LBond, 6)
        Case "Senior Unsecured"
            recoveryMean = 0.5113
            recoveryStdDev = 0.2545
            simulatedPortValue(Ls, LBond) = randomInvBetaDist(recoveryMean,
                recoveryStdDev) * portHldg(LBond, 6)
        Case "Senior Subordinated"
            recoveryMean = 0.3852
            recoveryStdDev = 0.2381
            simulatedPortValue(Ls, LBond) = randomInvBetaDist(recoveryMean,
                recoveryStdDev) * portHldg(LBond, 6)
        Case "Subordinated"
            recoveryMean = 0.3274
            recoveryStdDev = 0.2018
            simulatedPortValue(Ls, LBond) = randomInvBetaDist(recoveryMean,
                recoveryStdDev) * portHldg(LBond, 6)
        Case "Junior Subordinated"
            recoveryMean = 0.1709
            recoveryStdDev = 0.109
            simulatedPortValue(Ls, LBond) = randomInvBetaDist(recoveryMean,
                recoveryStdDev) * portHldg(LBond, 6)
    End Select
End If
```

```
      Next LBond

    Next Ls

End Sub
```

Code 12.2: VBA codes of the simPortValue() routine.

```
Sub CreditEngine()

    Dim assetThresholdMatrix(1 To 7, 1 To 7) As Double
    Dim LInitRating As Integer
    Dim LThreshold As Integer
    Dim LEndRating As Integer

    Call calAssetThreshold(assetThresholdMatrix)

    For LThreshold = 1 To 7
      For LInitRating = 1 To 7
        Worksheets("Reference").Range("L4").Offset(LInitRating - 1, LThreshold - 1).Value =
          assetThresholdMatrix(LInitRating, LThreshold)
      Next LInitRating
    Next LThreshold

'- - - - - - - - - - - - - - - - - - - - - - - - - - - - - - - - - -
    Dim nbond As Integer: nbond = Worksheets("InputParameters").Range("B2").Value
    Dim portHldg() As Variant: ReDim portHldg(1 To nbond, 1 To 6)
    Dim oneYearForwardPortValues() As Double: ReDim oneYearForwardPortValues(1 To
      nbond, 1 To 8)
    Dim oneYearForwardBondValues(1 To 8) As Double
    Dim portAssetThreshold() As Double: ReDim portAssetThreshold(1 To nbond, 1 To 7)
    Dim couponRate As Double
    Dim yearToMaturity As Integer
    Dim LBond As Integer
    Dim k As Integer

    For LBond = 1 To nbond

'reading in the content of the bond portfolio

      For k = 1 To 6
        portHldg(LBond, k) = Worksheets("InputParameters").Range("D4").Offset(LBond - 1,
          k - 1).Value
      Next k

'evaluating the one year bond values for each bond in the portfolio

      couponRate = portHldg(LBond, 4)
      yearToMaturity = portHldg(LBond, 5)
```

```
Call calForwardBondValues(couponRate, yearToMaturity, oneYearForwardBondValues)
For LEndRating = 1 To 8
   oneYearForwardPortValues(LBond, LEndRating) = oneYearForwardBondValues
   (LEndRating)
   Worksheets("InputParameters").Range("K4").Offset(LBond - 1, LEndRating - 1) =
   oneYearForwardPortValues(LBond, LEndRating)
Next LEndRating
```

'setting up the asset return threshold for each bond in the portfolio

```
Select Case portHldg(LBond, 2)
   Case "AAA"
      LInitRating = 1
   Case "AA"
      LInitRating = 2
   Case "A"
      LInitRating = 3
   Case "BBB"
      LInitRating = 4
   Case "BB"
      LInitRating = 5
   Case "B"
      LInitRating = 6
   Case "CCC"
      LInitRating = 7
End Select
For LThreshold = 1 To 7
   portAssetThreshold(LBond, LThreshold) = assetThresholdMatrix(LInitRating,
   LThreshold)
Next LThreshold

Next LBond
```

```
'-----------------------------------
'generating an array of correlated random variables

Dim numOfIterations As Integer: numOfIterations = Worksheets("OutputResult").Range
   ("B2").Value
Dim choleskyMatrix() As Double: choleskyMatrix() = CholeskyDecom(Worksheets
   ("InputParameters").Range(Worksheets("InputParameters").Range("B5").Value))
Dim numOfFactors As Integer: numOfFactors = UBound(choleskyMatrix(), 1)
Dim randomArray() As Double: ReDim randomArray(1 To numOfIterations, 1 To
   numOfFactors)
Dim corRandomArray() As Double: ReDim corRandomArray(1 To numOfIterations, 1 To
   numOfFactors)

seed = 5678

randomArray() = invStdNorRandomArray(numOfIterations, numOfFactors)

corRandomArray() = corInvStdNorRandomArray(randomArray, choleskyMatrix)
```

```vba
'------------------------------------
'mapping of scenarios

    Dim simulatedPortValue() As Double: ReDim simulatedPortValue(1 To numOfIterations, 1
        To nbond)

    Call simPortValue(numOfIterations, corRandomArray, nbond, portHldg,
        portAssetThreshold, oneYearForwardPortValues, simulatedPortValue)

'------------------------------------
'writing out the standalone risk number

    Dim tempArray() As Variant: ReDim tempArray(1 To numOfIterations)
    Dim Ls As Integer
    Dim mean As Double, stdev As Double

    For LBond = 1 To nbond
        Worksheets("OutputResult").Range("D4").Offset(LBond - 1, 0) = portHldg(LBond, 1)
        Worksheets("OutputResult").Range("E4").Offset(LBond - 1, 0) = portHldg(LBond, 2)
        For Ls = 1 To numOfIterations
            tempArray(Ls) = simulatedPortValue(Ls, LBond)
        Next Ls
        mean = WorksheetFunction.Average(tempArray)
        stdev = WorksheetFunction.stdev(tempArray)
        Worksheets("OutputResult").Range("F4").Offset(LBond - 1, 0) = stdev
        If mean <> 0 Then
            Worksheets("OutputResult").Range("G4").Offset(LBond - 1, 0) = stdev / mean
        End If
    Next LBond

'------------------------------------
'writing out the overall risk number

    For Ls = 1 To numOfIterations
        tempArray(Ls) = 0
        For LBond = 1 To nbond
            tempArray(Ls) = tempArray(Ls) + simulatedPortValue(Ls, LBond)
        Next LBond
    Next Ls

    mean = WorksheetFunction.Average(tempArray)
    stdev = WorksheetFunction.stdev(tempArray)
    Worksheets("OutputResult").Range("B4").Value = mean
    Worksheets("OutputResult").Range("B5").Value = stdev
    Worksheets("OutputResult").Range("B6").Value = stdev / mean
    Worksheets("OutputResult").Range("B7").Value = WorksheetFunction.Percentile
        (tempArray, 0.05)
    Worksheets("OutputResult").Range("B8").Value = WorksheetFunction.Percentile
        (tempArray, 0.01)
```

```
'- - - - - - - - - - - - - - - - - - - - - - - - - - - - - - - - - - -
'writing out the marginal risk number

  Dim tempsave As Double
  Dim Lptr As Integer

  For Lptr = 1 To nbond
    tempsave = portHldg(Lptr, 6)
    portHldg(Lptr, 6) = 0
    Call simPortValue(numOfIterations, corRandomArray, nbond, portHldg,
      portAssetThreshold, oneYearForwardPortValues, simulatedPortValue)
    For Ls = 1 To numOfIterations
      tempArray(Ls) = 0
      For LBond = 1 To nbond
        tempArray(Ls) = tempArray(Ls) + simulatedPortValue(Ls, LBond)
      Next LBond
    Next Ls
    stdev = WorksheetFunction.stdev(tempArray)
    Worksheets("OutputResult").Range("H4").Offset(Lptr - 1, 0) = Worksheets
      ("OutputResult").Range("B5").Value - stdev
    Worksheets("OutputResult").Range("I4").Offset(Lptr - 1, 0) = (Worksheets
      ("OutputResult").Range("B5").Value - stdev) _ / Worksheets("OutputResult")
          .Range("B4").Value
    portHldg(Lptr, 6) = tempsave
  Next Lptr

End Sub
```

Code 12.3: *VBA codes of the creditEngine() routine.*

```
Sub calAssetThreshold(ByRef assetThresholdMatrix() As Double)

  Dim tranMatrix(1 To 7, 1 To 8) As Double
  Dim LInitRating As Integer
  Dim LEndRating As Integer
  Dim LThreshold As Integer
  Dim k As Integer
  Dim tempProb As Double

'reading in the one year transition matrix

  For LInitRating = 1 To 7
    For LEndRating = 1 To 8
      tranMatrix(LInitRating, LEndRating) = Worksheets("Reference").Range("B4").Offset
        (LInitRating - 1, LEndRating - 1).Value / 100
    Next LEndRating
  Next LInitRating

'evaluating the asset return threshold matrix
```

```
     For LInitRating = 1 To 7
       For LThreshold = 7 To 1 Step -1
         tempProb = 0
         For k = 7 To LThreshold Step -1
           tempProb = tempProb + WorksheetFunction.Max(tranMatrix(LInitRating, k + 1),
             0.0000000001) `1E-10 is used to avoid zero
         Next k
         assetThresholdMatrix(LInitRating, LThreshold) = WorksheetFunction.NormSInv
           (tempProb)
       Next LThreshold
     Next LInitRating
End Sub
```

```
Sub calForwardBondValues(couponRate As Double, yearToMaturity As Integer,
   oneYearForwardBondValues() As Double)

   Dim oneYearForwardCurves(1 To 7, 1 To 4) As Double
   Dim LEndRating As Integer
   Dim LYear As Integer
   Dim k As Integer
   Dim sum As Double

'reading in the one year forward zero curve for different year end non-default ratings
   For LEndRating = 1 To 7
     For LYear = 1 To 4
       oneYearForwardCurves(LEndRating, LYear) = Worksheets("Reference").Range
         ("B17").Offset(LEndRating - 1, LYear - 1).Value / 100
     Next LYear
   Next LEndRating

'evaluating the one year bond values for different year end ratings
   For LEndRating = 1 To 7
     sum = couponRate * 100
     For k = 1 To yearToMaturity - 1
       sum = sum + couponRate * 100 / ((1 + oneYearForwardCurves(LEndRating, k)) ^ k)
       If k = yearToMaturity - 1 Then
         sum = sum + 100 / ((1 + oneYearForwardCurves(LEndRating, k)) ^ k)
       End If
     Next k
     oneYearForwardBondValues(LEndRating) = sum
   Next LEndRating

   oneYearForwardBondValues(8) = 0

End Sub
```

Code 12.4: VBA codes of the calAssetThreshold() and calForwardBondValues() routines.

REVIEW QUESTIONS

1. The CreditMetrics model uses the correlation between firms' equity returns as a proxy for the correlation of asset returns. In the implementation of the model, the correlation used was arbitrary. Select three to five large cap firms, preferred in different countries and industries, compute their correlations using their equity data; then implement the CreditMetrics model with their underlying bond data.

2. Select a global benchmark index such as the MSCI All Country World Index (ACWI) or the Global Dow index (GDOW); then apply the firms' volatilities of the chosen index with their country-industry pairs to compute the correlations, and implement the CreditMetrics model. Contrast the result against that of Question 1.

ENDNOTES

1. "CreditMetrics^{TM} – Technical Document," J.P. Morgan & Co., 1997.
2. Refer to CreditMetrics.xls.
3. Robert C. Merton, "On the Pricing of Corporate Debt: The Risk Structure of Interest Rates," *Journal of Finance* 29, No. 2 (1974): 449–470.
4. Because the volatility of an asset return does not affect the joint probabilities of credit rating changes, so the asset return threshold values can be applied.
5. The joint distribution of the asset returns is assumed to be multivariate normal.
6. It is referred to as a credit rating migration outcome where a new credit rating reaches the risk horizon.
7. Since the beta distribution produces numbers between zero and one, so meaningful recovery rates would be chosen.
8. The recovery rate of a given obligor is independent of all other asset values within the portfolio.
9. Refer to Section 8.5 of "CreditMetrics^{TM} – Technical Document," J.P. Morgan & Co., 1997.
10. Carty & Lieberman [96a] — Moody's Investors Service.

## CHAPTER 13

KMV–Merton Model

13.1 KMV–MERTON MODEL OF CREDIT RISK

Credit risk is the risk that a debtor fails to meet its repayments according to a pre-determined schedule, either incapably or unwillingly. In this chapter, the main focus is on the credit risk of a publicly traded firm. Many practitioners and academics have carried out research in forecasting the credit default of a firm. One key model that has been broadly applied is the structural model developed by Merton.[1] The model uses a firm's structural variables such as liability and equity to determine its default probability. A firm is considered to be in default when its assets are not sufficient to cover its debt at maturity. When the value of assets is greater than the value of debt, the firm should be able to make the debt repayment and the value of equity at this time is positive given by the accounting relationship:

$$\text{Asset} - \text{Liability} = \text{Equity}.$$

On the other hand, when the value of assets is less than the value of debt, the firm will default on the debt and the value of equity is zero as all assets are claimed by the bond owners as shown in Figure 13.1. The Merton model suggests that equity can be considered a call option on the value of the assets with strike price equal to the firm's debt. Assume that the value of assets follows a random log-normal process. It appears that the process is not directly observable. However, the value of assets and its volatility can be inferred from the market value of equity utilizing the Black–Scholes pricing of call options. Consequently, the probability of default can be calculated.

The crucial assumption of the Merton model is that the value of assets follows a random log-normal process given by:

$$\Delta A_t / A_t = \varepsilon(\mu_A \Delta t, \sigma_A \sqrt{\Delta t}) \tag{13.1}$$

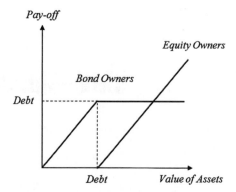

FIGURE 13.1 Pay-off to bond and equity owners.

where μ_A and σ_A are respectively the expected return and the volatility of assets. They are considered to be constant parameters. It is clear that neither of these parameters nor the value of assets are directly observable. Suppose that the firm has issued one zero-coupon bond that matures at time T. The value of equity can be considered a call option on the value of the assets with strike price equal to the notional value of the firm's debt L and maturity at time T. The payoff to equity owners at maturity is therefore equivalent to:

$$E_T = \max\{A_T - L, 0\}. \tag{13.2}$$

Consequently, the value of equity at any time t prior to the maturity can be calculated through the Black–Scholes pricing of call options as:

$$E_t = A_t \, N(d_1) - L \, e^{-r(T-t)} \, N(d_2) \tag{13.3}$$

where r is the risk-free interest rate. The terms d_1 and d_2 are given by:

$$d_1 = \frac{\ln(A_t/L) + (r + \frac{1}{2}\sigma_A^2)(T - t)}{\sigma_A \sqrt{T - t}} \tag{13.4}$$

$$d_2 = d_1 - \sigma_A \sqrt{T - t}. \tag{13.5}$$

The Black-Scholes pricing in (13.3) describes the value of equity as a function of the value of assets if the firm's debt at time T is L. It also generates the relationship between the volatility of equity and the volatility of assets through Ito's lemma as:[2]

$$\sigma_E = \left(\frac{A_t}{E_t}\right) N(d_1)\sigma_A. \tag{13.6}$$

For a publicly traded firm, the current value of equity is easily obtained from the market by calculating the market cap of the firm. Likewise, the current volatility of equity can also be estimated using a historical dataset of stock returns. The Merton model suggests that the current value of assets A_0 and its volatility σ_A can be inferred from the market data of equity using the two non-linear equations in (13.3) and (13.6) with $t = 0$. The probability that the firm will default on its debt L that matures at later time T can be calculated as:[3]

$$P_{default} = N(-D) \qquad (13.7)$$

where D is regarded as the distance to default from the mean value of assets in number of standard deviations given by:

$$D = \frac{\ln(A_0/L) + (\mu_A - \frac{1}{2}\sigma_A^2)T}{\sigma_A\sqrt{T}}. \qquad (13.8)$$

The expected return of assets μ_A in (13.8) remains to be determined by some other procedure.

EXAMPLE 13.1

Suppose we have collected the up-to-date monthly stock prices of a firm for the previous year. The current stock price of the firm is given in cell E14 (see Figure 13.2) with outstanding shares in cell F14. The current value of equity E_0 is then calculated to be E14*F14 = $52,000.00. The current volatility of equity σ_E can be estimated

	A	B	C	D	E	F	G	H
1				Date	Stock Prices	Outstanding Shares	Equity	Log Returns
2	Maturity (T)	1	(years)	10/31/2007	52.40	1000	52400	
3	Risk-Free Rate (r)	1.34%	(per year)	11/30/2007	52.80	1000	52800	0.76%
4	Debt (L)	$102,304.00		12/31/2007	53.25	1000	53250	0.85%
5	Equity (E₀)	$52,000.00		1/31/2008	61.75	1000	61750	14.81%
6	Equity Volatility (σₑ)	29.65%	(per year)	2/29/2008	61.50	1000	61500	-0.41%
7	Asset (A₀)	$152,942.22		3/31/2008	64.05	1000	64050	4.06%
8	Asset Volatility (σₐ)	10.08%	(per year)	4/30/2008	61.75	1000	61750	-3.66%
9				5/30/2008	70.50	1000	70500	13.25%
10	Precision	1.00E-08	Calculate	6/30/2008	66.80	1000	66800	-5.39%
11	PrecFlag	TRUE	Asset & Volatility	7/31/2008	64.10	1000	64100	-4.13%
12	Max. Dev.	8.70E-10		8/29/2008	63.50	1000	63500	-0.94%
13				9/30/2008	62.35	1000	62350	-1.83%
14	Asset Mean Return (μₐ)	2.50%	(per year)	10/31/2008	52.00	1000	52000	-18.15%
15	Distance to default (D)	4.19						
16	Default Probability (P default)	1.42E-05						
17								
18								

FIGURE 13.2 A simple implementation of the KMV–Merton model.

through the standard deviation of monthly historical returns on equity in cells H3:H14 as:

$$\text{STDEV}(H3 : H14)^* \ \mathbf{SQRT}(12) = 29.65 \text{ percent per year.}$$

The debt L that will have to be paid in $T = 1$ year is \$102,304.00. The risk-free interest rate r is 1.34 percent per year.

The inferred value of assets A_0 and its volatility σ_A from (13.3) and (13.6) can be determined by calling the Newton–Raphson procedure with two variables given by:

$$g_1(A_0, \sigma_A) = E_0 - [A_0 N(d_1) - L\, e^{-rT} N(d_2)]$$
$$g_2(A_0, \sigma_A) = \sigma_E - (A_0/E_0)\, N(d_1)\, \sigma_A$$

where $d_1 = \dfrac{\ln(A_0/L) + (r + \frac{1}{2}\sigma_A^2)T}{\sigma_A \sqrt{T}}$ and $d_2 = d_1 - \sigma_A \sqrt{T}$.

The search can be initiated from the point where A_0 is much greater than L such that both d_1 and d_2 are large. This gives the initial point of the search as $A_0 = E_0 + L$ and $\sigma_A = \sigma_E E_0/(E_0 + L)$. The VBA coding for this routine is given as follows:

```
Sub CalAssetVol()
    Dim x(1 To 2) As Double, n As Integer, prec As Double, precFlag As Boolean,
        maxDev As Double
    n = 2
    x(1) = Range("debt").Value + Range("equity").Value
    x(2) = Range("sigmaEquity").Value * Range("equity").Value / x(1)
    prec = Range("prec").Value
    Call NewtonRaphson(n, prec, x, precFlag, maxDev)
    Range("B7") = x(1)
    Range("B8") = x(2)
    Range("B11") = precFlag
    Range("B12") = maxDev
End Sub

Sub FunctionArray(n As Integer, x() As Double, ByRef g() As Double)
    Dim maturity As Double: maturity = Range("maturity").Value
    Dim debt As Double: debt = Range("debt").Value
    Dim equity As Double: equity = Range("equity").Value
    Dim sigmaEquity As Double: sigmaEquity = Range("sigmaEquity").Value
    Dim riskFree As Double: riskFree = Range("riskFree").Value
    Dim d1 As Double, d2 As Double
    d1 = (Log(x(1) / debt) + (riskFree + x(2) ^ 2 / 2) * maturity) / (x(2) * Sqr(maturity))
    d2 = d1 - x(2) * Sqr(maturity)
    With Application.WorksheetFunction
```

```
      g(1) = equity - x(1) * .NormSDist(d1) + debt * Exp(-riskFree * maturity) * .
         NormSDist(d2)
      g(2) = sigmaEquity - (x(1) / equity) * .NormSDist(d1) * x(2)
   End With
End Sub
```

The resulting values of $A_0 = \$152{,}942.22$ and $\sigma_A = 10.08$ percent per year are respectively displayed in cells B7 and B8. Suppose the expected return of asset is estimated to be $\mu_A = 2.50$ percent per year. The distance to default is calculated to be $D = 4.19$ and the probability of default $P_{default}$ in $T = 1$ year is determined to be 1.42×10^{-5}.

KMV Corporation has developed a practical application of Merton's model in predicting the default of a firm.[4] The goal of the KMV–Merton model is to generate the probability of default, referred to as the Expected Default Frequency (EDF), for the firm at any given time in the future. KMV claims that solving both equations (13.3) and (13.6) simultaneously for the current value of assets and its volatility will give bad results in practice. In particular, the linkage between equity volatility and asset volatility in (13.6) holds only instantaneously. The market leverage moves around far too much for (13.6) to provide reasonable results according to endnote 4. KMV suspends the full use of equation (13.6) and formulates an iterative procedure that simultaneously estimates all three parameters A_0, σ_A, and μ_A using (13.3).

In implementing the KMV–Merton model, the first step is to choose a forecasting horizon. It is common to consider a forecasting period of one year with $T = 1$. Next collect the up-to-date historical stock prices of the firm and calculate the values of equity $\{E(1), E(2), \ldots, E(m)\}$ for each day in the previous year. It should be noted that the last entry $E(m)$ in the series is presumably the current value of equity E_0 of the firm. Then gather the book values of the firm's aggregate liabilities as the notional values of the firm's debt $\{L(1), L(2), \ldots, L(m)\}$ in the same period. After that, gather the information about the risk-free interest rates $\{r(1), r(2), \ldots, r(m)\}$ with the same maturity term of T. The fifth step is to perform the following iterative procedure that simultaneously estimates all three parameters A_0, σ_A, and μ_A.

1. Take the initial guess of $\sigma_A = \sigma_E E(m)/[E(m) + L(m)]$ as in Example 13.1. The current volatility of equity σ_E can be estimated through the standard deviation of daily historical returns on equity $\{r_E(2), r_E(3), \ldots, r_E(m)\}$, where $r_E(i) = \ln[E(i)/E(i-1)]$, scaled up by a factor of $\sqrt{260}$ for 260 trading days per year.

2. Since Equation (13.3) must be true at any time in the past, we have:

$$E(i) = A(i)N(d_1) - L(i)e^{-r(i)T}N(d_2), \quad d_1 = \frac{\ln[A(i)/L(i)] + (r(i) + \frac{1}{2}\sigma_A^2)T}{\sigma_A\sqrt{T}}$$
$$d_2 = d_1 - \sigma_A\sqrt{T}$$

$$(13.9)$$

for $i = 1, 2, \ldots, m$. Given the trial estimate of σ_A, use (13.9) to generate a sequence of inferred asset values $\{A(1), A(2), \ldots, A(m)\}$ for each day in the previous year. Again, the term $A(m)$ represents the current value of assets A_0.

3. Calculate the daily returns on assets $\{r_A(2), r_A(3), \ldots, r_A(m)\}$, where $r_A(i) = \ln[A(i)/A(i-1)]$, for each day in the previous year. Update the estimates of σ_A and μ_A through the standard deviation and mean, respectively, of the return series.

4. Repeat (2) and (3) until the value of σ_A converges for which the absolute difference in adjacent estimates is less than the required precision.

(Ex).

The final step is to calculate the default probability or the EDF measure in (13.7) using $L(m)$ together with the estimated values of $A(m)$, σ_A and μ_A.

It should be noted that the procedure used in this chapter illustrates only the structure of the KMV–Merton model. A commercial implementation of the model is far more sophisticated with five major differences:

- Five classes of liabilities are used.
- Cash payouts are incorporated in the model.
- Default can take place at or before horizon.
- Equity is a perpetual call option on the underlying assets.
- Default barrier and distance to default in EDF mapping are empirically determined.

13.2 EXCEL AND VBA IMPLEMENTATION

The KMV–Merton model of credit risk can be implemented very easily in VBA. We first develop a routine called CalDefProb() that performs the above iteration and estimates the parameters $A(m)$, σ_A, and μ_A in the calculation of the default probability. The pseudo code of CalDefProb() is given by Code 13.1. It requires the input of the forecasting horizon T together with the market data $\{E(1), \ldots, E(m)\}$, $\{L(1), \ldots, L(m)\}$, and $\{r(1), \ldots, r(m)\}$. They are kept as common data at the module scope that can be accessed by other routines within the module. In Code 13.1, the iterative procedure that simultaneously estimates all three parameters A

(m), σ_A, and μ_A can be illustrated by the following flow diagram.

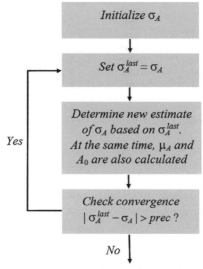

Initialize σ_A

Set $\sigma_A^{last} = \sigma_A$

Determine new estimate of σ_A based on σ_A^{last}. At the same time, μ_A and A_0 are also calculated

Check convergence $|\sigma_A^{last} - \sigma_A| > prec$?

Yes

No

Final σ_A with μ_A and A_0

The volatility of equity σ_E is first estimated through the standard deviation of daily returns on equity $\{r_E(2), r_E(3), \ldots, r_E(m)\}$, for which the initial guess for the volatility of assets σ_A can accordingly be defined. In an iterative procedure, it is useful to store the latest estimate of σ_A using another variable called σ_A^{last} such that the new estimate of σ_A can easily be compared for convergence. The latest σ_A^{last} will be used to generate a sequence of inferred asset values $\{A(1), A(2), \ldots, A(m)\}$ from (13.9). This can be achieved by calling the Newton-Raphson procedure successively for each i_{ptr}, running from 1 to m, with one variable x taken to be the inferred asset value. In generating $A(i_{ptr})$, the search can be initiated by setting $x = E(i_{ptr}) + L(i_{ptr})$ with required precision of $prec = 1 \times 10^{-8}$. The routine *FunctionArray()* evaluates the discrepancy in (13.9) with respect to the time pointer i_{ptr} by taking in the corresponding market data $E(i_{ptr})$, $L(i_{ptr})$, and $r(i_{ptr})$ together with the latest σ_A^{last} and maturity T. Both σ_A^{last} and i_{ptr} are kept as common data so that they can be accessed by *FunctionArray()* within the same module. It is then possible to update the estimates of σ_A and μ_A through the standard deviation and mean, respectively, of the daily returns on assets $\{r_A(2), r_A(3), \ldots, r_A(m)\}$ relative to the generated asset values. The new estimate of σ_A can be checked for convergence by comparing it with σ_A^{last} based on the same precision as adopted in the Newton–Raphson procedure. If the convergence condition has been satisfied, it will be taken as the final result of σ_A together with the new μ_A and $A(m)$.

	A	B	C	D	E	F
1	Date	Stock Prices	Outstanding Shares	Equity	Liability	Risk-Free Rate
2	11/1/2007	52.40	1000	52400.00	105039	3.89%
3	11/2/2007	52.15	1000	52150.00	105039	3.74%
4	11/5/2007	52.30	1000	52300.00	105039	3.86%
5	11/6/2007	52.40	1000	52400.00	105039	3.83%
249	10/29/2008	50.40	1000	50400.00	102304	1.41%
250	10/30/2008	55.00	1000	55000.00	102304	1.36%
251	10/31/2008	52.00	1000	52000.00	102304	1.34%
252						

FIGURE 13.3 The layout of the worksheet "Data."

Otherwise, repeat the procedure by going back to the statement where we assign σ_A^{last} to be the latest σ_A. It is then straightforward to evaluate the distance to default and default probability using (13.8) and (13.7) respectively once all three parameters have been estimated.

Figures 13.3 and 13.4 depict the spreadsheet design for the VBA implementation[5] of the KMV–Merton model. In Figure 13.3, market data are kept under the worksheet "Data" where we have collected the up-to-date (as of the date shown in A251) stock prices in column B, outstanding shares in column C, and aggregate liabilities in column E of the firm for each day in the previous year. Risk-free interest rates within the same time period are also collected in column F. The firm's equity for each day in column D can be calculated as the product of the corresponding entries in column B and column C in the same row. Figure 13.4 depicts the worksheet "KMV–Merton" that serves as the output interface of this implementation. The

	A	B	C	D
1				
2	Maturity (T)	1	(years)	
3	Risk-Free Rate (r_0)	1.34%	(per year)	
4	Debt (L_0)	$102,304.00		
5	Equity (E_0)	$52,000.00		
6	Equity Volatility (σ_E)	41.46%	(per year)	
7	Asset (A_0)	$152,916.72		
8	Asset Volatility (σ_A)	15.76%	(per year)	
9	Asset Mean Return (μ_A)	-0.33%	(per year)	
10				
11	Distance to default (D)	2.45		
12	Default Probability ($P_{default}$)	0.0071407	Default Probability	
13				
14				

FIGURE 13.4 The layout of the worksheet "KMV–Merton."

VBA code of CalDefProb() that incorporates the above spreadsheet design is given by Code 13.2.

```
# define the following module-level variables
```
$T, E(1:m), \quad L(1:m), r(1:m), i_{ptr}, \sigma_A^{last}$

CalDefProb( )

```
# input market data from Excel
    Read T, m, E(1 : m), L(1 : m), r(1 : m)
```

```
# estimate σ_E
```
$\quad$ For($i = 2$ to m){ $\quad r_E(i) = \ln(E(i) / E(i-1))$ $\quad$ }
$\quad \sigma_E =$ **STDEV**($r_E(2:m)$) $\times \sqrt{260}$

```
# define the initial guess for σ_A
```
$\quad \sigma_A = \sigma_E E(m)/[E(m) + L(m)]$

```
# save latest estimate of σ_A for comparison
# label this statement as the beginning of the iteration
```
$\quad$ *nextltr* : $\sigma_A^{last} = \sigma_A$

```
# use σ_A^last to generate { A(1), A(2), ..., A(m) } through the Newton-Raphson procedure
```
$\quad$ For($i_{ptr} = 1$ to m){ $\quad x = E(i_{ptr}) + L(i_{ptr})$
$\qquad\qquad\qquad\qquad prec = 1 \times 10^{-8}$
$\qquad\qquad\qquad\qquad$ Call *NewtonRaphson*(1 , *prec* , *x* , *precflag* , *maxdev*)
$\qquad\qquad\qquad\qquad A(i_{ptr}) = x$
$\qquad\qquad\quad$ }

```
# update the estimates of σ_A and μ_A
```
$\quad$ For($i = 2$ to m){ $\quad r_A(i) = \ln (A(i) / A(i-1))$ $\quad$ }
$\quad \sigma_A =$ **STDEV**($r_A(2:m)$) $\times \sqrt{260}$
$\quad \mu_A =$ **AVERAGE**($r_A(2:m)$) $\times 260$

```
# check convergence
```
$\quad$ If ($\quad |\sigma_A^{last} - \sigma_A| > prec$){ Go back to the statement labeled as *nextltr* }

```
# if convergence condition has been satisfied, evaluate distance to default and default
  probability
```
$$D = \frac{\ln[(A(m)/L(m))] + (\mu_A - \frac{1}{2}\sigma_A^2) T}{\sigma_A \sqrt{T}}$$

$P_{default} =$ **NORMSDIST**($- D$)

FunctionArray(n = 1 , x , g)

```
# use market data according to the time pointer i_ptr
    Take T_use = T
    Take E_use = E(i_ptr)
```

Take $L_{use} = L(i_{ptr})$
Take $r_{use} = r(i_{ptr})$

\# use latest estimate of σ_A
    Take $\sigma_{A,use} = \sigma_A^{last}$

\# evaluate the discrepancy in (13.9)

$$d_1 = \frac{\ln(x/L_{use}) + (r_{use} + \frac{1}{2}\sigma_{A,use}^2)T_{use}}{\sigma_{A,use}\sqrt{T_{use}}}$$

$$d_2 = d_1 - \sigma_{A,use}\sqrt{T_{use}}$$

$$g = E - [xN(d_1) - L_{use}\,e^{-r_{use}\,T_{use}}N(d_2)]$$

Code 13.1: Pseudo code of the CalDefProb() routine.

```
Option Explicit
Private Const mMax = 1000
Private maturity As Double
Private equity(1 To mMax) As Double
Private debt(1 To mMax) As Double
Private riskFree(1 To mMax) As Double
Private iptr As Integer
Private sigmaAssetLast As Double
```

```
Sub CalDefProb()
    maturity = Worksheets("KMV-Merton").Range("maturity").Value
    Dim m As Integer: m = WorksheetFunction.CountA(Worksheets("Data").Range("A:A")) - 1
    Dim i As Integer
    For i = 1 To m
        equity(i) = Worksheets("Data").Range("D2").Offset(i - 1, 0)
        debt(i) = Worksheets("Data").Range("E2").Offset(i - 1, 0)
        riskFree(i) = Worksheets("Data").Range("F2").Offset(i - 1, 0)
    Next i

    Dim equityReturn As Variant: ReDim equityReturn(2 To m)
    Dim sigmaEquity As Double
    Dim asset() As Double: ReDim asset(1 To m)
    Dim assetReturn As Variant: ReDim assetReturn(2 To m)
    Dim sigmaAsset As Double, meanAsset As Double
    Dim x(1 To 1) As Double, n As Integer, prec As Double, precFlag As Boolean, maxDev As
        Double

    For i = 2 To m: equityReturn(i) = Log(equity(i) / equity(i - 1)): Next i
    sigmaEquity = WorksheetFunction.StDev(equityReturn) * Sqr(260)

    sigmaAsset = sigmaEquity * equity(m) / (equity(m) + debt(m))
```

```
nextItr:    sigmaAssetLast = sigmaAsset
    For iptr = 1 To m
        x(1) = equity(iptr) + debt(iptr)
        n = 1
        prec = 0.00000001
        Call NewtonRaphson(n, prec, x, precFlag, maxDev)
        asset(iptr) = x(1)
    Next iptr

    For i = 2 To m: assetReturn(i) = Log(asset(i) / asset(i - 1)): Next i
    sigmaAsset = WorksheetFunction.StDev(assetReturn) * Sqr(260)
    meanAsset = WorksheetFunction.Average(assetReturn) * 260

    If (Abs(sigmaAssetLast - sigmaAsset) > prec) Then GoTo nextItr

    Dim disToDef As Double: disToDef = (Log(asset(m) / debt(m)) + (meanAsset - sigmaAsset
        ^ 2 / 2) * maturity) / (sigmaAsset * Sqr(maturity))
    Dim defProb As Double: defProb = WorksheetFunction.NormSDist(-disToDef)


    Worksheets("KMV-Merton").Range("B3").Value = riskFree(m)
    Worksheets("KMV-Merton").Range("B4").Value = debt(m)
    Worksheets("KMV-Merton").Range("B5").Value = equity(m)
    Worksheets("KMV-Merton").Range("B6").Value = sigmaEquity
    Worksheets("KMV-Merton").Range("B7").Value = asset(m)
    Worksheets("KMV-Merton").Range("B8").Value = sigmaAsset
    Worksheets("KMV-Merton").Range("B9").Value = meanAsset
    Worksheets("KMV-Merton").Range("B11").Value = disToDef
    Worksheets("KMV-Merton").Range("B12").Value = defProb
End Sub
```

```
Sub FunctionArray(n As Integer, x() As Double, ByRef g() As Double)
    Dim maturityUse As Double: maturityUse = maturity
    Dim equityUse As Double: equityUse = equity(iptr)
    Dim debtUse As Double: debtUse = debt(iptr)
    Dim riskFreeUse As Double: riskFreeUse = riskFree(iptr)
    Dim sigmaAssetUse As Double: sigmaAssetUse = sigmaAssetLast
    Dim d1 As Double, d2 As Double
    d1 = (Log(x(1) / debtUse) + (riskFreeUse + sigmaAssetUse ^ 2 / 2) * maturityUse) /
        (sigmaAssetUse * Sqr(maturityUse))
    d2 = d1 - sigmaAssetUse * Sqr(maturityUse)
    With Application.WorksheetFunction
        g(1) = equityUse - x(1) * .NormSDist(d1) + debtUse * Exp(-riskFreeUse * maturityUse)
            * .NormSDist(d2)
    End With
End Sub
```

Code 13.2: VBA code of the CalDefProb() routine.

REVIEW QUESTION

1. Throughout the chapter, a time horizon of one year is assumed. Therefore, the default probability is computed, looking forward one year time. The KMV–Merton model is so robust that it can straightforwardly compute the default probability of a five year time horizon. Select a publicly traded firm; adjust the necessary parameters in order to obtain the default probability of a five year time horizon. Compare the result again that of a one year time horizon.

ENDNOTES

1. Robert C. Merton, "On the Pricing of Corporate Debt: The Risk Structure of Interest Rates," *Journal of Finance* 29, No. 2 (1974): 449-470.
2. Consider E_t to be a function of A_t in (13.3). It follows from Ito's lemma that $\Delta E_t/E_t = \varepsilon(\mu_E \Delta t, \sigma_E \sqrt{\Delta t})$ with volatility $\sigma_E = (A_t/E_t)(\partial E/\partial A)\sigma_A$ and $\partial E/\partial A = N(d_1)$.
3. It can be shown that $\ln(A_T) = \varepsilon(\rho, v)$ is random normal with $\rho = \ln(A_0) + (\mu_A - \frac{1}{2}\sigma_A^2)T$ and $v = \sigma_A \sqrt{T}$. The probability that $A_T \leq L$ given A_0 at current time is given by

$$Prob(A_T \leq L) = N(-D), \quad D = [P - \ln(L)]/v.$$

4. P. Crosbie and J. Bohn, "Modeling Default Risk," Moody's KMV (2003).
5. Refer to KMVMerton.xls.

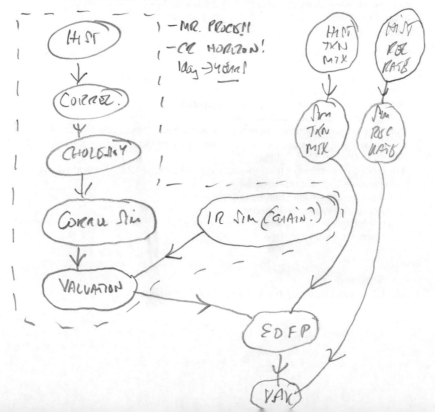

VBA Programming

A.1 INTRODUCTION

Excel is the most admired tool for financial planning, modeling, analysis, and forecasting. VBA (Visual Basic for Applications) is the programming language and environment for advanced users of Excel and other Microsoft Office products to automate computing operations and extend Excel functionalities. Users with the knowledge of Excel and VBA programming can establish and formulate complicated financial engineering models. Although there have been many books written about the usage of Excel and the basic skills of spreadsheet modeling, this book is written about the practical knowledge for constructing financial engineering models effectively with VBA programs. This appendix explains the key knowledge of VBA programming, as well as the essential components and structure of VBA programs. It also discusses advanced VBA techniques, including the usage of arrays and matrix computing. When you finish reading this appendix, you are ready to learn the practical knowledge and techniques of VBA programming required for financial engineering. To learn more, you may apply the VBA programming knowledge to establish professional financial models by going through the examples discussed in this book.

A.2 A BRIEF HISTORY OF VBA

VBA is a companion tool of Excel and other Microsoft Office products. Excel is a *de facto* computing tool for financial analysts, engineers, and practitioners. The first Excel release accompanied by VBA was Excel 5, which was released in 1993. It introduced the macro features in the form of

VBA programs. Macro can be considered a sequence of recorded keyboard and mouse actions. Running a macro is equivalent to reapplying the sequence of recorded actions on the underlying application. It can eliminate repetitive actions and automate the application.

In 1999, Excel 2000 introduced the important sixth version of VBA (VBA6), which incorporated some new language functions and object-oriented programming (OOP) features. OOP is a paradigm of modern programming languages that makes program development and maintenance easier by abstracting software components to objects and programming to object interactions. In this section of the book, there is a brief discussion of OOP and the important Excel Object Model. VBA6 continues to be the VBA version for Excel 2003 and the recent 2007 version. Although VBA6 is very robust, macro viruses written in VBA are still a serious security risk in Microsoft Office documents. The problem is due to the evolving architecture design of the script-based VBA languages. Therefore, newer versions of Excel always come with more and newer VBA security settings in order to fight against the potential attachment and risk of the macro virus.

Excel with VBA6 has proved to be quite successful due to the huge VBA adoption of Excel users. However, the VBA6 language and the integrated development environment (IDE) had only a few enhancements in later Excel versions. The enhancements were chiefly applied on the Excel object model for VBA in order to coordinate with the enhanced Excel features. Since 2000, Microsoft has been aggressively developing the .Net software technology and incorporating the technology into the new Microsoft applications so as to address the critical software issues of interoperability, Internet advancement, platform independence, simplified deployment, portability, and security. Microsoft intended to promote the new VB.Net alternatives, including Visual Studio Tools for Office (VSTO) and Visual Studio Tools for Applications (VSTA), in order to replace the old script-based VBA, but they did not offer the ease of development and deployment for *ad hoc* and tightly integrated solutions of the existing VBA. VBA users were reluctant to adopt and upgrade to the newer .Net alternatives because the efforts of intensive reprogramming for converting VBA programs into VB.Net programs overshadowed the .Net benefits. This appendix includes some suggestions regarding the programming practice that make VBA programs convertible to future releases.

A.3 ESSENTIAL EXCEL ELEMENTS FOR VBA

Spreadsheet modeling is a programming activity that includes the setting of formulas into the cells of spreadsheets. The automation through formulas in the cells can only satisfy the general needs of spreadsheet models. The flexibility is actually restricted by the static formulas written in the cells. With VBA programs, you can construct more powerful and dynamic spreadsheet models by programmatically accessing and altering the contents and properties of all Excel elements, including setting dynamic formulas for the cells. For example, users can use a VBA program to generate formulas inside the cells of a worksheet according to user inputs and build a dynamic binomial tree for projecting interest rates. In fact, the strength of VBA programs is the ability to dynamically interact with and manipulate the contents and properties of cells and all objects of Excel. Therefore, it is essential to firstly understand the ways to interact with the contents and properties of cells and ranges in VBA programs so as to program the dynamic behavior of sophisticated spreadsheet models. Here, we will review three key elements in Excel that are essential to VBA programs. They are cell references, named cells/ranges, and functions. In Excel, a cell reference is used for formulas to address the content of cells or ranges. A named cell/range is used for indirectly addressing a cell or a range. Worksheet Functions are used in formulas to perform some preset computing.

A.3.1 Excel Cell Reference

You may be experienced in working with Excel, but you may not be aware of all the important elements stored in a cell. In Excel, a cell may contain many elements including:

- a cell reference (we use the reference to address a cell or a range),
- a formula (a valid spreadsheet formula),
- a value (a constant, an element of an Excel array, or the computed value of the cell formula),
- a comment (which can be displayed in a comment box),
- cell formats or display formats (such as font, color, alignment, style, and so on),
- conditional rules and formats (for formatting cell display according to some rules),
- data validation rules (for validating user inputs filling into the cell),
- and so on.

The address of a cell in a worksheet is called a cell reference. We commonly use the cell references to address the content of cells or ranges as the operands or function arguments in Excel formulas. In VBA programs, we also need to use cell references to address the cells and ranges in Excel in order to programmatically access and alter their content and properties. There are two styles of cell reference. The commonly used reference style is the *A1 notation*, in which we use an English letter (or two/three letters) to represent the column of a cell and follow with a number to represent the row. For example, "D12" means the cell in the column D and the twelfth row of the working worksheet. The cell reference can be *relative* or *absolute*. For a relative reference, Excel will automatically shift the relative row and/or column when it copies a cell formula. For an absolute reference, Excel will always maintain the same row and/or column when it copies a cell formula. The prefix of the "$" sign is used to denote an absolute reference. Thus, there are four combinations of cell references:

- Relative reference (e.g. D12)
- Column absolute reference (e.g. $D12)
- Row absolute reference (e.g. D$12)
- (Full) Absolute reference (e.g. $D$12).

The second reference style is the *R1C1 notation*. The R1C1 notation uses a row number and a column number to represent the location of a cell. The number after the letter R refers to the row, and the number after the letter C refers to the column. For an absolute reference, R1C1 refers to the cell A1, R2C1 to the cell A2, R3C1 to the cell A3, R1C2 to the cell B1, R1C3 to the cell C1, and so on. For relative reference, a square bracket with an enclosed number specifies the relative position. For example, RC refers to the cell itself, R[1]C to the cell in the next row, R[-1]C to the cell in the previous row, RC[1] to the cell in the next column, RC[-1] to the cell in the previous column, and so on.

Usually, Excel displays formulas in the A1 style. *To change the style to R1C1 notation, click the Office button, click the Excel Options button, select Formulas, and select the R1C1 reference style option.* The location of the R1C1 reference style option in the Excel Options window is shown in Figure A.1. Then, Excel will present all formulas in the R1C1 style. When the worksheet is in the R1C1 style, you may notice that the top column of the worksheet shows the column numbers instead of the column letters. When you copy a cell with a cell formula to another cell, the copied formula in the R1C1 style will not have any changes. This is actually the copy mechanism of Excel that can maintain the correct cell references of the copied formulas.

Considering the example in Figure A.2, you may notice that the three formulas of Price x Qty in the R1C1 style are the same. In VBA programs, you may enter formulas into Excel cells using any reference style. Although it is common and intuitive to use the A1 style in Excel formulas, you will

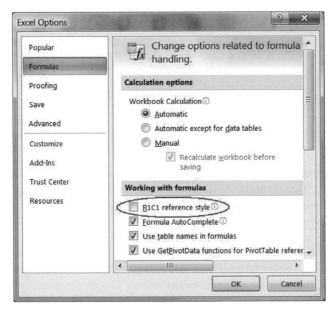

FIGURE A.1 Switch to the R1C1 reference style.

	A	B	C	D	E	F	G
1	*Original Values & Formulas in A1 Style:*				*Cells copied from A2:C6*		
2	Price	Qty	Total		Price	Qty	Total
3	22.3	12	=A3*B3		22.3	12	=E3*F3
4	33.4	23	=A4*B4		33.4	23	=E4*F4
5	44.5	34	=A5*B5		44.5	34	=E5*F5
6		Gross:	=SUM(C3:C5)			Gross:	=SUM(G3:G5)

	1	2	3	4	5	6	7
1	*Original Values & Formulas in R1C1 Style:*				*Cells copied from A2:C6*		
2	Price	Qty	Total		Price	Qty	Total
3	22.3	12	=RC[-2]*RC[-1]		22.3	12	=RC[-2]*RC[-1]
4	33.4	23	=RC[-2]*RC[-1]		33.4	23	=RC[-2]*RC[-1]
5	44.5	34	=RC[-2]*RC[-1]		44.5	34	=RC[-2]*RC[-1]
6		Gross:	=SUM(R[-3]C:R[-1]C)			Gross:	=SUM(R[-3]C:R[-1]C)

FIGURE A.2 An example of Excel formulas shown in different styles.

sometimes find it easier to enter formulas into Excel cells using the R1C1 style in VBA programs.

In VBA programming, there are several ways to refer to a cell or a range. The most common way is to use the Range object. To define a cell or range reference through the Range object, the syntax is similar to calling a function with arguments. By specifying the value of a cell or range as a string argument in the Range object, it can establish a link to the specified cells or ranges in VBA programs. Here are some examples:

Range("A3")	*refers to the cell A3 of the active worksheet*
Range("B12:C22")	*refers to the range B12:C22 of the active worksheet*
Range("B12","C22")	*refers to the same range B12:C22 of the active worksheet*
Range("A:C")	*refers to columns A through C*
Range("10:12")	*refers to rows 10 to 12*
Range("B12:C22,F12:G22")	*refers to the multiple ranges B12:C22 and F12:G22*
Worksheets(1).Range("B20:D30")	*refers to the range B20:D30 of the first worksheet*
Worksheets("Sheet2").Range("C2")	*refers to the cell C2 of the worksheet "Sheet2"*

VBA objects can contain collections of objects. For example, a workbook can contain multiple worksheets. Any object with a plural name generally means that it is a collection of objects of the same type. Thus, Worksheets means a collection of worksheets in a workbook. To address a specific item in a collection, we can use an index number or the exact item name as shown in the last two examples above. The index numbers of Excel objects usually begin from one onward.

The Range object includes many useful properties and methods. The comprehensive list of the properties and methods of the range can be found in Excel Help by searching "Range object members." Since VBA programs often access and alter the properties of ranges, it is necessary to be familiar with the usage of the available properties and methods of the range object. Some useful properties and methods are listed below:

Range("B3").Value	*refers to the value of the cell/range*
Range("B3").Font	*refers to the font object of the cell/range*
Range("B3").Column	*refers to the number of the first column of the range (i.e. 2)*
Range("B3:F30").Columns.Count	*returns the number of the column collection in the range*
Range("B3:F30").Columns(2)	*refers to the second column of the range*
Range("B3").Row	*refers to the number of the first row of the range (i.e. 3)*
Range("B3:F30").Rows.Count	*returns the number of the row collection in the range*
Range("B3:F30").Rows(2)	*refers to the second row of the range*
Range("B3").Formula	*refers to the A1-styled formula of the cell/range*
Range("B3").FormulaR1C1	*refers to the R1C1-styled formula of the cell/range*
Range("B3:F30").FormulaArray	*refers to the array formula in the range B3:F30*
Range("B3:F30").HasFormula	*returns True if all cells in the range contain formulas*
Range("B3:F30").HasArray	*returns True if all cells in the range are part of an array formula*
Range("B3:F30").Clear	*clears the entire object of the range B3:F30*
Range("B3:F30").ClearFormats	*clears the formats of the range B3:F30*
Range("B3:F30").ClearContents	*clears the values & formulas of the range B3:F30*
Range("B3:F30").Cells	*refers to the range object of all cells in the range B3:F30*
Range("B3:F30").Select	*selects the range B3:F30*
Selection.Copy	*copies the range to the Clipboard*
Selection.Copy(Range("H3:J30"))	

	copies the content in the selected range to the range H3:J30
Selection.Cells.Clear	*clears the entire object of all cells of the selected range*
Selection.Cells.ClearContents	*clears the values & formulas of all cells of the selected range*

An alternative approach to access the cells of Excel is to use the Cells property of the range object. Cells(row, column) can refer to a single cell using a pair of row and column index numbers. Although the usage is similar to the Range object, using the Cells property with index numbers is sometimes more convenient than using a string argument to specify a cell reference in VBA programs. Here are some examples that compare the usage of the Range object against the Cells(row, column) property:

The use of the Range object:	The equivalent use of the Cells(row,column) property:
Range("A3")	Cells(3,1)
Range("B12:C22")	Range(Cells(12,2), Cells(22,3))
Range("B12","C22")	Range(Cells(12,2), Cells(22,3))
Worksheets("Sheet2").Range("C2")	Worksheets("Sheet2").Cells(2,3)
Worksheets(1).Range("B20:D30")	Worksheets(1).Range(Worksheets(1).Cells(20,2), Worksheets(1).Cells(30,4))

In order to illustrate the usage of the Cells property with a pair of row and column index numbers, the following is a good VBA sample function that sums up all the values of a range of cells. The syntax and meaning of the program codes will be explained in A.5 "Basic VBA Programming Concepts."

```
Function SumOfRange(inRange As Range) As Double
    Dim rowcnt As Integer: rowcnt = inRange.Rows.Count
    Dim colcnt As Integer: colcnt = inRange.Columns.Count
    Dim sum As Integer, row As Integer, col As Integer
    For row = 1 To rowcnt
        For col = 1 To colcnt
            sum = sum + inRange.Cells(row, col).Value
    Next col, row
    SumOfRange = sum
End Function
```

A.3.2 Excel Defined Names

In Excel, a name can be defined to refer to a cell/range of a worksheet, a constant value, or a constant array. It is a good practice to define names for ranges and use the defined names in formulas, because it allows us to flexibly redefine the referred content of defined names without affecting the

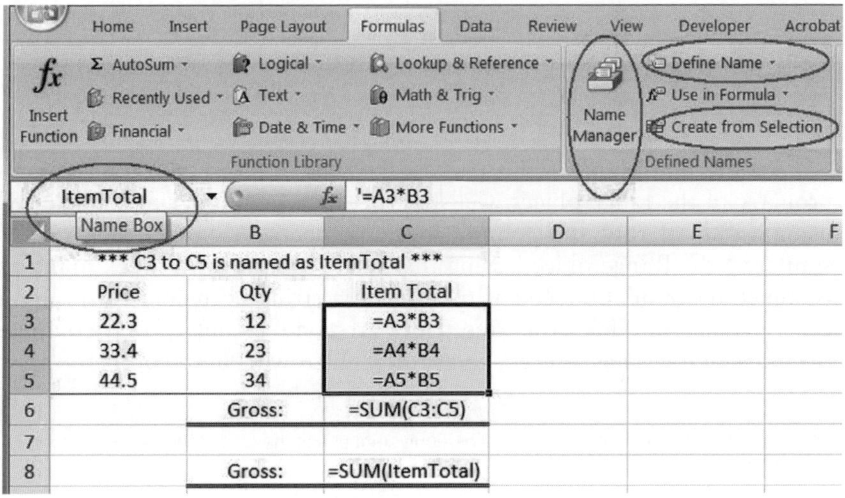

FIGURE A.3   An example of using defined names in a formula.

formulas. For example, as shown in Figure A.3, you may define a named range of C3:C5 as "ItemTotal" and set the formula of cell C8 as "=SUM (ItemTotal)." Then, the formula appears to be more meaningful. It is obvious that it means the sum of a list of item totals. The formula is always correct if the named range "ItemTotal" refers to the correct range of all item totals. There are four main ways to define names. The first way is to simply override the Name Box with a name once a cell or a range is selected. The second way is to use the Name Manager for manually creating, editing, and deleting names. The third way is to pop up the "Define Name" dialog to create a new name for a cell or range. The last way is to "Create from Selection" when a table range is selected. Figure A.3 shows the available functions for creating names under the Formulas tab in the ribbon.

The following steps demonstrate the use of "Create from Selection" for a table range:

1. Select a table range.
2. Click "Create from Selection" from the Defined Names group in the Formula tab.
3. Click "OK" with the options of "Top row" and "Left column" selected (or checked).
4. Then, nine defined names will be created automatically and accordingly as shown in Figure A.4.
5. Click "Name Manager" to check the defined names (as shown in Figure A.5).

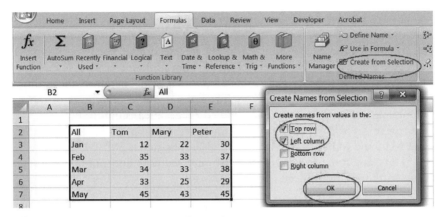

FIGURE A.4 Create named ranges from selection.

In VBA programs, the Range object can take defined names as the argument besides a reference of ranges. Using the defined names in the above example, we can refer to those named ranges as follows:

Range("Jan")	*refers to the range C3:E3*
Range("Mary")	*refers to the range D3:D7*
Range("All")	*refers to the range C3:E7*

In Excel, intersections and unions of ranges are applicable for the worksheet functions and formulas. They are workable as the argument of the Range object as well. The intersection is the common range covered by

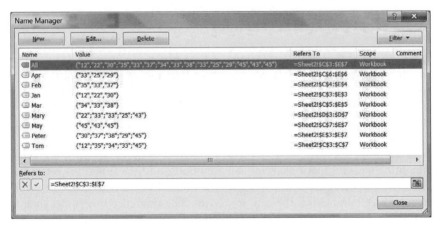

FIGURE A.5 Named ranges are shown in the Name Manager.

ranges. A space between two ranges or named ranges means intersection. For example, the formula "Tom Apr + Mary Apr" means the intersection of Tom (in column C) and Apr (in row 6) plus the intersection of Mary (in column D) and Apr (in row 6). The intersection of Tom and Apr is 33 (i.e. cell C6). The intersection of Mary and Apr is 25 (i.e. cell D6). Therefore, the addition of these two intersection cells is 58. The union is the combination of ranges. A comma between two ranges or named ranges means union. For example, the formula "SUM(Jan,Mar,May)" means the union of the named ranges Jan, Mar, and May (i.e. the row 3, 5, and 7). The sum is 302.

Here are some examples that use intersections and unions of named ranges in the Range object:

Range("Jan Apr")	*refers to the range C6:C6 (i.e. the cell C6)*
Range("Mary Apr")	*refers to the range D6:D6 (i.e. the cell D6)*
Range("Jan, Peter")	*refers to the union ranges C3:E3 and E3:E7*
Range("Mar, Mary")	*refers to the union ranges C5:E5 and D3:D7*
Range("Feb, Mar, Apr")	*refers to the range C4:E6*

It is a good practice to use defined names in Excel models, because the formulas are more meaningful than using symbolic cell references. Besides, we get the flexibility to redefine the referred ranges of the named ranges without affecting the formulas with those named ranges. It is also a good practice for VBA programs to refer to defined names instead of using static and symbolic reference cells or ranges. Thus, the same flexibility and readability can be applied to the VBA programs as well. The financial models discussed in this book will demonstrate the use of defined names in VBA programs.

A.3.3 Excel Worksheet Functions

Excel 2007 includes about 350 worksheet functions grouped into twelve main categories. Excel Help contains excellent information about the usage of the worksheet functions, including examples and cross-references to the related functions. Moreover, the Insert function dialog can guide users to fill in arguments into the required functions. Figure A.6 shows the Help window and the location of the Insert function button.

To build sophisticated financial models, it is necessary to understand the information functions, reference functions, and the functions related to matrix computing. The information functions allow users to query information of a cell and check the cell properties. The reference functions, such as Address, Areas, Column, Columns, Row, Rows, Indirect, and Offset, are useful for users to query the information of a range, and assign ranges with

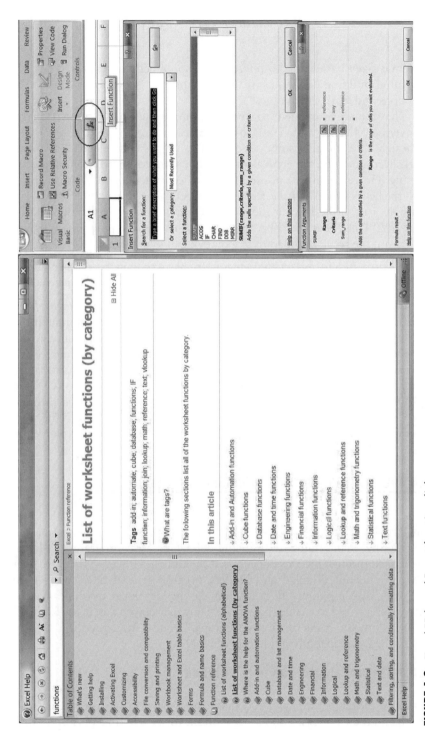

FIGURE A.6 Excel Help and Insert function dialog.

dynamic sizes based on the reference of some cells or ranges. They are helpful in building dynamic spreadsheet models. Users should look at the functions and learn their usages.

The functions related to matrix computing, including MDeterm, MInverse, MMult, and Transpose, are useful in financial engineering. Although VBA includes some set of VBA functions equivalent to the Excel worksheet functions, the equivalent VBA functions for matrix computing are missing. However, users can use the worksheet functions in VBA programs with the help of the *WorksheetFunction* object of the Application object. For example, to call the MMult function to compute the matrix multiplication of two VBA matrices (i.e. VBA two-dimensional arrays) in a VBA program and return the result in the form of a matrix will look like the following:

Dim matrix Result() as Double 'define a variable to contain the returned value
matrix Result = Application.Worksheet Function.MMult(matrix1, matrix2)

Worksheet functions can flexibly accept either Excel cells/ranges, VBA variables, or some VBA object properties as arguments. After computation, they can return a value or an array back to VBA. However, the interaction between VBA and Excel takes more resources and it is slow. Therefore, if intensive computation is required through the use of worksheet functions, users are advised to develop the equivalent user-defined functions (UDF) in VBA code instead of invoking the Excel worksheet functions through the WorksheetFunction object in VBA programs. This will avoid the slow interaction between Excel and VBA. The topic of UDF will be explained in A.4.6 "The Procedure to Create a VBA Function."

A.4 THE VBA DEVELOPMENT ENVIRONMENT (VBE)

The VBA Development Environment or Visual Basic Editor (VBE) is an integrated tool of Excel and Microsoft Office products. It is a separate tool for creating, maintaining, testing, and debugging VBA programs. VBE can be invoked through the Developer tab of the ribbon. However, the Developer tab is by default disabled and hidden, because general Excel users need not write VBA programs. In order to make the Developer tab appear in the ribbon, users need to enable the option "Show Developer Tab in the Ribbon" in the "Popular" pane of "Excel Options." Figure A.7 shows the steps to enable the Developer tab option in Excel 2007.

A.4.1 The Developer Tab in the Ribbon

Inside the Developer tab, you may find several groups of features. The Code group and the Controls group are important for developing VBA programs.

1. Click the Microsoft Office Button in the upper-left corner of Excel.
2. Click the "Excel Options" Button in the bottom of the drop-down menu.
3. Click "Popular" in the pop-up Excel Options window.
4. Select the "Show Developer tab in the Ribbon" check box, and then click "OK".
5. The Developer tab should be available and shown in the ribbon.
6. The Developer tab shows all developer features. For example,
   users can click the "Visual Basic" button to invoke the Visual Basic Editor.

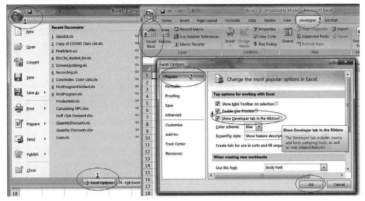

FIGURE A.7   The procedure to enable the Developer tab.

The Code group includes five buttons for users to invoke and manage VBA programs. The first button is for launching the Visual Basic editor (VBE). The second button is for opening the Macros dialog. A macro is a VBA subroutine that performs a sequence of recorded commands. Users can create, edit, and run macros through the Macros dialog. The Record Macro button is for recording mouse clicks and keystrokes to macros, so that we can replay the same sequence of commands later. The Use Relative References button is a switch to select whether macros should record the affected cells or range using absolute or relative references. Usually, we use relative references because the recorded macros can be more flexible for extension. Finally, the Macro Security button can open the Trust Center dialog for users to manage the Macro security settings. There are four macro settings as shown in Figure A.8. We usually select the "Enable all macros" option only during the development of VBA programs. It is necessary to select either the "Disable all macros with notification" option or the "Disable all macros except digitally signed macros" option in order to protect users from the attack of macro viruses. The screen of the Trust Center dialog showing the available options of Macro Settings can be seen in Figure A.8.

If the Macro Settings disable all macros, whenever an Excel file containing macros is opened, a security warning will be displayed in the line behind the ribbon as shown in Figure A.9. Users may click the Options button and

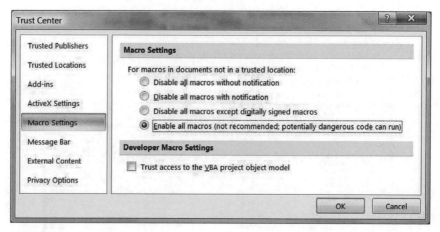

FIGURE A.8   The Trust Center.

select "Enable this content" of the Options dialog to allow the macros to be executed.

The Controls Group in the Developer tab contains buttons for inserting and managing user interface (UI) controls, such as buttons, combo boxes, check boxes, spin buttons, and so on, into a worksheet. There are two types of UI controls: Form controls and ActiveX controls. For the newly developed Excel applications, the Form controls should be used because they are the native components built into Excel 2007. ActiveX controls are components of external add-in modules, which are not part of Excel. ActiveX controls were the software component technology developed by Microsoft in 1996. The technology can extend the features of the Office products by adding in interoperable external modules. For general spreadsheet models, the native Form controls are sufficient and simple enough for designing input forms; it is not necessary to use the ActiveX controls and custom dialog boxes. Therefore, the spreadsheet models explained in this book use the Form controls only. You will learn how to use the Form controls with financial models in this book. To manage the inserted Form controls, users may right click on the Form control to choose the option "Assign Macro" or "Format Control," which can change the properties of the control. Figure A.10 is a simple example showing how to insert a button control into a worksheet and pop up the menu to assign a macro into the button control.

A.4.2 The Windows of VBE

As mentioned, the VBE is a programming environment for creating, maintaining, testing, and debugging VBA programs. To start the VBE, click the

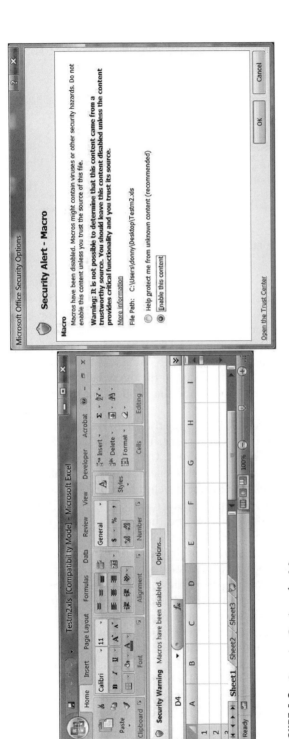

FIGURE A.9 Security Options for Macros.

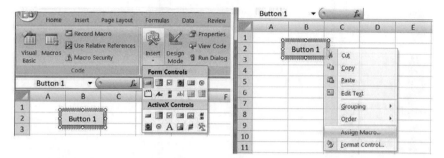

FIGURE A.10 Insert a button control into a worksheet.

"Visual Basic" button in the Code group of the Developer tab. You may notice that the invoked VBE application has a different look and style. The VBE with the old-fashioned look and style was designed for Excel 2000 and is still being used for Excel 2007. Although Microsoft is promoting the newer .Net software technologies and tools in order to purposefully replace the traditional VBA programming tool, VBE and VBA are provided with Excel 2007 for current Excel users due to the overwhelming adoption of VBA programs in spreadsheet models and the strong demand by existing Excel users.

The VBE, as shown in Figure A.11, has the traditional menu bar, button bar, and several windows inside the workspace. The View menu item of the menu bar contains a list of available windows. Users may arrange the location and display of the windows just like the general Windows applications. Four main windows are important for the development of VBA programs. The *Project Explorer* window, which is usually located in the top left region of the workspace, contains the structure and the components of the integrated VBA projects of the Excel application. Users can insert new programs (or modules) and organize the project structure in the Project Explorer. The *Properties* window, which is usually located directly below the Property Explorer, contains the properties of the active component of the VBA project. Users can directly rename the components and modify the properties of the component shown in the Properties window. The properties can determine the behaviors of the Excel application, such as the appearance of worksheets and the enablement of some spreadsheet features. The *Code* window displays the VBA source code of a program. Users create and maintain a VBA program in the Code window. Several Code windows can be opened simultaneously. A Code window is equivalent to the view of a program in the VBA project. The *Immediate* window is quite useful for testing and debugging programs. The Immediate window allows users to enter and execute simple VBA commands in order to test and investigate the

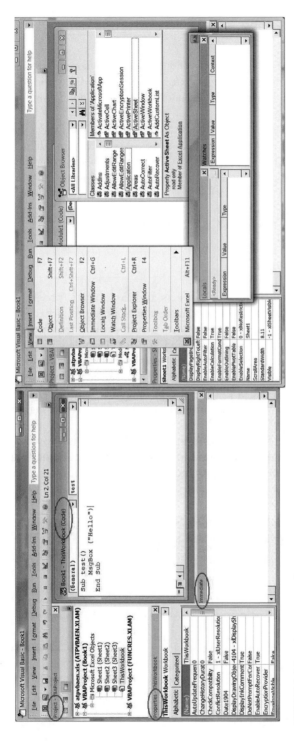

FIGURE A.11 The VBE windows.

program logic. Users can also insert debugging codes into programs so as to display and investigate debugging information in the Immediate window during program execution. Please read Appendix C on VBA debugging for more information on this topic.

Besides the explained four main windows, the Object Browser, the Locals window, and the Watch window are also useful in testing and debugging VBA programs. The Object Browser allows users to browse through the Excel Object Model. The Locals window and the Watch window can display the changing values of local or watched variables or expressions during program execution. More information can be found in Appendix B on the Excel Object Model and in Appendix C on VBA Debugging.

A.4.3 The Project Explorer

The Project Explorer presents all open projects and the objects (programs and modules) of the Excel application in a hierarchical structure, organized like folders and files. The root or base objects in the project tree are the workbooks being worked on and the attached add-ins. Double-clicking a tree folder can expand or collapse the folder. Double-clicking a worksheet item can open the Code window to display the VBA source codes. Right-clicking any item can trigger the pop-up menu for opening the project properties window, inserting new modules, importing, exporting, removing, or printing the file as shown in Figure A.12.

The project properties window contains two tab pages as shown in Figure A.13. The General tab allows users to change the project name (but it is usually not necessary and meaningful), add project description, attach a

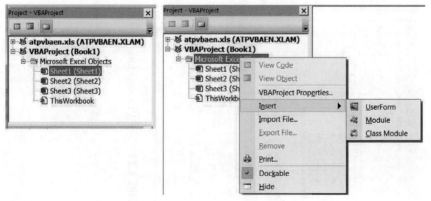

FIGURE A.12   A VBA Project structure.

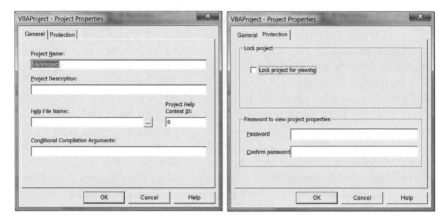

FIGURE A.13 VBA Project Properties.

help file, and specify compilation arguments (only for very advanced users). The Protection tab allows users to apply a password to protect the project properties from viewing, or lock the whole project. Once the project is locked, a correct password must be provided in order to expand the project tree and access the written VBA programs.

In the pop-up menu of the project, you may find the Insert menu item pointing to three types of program modules. They arc User Form, Module, and Class Module. A User Form is a custom VBA dialog box. It contains user-defined VBA codes for handling form-based activities. Users can create User Forms for acquiring user input and presenting computing output. Inside User Forms, users can freely design the screen layout and insert any available form controls, such as buttons, text boxes, spin buttons, and so on. A Module contains user-defined VBA functions, subroutines, and macros. We will demonstrate the procedures to create new modules containing functions and subroutines in A.4.5 and A.4.6. A Class Module contains user-defined classes. A class defines a group of properties and methods of the same type of objects. Programmers with competent knowledge of object-oriented programming will define classes in the Class Modules and create objects from the defined classes for handling reusable objects and complex models.

A.4.4 The VBA Project Structure

In the project window, each VBA project can have four folders to hold different types of user-developed VBA programs. The four folders are named Microsoft Excel Objects, Modules, Forms, and Class Modules. We can extend the features and functionalities of Excel by writing VBA programs in the project and linking the VBA programs with Excel objects. The developed programs are automatically stored and grouped into the corresponding folders according to their program types. However, the folders will be hidden if no files are stored in them. The Microsoft Excel Objects folder stores the VBA programs linked with and owned by the worksheet or chart objects. Each worksheet or chart object can have only one corresponding VBA program linked with it. The Modules folder keeps user-defined functions (UDF), macros, and VBA subroutines that are available to all worksheets, charts, and Excel objects, as well as the workbook. The Forms folder holds user-defined forms, also called User Forms. User Forms are user-defined dialog boxes for capturing inputs and presenting computation outputs. The advantages of using User Forms over the worksheets and charts are the highly customizable user interface and the independence from the Excel objects. However, it is simpler and more common to use and attach Form controls into worksheets instead of using User Forms. The last folder holds Class Modules. Creating user-defined classes can promote code reusability, but the usage of Class Modules requires developers with advanced programming knowledge and skills. Since program modules are good enough to satisfy the needs of the discussed financial engineering model, this book will not cover the topics of User Forms and Classes.

The only default folder available in the VBA project is the Microsoft Excel Objects folder, because there is a workbook and at least one worksheet defined in an Excel file and the corresponding program files will be automatically shown in the folder. Figure A.14 shows the Excel file "Test. xls" containing a workbook and three worksheets. Each worksheet or chart object will automatically have the corresponding program file attached to the Excel file. The program file of the workbook object has the default name of "ThisWorkbook." The default names of the worksheet program files are Sheet1, Sheet2, and onward, which correspond to the default names of the newly inserted worksheets. The program files allow developers to write VBA procedures into them and attach the subroutines with the pre-defined events in order to alter the behaviors of the Excel objects, including the workbook, worksheets, and charts. For example, there is a pre-defined Open event for the workbook object, which will be triggered whenever the Excel file is opened. If you would like to display a message dialog, such as showing the message "Good Morning," whenever the Excel file is opened, you may write a subroutine with the procedure name of "Workbook_ Open" in the program file of "ThisWorkbook" and include a MsgBox() statement in the subroutine. Then, the greeting message will be shown due to the automatic execution of the Workbook_Open subroutine whenever the Excel file is opened. The source code is shown in Figure A.14.

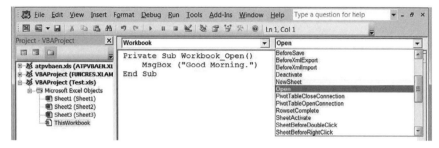

FIGURE A.14 Events of the Workbook.

A.4.5 The Procedure to Create a VBA Subroutine

There are two main types of procedures in a VBA program. They are VBA functions and subroutines. A function is a set of program statements that accepts arguments, performs some computing, and returns a computed result to the calling program statement. A subroutine contains program statements that execute in sequence and according to the flow control statements. Unlike functions, subroutines do not have any return value. Both functions and subroutines can define some input arguments, but it is not compulsory. Subroutines may invoke other subroutines or functions. Functions usually invoke other functions only. Table A.1 summarizes the main differences of functions and subroutines.

TABLE A.1 Differences between functions and subroutines.

	Functions	Subroutines
Require arguments	Optional, but usually required	Optional
Return values to the caller	Only one return value	Nil
Invoke other procedures	Usually other functions only	Subroutines and functions
Modify Excel properties	Not allowed	Allowed

The syntax of calling procedures is similar to using worksheet functions in Excel formulas. Arguments are enclosed in parentheses. To use the return value of a function, assign the function to a defined variable and enclose the arguments in parentheses. Figure A.15 utilizes the popular and useful function of *MsgBox* to illustrate the syntax of calling procedures.

Subroutines without any input arguments are also treated as "macros" and can be invoked in the macro function of Excel. To demonstrate how to call a macro in Excel, we insert a button control in a worksheet and link it

```
Sub Test()
    Dim pressedButton As VbMsgBoxResult
    'MsgBox is a useful function. According to the input arguments, a message box
    '  containing "HELLO" with a pair of YES and NO buttons will pop up
    '  and the user-pressed button will be returned and assigned into a variable
    pressedButton = MsgBox("Hello", vbYesNo)
    'Check if the YES button is pressed
    If pressedButton = vbYes Then
        MsgBox ("You pressed the YES button")
    Else
        MsgBox ("You pressed the NO button")
    End If
End Sub
```

FIGURE A.15   A sample subroutine.

to a macro. When users press the button, it will trigger the execution of the macro. As an example, let us go through the following basic steps to write a macro (i.e. an argument-less VBA subroutine) and invoke the macro by clicking on the button control attached in a worksheet.

1. Start an Excel application and Start the VBE by clicking the Visual Basic button in the Developer tab in the ribbon.
2. Expand the VBAProject folder shown in the Project Explorer.
3. Insert a new Module through the Insert item of the menu bar and use the default "Module1" as the module name. If the insertion is successful, Module1 should appear in the Modules folder.
4. Double-click Module1 to open the Code window of Module1 in the workspace.
5. Inside the Code window, type the following three VBA statements:
   Public Sub SayHello()
       MsgBox("Hello")
   End Sub
6. Now we have a macro (or an argument-less subroutine) with the name SayHello ready to be invoked. Before we link the macro with a button-control in the worksheet, we need to test the macro inside the VBE first in order to ensure the macro can execute correctly.
7. To test the SayHello macro, press the button with a green arrow icon as shown in Figure A.16. The VBE will execute the macro and, as a result, a message dialog with the message "Hello" will pop up as shown in the figure above because of the execution of the MsgBox statement.
8. To call the SayHello macro in Excel, go back to Excel and press the Macros button in the Developer tab. In the Macro window, you can find the SayHello macro shown in the list of Macro names.
9. Click the line SayHello, and press the Run button as shown in Figure A.17. If you get the same message pop-up, it indicates that you can successfully invoke the SayHello macro in Excel.

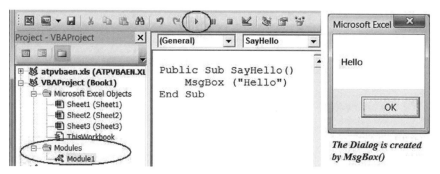

FIGURE A.16 Execute a macro in VBE.

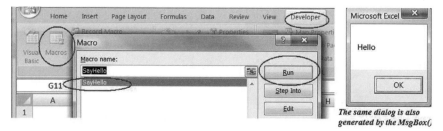

FIGURE A.17 Execute a macro in the Macro window.

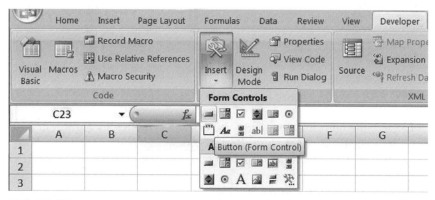

FIGURE A.18 Form Controls.

10. To link the SayHello macro with a button control, we need to insert a button control into a worksheet. Press the Insert button in the Developer tab. A list of available Form controls will be shown. There are 10 form controls as shown in Figure A.18. The first one is a button control.

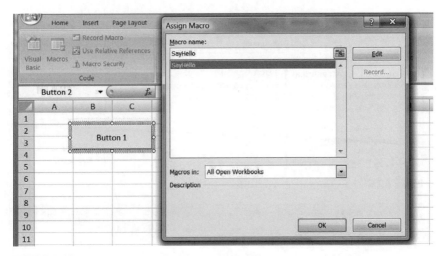

FIGURE A.19 Assign a macro to a button control.

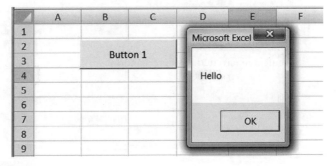

FIGURE A.20 Invoke a macro by pressing the button control.

11. Click the Button icon under Form Controls and use the mouse cursor to draw the region of the button in the worksheet.
12. Then, the Assign Macro window will pop up as shown in Figure A.19. Select SayHello and press OK.
13. Now, the button control labeled "Button 1" has been put on a worksheet and linked to the SayHello macro. Press the button and have the message dialog with "Hello" pop up. The "Hello" message window will pop up as in Figure A.20.

A.4.6 The Procedure to Create a VBA Function

Although Excel provides many built-in functions, they may not satisfy all requirements. VBA functions are also called user-defined functions (UDF) because they are callable in Excel formulas. Now, let us create a UDF in a VBA module. The example function *Triple* will accept a number and calculate the tripled value of the input number as the return value. Then, we can call the *Triple* function in an Excel formula. Here are the basic steps of creating VBA functions:

1. Start an Excel application and start the VBE by clicking the Visual Basic button in the Developer tab.
2. Expand the VBAProject folder shown in the Project Explorer.
3. Insert a new Module and use the default "Module1" as the module name. If the insertion is successful, Module1 should appear under the Modules folder.
4. Double-click Module1 to open the Code window of Module1 in the workspace.
5. Inside the Code window, type the VBA statements as shown in Figure A.21.
6. To test the Triple function, open the Immediate window through the View menu item.
7. Type "? Triple(1.23)" in the Immediate window and press Enter. The "?" mark shows the execution result of the command in the Immediate window immediately. You should get a result similar to Figure A.22.
8. To verify if the answer is correct, type "? 1.23 * 1.23 * 1.23". The "*" mark means multiplication. The Immediate window allows you to enter VBA commands and execute the commands immediately. You should get the same calculated result as shown in Figure A.23.
9. To use the Triple function in an Excel formula, activate the Excel application.
10. Select any cell, enter the formula "=Triple(1.23)", and you should get the same answer as in Figure A.24.
11. Now, let us check if the Triple function can accept a cell reference as the argument just like the common usage of the worksheet functions.

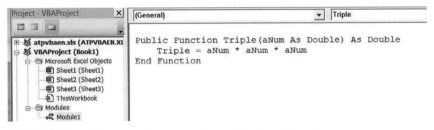

FIGURE A.21 A VBA function that can be used in Excel formulas.

```
Immediate
 ? Triple(1.23)
 1.860867
```

FIGURE A.22   Test a VBA function in the Immediate window.

```
Immediate
 ? Triple(1.23)
 1.860867
 ? 1.23 * 1.23 * 1.23
  1.860867
```

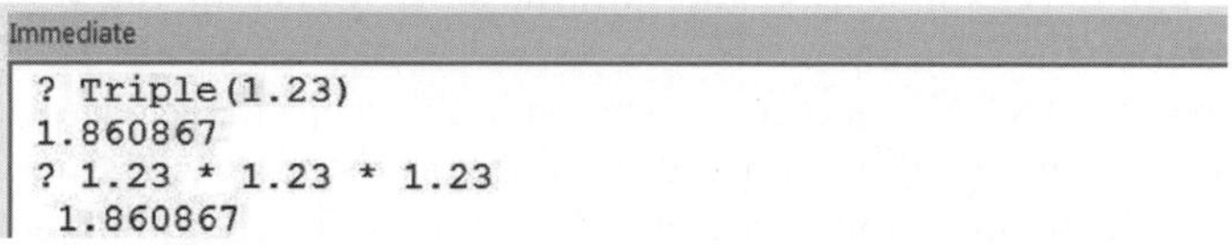

FIGURE A.23   Verify the function result in the Immediate window.

D1	▼	f_x	=Triple(1.23)	
	A	B	C	D	E
1				1.860867	

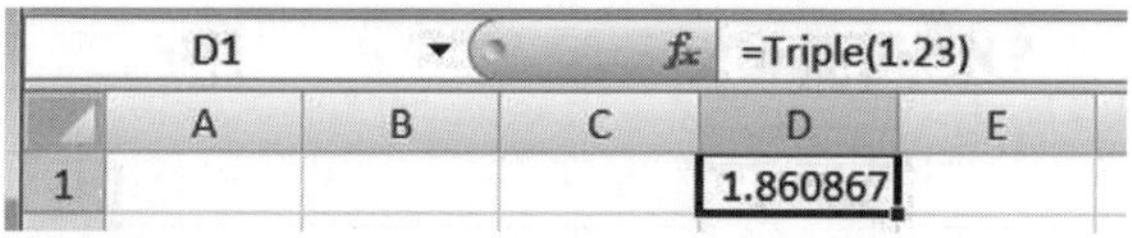

FIGURE A.24   Invoke the VBA function in an Excel formula.

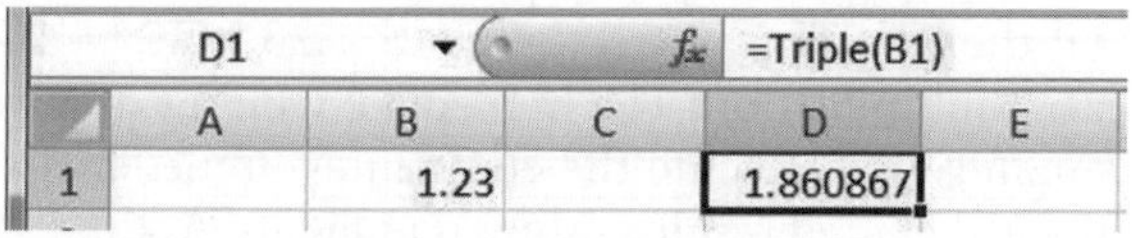

D1	▼	f_x	=Triple(B1)	
	A	B	C	D	E
1		1.23		1.860867	

FIGURE A.25   Pass an Excel cell value to the VBA function.

Select the cell B1 and enter "1.23". Select another cell and enter "=Triple(B1)". Figure A.25 shows the same calculation results.

A.5 BASIC VBA PROGRAMMING CONCEPTS

VBA, extended from Visual Basic, is a high-level programming language. In computing, a high-level programming language means that it includes many humanly-recognizable words, such as "if," "else," "for," "while," "do," and so on, as the constructs of program commands and statements. The reserved English words for program commands and statements are called keywords. They are used to hide the details of the internal processing, such as the operations of the central operation unit (CPU) and the access of computer components. Microsoft designed VBA to be friendlier than other popular languages, such as Java and C, because VBA adopts more English keywords instead of using symbols. For example, you may find many curly brackets {} in Java or C languages, but not in VBA programs. Yet, many skillful programmers prefer the symbol-rich Java or C-like languages because they consider typing and reading symbols instead of English words quicker and more intuitive.

VBA programs, or program modules as they can be called, are composed of VBA program statements. Program statements are instructions to manipulate the content of variables or object properties, perform some sort of mathematical calculation, make conditional decisions, recursively execute a sequence of statements, invoke other procedures, and so on. In English, a statement is delimited by a full stop or period. In VBA, each program statement should occupy a single line. No delimiter is required to denote the end of a statement. For multiple short statements, programmers may use a colon (:) to concatenate multiple statements into a single line. For a long statement, programmers may apply underscores (_) at the end of lines to split a statement into multiple lines. You may find examples of statement concatenation and statement continuation in Appendix C.

There are two levels of program statements: module-level and procedure-level. Module-level program statements are mainly declaration statements, which declare module-level variables and procedures of the module. Variables store constant values or computed results. Procedures define dedicated tasks to be performed and can contain any type of program statements. Procedures can be subroutines or functions. The declarative statements of procedures can declare procedure-level (local) variables only. Module-level variables are basically available for use by all procedures declared within the module. Procedure-level variables are available for use by the procedure only. When a procedure is called or invoked, the program statements will be executed in the defined sequence in order to achieve the dedicated task of the procedure.

Inside a program module, users may make explanatory remarks or comments anywhere. Since it is difficult to understand the purpose and design of a program by solely reading the program statements, comments are useful plain descriptions that explain the purpose of the program and the design of the program logic. VBA supports comments in English or other languages. Comments are useful for programmers to maintain and extend the programs. Any text after a single quotation mark (') or the REM keyword are considered VBA remarks or comments. The VBA editor will show the text comments in green to indicate that those comments will be ignored during program compilation and execution. In summary, a VBA program module will have the following structure:

Inside a Program Module, it includes:

- Declaration statements of module-level variables
- Declaration statements of procedures (i.e. subroutines or functions)
  ' Comments or remarks are used to explain the program design and logic

Inside a procedure (i.e. subroutine or function), it includes:

- Declaration statements of procedure-level (or local) variables
- Other program statements that
  - manipulate the content of variables or object properties
  - perform some sorts of calculation and decision analysis
  - control the sequence of program execution
  - invoke other procedures (subroutines or functions).

The program structure represents the logic and sequence of computing. There are no fixed pattern and style of program structure. The general structure of a procedure may include analyzing inputs, performing some computing based on the inputs in order to achieve the dedicate goal of the procedure, and finally presenting outputs. Shown in Figure A.26 below is an example of a factorial function, which illustrates the general structure and logic of a function.

The screen shown in Figure A.26 can be divided into three sections. The left side illustrates the project structure of the Excel application. Module1 in the Modules folder is the program module created for this

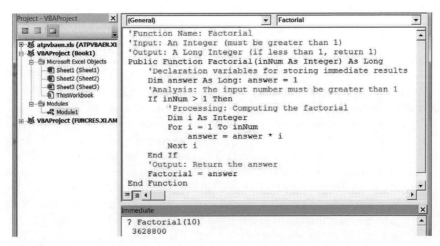

FIGURE A.26 A VBA function to calculate the factorial of a number.

example. The right side has two windows. The top window displays the VBA source code of the Factorial function written in Module1. The bottom window is called the Immediate window, which allows users to enter VBA commands for program testing. Here a VBA command is entered to test the calculation of Factorial(10). The answer 362,800 is immediately shown beneath the command.

Let us analyze the statements inside the Factorial function. It starts with some comments, which explain the design and logic of the function. It is a good programming practice to write comments in a consistent format and style. The Factorial function contains a block of program statements. The first statement is a Function declaration statement and the last statement is an End Function statement. They define the boundary of the function. Words that turn blue in VBE are keywords of VBA. The keywords have particular meanings in VBA. The processing logic of the function can be divided into four sections, which declare variables, analyze inputs, compute, and finally return an answer. Each section is annotated with some comments. The syntax of the program statements will be explained in this section later. Besides writing remarks or comments inside programs, program indentations are important because the space introduced at the beginning of statements can express the hierarchical levels or nested relationship of the statements. Each sub-level should have an additional indentation of four spaces. A consistent style of indented program statements is essential to facilitate the readability of the program.

Now, let us see an example of a subroutine with a similar program structure. The source code of the subroutine is shown in Figure A.27.

A module named LoanCalc is created in the Modules folder. A subroutine of CalculatePayment is written in the LoanCalc module. To test the subroutine, the example uses a worksheet with some defined names and then invokes the subroutine for calculation. The result of $18,871.23 is

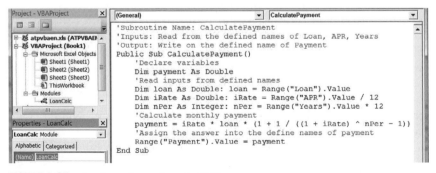

FIGURE A.27 A subroutine written in VBE.

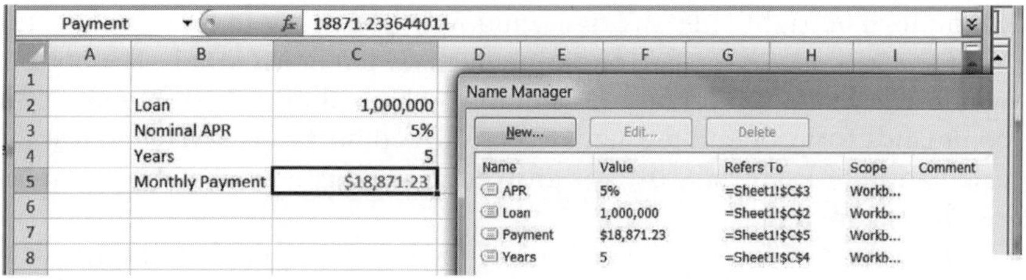

FIGURE A.28   The subroutine writes the payment value in the worksheet.

displayed in the named cell Payment. The worksheet for the test looks like Figure A.28.

Let us analyze the statements inside the subroutine. The Calculate Payment subroutine starts with some comments briefly explaining the source of inputs and the destination of the output. The subroutine accesses the content of worksheets through some defined names instead of specifying the exact cell references. It reads the values of the named cells Loan, APR, and Years, calculates the monthly payment, and finally assigns the calculated monthly payment to the value of the named cell Payment. Similar to a function, the first statement declares the beginning of the subroutine and the last statement of End Sub declares the ending boundary of the subroutine. Green words are comments and blue words are keywords. There are also four sections of program statements for declaring variables, reading inputs from Excel ranges, computing, and writing the output to a named cell. By following the same programming practices, explanatory comments, indented statements, and meaningful variable names are essential to facilitate the readability of the program.

By going through the above examples, we have briefly explained the basic program structure of a function and a subroutine. A good function should accept inputs only from the procedure arguments enclosed in parentheses and return a single result to the function caller. However, a subroutine may accept inputs from many different sources, such as the procedure arguments enclosed in parentheses, direct access of cell values of worksheets, inputs from dialog input boxes, or the content of an external file. Outputs of a subroutine are more versatile, such as writing to a cell, building a new worksheet, creating a new chart, displaying the result in a dialog box, printing out a report, or outputting a file. Only subroutines can have the access rights to write or override the values and properties of Excel elements, such as cells and ranges. We will demonstrate the usage of subroutines for various tasks in the discussed financial models of this book.

A.5.1 Variables and Data Types

When we build spreadsheet models, we use cells to store data and formulas. It is easy to read, write, and modify data and formulas in the cells. Cells can automatically provide enough storage for data and formulas. In VBA, we can still read, write, and modify data and formulas stored in the cells of Excel worksheets by means of the Range object, but it is more convenient to have native storage in VBA for storing data. VBA does not provide similar flexible storage as the cells in Excel. We need to declare variables to store and manipulate data in VBA programs. When a variable is declared, you need to provide a meaningful name and the data type to the variable. The variable name is the label used and referred to by the subsequent program statements to address the stored data. It is similar to the defined names in Excel. The name must begin with a letter and can be as many as 255 characters, although it is usually less than 20 characters. The characters can be letters, digits, and underscores. We often follow some naming convention for variables in order to maintain good programming discipline. For example, CamelCase is a common naming convention that combines words without spaces and capitalizes the first character of each word. For variable names, it is common to use a lowercase letter for the first character, such as interestRate, annual Rate, and costOfFund. For procedure names, it is advisable to keep the first character a capital letter and the first word as a verb so as to describe the functions of the procedures from the names, such as PrintTable, CalcInterest, and ReadFromSheet.

The data type of a variable describes the type of content and the preset usage of the data so that VBA can prepare and reserve enough memory storage for the data according to the data type. Besides, VBA can check the syntax and consistency of program statements according to the data types of the included variables. VBA supports eleven intrinsic data types. They are byte, boolean, currency, date, double, integer, long, object, single, string, and variant. Boolean variables can store the logic value of True or False only. Date variables can store dates ranging from January 1, 100 to December 31, 9999 with the time from 0:00:00 to 23:59:59. String variables can store strings with up to 64,000 characters.

There are several numeric types including Byte (from 0 to 255), Integer (from $-32,768$ to $32,767$), Long (from $-2,147,483,468$ to $2,147,483,467$), Single (single-precision, floating-point numbers that can record around eight digits of a number), Double (double-precision, floating-point numbers that can record around 16 digits of a number), and Currency (a large number but with maximum four decimals only). For financial engineering and computing, we should always use *Integer* for integer numbers and *Double* for decimal numbers. You will find our examples mainly use Integers and

Doubles. Occasionally, we need to use Long for storing larger integers that are larger than 32,767 or smaller than -32,767.

To declare a variable, we use the Dim keyword for procedure-level variables. For module-level variables, we can use the keywords Dim, Private, or Public. Although Dim and Private are the same, using the Private keyword to declare module-level variables can explicitly specify that the defined variables are privately available for all procedures within the same module only. They are protected from being used by the external procedures. The Public keyword is used to define public module-level variables. The public module-level variables are accessible by any procedure of any modules. Usually, we should consider that module-level variables are private, because public module-level variables can be accessed and modified by any procedures external to the module. In case there are errors, it will be difficult to debug and trace the changes of the public variables that are modified by external procedures. In fact, it is a poor programming practice to define and use variables with such broad and global scope. Programs with public variables are considered to be poor in software quality. To facilitate the use of private module-level variables, we should make use of public functions so that any changes can be managed by those functions instead of allowing any direct change of the values of module-level variables.

Here are some examples of variable declarations. Their data types are specified after the As keyword and commas are used to delimit the declarations of multiple variables within one program statement:

```
Dim numPeriods As Integer            'declare a variable and it is an integer
Dim isAnnuityDue As Boolean          'declare a variable and it is either TRUE or FALSE
'declare four variables and they are decimal numbers
Dim presentValue As Double, futureValue As Double
Dim constantPayment As Double, interestRate As Double
```

The data type of Object is a reference of any object. All objects in Excel are derived from and belong to the type of Object. All derived objects have their own properties and methods. In order to utilize those specific properties and methods, it is necessary to declare variables with specific class names (i.e. the type of the specific object group) instead of declaring them as the Object data type. The example shown in Figure A.29 declares a variable with the name currentRange as an object of the class Range, so that we can use currentRange to refer to a range in an Excel worksheet. The program sets currentRange referring to the current selected range of the active worksheet. It also means that the properties and methods of Range are applicable to currentRange. Thus, the subsequent statements can set the properties and invoke the methods of currentRange, which clear the formats of all cells of the range, turn on the bold style of the font, set the

```
Sub Test()
    Dim currentRange As Range
    Set currentRange = Application.Selection 'equivalent to the current selected range
    currentRange.ClearFormats                'clear all formats
    currentRange.Font.Bold = True            'bold the content
    currentRange.Font.Color = RGB(255, 0, 0) 'set color as Red
    With currentRange.Cells(1, 1).AddComment 'add comment at the first cell
        .Text ("The font is now bold red")
        .Visible = True
    End With
End Sub
```

FIGURE A.29   The subroutine demonstrates the use of the object type.

font color to red, add a comment at the first cell of the range, and make the comment visible.

Variant is a special data type for storing data with any data type. Similar to the data stored in the cells of Excel, variant can store data of any data type including integer, decimal number, string, date, and so on. Although it seems simple to declare all variables as variant and let VBA handle the different types of data during program execution, programs will suffer from the poor performance since extra computing is required for checking, extracting, and converting the data type of the variant variables every time they are accessed. Moreover, VBA cannot check any syntax errors of the program statements with variant variables during compilation. As a result, data with incorrect data type stored in the variant variables can cause runtime errors during program execution. Therefore, we need to be cautious if we consider using the variant data type. However, when you call the Excel matrix functions in VBA programs, it is necessary to declare variant variables to store the output arrays of the matrix functions, such as Transpose, Mmult, and MInverse, in which the returned results are actually a two-dimensional array of decimal numbers. The example shown in Figure A.30 demonstrates how to call the MInverse function of Excel in VBA and assign the returned value to a variable with the variant type. We will discuss the issues of Matrix functions in the VBA Arrays section in this appendix.

```
Sub test()
    Dim matrix As Variant           'matrix as a Vairant can store anything
    'matrix must be a Variant so that the returned value of the MInverse function
    'of the Excel appliction can be stored into it.
    matrix = Application.WorksheetFunction.MInverse(Range("A1:B2").Value)
    Range("C3:D4").Value = matrix    'show the inversed matrix in the Range of C3:D4
End Sub
```

FIGURE A.30   The subroutine demonstrates the use of the Variant type.

A.5.2 Declaration and Assignment Statements

In this section, we briefly describe the usage and syntax of the VBA declaration statements. Declaration statements are used to declare procedures, variables, enumerations, and user-defined data types of a program. First, let us talk about the declaration statements Function and Subroutine.

Function . . . **End** **Function**	It declares the name, arguments, and code that form the body of a Function procedure. The processing logic of the function is the VBA statements embedded inside the function construct. Arguments must be declared inside the parentheses so that they can be treated as the inputs to the function. All functions must return a value. Assigning a value to the name of a function is equivalent to setting the return value of the function. If the data type of the returned value is numeric, the default return value is zero. In the example function CalcSquareRoot, as shown in Figure A.31, if you pass a negative number to the function, the "Exit Function" statement will cause the immediate exit of the function and return a zero to the caller.

Statement Syntax:
[Public | Private] [Static] Function *FunctionName* [(*arg1*[, *arg2*] . . .)] [As type]

[*statements*] . . .
[*FunctionName* = *expression*]
[Exit Function]
[*statements*] . . .
[*FunctionName* = *expression*]
End Function

```
' Here is an example of a function
Function CalcSquareRoot(NumberArg As Double) As Double
    If NumberArg < 0 Then      ' Evaluate argument.
        Exit Function          ' Exit to calling procedure.
    Else
        CalcSquareRoot = Sqr(NumberArg) ' Return square root.
    End If
End Function
```

```
Immediate
 ? CalcSquareRoot(8)
  2.82842712474619
```

FIGURE A.31 A Function sample code.

Sub . . . **End Sub**	It declares the name, arguments, and code that form the body of a Sub procedure. The processing logic of the subroutine is the VBA statements embedded inside the Sub construct. Arguments must be declared inside the parentheses so that they can be treated as the inputs to the subroutine. The structure is similar to the function statement, but there is no return value. A sample subroutine is shown in Figure A.32.

Statement Syntax:
[Private | Public] [Static] Sub *SubName* [(*arg1*[, *arg2*] . . .)]
[*statements*] . . .
[Exit Sub]

```
                    [statements] . . .
                    End Sub


' Here is an example of Sub procedure with two arguments.
Sub CalcAndShowArea(Length As Double, Width As Double)
        Dim Area As Double       ' Declare local variable.
        If Length = 0 Or Width = 0 Then
            ' If either argument = 0
            Exit Sub             ' Exit Sub immediately.
        End If
        Area = Length * Width    ' Calculate area of rectangle.
        Debug.Print Area         ' Print Area to Immediate window.
End Sub
```

```
Immediate
Call CalcAndShowArea(10,20)
  200
```

FIGURE A.32   A Subroutine sample code.

As shown above, both Function and Sub can be prefixed with the keyword Private or Public. It declares the scope of the procedure available for being invoked by other procedures. Private procedures are available only to all procedures of the module in which they are declared. Public procedures are available to all procedures of all modules in the application. It also means that public procedures are available to all procedures that can access the module. If a procedure is static, the local (procedure-level) variables of the static procedure are preserved between calls. It also means that all local variables of static procedures are automatically static. The Exit statements inside the body of the procedures can cause the immediate break and exit of the procedure.

The following summarizes the general declaration statements of variables:

Option Explicit	It is used *at module-level* to force explicit declaration of all variables in that module. Without the *option explicit* statement, variables are automatically created when they are assigned with values the first time. It should be the first statement in all VBA programs. Even without this statement, we should maintain the good practice to declare all variables explicitly. Automatic creation of variables may cause confusion. Syntax: Option Explicit
Dim | Static	Procedure level variables are declared with either *Dim* or *Static*. Storage space is allocated according to the declared data types. Procedure level variables are accessible within the procedure only.

Procedure level variables declared with *Dim* will be cleared when the execution of the procedure is terminated with the End or Exit command. Only *Static* variables are retained between procedure calls.

Syntax: Dim | Static *varName* As *type* [, *varName* As *type*] . . .

Example: Dim numOfPeriods as Integer, strikePrice as Double

Static totalProcCalls as Integer, totalProcSum as Double

For the declaration of arrays, the dimensions should be declared within the parentheses after the variable name:

Examples: Dim costs(7) as Double, prices(8, 9) as Double

Static cost(7) as Double, prices(8, 9) as Double

Private |
Public

Module-level variables are declared with either *Private* or *Public*. Storage space is allocated according to the declared data type.

Private variables are available only to the module in which they are declared.

Although the *Dim* keyword is equivalent to the *Private* keyword, which can be used to declare private module-level variables, it is suggested to explicitly use the *Private* keyword.

Variables declared using the *Public* keyword are available to all procedures in all modules in all applications. However, we should consider declaring module-level variables as private variables first in order to protect them from any unexpected access by external programs.

Syntax: Public | Private *varName* As *type* [, *varName* As *type*] . . .

Example: Public grossIncome as Double, grossProfit as Double

Private totalCost as Double, totalIncome as Double

For the declaration of arrays, the dimensions should be declared within the parentheses after the variable name:

Examples: Private costs(7) as Double, prices(8, 9) as Double

Public costs(7) as Double, prices(8, 9) as Double

Const

It declares constants for use in place of literal values.

Constants are variables that cannot be altered once they have been defined.

At module level, constants can be private or public. Constant is private by default.

Syntax: [Public | Private] Const *constName* [As *type*] = *expression*

Example: Public Const PI = 3.14159

Enum . . .
. . .
End Enum

Enumeration is a related set of constants. They are used when working with many constants of the same type. It is declared in the *Enum* statement construct.

Enumerations are declared *at module level only*.

The use of enumerations can make program codes easier to read.

Enumerations can be private or public and are private by default.

Syntax:

[Public | Private] Enum *EnumName*

memberName [= *constantExpression*]

[*memberName* [= *constantExpression*]]

   . . .

End Enum

Example 1:
Enum Prompts
No = -1: Maybe = 0: Yes = 1
End Enum

    . . .

If userPreference = Prompts.Yes Then . . .

Example 2 - Enumeration Concatenation:
Enum FileRights
Create = 1: Read = 2
Write = 4: Delete = 8
End Enum

    . . .

Dim filePermission As FileRights
filePermission = FileRights.Read Or FileRights.Write
Example 3 - By default, the constants are automatically assigned numerical
values in order, starting with 0, then 1, and so on:
Enum BlackLevels
Light: Normal: Dark
End Enum

    . . .

Dim tvBlacklevel As BlackLevels
tvBlacklevel = BlackLevels.Dark

Type . . . | User-defined Type (UDT) groups related data elements together so that the
. . . | elements can be declared with a single declaration statement of the UDT.
End Type | The use of UDT can make programs easier to read.

The Type statement is used to define a UDT containing one or more
elements. It can only be declared *at module level*.
UDTs are public by default. Since a UDT does not contain any data, it is
harmless to let it be public and accessible by all modules.
UDT variables are declared with the Dim or Static statements at procedure
level and the Public or Private statements at module level.

Syntax:
[Public | Private] Type TypeName
elementName [(subscripts)] As type
[elementName [(subscripts)] As type]

    . . .

End Type

Example:
Type StockOption
CurrentPrice as Double
StrikePrice as Double
ExpiryDate as Date
End Type

    . . .

```
Dim euroOption As StockOption
euroOption.CurrentPrice = 10.12
euroOption.StrikePrice = 9.88
euroOption.ExpiryDate = #15 Jan 2009#
```

ReDim It is only used at *procedure level* to reallocate storage space for dynamic array variables that are declared at the module or procedure level.
The *Preserve* keyword is used to preserve the data in an existing array when the dimension sizes are redefined.

Syntax:
ReDim [Preserve] varName(subscripts) [As type] [, varname(subscripts) As [type]] . . .
Example: Dim myArray() as Integer 'Declare a dynamic array
     ReDim myArray(4, 5) 'Allocate 4 x 5 elements

Once we have declared variables, we can assign and save data to the variables. Two assignment statements are available in VBA. One is for the assignment of any basic data type and the other one is for object assignment. Assignment statements can be used at the procedure level only. The equal operator ($=$) is used to assign data into variables with any basic data type or properties of any objects. The left side of the equal operator is the variable name that will contain the computing result. The right side can be any numeric or string literal, constant, or formula-like expression. In programming, an operator is a code unit that performs an operation or evaluation on one or more value-returning code elements, such as literals, variables, constants, and so on. Such an operation can be an arithmetic operation; a string concatenation; a comparison that determines which of two values is greater; or a logical operation evaluating whether two expressions are both true. Please find more information in Appendix C, which includes a summary of VBA operators.

For assigning objects, we need to add the Set keyword in front of the assignment statement. The syntax of the Set statement also includes the equal operator. The right side of the equal operator should return an object reference with the class equal to the assigned object specified in the left side of the equal operator. It is remarkable that the Set keyword is omitted in the new VB.Net programming language in order to standardize and simplify the syntax of the assignment statements. As a result, VB.Net has only one type of assignment statement. Here are some examples of VBA assignment statements:

```
Dim int1 as Integer, int2 as integer, _
num1 as Double, num 2 as Double        ' Declare four numeric variables, 'and it is split into two
                                         lines by the underscore.
int1 = 101                             ' Assign and store 101 into the variable int1
num1 = 123.45                          ' Assign and store 123.45 into the variable num1
int2 = 100 * int2                      ' Compute 100 x 101 and store the result 10100 into int2
```

num2 = num1 + 5.5	' Compute 123.45 + 5.5 and store the result 128.95 into num2
Const PI as Double = 3.1416	' PI is a read-only constant with the value of 3.1416
num2 = PI + 5.5 + num1	' PI can be used for computation
Dim costRange As Range	' Declare a range object
Set costRange = Range("A10:B20")	'Assign the costRange equivalent to the range ' from A10 to B20 of the active worksheet
costRange.Value = 10	' Assign the value 10 to all cells from A10 to B20

The following is an example of a VBA program with variables declared in the two different levels. There are module-level and procedure-level variables.

```
' declare public module variables: accessible by external modules
Public varInt2 as Integer       ' varInt2 is a public integer number
Public varNum2 as Double        ' varNum2 is a public decimal number

' declare private module variables: accessible inside the Module only
Private varInt1 as Integer      ' varInt1 is a private integer number
Private varNum1 as Double       ' varNum1 is a private decimal number
Const PI as Double = 3.14159    ' PI is a constant (read only) and private by default

Function Test(input Int as Integer, input Num as Double) as Integer
    ' declare local variables: accessible inside the Test() Function only
    Dim int1 as Integer         ' int1 is a local integer number of the function
    Dim num1 as Double          ' num1 is a local decimal number of the function
    ' program statements may be placed here . . .
    ' program statements can access varInt1, varNum1, varInt2, and varNum2
End Function

Sub CallMe()
    ' declare local variables: accessible inside the CallMe() Subroutine only
    Dim int2 as Integer         ' int2 is a local integer number of the subroutine
    Dim num2 as Double          ' num2 is a local decimal number of the subroutine
    ' program statements may be placed here . . .
    ' program statements can access varInt1, varNum1, varInt2, and varNum2
End Sub
```

A.5.3 Flow Control Statements

Program statements are normally executed in sequence. However, there are flow control statements that allow programmers to determine and change the order of execution from the standard sequential flow of program execution. Flow control statements implement the core processing logic of a program. The flow control statements can be further divided into procedure-calling statements, conditional statements, and looping statements. The procedure-calling statement invokes the execution of other procedures. Once the execution of the called procedure is completed, it returns back the calling statement and the program continues the execution from the statement just below the calling statement. The syntax of the procedure-calling statement is simply the procedure name with arguments enclosed in parentheses. If the invoked procedure is a function, users may use the assignment statement to store the return value into a variable.

The conditional statements "If" and "Select Case" manage the execution of a set of statements that execute only if some condition is met. The looping statements "Do," "For," and "For Each" manage the recursive execution of a set of statements that will repeat or end when some condition is met. Besides, there are Exit statements that may break the execution of the looping statements and continue the execution from the statement just below the looping statement.

Conditional statements are useful for performing some actions based on some decisions. The *If* statement can be a single line statement or in the form of a construct with multiple lines of statements. All *If* statements need a condition that can be evaluated as either True or False. The condition specified in the If statement can be a complex expression with several comparison operators and/or logical operators. Please read Appendix C on the summary of VBA operators for more information. Here are some examples:

Examples of the single line If statement:
If Range("A10").Value = "HK"   **Then** interestRate = 0.05
If Range("A10").Value = "HK"   **Then** interestRate = 0.05   **Else** interestRate = 0.03
If interestRate > 0.05 **And** interestRate < 0.03   **Then** isValidRate = False
If Range("A10").Value = "HK" **Or** interestRate > 0.05   **Then** Range("C10").Value = "OK"

Examples of the If...Then...Else construct with multiple lines of statements:
If Range("A10").Value = "HK" **Then**   ' Simple If..Then construct
        interestRate = 0.05
        calcMethod = "Gauss"
End If

If interestRate > 0.05 And interestRate < 0.03 **Then**   ' If...Then...Else construct
        interestRate = 0.05
        calcMethod = "Gauss"
Else
        interestRate = 0.03
        calcMethod = "Standard"
End If
If interestRate < 0.03 **Then**   ' If...Then...ElseIf..Else construct
        marginRate = 0.02

```
ElseIf interestRate < 0.04 Then
        marginRate = 0.04
ElseIf interestRate < 0.05 Then
        marginRate = 0.06
Else
        marginRate = interestRate * 1.5
End If
```

All statement blocks can contain other statement blocks. We call these nested statements. Here is an example of a nested *If* statement.

```
If interestRate > 0.05 And interestRate < 0.03 Then    ' Nested If..Then...Else constructs
        If calcMethod = "Standard" Then
                marginRate = interestRate * 2.2
        Else
                marginRate = interestRate * 1.5
        End If
Else
        If calcMethod = "Standard" Then
                marginRate = interestRate * 5.6
        Else
                marginRate = interestRate * 7.8
        End If
End If
```

When there are many different conditions depending on the evaluation of the value of a variable or an expression, it becomes cumbersome to use numerous *ElseIf* statements in an *If* statement construct. VBA offers the *Select Case* statement construct to handle such situations. The *Case* statements inside the *Select Case* statement construct provide flexible and simple syntax to express conditions. Here are some examples:

Examples of the Select Case construct with multiple lines of statements:
```
Select Case interestCode      ' Decision on the numeric value of interestCode
Case 1, 2, 3, 4, 5            ' Case expression can be a constant or multiple constants
        interestRate = 0.02
Case 11 to 15                 ' Case expression can be a range using the keyword "to"
        interestRate = 0.03
Case 6 to 10, 16 to 20        ' Case expression can be multiple ranges delimited by a
                                comma
        interestRate = 0.04
Case Is < 30                  ' Case expression using the Is keyword and a logical operator
        interestRate = 0.05
Case Else                     ' The case beyond the above case expressions
        interestRate = 0.06
End Select
Select Case interestType      ' Decision on the string value of interestType
Case "A", "B", "C"            ' Case expression can be a constant or multiple constants
        interestRate = 0.02
```

Case "D" to "F"   ' Case expression can be a range using the keyword "to"
    interestRate = 0.03
Case "G", "H", "L" to "N"   ' Case expression can be multiple ranges delimited by a
                                     comma
    interestRate = 0.04
Case Is < "X"   ' Case expression using the Is keyword and a logical operator
    interestRate = 0.05
Case Else   ' The case beyond the above case expressions
    interestRate = 0.06
End Select

Looping allows recursive executions of a block of program statements. There are three basic looping statements. They are the Do . . . Loop statement, the For . . . Next statement, and the For Each . . . Next statement. In the construct of the *Do . . . Loop* statement, a condition can be applied at the beginning or the end of a loop in order to determine the exit point of the loop and proceed to the next line just below the loop. There are four approaches to apply condition checking to the Do . . . Loop. The examples shown in Figure A.33 demonstrate the four approaches by using four factorial functions. The factorial functions return exactly the same results and have similar processing logic but are different in syntax.

The While condition is equivalent to the opposite result of the Until condition. Thus, in the above example, While (nextNum <= endNum) is equivalent to Until Not (nextNum <= endNum), which is also equivalent to Until (nextNum > endNum). While is more often used than Until. As a guideline, it is better to avoid using negative operators, including Not and < >, in the condition expression because the negative logic is generally difficult to understand.

The While and Until condition checking can be placed after either the Do keyword or the Loop keyword. If the condition checking is placed after the Do keyword, the exit condition is checked first before going into the

```
Function Factorial1(endNum As Integer) As Integer
    Factorial1 = 1
    Dim nextNum As Integer: nextNum = 2
    Do While nextNum <= endNum
        Factorial1 = Factorial1 * nextNum
        nextNum = nextNum + 1
    Loop
End Function

Function Factorial2(endNum As Integer) As Integer
    Factorial2 = 1
    Dim nextNum As Integer: nextNum = 2
    Do Until nextNum > endNum
        Factorial2 = Factorial2 * nextNum
        nextNum = nextNum + 1
    Loop
End Function
```

```
Function Factorial3(endNum As Integer) As Integer
    Factorial3 = 1
    Dim nextNum As Integer: nextNum = 1
    Do
        Factorial3 = Factorial3 * nextNum
        nextNum = nextNum + 1
    Loop While nextNum <= endNum
End Function

Function Factorial4(endNum As Integer) As Integer
    Factorial4 = 1
    Dim nextNum As Integer: nextNum = 1
    Do
        Factorial4 = Factorial4 * nextNum
        nextNum = nextNum + 1
    Loop Until nextNum > endNum
End Function
```

FIGURE A.33   The Factorial functions coded in different looping program statements.

loop and executing any statements inside the loop. If the exit condition checking is placed after the Loop keyword, the loop will be executed once before the exit condition is checked. Therefore, in the example functions of Factorial3 and Factorial4, you may find that the initial value of nextNum is 1 instead of 2. If the nextNum is initialized as 2, Factorial3(1) or Factorial4(1) will return a wrong answer of 2 instead of the expected answer of 1, because the unconditional execution of the loop will take place in the first iteration. Since the first iteration of the loop will be executed unconditionally, the statement of "factorial = factorial × 1" will be executed once before any condition checking takes place. During the execution of the statements inside the loop, placing an Exit Loop statement inside the loop can cause the immediate exit of the loop and the continued program execution from the next statement just below the Loop statement. Among the four styles of loops, the Do While . . . Loop as illustrated in the Factorial1 function of Figure A.33 is most commonly used.

It is quite common to repeat a block of statements a specific number of times in a loop. It needs a variable to act as a counter and the counter will increase by 1 with each repetition of the loop. The *For . . . Next* statement block is designed for such a condition. Although the same goal can be achieved by using the Do While . . . Loop statement block, the For . . . Next statement construct will be simpler. As shown in Figure A.34, the example function of Factorial5 using the For . . . Next statement structure is functionally equal to the example function of Factorial1 using the Do While . . . Loop.

You may find it more intuitive to read the For . . . Next statement than the relatively cumbersome Do While . . . Loop statement. The single statement of "For (counter) = (the initial value) To (the final value) Step (the incremental amount)" already contains the set up of the initial value of the

```
Function Factorial5(endNum As Integer) As Integer
    Factorial5 = 1
    Dim nextNum As Integer
    For nextNum = 2 To endNum Step 1
        Factorial5 = Factorial5 * nextNum
    Next nextNum
End Function
```

```
Function Factorial1(endNum As Integer) As Integer
    Factorial1 = 1
    Dim nextNum As Integer: nextNum = 2
    Do While nextNum <= endNum
        Factorial1 = Factorial1 * nextNum
        nextNum = nextNum + 1
    Loop
End Function
```

FIGURE A.34 Two Factorial functions coded in a For loop and a Do loop.

counter, the exit condition in which the counter must be less than or equal to the final value, and the automatic increment of the counter with each repetition of the loop. The Step keyword is optional and equal to one by default. It specifies the incremental amount, which can be any positive or negative number. A negative Step amount actually specifies the decrement of the counter with each repetition of the loop. The final statement of the For loop is the Next statement. You may omit the counter variable after the Next keyword, but it is a better practice to explicitly specify the corresponding counter variable of the Next statement. This is because there may be several nested For loops with multiple Next statements. You will see this in the examples of this book.

The final looping statement is the "For Each" statement. It is used to handle the object items of an object collection. The syntax is similar to the "For . . . Next" statement, which repeats the execution of a set of statements for each object in an object collection instead of a counter. The advantage of using the "For Each" statement is that we do not have a variable for counting the current number of iterations. In programming, it is common to have a counter to keep track of the current number of iterations so that it can be used for calculating the index numbers pointing to the right elements of arrays. Thus, the statement is useful for looping through a single object collection only. If we need to use a loop counter for multiple objects or arrays during each iteration, we need to use the "For . . . Next" statement and refer to the objects or arrays by an index number, which is usually calculated from a loop counter. Let's use the example shown in Figure A.35 to explain the usage of the "For Each" statement.

The SumOfSelection subroutine can sum the valid numeric values of all cells of the currently selected range. The result will be displayed in a message box. The "cell" is a defined variable in the For Each looping statement referring to an individual cell in the cell collection of Selection.Cells during the repetitive execution of the loop. To test and use the SumOfSelection subroutine, users may select a range in a worksheet first, click the Macros button in the Developer tab of the ribbon, click SumOfSelction shown in

```
Sub SumOfSelection()
    'by default, the total vairable is initialized as zero
    Dim total As Double
    'Selection.Cells contains a collection of all cells of the selected range
    For Each cell In Selection.Cells
        'sum only those cells with a valid numeric value into the total variable
        If IsNumeric(cell.Value) Then total = total + cell.Value
    Next
    'display the result using a message box
    MsgBox ("Sum of Selection = " & Round(total, 2))
End Sub
```

FIGURE A.35 A subroutine with a For-Each loop.

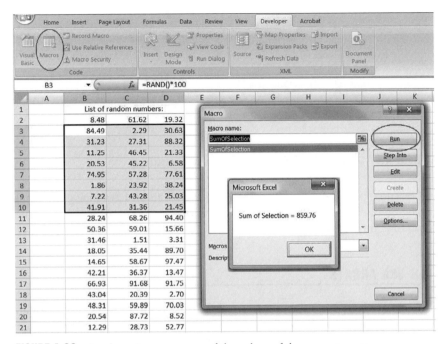

FIGURE A.36 A subroutine to sum up of the values of the current range.

the macro list, and press the Run button to invoke the SumOfSelection subroutine. Then the message box containing the summation result will pop up. Figure A.36 shows an example of the described operations.

Furthermore, it is common to have multiple levels of statements in programs. We call those embedded statements nested statements. As a guideline, the number of nested levels should not be more than five. Otherwise, it will be difficult to understand the program code and hard to maintain the program. If you write a program with many nested levels, a common solution is to create a function to contain a group of some inner statements so that the inner loops can be replaced by a function call. You will find many examples of nested statements in the financial models of this book. Figure A.37 is an example of nested statements with two levels of For loops and one level of Do loop.

The flow control statements are the important elements for implementing program logic. The combination of those statements can construct very complicated processing logic and fulfill the computation of very complicated mathematical functions and formulas. Understanding the introduced declaration, assignment, and flow control statements is just the initial stage

```
'This example illustrates the use of nested For and Do statements
Sub NestedExample()
    Dim random(3, 4, 5) As Double 'By default, the array is zero-based
    Dim x As Integer, y As Integer, z As Integer
    For x = 0 To UBound(random, 1) 'The upper bound of the first dimension
        For y = 0 To UBound(random, 2) 'The upper bound of the second dimension
            z = 0
            Do While z <= UBound(random, 3) 'The upper bound of the third dimension
                'Fill in all elements of the array with random numbers
                random(x, y, z) = Rnd() * 100
                z = z + 1
            Loop
    Next y, x
End Sub
```

FIGURE A.37 An example of nested program statements.

of learning programming. Reading good programs and practicing programming can help you to grasp the programming techniques for the construction of complicated financial models with VBA programs.

A.6 VBA ARRAYS

Arrays are important elements for VBA programming. An array is a data structure that consists of a series of elements of the same data type, such as integers, doubles, strings, objects, and so on. For example, suppose you need to store the monthly interest rates of a year in a variable. You could declare an array variable of 12 numeric elements to hold the 12 interest rates. The array structure helps us to group related elements together so that it is easy to address an individual element with the same variable name and an integer value as the index. In Excel, an array is equivalent to the stored values in a range of cells. Excel arrays are either one or two dimensions. A one-dimensional array is equivalent to a series of cells in a row or a column. A two-dimensional array is actually a range of cells arranged as a set of rows and columns. VBA supports arrays with more than one dimension. Although VBA arrays can be up to 60 dimensions, we often use one- or two-dimensional arrays only. Occasionally, we may use three- or four-dimensional arrays for rather complicated data structures.

There are two types of arrays in VBA: fixed-size arrays and dynamic arrays. A fixed-size array has a fixed number of elements when it is declared. A dynamic array has an unknown number of elements when it is declared. We can store data into the declared elements of the fixed-size arrays. We cannot store any data into the dynamic arrays because the number of elements is unknown. There are two ways to use dynamic arrays. First, we may use the ReDim statement to convert a dynamic array into a fixed-size array, and then we can store data into the declared elements of the converted array. The syntax of the ReDim statement is similar to the Dim statement. We will explain and demonstrate the use of the ReDim statement with examples. Second, the dynamic array can accept the array returned from a function. For example, we can declare a dynamic array to receive the array returned from the matrix functions MInverse or MMult.

All array dimensions have specified boundaries. The lower bound is zero by default, but can be preset by the Option Base statement or specified in the declaration statements. The Option Base statement is used only at the module level to declare the lower bound for array dimensions. The syntax of the statement is "Option Base 1." This means users can preset the index base of all arrays declared in the module to be 1 instead of the default 0. However, it is recommended not to override the default index base with the Option Base statement and to let the index base have the default value of 0. This is because the feature has been deprecated in the newer VB.Net language and all common program languages enforce the index base to be zero only. Therefore, *you should avoid changing the index base.*

As explained, we use the Dim statement to define variables. VBA uses the same Dim statement to define arrays. The dimensions of arrays are declared in a set of parentheses. The module-level arrays are declared with the same syntax, but we may use the keywords Private or Public instead of Dim to explicitly specify the scope of the arrays. Here are some examples of array declarations:

Dim interestRates(1 to 12) as Double	It declares interestRates as an array of 12 numbers. The index of the first element is 1 and the index of the last element is 12.
Dim rates2(0 to 11) as Double	It declares rates2 as an array of 12 numbers. The index of the first element is 0 and the index of the last element is 11.
Dim rates3(3 to 14) as Double	It declares rates3 as an array of 12 numbers. The index of the first element is 3 and the index of the last element is 14.
Dim rates4(1 to 4, 1 to 12) as Double	It declares rates4 as a two-dimensional array of 4 x 12 numbers. The index base of all dimensions is 1.
Dim rates5(0 to 4, 0 to 12) as Double	It declares rates5 as a two-dimensional array of 5 x 13 numbers. The index base of all dimensions is 0.
Dim rates6(5,6,7) as Double	It declares rates6 as a three-dimensional array. The index base is either equal to the default 0 or based on the Option Base statement.
Dim rates7() as Double	It declares rates7 as a dynamic array with unknown number of elements and dimensions. It should be redefined or resized later.
ReDim rates7(0 to 5, 0 to 6) as Double	It re-declares rates7 as a two-dimensional array of 6 x 7 numbers. The index base of all dimensions is 0. The previous dimensions of rates7 are ignored.

As shown in the above examples, the number of dimensions and the dimension sizes are declared inside the parentheses. A comma is the delimiter of the dimensions. We can use the keyword "to" to specify the first index number and the last index number (or the lower bound and the upper bound) of dimensions. If you omit the first index number and the keyword "to," the first index will be equal to the default 0 or based on the Option Base statement. VBA allows users to set the index base as one with the Option Base statement because all Excel object collections are indexed from one and Microsoft considers that it is more natural to use one as the first index. However, it is an interesting and confusing feature of VBA to allow programmers to determine the index base of arrays, because the common practice of modern programming languages restricts the index base of arrays to zero. Moreover, if you read a program with arrays of different index bases, you will get confused and find it difficult to maintain the program. It is a controversial topic whether it is essential to allow arrays with different index bases in a program and whether one is the better index base than zero. Microsoft concluded the arguments in the new VB.Net programming language (the next generation of VB) and decided to follow the general practice of modern programming languages that all indexes should be zero-based only. In the new VB.Net, the index base of all arrays is only zero. The Option Base statement has been removed because it is not allowed to change the index base. If the first index of the dimension is specified in the array declaration statement, it should be declared as zero although it is redundant. In order to ensure all new written VBA programs are easily upgradeable to the later versions of VB, it is better to follow the new syntax of the array declaration and the management of arrays in VB.Net. Two approaches are proposed. First, we take the default zero and should not use the Option Base statement in any modules so that it is not necessary to specify the initial indexes of arrays. Second, we always specify the first index of dimensions as zero in order to eliminate the confusion that may lead from the Option Base statement. Here are examples:

```
'First Approach (use the default 0):        'Second Approach:
Dim array1(12) as Double                     Dim array1(0 to 12) as Double
Dim array2(3,4,5) as Double                  Dim array2(0 to 3, 0 to 4, 0 to 5) as Double
```

The following two procedures are good examples to demonstrate the manipulation of array-related statements with VBA statements. The first procedure is the CloneMatrix() function that accepts a two-dimensional Double array, makes a clone of the input array, and returns the created clone array to the caller. The second procedure is a subroutine for testing the CloneMatrix() function. It creates a two-dimensional Double array with 3×4 elements, fills the elements of the array with some numeric values, calls the CloneMatrix() function to make a clone of the array, and finally prints out the elements of the clone in order to verify if the generated clone array is exactly equal to the original array.

```
'The function will accept an input array and return a Double array
Function CloneMatrix(matrix() As Double) As Double()
    Dim clone() As Double                                    'define a dynamic double array
    Dim rowLowBound As Integer: rowLowBound = LBound(matrix, 1)   'get the lower bound of 1st dim.
    Dim rowUpBound As Integer: rowUpBound = UBound(matrix, 1)     'get the upper bound of 1st dim.
    Dim colLowBound As Integer: colLowBound = LBound(matrix, 2)   'get the lower bound of 2nd dim.
    Dim colUpBound As Integer: colUpBound = UBound(matrix, 2)     'get the upper bound of 2nd dim.

    'Redefine the dynamic double array according to the dimensions of the input array
    ReDim clone(rowLowBound To rowUpBound, colLowBound To colUpBound)
    Dim x As Integer, y As Integer
    For x = rowLowBound To rowUpBound          'loop for each row (1st dimension) of the input array
        For y = colLowBound To colUpBound      'loop for each column (2nd dimension) of the input array
            clone(x, y) = matrix(x, y)         'copy each element value into the clone array
    Next y, x
    CloneMatrix = clone                        'return the created clone to the caller
End Function
```

The CloneMatrix() function accepts a dynamic array of Doubles because it can flexibly accept an input array with any dimensions and any sizes. The syntax of "As Double()" specifies the return value of the function is a dynamic array of Doubles. Here, the function treats the input array as a two-dimensional array. For convenience, it also treats the first dimension as a row and the second dimension as a column. The first statement in the function defines "clone" as a dynamic array of Doubles because the sizes of "clone" are unknown when the function is written. "Clone" will be the return value of the function. In order to get the boundary information of the dimensions of the input array, the two useful VBA functions of LBound () and UBound() are used to examine the lower and the upper boundary of each dimension. Once the sizes of the input array are found, "clone" can be redefined to be a fix-sized array. Since the input array has two dimensions, the function uses two for-loops to iterate through all elements of the input array and copy the element values of the input array into the cloned array. Finally, the function sets the cloned array as the return value.

The TestClone() subroutine creates a fixed-size, two-dimensional array with 3×4 elements named "matrix." Then two for-loops are used to generate numbers and store the numbers into the elements of "matrix." The formula for the generated numbers is not important. It only aims at generating different numbers for elements with different rows and columns only. Then a new dynamic array named "newMatrix" is defined and a cloned array generated from the CloneMatrix() function is assigned to "newMatrix." Finally, the debug.print() function is used to print out the values inside the cloned array in order to ensure the input array can be successfully copied into the clone.

The above examples summarize the basic coding techniques of defining arrays, redefining dynamic arrays, assigning values into the elements of arrays, extracting the element values from arrays, examining the sizes of arrays, defining an array as the input parameter of a function, defining an array as the return value of a function, and invoking a function with arguments of arrays. Those are the common manipulations of arrays in VBA.

A.7 USING WORKSHEET MATRIX FUNCTIONS IN VBA

There are four matrix functions in Excel. In Excel, a matrix is equal to a range of cells with rows and columns. The MDeterm function returns the determinant of a matrix, which is a decimal number. The other three functions return a new matrix. The Transpose function returns a transposed matrix. The MInverse function returns a new matrix, which is the inverse of the input matrix. The MMult function returns a new matrix, which is the multiplication of two input matrices. In VBA, it is easy to use those matrix functions by means of the WorksheetFunction object. Those matrix functions are smart enough to accept either Excel ranges or VBA arrays with any index base. The following example uses a function to demonstrate how to call worksheet matrix functions in VBA:

```
Function TestMatrix(xlRange As Range) As Double
    Dim rowCount As Integer: rowCount = xlRange.Rows.Count
    Dim colCount As Integer: colCount = xlRange.Columns.Count
    'Define a VBA array depending on the dimensions of the input Excel Range
    Dim vbArray() As Double: ReDim vbArray(0 To colCount - 1, 0 To rowCount - 1)
    Dim row As Integer, col As Integer
        For row = 1 To rowCount
        For col = 1 To colCount
            vbArray(col - 1, row - 1) = Math.Sqr(xlRange(row, col).Value)
    Next col, row
    Dim newMatrix As Variant
    With Application.WorksheetFunction
        'newMatrix will be a symmetric matrix (i.e. Rows.Count = Columns.Count)
        newMatrix = .MMult(xlRange, vbArray)
        newMatrix = .Transpose(newMatrix)
        newMatrix = .MInverse(newMatrix) 'Minverse only works with a symmetric matrix
        TestMatrix = .MDeterm(newMatrix) 'MDeterm will return a decimal number only
    End With
End Function
```

"TestMatrix" is just a function to demonstrate how to call the four worksheet matrix functions in VBA. The computations of this example are for demonstration only and have no real application. The function accepts a range as the argument. The first statement defines the rowCount variable to record the number of rows in the input range. The second statement defines the colCount variable to record the number of columns in the input range. Since the function will call the MMult function to multiply two matrices with the first argument being the input range and the second argument being a VBA array, the third statement creates a VBA array with appropriate dimensions that make the matrix multiplication applicable. The fourth statement defines the vbArray variable (a VBA array) with the row dimension equal to the number of columns in the input range and the column dimension equal to the number of rows in the input range. The fifth to ninth statements use two nested For loops to assign some values into the VBA array. The 10th statement prepares the newMatrix variant to store the return matrix from the worksheet matrix functions. The rest of the statements demonstrate the invocation of the four worksheet matrix statements. The final result comes from the return decimal number of the MDeterm function. To test the function, users may randomly assign numbers into a range of cells. The range can be any number of rows and columns. In Figure A.38, we generated a set of numbers into the range B2:B5. Then, users may select a cell and enter the formula "=TestMatrix(B2:D5)". The computed result of the TestMatrix function is a large negative number, which is shown in the cell B7.

Furthermore, we designed a function that can generate random numbers into a range of cells instead of a single value, which is similar to the return array of MMult, MInverse, and MTranpose. The function is named GenRandomMatrix, as can be seen in Figure A.38. The output of the function is a two-dimensional array of numbers instead of a single value. In order to put the array of numbers into a range of cells, we need to apply the function in an array formula. In our example, we select the range B2:D5, enter the formula "=GenRandomMatrix()", and press CTRL-ALT-Enter in

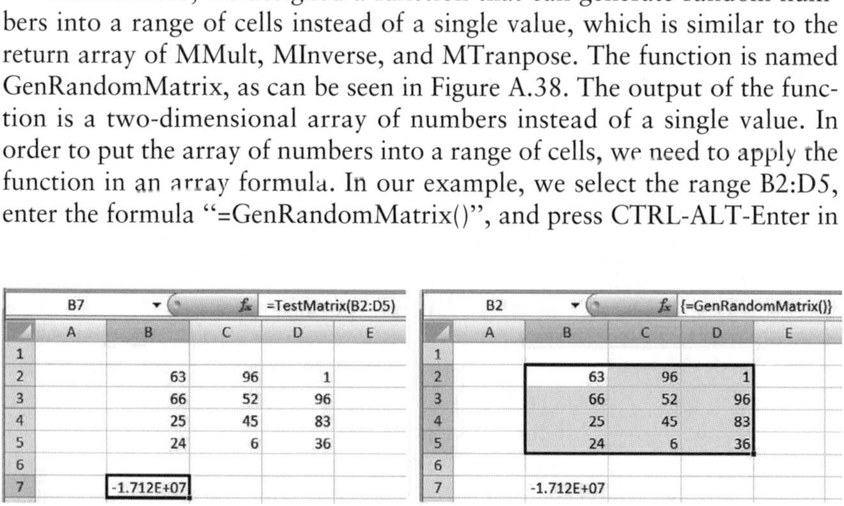

FIGURE A.38 Two user-define matrix functions: TestMatrix() and GenRandomMatrix().

order to define the formula as an array formula. The source code of the function is as follows:

```
Function GenRandomMatrix() As Double()
  'Application.Caller is equivalent to the range applying the function
  Dim rowCount As Integer: rowCount = Application.Caller.Rows.Count
  Dim colCount As Integer: colCount = Application.Caller.Columns.Count
  Dim vbArray() As Double: ReDim vbArray(0 To rowCount - 1, 0 To colCount - 1)
  Dim row As Integer, col As Integer
  For row = 0 To rowCount - 1
    For col = 0 To colCount - 1
    'Generate a random number between 0 to 100
      vbArray(row, col) = Int(Math.Rnd() * 100)
  Next col, row
  GenRandomMatrix = vbArray 'The return result is a two-dimensional array of numbers
End Function
```

"GenRandomMatrix" is a function to generate random numbers and return a two-dimensional array of random numbers. Therefore, the return value of the function is defined as Double(). The function needs not accept any argument. The second statement defines the rowCount variable to record the number of rows in the range that is selected to contain the generated random number. The range is defined in Application.Caller. The third statement defines the colCount variable to record the number of columns in the range of the Application.Caller. The fourth statement defines the vbArray variable (a VBA array) with the same dimensions as the Application. Caller. The fifth to ninth statements use two nested for loops to assign generated random numbers into the VBA array. The final statement assigns the VBA array of random numbers as the return values. By using the Excel array formula, the array of numbers can be assigned to the range of cells accordingly.

Although we may call worksheet functions in VBA programs, the new matrices returned from those matrix functions are all with index base one instead of zero, because the index base of all Excel collections and ranges start from one instead of zero. It would be very confusing and lead to many mistakes if VBA programs mixed different index-based arrays. To solve this problem, it is necessary to ensure the index-base of all arrays is zero. For any non-zero based arrays, we need a function to convert them into zero-based arrays. For any matrix functions, we need alternative functions to perform the same operations but the return arrays are all zero-based. We have created a module with the name "Matrix." The Matrix module includes five functions that can satisfy the described requirements. The function structure and the purpose of the functions are as follows:

Function Structure	Function Description
Convert(matrix1 As Variant) As Double()	Convert an input array with any index base into a zero-based array
Transpose(matrix1 As Variant) As Double()	Transpose an input array with any index base into a transposed zero-based array
Inverse(matrix1 As Variant) As Double()	Inverse an input array with any index base into an inverse zero-based array
Multiply(matrix1 As Variant, matrix2 As Variant) As Double()	Multiply two input arrays with any index base and return a new zero-based array
Determinant(matrix1 As Variant) As Double	Calculate the determinant of an input array with any index base and return a decimal number

The following shows the source code of the Convert function:

```
'All variant inputs can be Range().value of Excel or a VBA two-dimensional double array
Public Function Convert(matrix1 As Variant) As Double()
    Dim rowLBound As Integer, colLBound As Integer
    Dim rowUBound As Integer, colUBound As Integer
    rowLBound = LBound(matrix1, 1)
    colLBound = LBound(matrix1, 2)
    rowUBound = UBound(matrix1, 1) - rowLBound
    colUBound = UBound(matrix1, 2) - colLBound
    Dim newMatrix() As Double
    ReDim newMatrix(0 To rowUBound, 0 To colUBound)
    Dim row As Integer, col As Integer
    For row = 0 To rowUBound
        For col = 0 To colUBound
            newMatrix(row, col) = matrix1(row + rowLBound, col + colLBound)
    Next col, row
    Convert = newMatrix
End Function
```

Let's go through the Convert function. The function is declared as Public so that it is available for use by any procedure. Only one input is declared as Variant and is named "matrix1." It must be a Variant, so that it can refer to the Value of an Excel range or a VBA two-dimensional array. We will have a subroutine to test the function and demonstrate that the function can flexibly accept an Excel range or a VBA two-dimensional array as the input argument. As we treat those functions as matrix functions, we treat the dimensions of the matrices as rows and columns. The first statement of the Convert function declares variables to contain the lower bounds of matrix1. The second statement declares variables to store the upper bounds of the result matrix. The third to sixth statements get and calculate the bound values. The seventh statement declares "newMatrix" to be the matrix to contain the converted matrix. The eighth statement redefines the dimensions of "newMatrix" so that it can match the size of "matrix1" and be zero-based. The ninth to 13th statements use two nested For loops to copy the content of the items from "matrix1" to "newMatrix." The final statement simply sets the return value equal to "newMatrix." To test the Convert function, we designed a Private subroutine named "TestConvert," which is written in the same module. It is private because the subroutine is just for testing purposes and it should not be available for other procedures. The source code of the subroutine is as follows:

```
'This tests the Matrix.Convert() function
Private Sub TestConvert()
    'Input array in the range(B2:D4)
    Dim matrix1() As Double, matrix2() As Double
    'Accept input as Range(:).Value
    matrix1 = matrix.Convert(Range("B2:D4").Value)
    Range("F1").Value = "Output of Matrix.Convert(Range(""B2:D4"").Value)"
    Range("F2:H4").Value = matrix1
    'Accept input as Double(,) array
    matrix2 = matrix.Convert(matrix1)
    Range("K1").Value = "Output of Matrix.Convert(Double(,))"
    Range("K2:M4").Value = matrix2
    'Show the output dimensions
    Debug.Print ("Row: " & LBound(matrix2, 1) & " to " & UBound(matrix2, 1))
    Debug.Print ("Col: " & LBound(matrix2, 2) & " to " & UBound(matrix2, 2))
End Sub
```

We will not describe the design of the testing subroutine, but it is remarkable to take a look at the fourth, eighth, and tenth statements. They demonstrate the usage of the Convert function. The third statement, "matrix.Convert(Range("B2:D4").Value)," returns a zero-based array from an Excel range. The sixth statement, "matrix.Convert(matrix1)," returns a zero-based array from a VBA two-dimensional array. The tenth statement demonstrates that the return array of the Convert function can be assigned to an Excel range. Thus, the flexibility of the function is similar to the usage of the Excel matrix functions.

Now, let us take a look at the source code of the Transpose function and the TestTranspose subroutine:

```
Public Function Transpose(matrix1 As Variant) As Double()
    Dim rowLBound As Integer, colLBound As Integer
    Dim rowUBound As Integer, colUBound As Integer
    rowLBound = LBound(matrix1, 2)
    colLBound = LBound(matrix1, 1)
    rowUBound = UBound(matrix1, 2) - rowLBound
    colUBound = UBound(matrix1, 1) - colLBound
    Dim newMatrix() As Double
    ReDim newMatrix(0 To rowUBound, 0 To colUBound)
```

```
Dim row As Integer, col As Integer
  For row = 0 To rowUBound
    For col = 0 To colUBound
        newMatrix(row, col) = matrix1(col + colLBound, row + rowLBound)
  Next col, row
  Transpose = newMatrix
End Function
```

```
'This tests the Matrix.Transpose() function
Private Sub TestTranspose()
    Range("B5").Value = "Excel Formula: {Transpose(B2:D4)}"
    Range("B6:D8").Select
    Selection.FormulaArray = "=TRANSPOSE(B2:D4)"
    Dim matrix1() As Double, matrix2() As Double
    'Accept input as Range(:).Value
    matrix1 = matrix.Transpose(Range("B2:D4").Value)
    Range("F5").Value = "Output of Matrix.Transpose(Range(""B2:D4"").Value)"
    Range("F6:H8").Value = matrix1
    'Accept input as Double(,) array
    matrix2 = matrix.Transpose(matrix1)
    Range("K5").Value = "Output of Matrix.Transpose(Double(,))"
    Range("K6:M8").Value = matrix2
    'Show the output dimensions
    Debug.Print ("Row: " & LBound(matrix2, 1) & " to " & UBound(matrix2, 1))
    Debug.Print ("Col: " & LBound(matrix2, 2) & " to " & UBound(matrix2, 2))
End Sub
```

You may notice that the statements of the Transpose function are similar to the statements of the Convert function. Actually, their processing logic is similar. The main differences are simply the transposed dimensions and the transposed placement of the copied values. Since the usage of the Transpose function is similar to the Convert function as well, the Test-Transpose subroutine also looks similar to the TestConvert subroutine. "matrix.Transpose(Range("B2:D4").Value)" returns a zero-based transposed array from an Excel range. "matrix.Transpose (matrix1)" returns a zero-based transposed array from a VBA two-dimensional array. "Range ("K6:M8").Value = matrix2" demonstrates that the returned array of the Tranpose function can be assigned into an Excel range.

Corresponding to the MInverse, MMult, and MDeterm functions in Excel, the Matrix module includes the Inverse, Mulitply, and Determinant functions. They simply invoke the equivalent worksheet functions and use the Convert function of the Matrix module to convert the returned array into a zero-based array. Here is the source code of these functions:

```
Public Function Inverse(matrix1 As Variant) As Double()
    Dim newMatrix As Variant
```

```
    newMatrix = Excel.WorksheetFunction.MInverse(matrix1)
    Inverse = Convert(newMatrix)
End Function

Public Function Multiply(matrix1 As Variant, matrix2 As Variant) As Double()
    Dim newMatrix As Variant
    newMatrix = Excel.WorksheetFunction.MMult(matrix1, matrix2)
    Multiply = Convert(newMatrix)
End Function

Public Function Determinant(matrix1 As Variant) As Double
    Determinant = Excel.WorksheetFunction.MDeterm(matrix1)
End Function
```

It is remarkable that the Multiply function accepts two arguments and both of them must be declared Variant so that the function applies a matrix multiplication to both matrices. The Matrix module also includes several private subroutines for testing those matrix functions. Here is the source code of those functions:

```
'This tests the Matrix.Inverse() function
    Private Sub TestInverse()
    Range("B9").Value = "Excel Formula: {MInverse(B2:D4)}"
    Range("B10:D12").Select
    Selection.FormulaArray = "=MINVERSE(B2:D4)"
    Dim matrix1() As Double, matrix2() As Double
    'Accept input as Range(:).Value
    matrix1 = matrix.Inverse(Range("B2:D4").Value)
    Range("F9").Value = "Output of Matrix.Inverse(Range(""B2:D4"").Value)"
    Range("F10:H12").Value = matrix1
    'Accept input as Double(,) array
    matrix2 = matrix.Inverse(matrix1)
    Range("K9").Value = "Output of Matrix.Inverse(Double(,))"
    Range("K10:M12").Value = matrix2
    'Show the output dimensions
    Debug.Print ("Row: " & LBound(matrix2, 1) & " to " & UBound(matrix2, 1))
    Debug.Print ("Col: " & LBound(matrix2, 2) & " to " & UBound(matrix2, 2))
End Sub

'This tests the Matrix.Multiply() function
Private Sub TestMultiply()
    Range("B14:H21").Clear
    Range("B14").Value = "Excel Formula: {MMult(B2:D4,B6:D8)}"
    Range("B15:D17").Select
    Selection.FormulaArray = "=MMult(B2:D4,B6:D8)"
    Range("B18").Value = "Excel Formula: {MMult(B15:D17,B10:D12)}"
    Range("B19:D21").Select
    Selection.FormulaArray = "=MMult(B15:D17,B10:D12)"
    Dim matrix1() As Double, matrix2() As Double
```

```
'Accept input as Range(:).Value
matrix1 = matrix.Multiply(Range("B2:D4").Value, Range("B6:D8").Value)
Range("F14").Value = "Output of Matrix.Multiply(Range(""B2:D4"").Value,Range(""B6:
    D8"").Value)"
Range("F15:H17").Value = matrix1
'Accept input as Double(,) array
matrix2 = matrix.Multiply(matrix1, Range("B10:D12").Value)
Range("F18").Value = "Output of Matrix.Multiply(Double(,),Range(""B10:D12"").Value)"
Range("F19:H21").Value = matrix2
'Show the output dimensions
Debug.Print ("Row: " & LBound(matrix2, 1) & " to " & UBound(matrix2, 1))
Debug.Print ("Col: " & LBound(matrix2, 2) & " to " & UBound(matrix2, 2))
Debug.Print ("Row: " & LBound(matrix1, 1) & " to " & UBound(matrix1, 1))
Debug.Print ("Col: " & LBound(matrix1, 2) & " to " & UBound(matrix1, 2))
End Sub

Private Sub TestAll()
    Range("A1:M21").Clear
    Range("B1").Value = "Input Range(B2:D4):"
    Dim inputArray(0 To 2, 0 To 2) As Double
    inputArray(0, 0) = 1
    inputArray(0, 1) = 2
    inputArray(0, 2) = 4
    inputArray(1, 0) = 3
    inputArray(1, 1) = 5
    inputArray(1, 2) = 7
    inputArray(2, 0) = 6
    inputArray(2, 1) = 8
    inputArray(2, 2) = 9
    Range("B2:D4").Value = inputArray
    Call TestConvert
    Call TestTranspose
    Call TestInverse
    Call TestMultiply
    Range("B2:D4").Select
End Sub
```

There is a TestAll subroutine that is usable for testing all matrix functions in the Matrix module. It creates a 3 x 3 array with assigned values from one to nine, and then calls the testing subroutines of TestConvert, TestTranspose, TestInverse, and TestMultiply. The testing results are displayed in a worksheet for verification. Figure A.39 shows the worksheet containing the testing results of all matrix functions.

A.8 SUMMARY

In this appendix, we have reviewed three important elements in Excel that are essential in VBA programs. Cell references can be in the A1 style or the

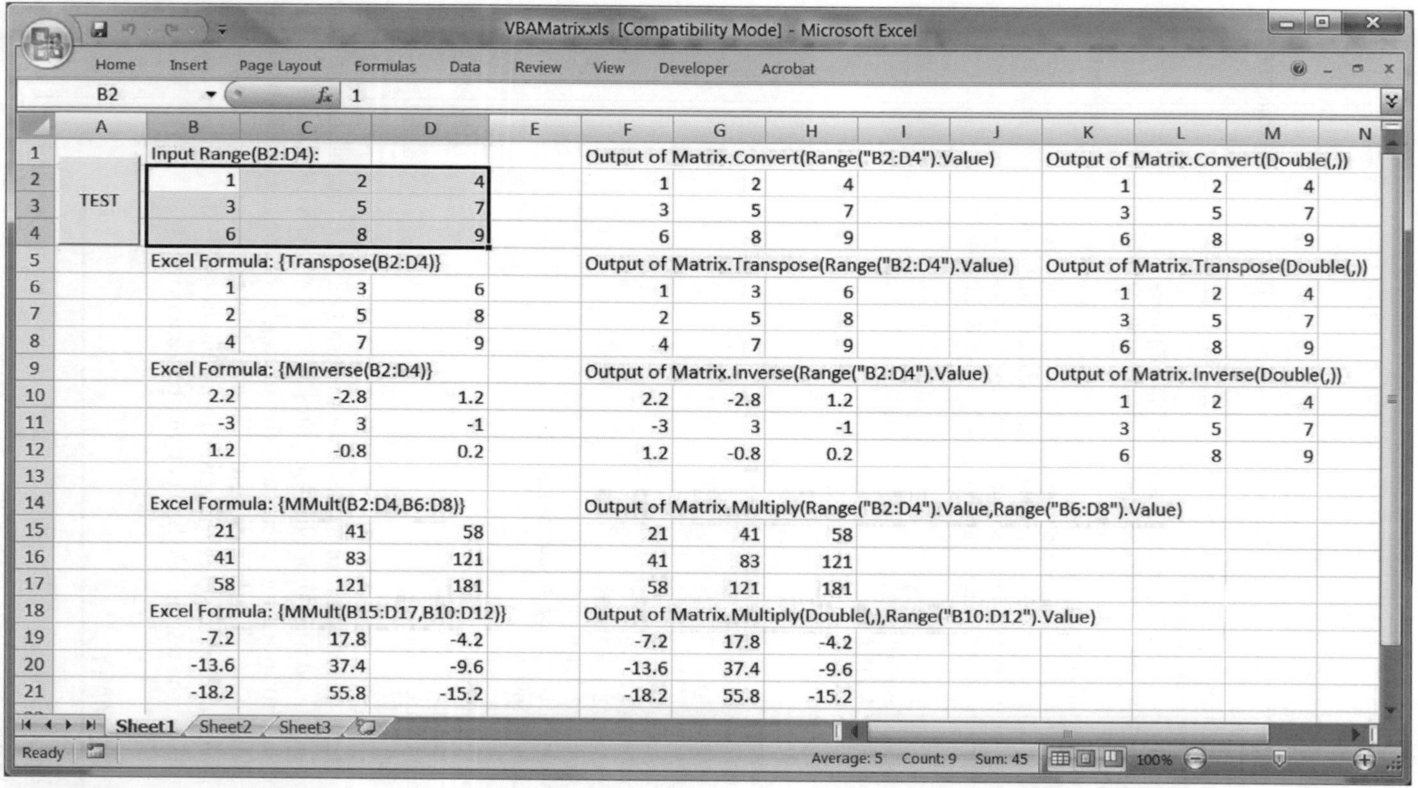

VBAMatrix.xls [Compatibility Mode] - Microsoft Excel

Home   Insert   Page Layout   Formulas   Data   Review   View   Developer   Acrobat

B2   fx   1

Input Range(B2:D4):

	1	2	4
TEST	3	5	7
	6	8	9

Output of Matrix.Convert(Range("B2:D4"),Value)

1	2	4
3	5	7
6	8	9

Output of Matrix.Convert(Double(,))

1	2	4
3	5	7
6	8	9

Excel Formula: {Transpose(B2:D4)}

1	3	6
2	5	8
4	7	9

Output of Matrix.Transpose(Range("B2:D4"),Value)

1	3	6
2	5	8
4	7	9

Output of Matrix.Transpose(Double(,))

1	2	4
3	5	7
6	8	9

Excel Formula: {MInverse(B2:D4)}

2.2	-2.8	1.2
-3	3	-1
1.2	-0.8	0.2

Output of Matrix.Inverse(Range("B2:D4"),Value)

2.2	-2.8	1.2
-3	3	-1
1.2	-0.8	0.2

Output of Matrix.Inverse(Double(,))

1	2	4
3	5	7
6	8	9

Excel Formula: {MMult(B2:D4,B6:D8)}

21	41	58
41	83	121
58	121	181

Output of Matrix.Multiply(Range("B2:D4"),Value,Range("B6:D8"),Value)

21	41	58
41	83	121
58	121	181

Excel Formula: {MMult(B15:D17,B10:D12)}

-7.2	17.8	-4.2
-13.6	37.4	-9.6
-18.2	55.8	-15.2

Output of Matrix.Multiply(Double(,),Range("B10:D12"),Value)

-7.2	17.8	-4.2
-13.6	37.4	-9.6
-18.2	55.8	-15.2

Sheet1   Sheet2   Sheet3

Ready   Average: 5   Count: 9   Sum: 45   100%

FIGURE A.39 The test output of all matrix functions.

R1C1 style. Both styles are useful when we insert formulas into Excel cells with VBA programs. Using defined names is a good programming practice because it makes formulas readable and meaningful. It is more dynamic and flexible to change the referenced cells and ranges of the defined names. Excel includes comprehensive worksheet functions that we can invoke in VBA programs. The matrix functions are especially useful in financial models. VBA programs are developed in the VBA development environment (VBE). There are many features and windows for programmers to manage their projects and programs.

Modules, procedures, variables, and program statements are the constructs of VBA programs. Generally, there are two types of procedures in modules. They are subroutines and functions. Variables can be module-level or procedure-level. There are many data types of variables. For numeric data types, we should define variables as Integer for integer numbers and Double for decimal numbers. If we need to use large integer numbers, we may define those variables as Long.

Declaration statements are used to declare procedures and variables. Variables can be declared with different scopes. Constant variables are declared as read only. Static variables are declared to store and retain values between procedure calls. Use of enumerations and types can gather related variables and make programs more readable. Assignment statements are used to assign values into variables of any basic data type and set object references into object variables. There are two main types of flow control statements. Conditional statements include the "If" and "Select" statements that execute a block of statements based on some conditions. The main looping statements are "Do . . . Loop", "For . . . Next", and "For Each . . . Next" statement constructs that manage the recursive execution of a set of statements that will repeat or end when some condition is met. The program logic of a program is mainly constructed by those declaration, assignment, and flow control statements.

Finally, VBA arrays are complicated components of a program. We have discussed and introduced the basic techniques of utilizing the arrays. Matrix functions are important for financial computing. Although there are some discrepancies in Excel arrays and VBA arrays, we have proposed a solution for several VBA matrix functions and grouped them into a single module for your reference.

This appendix briefly explains the main VBA programming knowledge and techniques for beginners so that they may understand VBA programs and read the VBA programs of this book. More summarized information regarding VBA features can be found in the following appendices (Appendices B to G).

The Excel Object Model

In early software languages such as the influential C language, functions and variables are the basic building blocks of a program. Functions contain the computing logic of a program. Variables contain data and computing results. It is not easy for programmers to manage hundreds and thousands of functions and variables in a large program. In modern object-oriented programming (OOP), such as VBA, a computer program is made up of a collection of objects that interact with each other. The object concept is borrowed from our experience in the real world, in which activities are regarded as the interaction between objects. The object abstraction in software can help programmers to better organize and manage a large amount of software components in programs including functions and variables. Besides, the new features in OOP facilitate the reusability of program codes. In OOP, related functions grouped inside an object are called object methods; while variables of an object are called object properties. The object *methods and properties* determine the behavior and capability of the object. For example, an open Excel file is treated as a workbook object in VBA programs. There are hundreds of properties in a workbook object that determine its behavior and capability. "Password" is one of the properties of a workbook object. Setting a value into the password property can protect the workbook from being viewed. A valid password must be provided in order to view the content of the workbook. There are also hundreds of methods in a workbook object. "Close" is a method available in a workbook object. Calling the Close method can close the open Excel file immediately.

Objects may contain other objects. Their relationships are organized in the form of a tree-structured model. In Excel, the whole application is organized and presented as a large set of Excel objects. The Excel operation is carried out by the interactions of these Excel objects. *The Excel Object Model* is the reference model of the Excel objects that describes the characteristics of the objects and represents the hierarchical relationships of the objects. The object acts like a container holding properties, methods, and even other objects. In order to control the Excel operations and manage the behaviors, we write VBA programs to access, examine, and manipulate the Excel Object Model. For example, the Application object represents the entire Excel application that contains many objects including a collection of workbook objects. A workbook object represents an open Excel file that contains many objects including a collection of worksheet objects. A worksheet object contains the columns, rows, names, cells, ranges, and so on. Their relationships are formulated as a hierarchical structure in the Excel Object Model. In VBA programs, we examine an object by traversing and specifying its hierarchical position using a dot (a full-stop) as a separator. The following code example is a recorded macro. All VBA statements in the macro refer to the properties or methods of some objects, which use some dots to express the hierarchical relationship from the higher level to the lower level of the addressed objects:

Sub Macro1()	*Explanation:*
Application.Calculation = xlManual	*Set the Calculation property as Manual*
Range("data").Select	*Select the range named data*
Selection.Font.Bold = True	*Turn on the Bold property of the Selection*
Selection.Font.Underline = xlUnderlineStyleSingle	*Set the Underline property as a single line*
Range("total").Select	*Select the cell named total*
ActiveCell.FormulaR1C1 = "=SUM(data)"	*Define the formula equal to the sum of a range*
Application.Calculate	*Call the method Calculate to compute immediately*
Application.Calculation = xlAutomatic	*Set the Calculation property back to Automatic*
End Sub	

The objects of the Excel Object Model are organized in multiple levels. To access the right object, we usually need to traverse from a higher level object down to the objects in the lower levels. For example, the VBA code to assign a value into the content of the range B3:D6 in the second worksheet of the workbook "book1.xls" is as follows:

```
Application.Workbooks("book1.xls").Worksheets(2).Range("B3:D6").Value = 123.
```

There is a With statement in VBA that lets us specify an object or user-defined type once for the entire series of statements. The With statement makes your procedures run faster and helps you avoid repetitive typing. The following works on the range B3:D6.

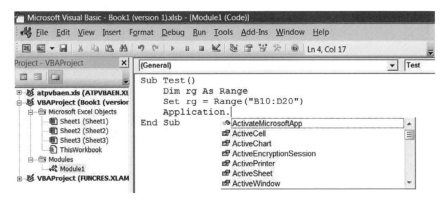

FIGURE B.1 VBA Editor.

```
Sub FormatRange()
   With Workbooks("book1.xls").Worksheets(2).Range("B3:D6")
      .Value = 30
      .Font.Bold = True
      .Font.Underline = xlUnderlineStyleSingle
   End With
End Sub
```

Acquiring the knowledge of the available objects, object collections, methods, and properties of the Excel Object Model is the key to control and master the Excel application with VBA programs. Since the Excel Object Model is huge in scope, it is not possible to memorize all of them. There are three common ways to get the information and help of the Excel Object Model during VBA programming. Firstly, in the VBA program editor, the intelligent pop-up list box of object members can give users some hints about available properties and methods regarding the object they are editing as shown in Figure B.1. The intelligent pop-up hint is a handy aid and must-have feature of OOP program editors.

Secondly, users may use Excel Help. Excel Help includes comprehensive documentation of the Excel Object Model. It illustrates the objects and their relationships in a clear hierarchical structure. It describes the available objects, their properties, methods, and collections of objects, as well as some helpful sample codes to illustrate their functions and usages. It is recommended to check the object information with Excel Help in order to facilitate your VBA program development. Please try to browse Excel Help for some important objects, such as Application, Workbook, and Worksheet, and the useful properties of Range, Cells, and so on. Figure B.2 shows a section of the hierarchy of the Excel Object Model in Excel Help. Users

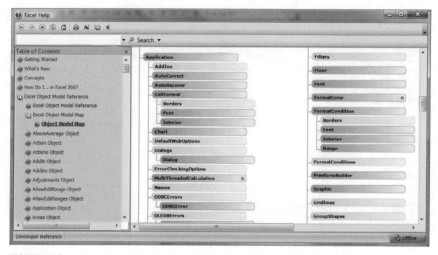

FIGURE B.2 The illustrated hierarchy of the Excel Object Model in Excel Help.

can search and browse the help page of any Excel object in Excel Help. For example, Figure B.3 shows the help page of the Range object.

Finally, users can use the Macro recorder to record Excel operations and examine the generated Macros (i.e. VBA argument-less subroutines) in order to understand the properties and methods used for the recorded operations. Figure B.4 shows the button location of Record Macro in the

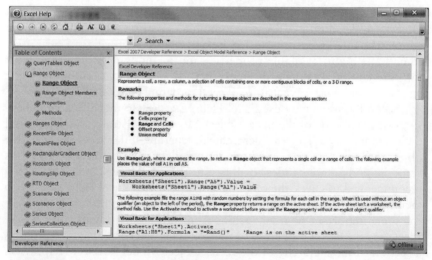

FIGURE B.3 Excel Help for the Range Object.

FIGURE B.4   The Developer tab.

Developer tab. The Macro recorder can automatically generate VBA code containing the affected object properties and invoked object methods corresponding to the manual operations of the user. Learning from the generated VBA code, users may modify the generated VBA code and copy the code into other programs. Some examples are shown in appendix A.

In conclusion, Excel represents all software components as objects and the object relationship in the form of the Excel Object Model. Programmers with the knowledge of how to access the objects, invoke the methods, and set the properties can effectively and fully control the Excel application.

VBA Debugging Tools

When writing VBA programs, it is necessary to ensure all written codes can be executed as expected and no side operations or effects will be generated. The VBA editor can help you with code editing, syntax checking, and program compiling. Even if the written programs can achieve clean compilations without errors, it is necessary to conduct comprehensive testing and debugging in order to ensure the program logic is accurate. This section will briefly introduce and describe two debugging commands and three basic diagnostic tools available in the VBE that can help programmers in testing and debugging.

The *Immediate Window* in the VBE allows programmers to enter commands and display debug information. During program execution, programmers can set break points at program statements. When an executing VBA program reaches a break point, the program will pause, and we call the state of the paused program break mode. Figure C.1 shows that the sample function has entered the break mode before the execution of the statement "sum = sum * count" and the programmer has just entered several *ad-hoc* comments in the Immediate Window in order to examine the present values of the variables.

In break mode, the question mark (?) command in the Immediate Window allows programmers to examine the values of variables or object properties. Simply type a question mark followed by a variable name or an object property in the Immediate Window and press Enter. VBA will display the latest contents of the variable or the object property in the next line. Figure C.2 illustrates three examples.

You can also execute VBA commands in the Immediate Window, but each VBA statement will be executed once you press the Enter key at the end of the VBA statement. Simply type a VBA command and press Enter. No question mark (?) is necessary to prefix the command.

```
(General)                                                    ▼  factorial

Function factorial(num As Integer)
    Dim count As Integer, sum As Integer
    sum = 1
    For count = 2 To num
        sum = sum * count
        'Show debug data on the immediate window
        Debug.Print ("Working Sum = " & sum)
    Next
    factorial = sum
End Function
```

```
Immediate
? Factorial(5)
Working Sum = 2
? Count
 3
Working Sum = 6
? Count
 4
```

FIGURE C.1 Program pauses in a break point.

```
Immediate
? ActiveSheet.Name
Sheet2
? ActiveCell.Value
 123
? Count
 4
```

FIGURE C.2 Debug with the Immediate Window.

```
Immediate
Range("A1").Value = 123
WorkSheets("Sheet2").Activate
```

FIGURE C.3 Execute VBA statements in the Immediate Window.

Figure C.3 demonstrates how to set a property and invoke a method in the Immediate Window.

If you want to execute multiple VBA statements, you can combine the statements with colons ":". Figure C.4 concatenates five statements including a recursive "For" loop.

Debug.Print() is a very useful VBA command to display messages or variable values in the Immediate Window. The Debug.Print() command works without affecting other operations in the program, even though the

```
Immediate
x=1: For Y = 1 to 10: X = X * Y: Next Y: Debug.Print(X)
 3628800
```

FIGURE C.4 Execute multiple VBA statements.

VBE is not executing. You may include as many Debug.Print() commands as required in programs so as to display enough data and messages in the Immediate Window for tracking the program progress and value changes of variables. By examining the displayed values and the display sequence, you may track the execution of programs and the change of variables during program execution. Figure C.5 prints out the values of "sum" to the Immediate Window during the execution of the For loop.

Debug.Assert() is another useful VBA command that can pause the execution of a program when the specified condition is evaluated as False. For example, Debug.Assert(ActiveSheet.Name="Sheet1") can cause a pause of the program if the active worksheet is not "Sheet1." However, unlike the Debug.Print() command, this command should be used during program testing and debugging only. All Debug.Assert() statements should be removed or disabled when the program is released for production or to end users. This is because end users will not know how to respond in case

```
(General)                                        ▼  factorial
Function factorial(num As Integer)
    Dim count As Integer, sum As Integer
    Debug.Print ("Start For Loop")
    sum = 1
    For count = 2 To num
        sum = sum * count
        'Show debug data on the immediate window
        Debug.Print ("Working Sum = " & sum)
    Next
    Debug.Print ("End For Loop")
    factorial = sum
End Function
```

```
Immediate
? factorial(5)
Start For Loop
Working Sum = 2
Working Sum = 6
Working Sum = 24
Working Sum = 120
End For Loop
 120
```

FIGURE C.5 Use Debug.Print for debugging.

the program is paused by a Debug.Assert() statement and waits for user instructions in the VBE.

User-defined Break Points can be set at any line of VBA statements. They tell VBA to pause execution immediately before the VBA statement containing the break point. To put or remove a break point in a line of code, place the cursor on that line and press F9 or choose "Toggle Break-point" from the Debug menu. The lines with a brick colored background are lines with break points. A line with a break point will appear with a yellow background immediately before the line of code is executed. In the break mode, users can resume program execution by pressing F5, or choosing "Continue" from the Run menu, or stepping through the code line by line by pressing F8, or Shift-F8 to "Step Over" the procedure call. In contrast to Debug.Assert() break commands, user-defined break points are not saved in the workbook file. Break points are preserved as long as the file is opened. They are removed when the file is closed.

The *Locals Window* is a useful tool for displaying the latest values of the executing procedure's local variables and the global variables declared at the module/program level. This makes it easy for programmers to examine the changes in local variables when they are stepping through the program line by line. Variables in the Locals Windows are read-only. If programmers want to alter the values of any variables for testing, they can enter commands in the Immediate Window and alter the values. Figure C.6 demonstrates a user stepping through the Test() subroutine, reading the debug output in the Immediate Window, and checking the variables in the Locals Window.

Finally, if users want to watch only a specific variable or expression, and cause program execution to pause when the value being watched is True or changes, the *Watches Window* allows users to add "Watches" of variables or expressions. The Watches Window can be invoked through the Debug item of the menu as shown in Figure C.7.

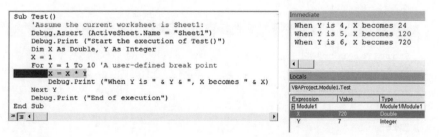

FIGURE C.6 The Locals Window.

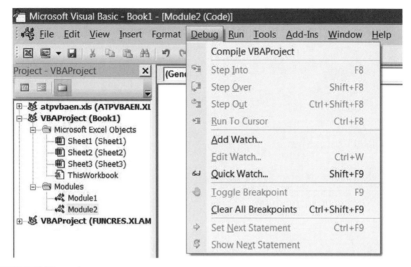

FIGURE C.7 Debug menu items.

FIGURE C.8 The Watches Window.

Right-click the Watches Window to edit, add, and delete watches. For example, there are two variables and one expression being watched in Figure C.8.

Summary of VBA Operators

An operator is a symbol or code element that performs an operation on one or more code elements that hold values. Value elements include variables, constants, literals, properties, and expressions. An expression is a series of value elements combined with operators, which yields a new value. The operators act on the value elements by performing calculations, comparisons, or other operations. VBA operators can be classified into five main categories: arithmetic operators, comparison operators, logical operators, assignment operators, and miscellaneous operators.

Arithmetic Operators (the result is either a decimal number or an integer):

		In the following examples, x and y can be any numeric value, variable, or expression	
+	Addition	x + y	(e.g. 13.5 + 5 returns 18.5)
−	Subtraction	x − y	(e.g. 13.5 − 5 returns 8.5)
*	Multiplication	x * y	(e.g. 13.5 * 5 returns 67.5)
/	Division (returns a numeric value)	"x / y"	(e.g. 13.5/5 returns 2.7)
\	Integer Division (returns an integer quotient)	"x \ y"	(e.g. 13.5\5 returns 2)
mod	Modulus Arithmetic (returns an integer remainder)	x mod y	(e.g. 13.5 mod 5 returns 4)
^	Exponentiation	x ^ y	(e.g. 2 ^ 3 returns 8)

Comparison Operators (the result is either True or False):

		In the following examples, x and y can be any boolean/logical value, variable, or expression.
=	Equal to	If x = y Then . . .
< >	Not equal to	If x < > y Then . . .
>	Greater than	If x > y Then . . .
> =	Greater than or equal to	If x > = y Then . . .
<	Less than	If x < y Then . . .
< =	Less than or equal to	If x < = y Then . . .
Is	Object Reference Comparison	If object1 Is object2 Then . . . returns True if object1 and object2 both refer to the same object, otherwise returns False.
Like	String Pattern Comparison	If string Like pattern Then . . . e.g. "Visual Basic" Like "Visual*"returns True because the string "Visual Basic" can match with the pattern of "Visual*" where the pattern symbol of "*" means any characters. The pattern symbols can be: ? Any single character. * Zero or more characters. # Any single digit (0–9). [charlist] Any single character in charlist. [!charlist] Any single character not in charlist.

Logical Operators (the result is either True or False):

		In the following examples, x and y can be any boolean/logical value, variable, or expression.	
Not	Negation	If Not x Then . . .	Not is a unary operator. It returns the opposite logical result of the evaluated expression.
And	Conjunction	If x And y Then . . .	Returns True if both expressions are evaluated to be True, otherwise returns False.
Or	Disjunction	If x Or y Then . . .	Returns False if both expressions are evaluated to be False, otherwise returns True.

Xor	Exclusion	If x Xor y Then . . .	Returns True if both expressions are evaluated to be different, otherwise returns False.
Eqv	Equivalence	If x Eqv y Then . . .	Returns True if both expressions are evaluated to be the same, otherwise returns False.
Imp	Implication	If x Imp y Then . . .	Returns False only if "True Imp False," otherwise returns True. (It is rarely used.)

Assignment Operators (there is only one assignment operator in VBA):

=	Assignment	e.g. x = y where x is a variable or a writable property and y can be any numeric, logical, string literal, constant, or expression. x and y must be with the same data type.

Miscellaneous Operators:

&	String Concatenation	e.g. "Good" & "Morning" returns "Good Morning"
:	Statement Concatenation	e.g. For x = 1 to 10: y = y * x: Next x where the two colon characters concatenate three VBA statements into one single line.
_	Statement Continuation	e.g. WorkBooks("MyBook.xls")_ .Worksheets("Sheet1")_ .Range("B10:B20")_ .Value = 100 where the three underscore characters indicate the VBA statement continues on the next lines.
'	Remark or Comment	e.g. Range("loan").Value = var1 'To assign the loan value where the single quote character indicates that the content after the single quote contains explanatory remarks or comments only. The VBA compiler should ignore the comments.
AddressOf		It is a unary operator that causes the address of the procedure it precedes to be passed to an API procedure that expects a function pointer at that position in the argument list. It can be used for the integration with other Dynamic Load Libraries (DLLs) compiled with Microsoft Visual C++ (or similar tools).

Summary of VBA Functions

Date and Time Functions:

Date to string conversion	Format FormatDateTime MonthName WeekdayName
Current date or time	Date Now Time Timer
Date calculation	DateAdd DateDiff
Date or time generation	DateSerial DateValue TimeSerial TimeValue
Part of a date or time	DatePart Day Hour Minute Month Second Weekday Year

Data Type Functions:

Data type conversion	CBool CByte CCur CDate CDbl CDec CInt CLng CSng CStr CVar CVErr
Data type information	IsArray IsDate IsEmpty IsError IsMissing IsNull IsNumeric IsObject LBound RBound TypeName VarType

Directory and File Functions:

Directory functions	CurDir Dir
File attributes	FileAttr FileDateTime FileLen GetAttr
File operations	EOF FreeFile Input Loc LOF Seek Spc Tab

Financial Functions:

Depreciation calculation	DDB SLN SYD
Investment calculation	FV IPmt IRR MIRR NPer NPV Pmt PPmt PV Rate
Numeric to strings	Format FormatCurrency FormatNumber FormatPercent

Mathematical Functions:

General functions	Exp Log Sqr
Numeric conversion	Abs Fix Int Round Sgn
Trigonometric functions	Atn Cos Sin Tan

Miscellaneous Functions:

ActiveX objects	CreateObject GetObject
Array functions	IsArray Array Filter Split
Execution	CallByName Shell
Logical functions	Choose IIf Switch
Random numbers	Randomize Rnd
Registry manipulation	DeleteSetting GetAllSettings GetSetting SaveSetting
Screen I/O	InputBox MsgBox
System color code	QBColor RGB
System information	Environ

String Functions:

String creation	Format Chr Hex Join Oct Space Str String
String comparison	InStr InStrRev StrComp
String conversion	Asc LCase Len StrConv UCase Val
String manipulation	Left LTrim Mid Replace Right RTrim StrReverse Trim

Summary of VBA Statements

The following table summarizes the VBA statements and their categories. The statements with the underlined category are important for new learners.

Statement	Category	Description
AppActivate	System	Activates an application window.
Beep	Miscellaneous	Generates a beep sound.
Call	Flow Control	Invokes an internal Sub procedure or a Function.
Call	System	Invokes an external procedure in a dynamic-link library (DLL).
ChDir	File Operation	Changes the current directory or folder.
ChDrive	File Operation	Changes the current drive.
Close	File Operation	Concludes input/output to an open file.
Const	<u>Declaration</u>	Declares constants. Constants can retain their values throughout the execution of a program. Constants can be public or private.
Date	System	Sets the current system date.
Declare	System	Used at module level to declare reference to external procedures (Sub or Function) in a dynamic-link library (DLL).

(Continued)

(Continued)

Statement	Category	Description
Deftype	Declaration	Used at module level to set the default data type for variables according to the names (not advised to use).
DeleteSetting	System	Deletes a section or key setting from an application's entry in the Windows registry.
Dim	Declaration	Declares variables and allocates storage space.
Do {While | Until} condition . . . Loop Do . . . Loop {While | Until} condition	Flow Control	Conditionally repeats a block of statements. Uses Exit Do to exit a Do loop.
End	Flow Control	Ends a procedure or block; which includes End (terminates execution immediately—it closes any files and clears variables), End Function, End If, End Property, End Select, End Sub, End Type, and End With.
Enum	Declaration	Declares a type for an enumeration.
Erase	Assignment	Reinitializes the elements of fixed-sized arrays.
Error	Error Handling	Simulates the occurrence of an error.
Event	Declaration	Declares a user-defined event.
Exit	Flow Control	Exits a block of statements, which includes Exit Do, Exit For, Exit Function, Exit Property, and Exit Sub.
FileCopy	File Operation	Copies a file.
For Each . . . Next	Flow Control	Repeats a group of statements for each element in an array or collection. Uses Exit For to exit a For loop.

For . . . Next	Flow Control	Repeats a group of statements a specified number of times. Uses Exit For to exit a For loop.
Function . . . . . . End Function	Declaration	Declares the name, arguments and code that form the body of a function procedure. Uses Exit Function to exit a function.
Get	File Operation	Reads data from an open file into a variable.
GoSub *label* . . . *label*: . . . Return	Flow Control	Branches to and returns from a subroutine within a procedure. GoSub is not a well structured flow control statement. If possible, consider using other flow control statements.
GoTo *label* . . . *label*: . . .	Flow Control	Branches unconditionally to a specified (labeled) line within a procedure. GoTo is not a well structured flow control statement. If possible, consider using other flow control statements.

If . . . Then . . . Else
 If . . . Then
 . . .
 ElseIf . . . Then
 . . .
 Else
 . . . End If
	Flow Control	Conditionally executes a group of statements, depending on the evaluated condition.

Implements	Class	Specifies an interface or class that will be implemented in the class module in which it appears.
Input #	File Operation	Reads data from an open sequential file and assigns the data to variables.
Kill	File Operation	Deletes files.
Let	Assignment	Assigns the value of an expression to a variable or property. Explicit use of the Let keyword is a matter of style, but it is usually omitted.

(Continued)

(*Continued*)

Statement	Category	Description
Line Input #	File Operation	Reads a single line from an open file and assigns it to a string variable.
Load	Class	Loads an object into memory.
Lock	File Operation	Controls access by other processes to all or part of a file opened using the Open statement.
LSet	Assignment	Left aligns a string within a string variable. LSet replaces any leftover characters in the string variable with spaces.
Mid	Assignment	Replaces a specified number of characters in a string variable with characters from another string. Use the MidB statement with byte data contained in a string.
MkDir	File Operation	Creates a new directory or folder.
Name	File Operation	Renames a disk file, directory, or folder.
On Error GoTo *label* . . . *label*: . . . Resume [Next]	Error Handling	Enables an error-handling routine and specifies the location of the routine within a procedure. On Error GoTo 0—Disables any enabled error handler. On Error Resume Next—Defers error trapping.
On . . . GoSub On . . . GoTo	Flow Control	Branches to one of several specified (labeled) lines, depending on the value of an expression.
Open	File Operation	Enables input/output to a file.
Option Base {0|1}	Declaration	Used at module level to declare the default lower bound for array subscripts. It is advisable to use Option Base 0.
Option Compare	Declaration	Used at module level to declare the default comparison method to use when string data is compared.

Option Explicit	Declaration	Used at module level to force explicit declaration of all variables in that module.
Option Private	Declaration	Prevents a module's contents from being referenced outside its project.
Print #	File Operation	Writes display-formatted data to an open file.
Private	Declaration	Used at module level to declare private variables and allocate storage space.
Property Get	Class	Declares the name, arguments, and code that form the body of a Property procedure, which gets the value of a property.
Property Let	Class	Declares the name, arguments, and code that form the body of a Property Let procedure, which assigns a value to a property.
Property Set	Class	Declares the name, arguments, and code that form the body of a Property procedure, which sets a reference to an object.
Public	Declaration	Used at module level to declare public variables and allocate storage space.
Put	File Operation	Writes data from a variable to a disk file.
RaiseEvent	Class	Fires an event declared at module level within a class, form, or document.
Randomize	Miscellaneous	Initializes the random-number generator.
ReDim	Declaration	Used at procedure level to reallocate storage space for dynamic array variables.
Rem	Miscellaneous	Used to include explanatory remarks in a program.

(Continued)

(Continued)

Statement	Category	Description
Reset	File Operation	Closes all disk files opened using the Open statement.
Resume	Error Handling	Resumes execution after an error-handling routine is finished. Resume—resumes with the error statement. Resume Next—resumes with the statement immediately following the error statement.
RmDir	File Operation	Removes an existing directory or folder.
RSet	Assignment	Right aligns a string within a string variable.
SaveSetting	System	Saves or creates an application entry in the application's entry in the Windows registry.
Seek	File Operation	Sets the position for the next read/write operation within an open file.
Select Case . . . Case . . . Case Else . . . End Select	Flow Control	Conditionally executes one of several groups of statements.
SendKeys	System	Sends one or more keystrokes to the active window as if typed at the keyboard.
Set	Assignment	Assigns an object reference to a variable or property.
SetAttr	File Operation	Sets attribute information for a file.
Static	Declaration	Used at procedure level to declare variables and allocate storage space. Variables declared with the Static statement retain their values as long as the code is running.
Stop	Flow Control	Suspends execution. (It doesn't close any files or clear variables.)

Sub . . . End Sub	Declaration	Declares the name, arguments, and code that form the body of a Sub procedure.
Time	System	Sets the system time.
Type	Declaration	Used at module level to define a user-defined data type containing one or more elements.
Unload	Class	Removes an object from memory.
Unlock	File Operation	Controls access by other processes to all or part of a file opened using the Open statement.
While . . . Wend	Flow Control	Same as Do While . . . Loop. (This is the old syntax of the Do While . . . Loop.)
Width #	File Operation	Assigns an output line width to an open file.
With . . . . . . End With	Miscellaneous	Executes a series of statements on a single object or a user-defined type.
Write #	File Operation	Writes data to an open file.

The following table explains the eight main categories of VBA statements.

Category of VBA statements	Description
Assignment	This category relates to the assignment of variables, strings, arrays, and objects. It is remarkable that the string-related assignment statements can be replaced by the VBA string functions. The Let keyword is optional and can be omitted in the assignment statement. Erase is only for reinitializing the elements of fixed-size arrays and releasing dynamic-array storage space. The "*Set*" statement, which assigns an object reference to a variable or property, should be used for object assignment.

(Continued)

(Continued)

Category of VBA statements	Description
Class	This category relates to the object-oriented statements for declaring classes, properties, interfaces, and events, as well as the loading and unloading of objects. Since the construction of user-defined classes is an advanced topic for general users, it is not covered in this book.
Declaration	It is an important category, which relates to the declaration of variables, procedures, enumerations, types, arrays, and all Option statements.
Error Handling	This category relates to the main error handling statements.
File Operation	File operation statements are not covered in this book.
Miscellaneous	There are only four statements in this category: *Beep* is used to generate a beep sound to alert a user. *Rem* is used to include explanatory remarks and is equivalent to the single quote (') command. *Randomize* initializes the random-number generator with an optional number argument. *With . . . End With* lets an object or user-defined type be specified once for a series of statements. With statements make procedures run faster and eliminate the repetitive typing of the object/type name inside the With block.
Flow Control	This is an important category, which relates to the statements of program flow control. However, users should avoid using the *Goto or GoSub* related statements, because a program with many *Goto/ GoSub* statements is difficult to read and follow.
System	The System category contains system-related statements. Additional knowledge of system functions and integration with external libraries is required to understand the usage of the system statements.

Excel Array Formula

The Excel array formula is a powerful feature that many users may not be aware of. An array formula is an Excel formula that works with a series of data values, including a range of cells, an array constant, a named range, or a named array constant, rather than a single data value. The series of data is treated as a two-dimensional array with the dimensions of rows and columns. Effective use of array formulas can simplify some repetitive formulas. Figure G.1 illustrates the use of array formulas in the ranges K2: L6 and N2:O6.

The simple Excel formulas in the range E2:F6 are shown in the range H2:I6. They are the simple calculations of the Sine function. We can use the single array formula {=SIN(B2:C6)} in the range K2:L6 to replace the 10 formulas used in the range E2:F6 and get the same result set. The curly bracket enclosing the Excel formula indicates that the formulas in the range are treated as an array formula. Any changes in the range B2:C6 can trigger the automatic recalculation of the array formula for the range K2:L6, which is equivalent to using multiple simple formulas. The array formula in the range N2:O6 uses an array constant as the argument for the Sine function, instead of referring to the values in the range B2:C6. The array constant should be enclosed within the curly bracket. Columns in the array constant are delimited by commas, for example {01, 0.2}. Rows in the

K2				f_x {=SIN(B2:C6)}									
	A	B	C	D	E	F	G	H	I	J	K	L	M	N	O
1		Radians			The Sine of Radians			Applied Formulas in E2:F6			Using Array Formula			With An Array Constant	
2		0.1	0.2		0.09983	0.19867		=sin(B2)	=sin(C2)		0.09983	0.19867		0.09983	0.19867
3		0.3	0.4		0.29552	0.38942		=sin(B3)	=sin(C3)		0.29552	0.38942		0.29552	0.38942
4		0.5	0.6		0.47943	0.56464		=sin(B4)	=sin(C4)		0.47943	0.56464		0.47943	0.56464
5		0.7	0.8		0.64422	0.71736		=sin(B5)	=sin(C5)		0.64422	0.71736		0.64422	0.71736
6		0.9	1.0		0.78333	0.84147		=sin(B6)	=sin(C6)		0.78333	0.84147		0.78333	0.84147
7								{=SIN(B2:C6)}			{=SIN({0.1,0.2;0.3,0.4;0.5,0.6;0.7,0.8;0.9,1})}				
8															

FIGURE G.1 Sample array formulas.

array constant are delimited by semi-colons, for example {0.1; 0.3; 0.5; 0.7; 0.9} represents an array of five rows in one column. Columns are specified with each row, for example {0.1, 0.2; 0.3, 0.4; 0.5, 0.6; 0.7, 0.8; 0.9, 1} represents an array of five rows in two columns. Users may name an array constant and use the named array constant in array formulas, which is similar to the usage of named cells or named ranges.

An array formula can perform multiple and iterative calculations based on the number of items in an array. The operation is similar to an automatically established loop of "For each item in array . . . Next" inside an array formula. There are two common usages of array formulas. First, as demonstrated in the previous example, the array formula can return an array of values as the result set and display the result set in multiple cells accordingly. Second, there are some functions, typically using SUM, AVERAGE, or COUNT, that work with an array or series of data, aggregate them, and return a single aggregated value to a single cell. We can apply an array formula to a single cell with those aggregation functions. In this type of single-cell array formula, the result calculated from the arrays is just a single value. The following example illustrates the usage of both multi-cell and single-cell array formulas (see Figure G.2). Consider there are two columns of data. Column one contains a list of prices stored in the range A2:A6 and column two contains the corresponding quantities of item sold stored in the range B2:B6. To calculate the item total or row total, we generally multiply the first price with the first quantity (A2*B2) and then copy the formula into all the rest of the rows as shown in column C. The total amount in C7 is equal to the sum of all item totals, in which the formula is simply =SUM(C2:C6).

Alternatively, you can use multi-cell array formulas to calculate the item totals by selecting D2:D6, entering the formula =A2:A6*B2:B6, then pressing Control+Shift+Enter. If you want to alter the multi-cell array formula, you must select the entire range of the array formula again so that you may apply changes to the range. The individual cells within an array formula are protected against modification. To calculate the sum of the price and quantity pair products, you can use a single-cell array formula by entering the formula =SUM(A2:A6*B2:B6) in cell D7, then pressing Control+Shift+Enter. You may notice a curly bracket is added automatically to illustrate the entered formula is treated as an array formula (see Figure G.3).

The single-cell array formula {=SUM(A2:A6*B2:B6)} indeed calculates the result in a single step only without the need to calculate each individual result ahead. The formula is actually equivalent to "=SUM(A2*B2, A3*B3, A4*B4, A5*B5, A6*B6)." The single-step operation of the single-cell array formula is equivalent to iterating the calculation of each item of the arrays in the array formula, saving the calculated values in some temporary

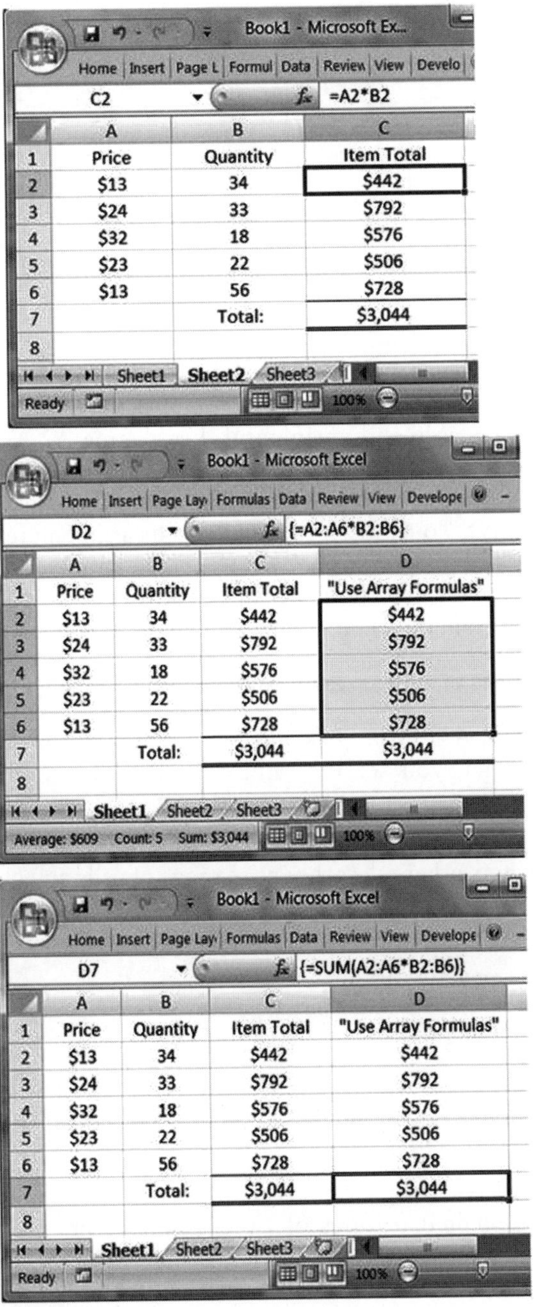

FIGURE G.2 Use of array formulas.

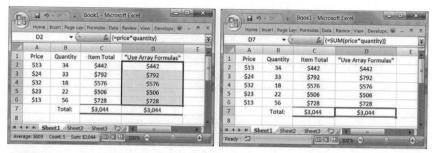

FIGURE G.3 Array formulas with named ranges.

memory, and calculating the sum of the values stored in the memory. You can use named ranges and named array constants in array formulas to make them more readable and meaningful. Let's name A2:A6 price and B2:B6 quantity. Then change the multi-cell array formulas in the range D2:D6 to ={price*quantity} and the single-cell array formula in D7 to =SUM (price*quantity). You will get the same results as in Figure G.3.

Although both approaches can achieve the same results, array formulas have both benefits and drawbacks. The advantages and disadvantages of using array formulas can be summarized in the following points:

Advantages of using array formulas:

Consistency—If you click any of the cells within a multi-cell array formula, you see the same formula. That consistency can help ensure greater accuracy.

Safety—You cannot overwrite part of a multi-cell array formula. You have to either select the entire range of cells and change the formula for the entire array, or leave it as is.

Simplicity—A single-cell array formula can be equivalent to several intermediate formulas.

Disadvantages of using array formulas:

Error-prone—If you forget to use Control+Shift+Enter for array formulas, Excel will miscalculate. Moreover, debugging an array formula is difficult.

Complexity—Array formulas are powerful, but they are one of the least documented features of Excel. Other users may not understand your array formulas. If other people need to modify your workbooks, you should include enough documentation of your array formulas and make sure they understand how to change them.

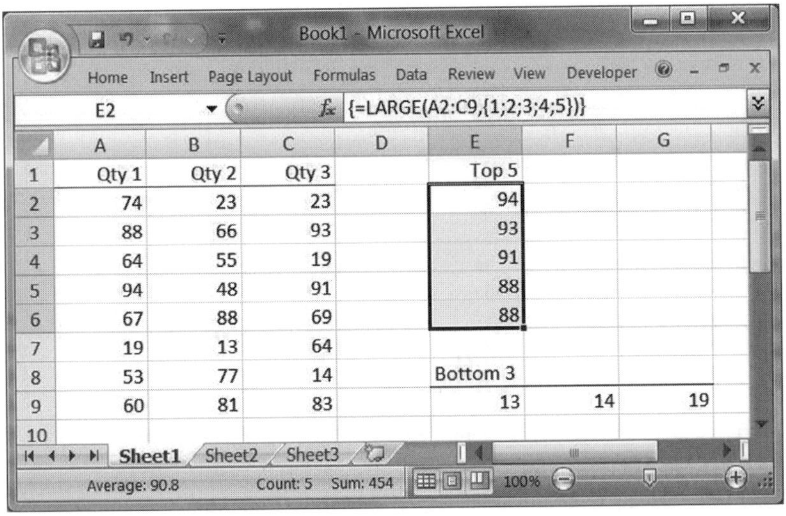

FIGURE G.4 Use of array formulas with the Small and Large functions.

Now, let's use the following four examples to illustrate the powerful usage of array formulas:

Finding the top and bottom numbers of a range: In the worksheet shown in Figure G.4, there are three sets of quantities listed in column A, B, and C. To find the top five numbers inside the range A2:C9 and display the answers vertically, we need to apply an array formula with a range and an array constant as the arguments. Let us select the vertical range E2:E6 and enter the array formula {=LARGE(A2:C9,{1;2;3;4;5})} into the range. Remember to press Control+Shift+Enter in order to apply the array formula into the range. The outer curly bracket is added automatically to enclose the array formula. The top five numbers will be displayed vertically. Similarly, we may find the bottom three numbers in the range, but display the answers horizontally. Let us select the horizontal range E9:G9 and enter the array formula {=SMALL(A2:C9,{1,2,3})} into the range. The bottom three numbers will be displayed horizontally. You may notice that the delimiters used by the array constants are determined by the expected direction of the displayed result. A comma is used for separating columns and displaying the results horizontally, while a semi-colon is used for separating rows and displaying the results vertically.

Using the IF function for conditional aggregation: In the worksheet shown in Figure G.5, a simple array formula {=AVERAGE (B2:B9 – C2:C9)} is used to calculate the average difference of all rows, which is equivalent to the average difference between the list price of column B and the sale

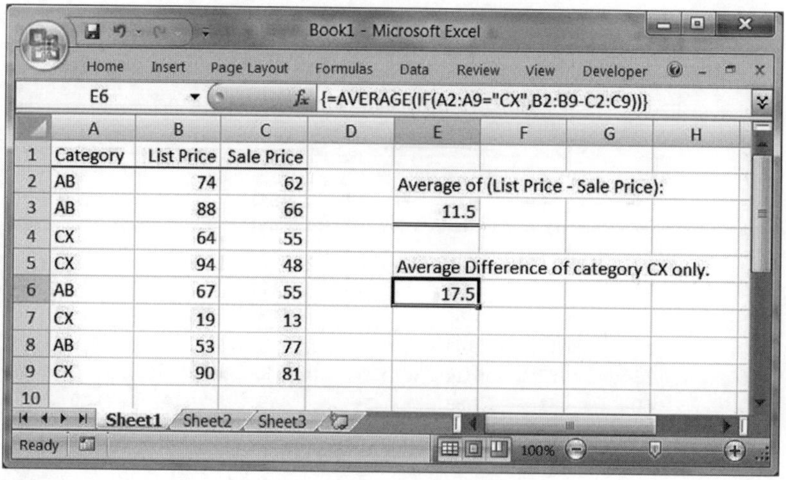

FIGURE G.5 Use of array formulas with the Average function.

price of column C. The array formula is applied in the cell E3 and the calculated value is 11.5. Moreover, we may use the IF function to apply some conditions to the calculation. Here, we calculate the average difference of the category CX only. In the cell E6, the single-cell array formula is {=AVERAGE(IF(A2:A9="CX",B2:B9 – C2:C9))} and the calculated value is 17.5 (see Figure G.5). Excel is smart enough to iterate the conditions specified inside the IF function of the array formula in order to compete the calculation.

Using multiple IF functions for conditional aggregation: This example applies more complicated conditions with several IF functions. Let's say we only want to calculate the average difference of the category CX and the difference should be more than eight. You will probably consider using the IF function with the AND function in the array function as shown in cell E3 of Figure G.6. The cell F3 illustrates the array formula applied in the cell E3. The array formula will always return 0. This is because both the AND function and the OR function cannot work properly in array formulas and the input is treated as a series of arguments instead of arrays. This also happens in other aggregation functions, such as SUM, AVERAGE, and COUNT. Thus, you need to consider an alternative approach. In this example, we use multiple IF functions to work for the AND operation. In the cell E7, we use two IF functions in the array formula {=AVERAGE(IF(A2:A9="CX",IF((B2:B9-C2:C9)>8,B2:B9-C2:C9)))} in order to handle the AND condition. Then you can get the expected answer 21.33.

Using the AND function for a single-cell array formula: As explained, the AND function can accept a series of arguments, which are similar to

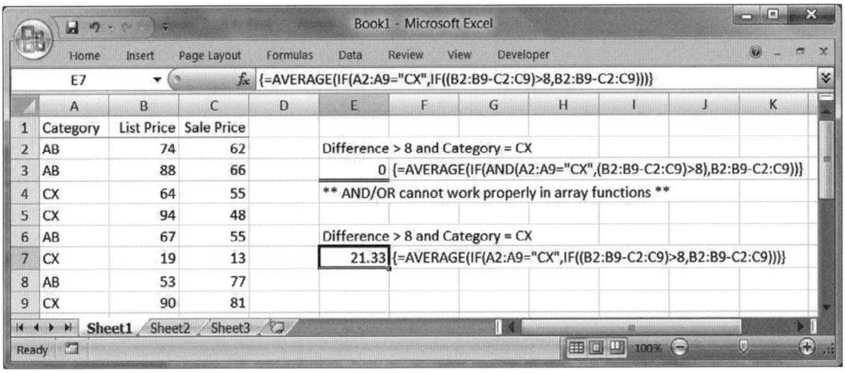

FIGURE G.6 Use of array formulas with the If function.

those aggregation functions. Figure G.7 illustrates the possible usage of the AND function in the single-cell array formula, similar to the usage of the aggregation functions. The example intends to check the presence of specified values in E2:F6 (1 to 10) against the range A1:C6. True should be returned only if the values in the range A1:C6 cover all numbers from 1 to 10. The array formula used in F8 is {=AND(COUNTIF(A1:C6,E2:F6))}. Since the first argument of COUNTIF is a range, A1:C6 will be considered a fixed argument for all iterations of the array formula. The second argument of COUNTIF is a single value that specifies the criteria. Thus, each item in the

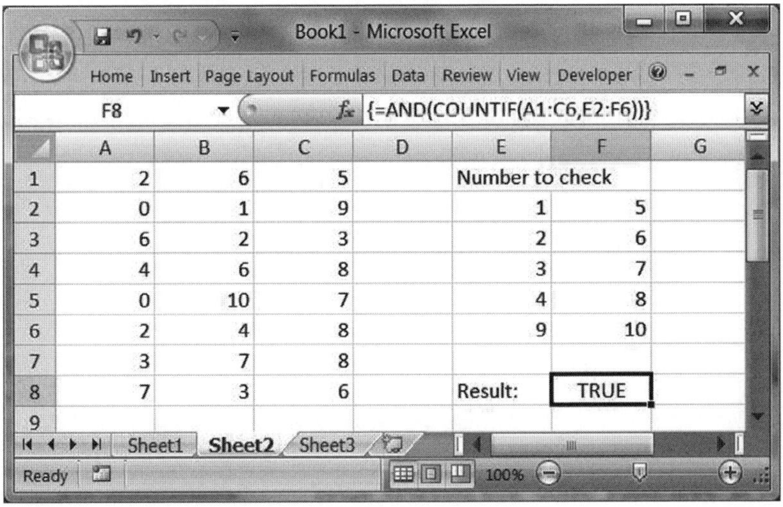

FIGURE G.7 Using the AND function for a single-cell array formula.

range E2:F6 will be considered a single value of the array during the iterations in the array formula. The array formula will iterate from 1 to 10 to check against the existence of the specified number in the range A1:C6. Countif will produce 0 (i.e. False) if the specified number cannot be found inside A1:C6. Otherwise, the number of occurrences of the specified number in A1:C6 will be returned. Any positive number will be considered True. Only if all values returned from the iterations of COUNTIF are positive integers, the AND function will produce True.

Index